Who Owns the Media?

Global Trends and Local Resistances

Edited by
Pradip N. **Thomas** and **Zaharom** Nain

with a Foreword by
Peter **Golding**

and contributions from
Sasha **Costanza-Chock**, Hopeton S. **Dunn**, Ana **Fiol**,
Cees J. **Hamelink**, William **Hueva**, Robert W. **McChesney**,
Jubril **Mohammed**, Mohammed **Musa**, Francis B. **Nyamnjoh**,
Seán **Ó Siochrú**, Dan **Schiller**, Slavko **Splichal**,
Ruth **Teer-Tomaselli**, Pradip N. **Thomas**,
Keyan **Tomaselli**, **Wang** Lay Kim,
Zaharom Nain, Yuezhi **Zhao**

SOUTHBOUND
P e n a n g

Zed Books
London and New York

WACC
L o n d o n

Published by
Southbound Sdn. Bhd.
Suite 20F, Northam House
55 Jalan Sultan Ahmad Shah
10050 Penang
Malaysia
Fax: 604-228 1758

E-mail: Books@southbound.com.my
Internet: http://www.southbound.com.my

Published in collaboration with Zed Books Ltd,
7 Cynthia St, London, N1 9JF, UK and
Room 400, 175 Fifth Avenue, New York,
NY 10010, USA in 2002.

http://www.zedbooks.co.uk

Distributed in the USA by Palgrave, a division of
St Martin's Press, LLC, 175 Fifth Avenue, New York, NY 10010.

A catalogue record for this book is available from the British Library.

US CIP is available from the Library of Congress.

ISBN 1 84277 468 9 hb
ISBN 1 84277 469 7 pb

Typeset by Chin Kooi Hong
in Baskerville 9.5/11.5 points
Cover design by C-Square Sdn. Bhd.
Pre-press services by Eefar Lithographic Sdn. Bhd., Penang, Malaysia
Printed by Jutaprint, Penang, Malaysia.

Perpustakaan Negara Malaysia Cataloguing-in-Publication Data

Who owns the media? : Gobal trends and local resistances / edited
    by Pradip N. Thomas and Zaharom Nain with foreword by Peter Golding.
    Includes index
    ISBN 983-9054-42-2
    1. Mass media – Political aspects. 2. Mass media policy.
    I. Thomas, Pradip N. II. Zaharom Nain. III. Golding, Peter.
    302.23

Contents

Foreword
Peter Golding   v

Editors' Preface   xi

Part 1 • Theory and policies

The political economy of international communications
Robert W. McChesney   3

Global institutions and the democratization of media
Seán Ó Siochrú   23

Intellectual property rights
Cees J. Hamelink   43

Part 2 • Regional and country case studies

**Privatization: The cost of media democratization
in East and Central Europe?**
Slavko Splichal   51

**The politics of the media in the English-speaking
Caribbean**
Hopeton S. Dunn   69

**The political economy of media in Southern Africa,
1990–2001**
William Hueva, Keyan Tomaselli and Ruth Teer-Tomaselli   97

**Media ownership and control in Africa in the
age of globalization**
Francis B. Nyamnjoh   119

Media and neoliberalism in Latin America
Ana Fiol   135

Communications and the crisis: From Neoliberal to authoritarian development?
Dan Schiller   159

The state, the market, and media control in China
Yuezhi Zhao   179

Media ownership and communication rights in India
Pradip N. Thomas   213

The political economy of media ownership in Nigeria
Mohammed Musa and Jubril Mohammed   227

Ownership, control and the Malaysian media
Zaharom Nain and Wang Lay Kim   249

Part 3 • Democratic communication futures

The whole world is watching: Online surveillance of social movement organizations
Sasha Costanza-Chock   271

Agendas for research and strategies for intervention
Pradip N. Thomas   293

Contributors   307

Index   311

Foreword

Peter Golding

This Foreword was written on the eve of the World Summit on the Information Society. With phase one held in Geneva in 2003, and the second phase to be held in Tunis in 2005, this massive gathering under the direct auspices of the International Telecommunications Union, and less directly the United Nations, brings together the great and the good, as well as the fairly great and the not so good, Heads of State, Executive Heads of United Nations agencies, industry leaders, non-governmental organizations, media representatives and civil society. Their allotted task is to assess the progress and future of a world which "is undergoing a fundamental transformation as the industrial society that marked the 20th century rapidly gives way to the information society of the 21st century".

This is no small task. But it is the most conspicuous manifestation of a powerful nostrum, that we live in a world that is rapidly undergoing irreversible and essential changes in the way we work, play, relate, travel, and conduct our politics and culture. The Summit arrives a quarter of a century after the report of its International Commission for the Study of Communication Problems was first submitted to UNESCO. When published in 1980 as *Many Voices, One World* and known thereafter as the MacBride Report in recognition of its doughty chair, the Irish diplomat Sean MacBride, the report was both the distillation and the propellant of a growing recognition that world communications had become a major facet of global inequalities, and were increasingly a vehicle by which such inequalities would become intensified. Thus, demands for a New World Information and Communication Order became clamourous, to the intense annoyance of the USA and others, then as now loyally following the American lead, and prompting their withdrawal from UNESCO altogether. The dust on that row did not settle for 20 years, and is still swirling today. What has changed in that quarter century is not the problem, nor its primary proponents, both victors and victims. But we now have "new technology".

Governments and corporations alike have become focused obsessively on the need to position themselves assertively and victoriously in the jostle at the forefront of the new society. The phenomenal growth of domestic computing, mobile telephony, and especially the Internet, have generated a dizzying euphoria about the imminent arrival of a new global society of equality, abundance, connectivity, and order.

It is a curious paradox of radical scholarship that, basking in and often celebrating this heady sense of arrival at tomorrow, questions about the ownership and control of the vast corporations that both benefit from and direct the new order have receded from prominence, at just the time when conglomerate elephantiasis is reaching new extremes. In the UK as I write, the virtual unification into one company of commercial terrestrial television is being complemented by liberal legislation opening the door to significantly extended intervention in the UK broadcasting market by that exemplar of corporate cultural commerce, Rupert Murdoch. It is worth asking just why there is such academic as well as political indifference to these issues.

Two broad assumptions are behind such a sanguine disregard: the presumption that an information society is upon us, and a mythology that the changes are entirely benign. The arrival of an 'information society' is but the latest branding of a sense of lurching into a new age that follows the labelling of our times as 'post-industrial' 'post-modern', or simply post millennial. At its heart is a curious obsession with technology, and especially communication technologies. This is a complex debate, and no simple dismissal of such attempts at periodicity will do. But we need to distinguish two very different forms of technology to understand these changes. Elsewhere I have simplistically referred to these as Technology One and Technology Two. The first, Technology One, allows existing social action and process to occur more speedily, more efficiently, or conveniently. Technology Two enables wholly new forms of activity previously impracticable or even inconceivable. In essence many new information and communication technologies (ICT) are more obviously Technology One than Technology Two. The introduction and development of telecommunications in the 19th century had profound consequences for the growth and form of imperialism which dwarf the impact of email and mobile telephony. The completion of the human genome project, and advances in microbiology and genetics, on the other hand, are enabling – for better or for worse – changes in our capacity to alter our own biologies and environment in ways whose consequences we cannot yet even comprehend or anticipate (Golding, 2000).

Of course, this is to simplify a complex debate. But over-enthusiasm about the benefits and importance of new communication technologies is one danger which can generate indifference to their political economy. The other is a set of mythologies about the "information society" which can easily degenerate into a Panglossian assessment of what the new order entails. These include the notion that we are floating in a "weightless economy", in which global trade is now dominated so much by information and knowledge goods that traditional inequities and obstacles to development will simply become irrelevant. In this vision universal mobility, ever-growing travel, and cultural internationalism combine to create a wholly new order. In this vein the social theorist John Urry has suggested, "Television and travel, the mobile and the modern, seem to be producing a global village, blurring what is private and what is public, what is front stage and what is back stage, what is near and what is far"(Urry, 1999, 2000). Intensifying mobility, usually involving the same rich segment of the population travelling further and more frequently, and the ubiquitous intrusion of mobile telephony into the lives of large segments of European youth, do not yet speak, however, of a cultural and social transformation. It is sometimes salutary to remember, for those of us living in societies or milieux suffused with the gadgetry of the information rich, that only in 2001 did we reach the point where there was one telephone line per 100 people in the world. One consequence of the global inequity in communications development continues to be found in Africa, where 10% of the world's population provides less than 1% of the global online netizenry.

Equally troubling is the presumption that the new society is one of vanishing inequities and poverty, as abundance and inclusivity blossom from its fertile soil. One refrain within this discourse is an insistence on the disappearance of traditional and familiar patterns of stratification, whether of classes within societies, or between societies globally. Yet in a world where over one billion people continue to exist on less than a dollar a day, while in the world's richest society, the United States, 34.6 million people, one in eight of the population, are below the poverty line, and more than nine million are categorized by the US department of agriculture as experiencing real hunger, it is difficult to define away or ignore the mundane but cruel continuities of inequity and want.

The conglomerate capitalist control over cultural and communications industries represents and expresses the triumph of private profit over collective need, corporate strategy over democratic direction. As the familiar litany of the diversified mega-corporations who control communications rolls onward – AOL, Time Warner, Disney, General Electric, News Corporation, Viacom, Vivendi, Sony, Bertelsmann, AT&T, – hardly hidden or blushing violets, and all making frequent guest appearances among the pages of this book, it is important to resist a disabling and demoralizing determinism that can follow from such stark analysis.

Popular unease and dissatisfaction with the oligopolistic powers and dominatory tendencies of such companies is far from dead. In the United States throughout 2003 the Federal Communications Commission (FCC) found itself at the centre of a storm of controversy and splits after some three million Americans contacted them to demand the retention of controls over media monopoly power. According to McChesney and Nichols "media ownership has been the second most discussed issue by constituents in 2003, trailing only the war in Iraq" (McChesney and Nichols, 2003). Local resistance and increasing 'media awareness' make acceptance of the corporate control of cultural production and distribution variably but increasingly problematic.

There are numerous uncertainties and contradictions from which we may draw some comfort, or to which at the very least analytical attention should be paid. Three examples of such contradictory tendencies may make the point. First, new technologies present radical opportunities that are not always the sole preserve of the conglomerates. Broadband makes possible the widespread and rapid distribution of the robustly seditious as well as the hard sell. Low power FM radio is a vital resource for community groups and social movements, for whom the Internet too has become a nerve system of unprecedented value. Initiatives like the Digital Destiny campaign of the Centre for Digital Democracy exemplify the potential of innovative, progressive, and inventive exploitation of the technological possibilities of new communications resources. Yet the inequity inherent in the larger picture is difficult to ignore. As a report for the World Bank recently notes, "global investment in incremental infrastructure over the next decade is expected to reach US$ 1.5 trillion. By 2010, over 700 million Internet accounts, 1.3 billion mobile phone subscribers, and nearly 1.5 billion main lines in service are expected in these [leading] markets, and communications revenues will explode to over US$ 1.7 trillion in 2010, a result of the sector entering many more facets of daily commerce and society" (Pyramid Research, 2000). Yet in poor countries "moderate literacy rates, low income levels and economic and social conditions...discourage ready availability of financial capital. The result is a relatively high incremental cost to participate in the Internet revolution, as factored in the costs is the cost of connectivity itself. These countries are impeded from participating in the Internet revolution, and thus are unable to capitalize upon the accelerated velocity of development it can bring with it" (ibid). There will continue to be no commercial imperative to invest in the communications infrastructure of such countries other than for the benefit and use of wealthier elites, perpetuating and deepening divisions that already exist.

Second, as the editors of this volume point out, all is not seamless success for the global giants of the communications sector. To watch the stumbling uncertainty of the AOL-Time Warner merger, to the point where in 2003 the company posted a US$54 billion quarterly loss and chairman Steve Case was forced to stand down, may mean no more than a reversion to the former company name of Time Warner, while the difficulties faced by Rupert Murdoch in imposing his son as CEO of BskyB in late 2003 may simply illustrate the irritation of old money – the institutional and city investors for whom a dynasty is a charmless and unconvincing approach to sound venture capitalism. But there may be more than *schadenfreude* to be derived from these occasional glimpses of grit in the machinery of corporate communications.

Third, the global reach of the media giants plays alongside a tentative but optimistic search for a new and international sensitivity, a hesitant sense of a global commons, to be found in debates about cosmopolitan citizenship, or what Arjun Appadurai refers to as "diasporic public spheres", distilled from the remnants of a "postnational political world" Appadurai (1996: 21–22). On the one hand the flat uniformity of a branded world beset by MTV, Disney, and a designer youth culture manufactured through the synergistic efficiencies of conglomerate cultural manufacture, offers little to utopian futurology. On the other hand the inevitable border-challenging effects of a globalized cultural diet, whether in language or entertainment, has in embryo the potential, or so many would hope, for a new cosmopolitanism quite beyond the designs and strategies of its creators.

These are complex issues. As always, before action comes understanding. To that end the essays in this volume make an informed, stimulating, and important contribution. Not only do their authors provide a timely return to crucial issues of media ownership, they provide the evidence and arguments that can take us beyond either wonder or despair at the litany of conglomeration that has become so familiar in describing the media industries. It is an invaluable resource and a welcome reminder of the central and vital role of understanding and challenging the political economy of the media in the 21st century.

References

Appadurai, A. (1996) *Modernity at large: Cultural dimensions of globalization*, Minneapolis: University of Minnesota Press.

Golding, P. (2000) Forthcoming features: Information and communications technologies and the sociology of the future, *Sociology*, 34, 1, 165–184.

McChesney, R., and Nichols, J. (2003) Up in flames, *The Nation*, 2 November.

Pyramid Research (2000) Global information infrastructure. Report for World Bank.

Urry, J. (1999) *Sociology beyond societies: Mobilities for the next century*. London: Routledge.

Urry, J. (2000) The global media and cosmopolitanism. Retrieved 4 November, from http://www.comp.lancs.ac.uk/sociology/soc056ju.html.

Editors' Preface

Issues related to media ownership and control ought to be of public concern. Not only have the media become dominant players in the cultural environments that we inhabit but mediation has become central to the way we live out our lives today. It would therefore seem obvious that an influence of such magnitude ought to be accountable to their major clients, the global public. This, however, is not the case and the essays included in this volume amply demonstrate this misfit between media ownership and public accountability.

While critical media researchers can be accused of behaving like excessively pessimistic witch doctors, they do nevertheless need to be applauded for systematically exploring and exposing the problematic relationship between culture and economics today, 'culture's' tenuous relationship with international and national politics, the commodification of culture, the precise nature of the global media grab and its consequences for global and local cultural environments. By foregrounding the analyses of media structures, they have also attempted to account for the persistent disjunctures, the slippages, the gaps, between the communitarian visions of democracy and its (un)translatability within the current global economic order.

These explorations have revealed the other side of the "bubble", the systemic flaws, corporate culpability and state complicity that are all too often glossed over by, or excluded from, popular media accounts of reality. A number of these studies have also revealed the multifaceted nature of resistance, the stories of extraordinary people using ordinary technologies to create media environments and media cultures of their choice. The many essays in this volume can be read as attempts to audit media practices within the matrix of global policies and national responses.

This volume of essays on the political economy of communications is largely the outcome of a series of workshops on media ownership and control that was organized by the London-based World Association for Christian Communications (WACC) between 1997 and 2001. WACC is an ecumenical non-governmental organization (NGO) that has long been involved in advocating the right to communicate. These workshops were held in Durban, Mexico City, Kathmandu, Kingston, Piran, Bangkok, Yaounde and Nadi. The main objective of these workshops was to map global and national media ownership trends within an economic climate characterized by deregulation, reregulation and privatization. Taken collectively, the many case studies that were presented at these workshops revealed a by now familiar pattern of media ownership trends characterized by "(a) the denationalisation and transnationalisation of telecommunications; (b) the privatisation and commercialisation of the public services of radio and television; (c) processes of deregulation and re-regulation (that led to the liberalising of media ownership through the granting of licenses, the opening of domestic media to non-national investments, the harmonisation of domestic and international media policies); (d) the integration of media horizontally and vertically within national frontiers leading to concentration and to increased links between local conglomerates, governments and transnational corporations; (e) attempts by powerful, regional media corporations to increase their terrestrial presence and (f) the transnationalisation and conglomeration of culture industries (through the ownership of networks, distribution channels and production/ content" (2001: 3).[1]

This volume is divided into three sections and contains fifteen essays. The three essays in Section 1 provide an overview of the some of the key global institutions and trends that are characteristic features of the contemporary political economy of global communications. These include global media governance structures and the emerging intellectual property rights (IPR) regime. Section 2 highlights numerous regional and national case studies of media ownership. Taken together, these case studies present a panoramic introduction to the correspondences between, and the specificities of, media ownership trends in various parts of the world. Section 3 looks forward and the two essays in this part deal with resistance, counter-resistance, advocacy and research priorities for just media futures. Combining theory and empirical information, these essays illuminate the blindspots of mainstream media analyses while advancing the project of media democratization.

Due to the pressures of space, we regret our inability to include in this volume all the case studies that were presented during the eight workshops. Many of these have been published in journals like *Javnost*, *Media Development* and in the recently published edited volume *Media and Democratic Renewal in Southern Africa*.[2] However, the essays included in

1. WACC (2001) *Media Ownership and Citizen Access: A Global Overview*,\. London: WACC Publications, 2001.

2. Keyan Tomaselli and Hopeton Dunn, (eds), (2002). *Media and Democratic Renewal in Southern Africa: New Approaches to Political Economy*. Denver, Colorado: International Academic Publishers.

this volume stand as a testimony to the variety, diversity and quality of the papers presented at these workshops. We are grateful to the authors who were not involved in the workshops but who nevertheless consented to share their insights and expertise through this publication. Last but not least, we are grateful to WACC for enabling a variety of spaces for the exploration of the right to communicate.

Pradip N. Thomas and Zaharom Nain

Theory and Policies

The Political Economy of
International Communications

Robert W. McChesney

It is axiomatic in nearly all variants of social and political theory that media and communication systems are cornerstones of modern societies. In political terms, they may serve to enhance democracy, or to deny it, or some combination of the two. Less commented upon, though no less significant, media and communication systems have emerged as central areas for profit making on modern capitalist societies. Much of the study of media, therefore, assesses the relationship of media and communication as private activities to the broader and necessary social and political duties that media systems perform. It is a central and recurring theme in media studies. In this chapter I will present a brief overview of recent developments in the global media system, and their relationship to the political economy. I argue that media is central to the emerging global economy as well as to any notion of political democracy, and that this dual life is a central tension on the world stage. I conclude that it is imperative that citizens organize to create new media policies that will better preserve and promote democratic values.

Before doing that, however, I think it important to debunk some of the mythology that impedes the ability of scholars to do clear analysis, and for citizens to be effective participants in media policy making. This is the mythology of the "free press" that emerged most dynamically in the United States, but now with the rise of neoliberalism and the global media system, it has become, increasingly, an international product. These bogus assumptions about government and private sector in media fog our ability to see the actual power relations at hand, and therefore inhibit our capacity to move toward establishing a more democratic and humane media system, and a more democratic and humane society. They take what is a complex and difficult problem for any society – how best to organize media to protect core values – and turn it into a simplistic and vulgar equation. There are several reasons for this faulty framework, but one stands out at the top of the list: the power of the dominant media corporations to defend their interests and propagate a mythology to protect their very privileged role in society. To do the mythology justice requires that the first portion of the paper focus on the United States.

The mythology of the free press in the United States

The conventional view of the proper relationship of the government to the media, as it developed in the United States, is well known to us all: the free press is generated by private citizens independent of government censorship and control. By logical deduction, this means that media and communication are, in effect, a function to be provided by profit-seeking businesses competing in the marketplace. The First Amendment to the US constitution guarantees this freedom, and as long as the government keeps its hands off the media, a society's flow of information and ideas will be safe. Without government intervention, a healthy media system will invariably rise from the rich soil of political freedom. Let the government intervene, no matter how well intended the intervention may seem, and alarm bells should go off in the minds of all liberal and right-thinking people. The government and the private media are by nature in conflict. To paraphrase the immortal words of Thomas Jefferson, if a society could have either media or government but not both, the sane choice for free people are media.

It is rare to encounter more nonsense in a single paragraph than in what you just read. It is not that the antagonism between the government and private media does not exist. Nor is it the very legitimate concern about state suppression of the press. To the contrary, what is absurd about this conventional framing is the notion that the state plays little or no role in establishing the press system, and that the state-media relations naturally tend to be antagonistic, with the consequence being a healthy and viable democratic political culture.

In the United States, as elsewhere, the state has always been a crucial and necessary player in the formation of the media system. Postal subsidies predating the revolution and important to this day stimulated the rise of the newspaper and magazine industries. Government printing contracts subsidized the partisan press until the middle of the 19th century. Libraries and schools purchased books and created readers for them. Copyright – a policy allowing authors limited right to monopolistic control over their output – was considered such an important policy that it was written into the constitution. Without the government sanctioned and enforced monopolies provided by copyright, which was intended to preserve a public domain as much as protect authors, the modern commercial media system as we know it would be unthinkable. So much for the idea that the private media system springs "naturally" from freedom's soil.

And that's not the half of it. When broadcasting came along the government allocated monopoly rights to extraordinarily valuable spectrum. It did likewise in granting monopoly rights to cable television franchises a few decades later. Although the government received not one penny in return for these monopoly rights, the value of this transfer of public property to private hands is placed in the hundreds of billions of dollars, *if not more*. Of the eight or nine massive media conglomerates that dominate the US (and, increasingly, global) media system, the clear majority was built upon the superprofits and leverage generated by having a radio, TV or cable monopoly license. It is even more the case that the government has directly created our systems of telecommunication, from telegraphy and telephony to wireless. Once these firms wrest these valuable monopoly licenses, their PR flacks and executives – with no sense of irony – will sometimes sound the alarm bells about "government intervention" in the "free market", if some regulator discusses an unfavourable regulation. In the corporate view, their privileges were won by seeming immaculate conception, and should be regarded as natural and inviolable thereafter.

So the question is not whether the government plays a role in establishing our media and communication systems, because it plays a foundational role. The question is in whose interests and for what values are government policies in communication meant to encourage? When one puts the questions this way, it has the effect of turning over what seemed like an unmovable rock and revealing the very seamy underside of US democracy. I think any serious review of the history of US communication policy making comes to only one conclusion: it is extraordinarily corrupt and dominated by very powerful special interests who do everything in their immense power to prevent any informed public participation. So it was in the 1920s and 1930s when a handful of private interests stole the airwaves and established commercial broadcasting in the United States, and so it has been ever since. Today the regulatory and policy making process is arguably more corrupt than ever, as tens of millions of dollars have made members of Congress and regulators virtual lapdogs of the powerful corporate lobbies, and the overwhelming majority of the public – conservatively 99.8% – has no clue that policies are being made in their name but without their informed consent.

This sort of corruption would have been unimaginable to the nation's founders, and much of that has to do with the way in which capitalism has developed in the United States over the past 200 years. The media system has gone from being a local and small scale enterprise during the nation's first few generations to becoming a very concentrated and lucrative area for generating massive profit by the end of the 19th century. Newspapers had been highly partisan institutions closely connected to the political process for the first 50–100 years on the republic's history. By the Progressive Era, newspapers – still the dominant news medium – were held in big chains and most communities had but a single newspaper or a duopoly. This generated the first and perhaps only truly great crisis in US media. The traditional partisanship of the press, where the editorial perspective of the paper invariably reflected the perspective of the owner, would no longer work. It was one thing to have highly partisan journalism in competitive markets where a broad range of views were available and where a new newspaper could be launched without massive amounts of capital. It was quite another thing to have highly partisan journalism in monopolistic markets where barriers to entry prevented any new competition. In that environment, highly partisan journalism was suspect from a democratic perspective. We should add that the partisanship was generally of a stridently pro-capitalist, anti-labour perspective.

This was nothing short of a legitimacy crisis for capitalist media in a democratic society. There was much sentiment among progressives and socialists to radically transform the press system to make it a non-profit institution under the control of communities. The ultimate solution was much less radical: it was the emergence of a newfangled idea called professional journalism, which was to be non-partisan, politically neutral and, to its most fervent acolytes, objective. For the first time the editorial content in the news media would not automatically reflect the viewpoints of the owner (or, increasingly, the advertiser). Journalism would be produced by trained professionals who would not even let their own values cloud their professional trained judgement. There were no journalism schools in the United States in 1900; by the First World War I all the major journalism schools had been established, almost always at the behest of powerful publishers.

In the conventional wisdom, professional journalism solved the problem of monopoly capitalist control over the media for a democratic society, and we all live happily ever after. It does no such thing, however. Along side its merits, which are trumpeted to all corners of the kingdom, professional journalism also tends to generate a tepid journalism that reflects the range of existing elite opinion. It therefore reinforces conventional business-as-usual politics and marginalizes the new, the critical and the radical, especially if they are threatening to entrenched economic interests. It presupposes the capitalist status quo as the natural and proper democratic ordering of social life. On the most ominous work of the state that requires the greatest democratic monitoring – engaging in war – professional journalism has proven to be mostly a stenographer to those in power. All in all, it provides little threat to the "weak" democracy that characterizes the United States today, typified by corrupt policies combined with rampant citizen ignorance and depoliticization.

In short, when one combines all of the above the idea that our private press system has an adversarial relationship with a government hell-bent on socialism is ludicrous. It is the stuff of fairy tales. They are far better seen as being in cahoots with each other, and both far more adept at serving those who sit atop the social pyramid, than those who are found closer to the bottom. As I said, this is a "weak" democracy, by traditional standards. Indeed the main defense of the current calibre of democracy in the United States is that it is the best we can hope for.

The U.S. system goes global

I spend so much time on the United States because it is the US model of media and regulation that is being exported across the planet. The nature of media policy debates have been similar in many nations of the world, except that public interest advocates tended to be somewhat more successful and corporate media interests were not as effective. The emergence of powerful systems of public broadcasting in most of the world's democracies in the 20th century was a testament to that. As far as issues of global communication policy – telegraphy, telephony, spectrum allocation, etc. – were concerned, these were hashed out among the nation-states, almost always at the elite level with minimal public involvement. The most powerful nations invariably rule the negotiations, Britain before the First World War, and the United States since 1945. The US government, in particular, has aggressively acted as if only a profit-driven media system as in the United States, with US style professional journalism, can be considered acceptable for a free society. As many nations come up short in that department, the US government has graciously worked to eliminate barriers to give the world's people greater exposure to US based commercial media.

The odd men out, so the speak, in this arrangement, have been the world's poor nations. Prior to the 1960s most of them were colonies and the rest were semi-colonies, so their media systems were designed to suit the needs of the colonial masters. Following the wave of national independence in the 1960s, the so-called Third World nations organized a campaign to establish a New World Information and Communication Order (NWICO). The idea was to have the west provide the resources to the poor nations so they could establish viable communication systems of their own, and be genuinely independent of their former colonizers. This program was far from perfect or well-organized, but, regardless of that, it met with an icy response from the West. The United States and Britain, under Reagan and Thatcher, withdrew from UNESCO in protest. The movement, never much of a threat to begin with, disintegrated.

Since the 1980s the trajectory in the global political economy has gone directly against notions like the NWICO. We then entered the age of neoliberalism, or corporate globalization. Neoliberalism refers to the set of national and international policies that call for business domination of all social affairs with minimal countervailing force. The market became the fount of all that was good and true in the word. Profit-seeking corporations and globe-trotting investors were the heroes of economic development. Unions, tariffs, taxes, public investment, and regulations – anything that got in the way of these forces – were the evil demons on the world stage. Government was to be lean and mean, at least with regard to serving the interests of the poor or working class. With regard to the needs of the wealthy and large corporations, governments were to be sympathetic and benevolent, though this point was not to be given much attention. The idea that people could govern their lives through informed self-government and a vibrant public sphere was dismissed as overrated; after all, such political cultures invariably interfered with the market, and tended therefore to be economically inefficient. Instead people were only to be trusted in the market as buyers and sellers. Everything else was bunk. The US corporate system, in short, was being exported to the world, albeit in global clothing.

Few industries have been as transformed by this process as the media. Prior to the 1980s and 1990s, national media systems were typified by domestically owned radio, television and newspaper industries. There were considerable import markets for films, TV shows, music, and books, and these markets tended to be dominated by US-based firms. But local commercial interests, sometimes combined with a state-affiliated broadcasting service, were the dominant forces in the media system. In this environment, the key concern was to allow the press freedom to operate without government coercion or censorship. This remains a problem across the planet, with recent press-state struggles taking place in Russia, Hungary, and Angola, to mention but a few (Cullison, 2000; Gordon, 2000; Swarns, 2000; Wright, 2000). A familiar theme as well, dealt with how the dominant commercial media often had a cozy and corrupt relationship with the dominant political forces (*The Economist*, 11 March 2000; Preston, 2000; Tyler, 2000).

All of this is changing, and changing rapidly, in present times. The nature of the traditional concerns remains, but their context has changed considerably. In the past, media systems were primarily national; but recently, a global commercial media market has emerged. To grasp media today and in the future, one must start with understanding the global system, and then factor in differences at the national and local levels. "What you are seeing," says Christopher Dixon, media analyst for the investment firm PaineWebber, "is the creation of a global oligopoly. It happened to the oil and automotive industries earlier this century; now it is happening to the entertainment industry."

This global oligopoly has two distinct but related facets. First, it means the dominant companies – roughly one-half US-based, but all with significant US operations – are moving across the planet at breakneck speed. The point is to capitalize on the potential for growth abroad – and not get outflanked by competitors – since the US market is well developed and only permits incremental expansion. As Viacom CEO Sumner Redstone has put it, "Companies are focusing on those markets promising the best return, which means overseas." Frank Biondi, former chairman of Vivendi's Universal Studios, asserts that "99 per cent of the success of these companies long-term is going to be successful execution offshore."

The dominant media firms increasingly view themselves as global entities. Bertelsmann CEO Thomas Middelhoff bristled when, in 1998, some said it was improper for a German firm to control 15% of both the US book publishing and music markets. "We're not foreign. We're international," Middelhoff said. "I'm an American with a German passport." In 2000 Middelhoff proclaimed that Bertelsmann was no longer a German company. "We are really the most global media company" (Kirkpatrick, 2000b). Likewise, AOL-Time Warner's Gerald Levin stated, "We do not want to be viewed as an American company. We think globally" (Schechter, 2000). Second, convergence and consolidation are the order of the day. Specific media industries are becoming more and more concentrated, and the dominant players in each media industry increasingly are subsidiaries of huge global media conglomerates. For one small example, the US market for educational publishing is now controlled by four firms, whereas it had two dozen viable players as recently as 1980 (*The Economist* 5 August 2000).

The level of mergers and acquisitions is breathtaking. In the first half of 2000, the number of merger deals in global media, Internet, and telecommunications totalled $300 billion, triple the figure for the first six months of 1999, and exponentially higher than the figure from ten years earlier (Mermigas, 2000a). The logic guiding media firms in all of this is clear: get very big very quickly, or get swallowed up by someone else. This is similar to trends taking place in many other industries. "There will be less than a handful of end-game winners," the CEO of Chase Manhattan announced in September 2000. "We want to be an end-game winner" (*Business Weekly*, 2000). But in few industries has the level of concentration been as stunning as in media. In short order, the global media market has come to be dominated by nine transnational corporations: General Electric (owner of NBC), AT&T/Liberty Media, Disney, AOL-Time Warner, Sony, News Corporation, Viacom, Vivendi, and Bertelsmann. None of these companies existed in its present form as recently as 15 years ago; yet all of them ranked among the largest 200 non-financial firms in the world for 2000 (*Wall Street Journal*, 2000). Of the nine, only five are truly US firms, though all of them have core operations there. Between them, these nine companies own: the major

US film studios; the US television networks; 80–85% of the global music market; the majority of satellite broadcasting world-wide; all or part of a majority of cable broadcasting systems; a significant percentage of book publishing and commercial magazine publishing; all or part of most of the commercial cable TV channels in the US and world-wide; a significant portion of European terrestrial television; and on and on and on.

By nearly all accounts, the level of concentration is only going to increase in the future. "I'm a great believer that we are going to a world of vertically integrated companies where only the big survive," said Gordon Crawford, an executive of Capital Research & Management, a mutual fund that is among the largest shareholders in many of the nine firms listed above (Bianco, 2000). For firms to survive, *Business Week* observes, speed is of the essence. "Time is short", (Ibid). "In a world moving to five, six, seven media companies, you don't want to be in a position where you have to count on others," Peter Chernin, the president of News Corporation, states. "You need to have enough marketplace dominance that people are forced to deal with you." Chernin elaborates: "There are great arguments about whether content is king or distribution is king. At the end of the day, scale is king. If you can spread your costs over a large base, you can outbid your competitors for programming and other assets you want to buy" (Hansell, 2000). By 2000, massive cross-border deals – like Pearson merging its TV operations with CLT and Bertelsmann, or Vivendi purchasing Universal – were increasing in prominence (Mermigas, 2000b).

Chernin's firm, Rupert Murdoch's News Corporation, may be the most aggressive global trailblazer, although cases could be made for Sony, Bertelsmann or AOL-Time Warner. Murdoch spun off Sky Global Networks in 2000, consolidating his satellite TV services that run from Asia to Europe to Latin America (Goldsmith and Dawtrey, 2000). His Star TV dominates in Asia with 30 channels in seven languages (Jacob, 2000). News Corp.'s TV service for China, Phoenix TV, in which it has a 45 per cent stake, now reaches 45 million homes there and has enjoyed an 80% increase in advertising revenues in the past year (Groves, 2000). And this barely begins to describe News Corp.'s entire portfolio of assets: Twentieth Century Fox films, Fox TV network, HarperCollins publishers, TV stations, cable TV channels, magazines, over 130 newspapers, and professional sport teams.

Why has this taken place? The conventional explanation is technology or, in other words, radical improvements in communications technology that make global media empires feasible and lucrative in a manner unthinkable in the past. This is similar to the technological explanation for globalization writ large. However, this is only a partial explanation, at best. The real force has been a shift to neoliberalism, which means the relaxation or elimination of barriers to commercial exploitation of media, and concentrated media ownership. There is nothing inherent in the technology that required neoliberalism; new digital communications could have been used, for example, to simply enhance public service media had a society elected to do so. With neoliberal values, however, television, which had been a non-commercial preserve in many nations, suddenly became subject to transnational commercial development and was thrust into the centre of the emerging global media system.

Once the national deregulation of media took place in major nations like the United States and Britain, it was followed by transnational measures like the North American Free Trade Agreement (NAFTA) and the World Trade Organization (WTO), all intent on establishing regional and global marketplaces. This has laid the foundation for the creation of the global media system, dominated by the aforementioned conglomerates. Now in place, the system has its own logic. Firms must become larger and diversified to reduce risk and enhance profit-making opportunities, and they must straddle the globe so as never to be outflanked by competitors. The upside is high; this is a market that some anticipate will have trillions of dollars in annual revenues within a decade. If that is to be the case, those companies that sit atop the field will almost certainly rank among the two or three dozen largest in the world.

The development of the global media system has not been unopposed in elite policy making forums. While media conglomerates press for policies to facilitate their domination of markets throughout the world, strong traditions of protection for domestic media and cultural industries persist. Nations ranging from Norway, Denmark and Spain to Mexico, South Africa and South Korea keep their small domestic film production industries alive with government subsidies. In the summer of 1998 culture ministers from 20 nations, including Brazil, Mexico, Sweden, Italy and Ivory Coast, met in Ottawa to discuss how they could "build some ground rules" to protect their cultural fare from "the Hollywood juggernaut". Their main recommendation was to keep culture out of the control of the WTO. A similar 1998 gathering, sponsored by UNESCO in Stockholm, recommended that culture be granted special exemptions in global trade deals. Nevertheless, the trend is clearly in the direction of opening markets.

Proponents of neoliberalism in every country argue that cultural trade barriers and regulations harm consumers, and that subsidies inhibit the ability of nations to develop their own competitive media firms. There are often strong commercial-media lobbies within nations that believe they have more to gain by opening up their borders than by maintaining trade barriers. In 1998, for example, when the British government proposed a voluntary levy on film and theatre revenues (mostly Hollywood films) to benefit the British commercial film industry, British broadcasters, not wishing to antagonize the firms who supply their programming, lobbied against the measure until it died. If the WTO is explicitly a pro-commercial organization, the International Telecommunication Union (ITU) has only become one after a long march from its traditional commitment to public service values in telecommunications (Molony, 1999).

The European Commission, the executive arm of the European Union, too, finds itself in the middle of what controversy exists concerning media policy, and it has considerably more power than the ITU. On the one hand, the EC is committed to building powerful pan-European media giants that can go toe-to-toe with the US-based giants. On the other hand, it is committed to maintaining some semblance of competitive markets, so it occasionally rejects proposed media mergers as being anti-competitive (Stern, 2000c). The wave of commercialization of European media has put the EU in the position of condemning some of the traditional subsidies to public service broadcasters as "noncompetitive," which is a source of considerable controversy (Stern, 2000a; Stern, 2000b). Public service broadcasting, once the media centrepiece of European social democracy, is now on the defensive and increasingly reduced to locating a semi-commercial niche in the global system (Goldsmith, 2000; Larsen, 2000). Yet, as a quasi-democratic institution, the EU is subject to some popular pressure that is unsympathetic to commercial interests.

Perhaps the best way to understand how closely the global commercial media system is linked to the neoliberal global capitalist economy is to consider the role of advertising. Advertising is a business expense made preponderantly by the largest firms in the economy. The commercial media system is the necessary transmission belt for business to market their wares across the world; indeed globalization as we know it could not exist without it. A whopping three-quarters of global spending on advertising ends up in the pockets of a mere 20 media companies (*The Economist* 11 March 2000). Ad spending has grown by leaps and bounds in the past decade as TV has been opened to commercial exploitation and is growing at more than twice the rate of GDP growth (Tomkins, 2000). Five or six super-ad agencies have emerged in the past decade to dominate this $350 billion global industry. The consolidation in the global advertising industry is just as pronounced as that in global media, and the two are related. "Mega-agencies are in a wonderful position to handle the business of mega-clients," one ad executive notes (Elliott, 2000). It is "absolutely necessary...for agencies to consolidate. Big is the mantra. So big it must be," another executive stated (Teinowitz and Linnett, 2000).

A second tier of less than 100 firms that are national or regional powerhouses rounds out the global media market. Sometimes these second-tier firms control niche markets, like business or trade publishing.

Between one-third and one-half of these second-tier firms come from North America; most of the rest are from Western Europe and Japan. Many national and regional conglomerates have been established on the backs of publishing or television empires, as in the case of Denmark's Egmont. Each of these second-tier firms is a giant in its own right, often ranking among the thousand largest companies in the world and doing more than $1 billion per year in business. The roster of second-tier media firms from North America includes Dow Jones, Gannett, Knight-Ridder, Hearst and Advance Publications, and among those from Europe are the Kirch Group, Mediaset, Prisa, Pearson, Reuters, and Reed Elsevier. The Japanese companies, aside from Sony, remain almost exclusively domestic producers.

This second tier has also crystallized rather quickly; across the globe there has been a shakeout in national and regional media markets with small firms getting eaten by medium firms and medium firms being swallowed by big firms. Compared with 10 or 20 years ago, a much smaller number of much larger firms now dominate the media at a national and regional level. In Britain, for example, one of the few remaining independent book publishers, Fourth Estate, was sold to Murdoch's HarperCollins in 2000 (Kirkpatrick, 2000a). A wave of mergers has left German television – the second largest TV market in the world – the private realm of Bertelsmann and Kirch (Rohwedder, 2000). Indeed, a wave of mergers has left all of European terrestrial television dominated by five firms, three of which rank in the global first tier (Reed, 2000). The situation may be most stark in New Zealand where the newspaper industry is largely the province of the Australian-American Rupert Murdoch and the Irishman Tony O'Reilly, who also dominates New Zealand's commercial-radio broadcasting and has major stakes in magazine publishing. Murdoch also controls pay television. In short, the rulers of New Zealand's media system could squeeze into a closet.

Second-tier corporations, like those in the first-tier, need to reach beyond national borders. "The borders are gone. We have to grow," the Chairman of Canada's CanWest Global Communications states in 2000. "We don't intend to be one of the corpses lying beside the information highway" (Brooke, 2000). "We have to be Columbia or Warner Brothers one day" (Cherney, 2000). The CEO of Bonnier, Sweden's largest media conglomerate, says that to survive, "we want to be the leading media company in Northern Europe" (Brown-Humes, 2000). Australian media moguls, following the path blazed by Murdoch, have the mantra "Expand or die." As one puts it, "You really can't continue to grow as an Australian supplier in Australia." Mediaset, the Berlusconi-owned Italian TV power, is angling to expand into the rest of Europe and Latin America. Perhaps the most striking example of second-tier globalization is Hicks, Muse, Tate

and Furst, the US radio/publishing/TV/billboard/movie theatre power
that has been constructed almost overnight. Between 1998 and 2000 it
spent well over $2 billion purchasing media assets in Mexico, Argentina,
Brazil, and Venezuela (Sutter, 2000).

Second-tier media firms are hardly "oppositional" to the global system.
This is true as well in developing countries. Mexico's Televisa, Brazil's
Globo, Argentina's Clarin and Venezuela's Cisneros Group, for example,
are among the world's 60 or 70 largest media corporations. These firms
tend to dominate their own national and regional media markets, which
have been experiencing rapid consolidation as well. They have extensive
ties and joint ventures with the largest media transnational corporations
(TNCs) as well as with Wall Street investment banks. In Latin America,
for example, the second-tier firms work closely with the US giants who
are carving up the commercial media pie among themselves. Televisa or
Globo can offer News Corp., for example, local domination of the
politicians and the impression of local control over their joint ventures.
And like second-tier media firms elsewhere, they are also establishing
global operations, especially in nations that speak the same language. As
a result, the second-tier media firms in the developing nations tend to
have distinctly pro-business political agendas and to support expansion
of the global media market, which puts them at odds with large segments
of the population in their home countries.

Together, the 60 or 70 first- and second-tier giants control much of the
world's media: book, magazine and newspaper publishing; music
recording; TV production; TV stations and cable channels; satellite TV
systems; film production; and motion picture theatres. But the system is
still very much in formation. The end result of all this activity by second-
tier media firms may well be the eventual creation of one or two more
giants, and it almost certainly means the number of viable media players
in the system will continue to plummet. Some new second-tier firms are
emerging, especially in lucrative Asian markets, and there will probably
be further upheaval among the ranks of the first-tier media giants. And
corporations get no guarantee of success merely by going global. The
point is that they have no choice in the matter. Some, perhaps many, will
falter as they accrue too much debt or as they enter unprofitable ventures.
However, we are likely closer to the end of the process of establishing a
stable global media market than to the beginning. And as it takes shape,
there is a distinct likelihood that the leading media firms in the world will
find themselves in a very profitable position. That is what they are racing
to secure.

The global media system is fundamentally non-competitive in any
meaningful economic sense of the term. Many of the largest media firms
have some of the same major shareholders, own portions of one another,

or have interlocking boards of directors. When *Variety* compiled its list of the fifty largest global media firms for 1997, it observed that "merger mania" and cross-ownership had "resulted in a complex web of interrelationships" that would "make you dizzy." The global market strongly encourages corporations to establish equity joint ventures in which the media giants all own a part of an enterprise. This way, firms reduce competition and risk and increase the chance of profitability. As the CEO of Sogecable, Spain's largest media firm and one of the twelve largest private media companies in Europe, expressed it to *Variety*, the strategy is "not to compete with international companies but to join them."

In some respects, the global media market more closely resembles a cartel than it does the competitive marketplace found in economics textbooks. This point cannot be overemphasized. In competitive markets, in theory, numerous producers work hard and are largely oblivious to each other as they sell what they produce at the market price, over which they have no control. This fairy tale, still regularly regurgitated as being an apt description of our economy, is ludicrous when applied to the global media system. The leading CEOs are all on a first name basis and they regularly converse. Even those on unfriendly terms, like Murdoch and AOL-Time Warner's Ted Turner, understand they have to work together for the "greater good." "Sometimes you have to grit your teeth and treat your enemy as your friend," the former president of Universal, Frank Biondi, concedes (Grover and Siklos, 1999). The head of Venezuela's huge Cisneros group, which is locked in combat over Latin American satellite TV with News Corporation, explains about Murdoch: "We're friends. We're always talking" (Hoag, 2000). Moreover, all the first and second tier media firms are connected through their reliance upon a few investment banks like Morgan Stanley and Goldman Sachs that quarterback most of the huge media mergers. Those two banks alone put together 52 media and telecom deals valued at $450 billion in the first quarter of 2000, and 138 deals worth $433 billion in all of 1999 (Mermigas, 2000b). This conscious co-ordination does not simply affect economic behaviour; it makes the media giants particularly effective political lobbyists at the national, regional, and global levels.

Global corporate media, culture and politics

But what about media content? Global conglomerates can at times have a progressive impact on culture, especially when they enter nations that had been tightly controlled by corrupt, crony-controlled media systems (as in much of Latin America) or nations that had significant state censorship over media (as in parts of Asia). The global commercial media system is radical in that it will respect no tradition or custom, on balance, if it stands in the way of profits. But ultimately it is politically conservative, because the media giants are significant beneficiaries of the current social structure around the world, and any upheaval in property or social relations, particularly to the extent that it reduces the power of business, is not in their interest.

The "Hollywood juggernaut", or the spectre of US cultural imperialism, remains a central concern in many countries for obvious reasons. Exports of US films and TV shows increased by 22% in 1999 (Guider, 2000), and the list of the top 125 grossing films for 1999 is made up almost entirely of Hollywood fare (D'Alessandro, 2000). When one goes nation by nation, even a "cultural nationalist" country like France had nine of its top 10 grossing films in 1999 produced by the Hollywood giants (Grey, 2000). "Many leftist intellectuals in Paris are decrying American films, but the French people are eating them up," a Hollywood producer noted (Lyman, 2000). Likewise, in Italy, the replacement of single-screen theatres by "multiplexes" has contributed to a dramatic decline in local film box office revenues (Rooney, 2000). The moral of the story for many European filmmakers is that you have to work in English and employ Hollywood moviemaking conventions to succeed (Foreman, 2000). In Latin America, channels controlled by media giants overwhelm local cable television and the de facto capital for the region is Miami (*TV International*, 2000).

But there are problems with leaving the discussion at this point. The notion that corporate media firms are merely purveyors of US culture is ever less plausible as the media system becomes increasingly concentrated, commercialized, and globalized. The global media system is better understood as one that advances corporate and commercial interests and values and denigrates or ignores that which cannot be incorporated into its mission. There is no discernible difference in the firms' content, whether they are owned by shareholders in Japan or France or have corporate headquarters in New York or Sydney.

As the media conglomerates spread their tentacles, there is reason to believe they will encourage popular tastes to become more uniform in at least some forms of media. Based on conversations with Hollywood executives, *Variety* editor Peter Bart concluded, "the world film-going audience is fast becoming more homogeneous." Whereas action movies had once been the only sure-fire global fare – with comedies considerably more difficult to export – by the late 1990s, comedies like *My Best Friend's Wedding* and *The Full Monty* were doing between $160 million and $200 million in non-US box-office sales

When audiences appear to prefer locally made fare, the global media corporations, rather than flee in despair, globalize their production. Sony has been at the forefront of this, producing films with local companies in China, France, India, and Mexico, to name but a few (Brodesser, 2000;

Duke, 2000b). India's acclaimed domestic film industry – "Bollywood" – is also developing close ties to the global media giants (*The Economist* 12 August 2000). This process is even more visible in the music industry. Music has always been the least capital-intensive of the electronic media and therefore the most open to experimentation and new ideas. US recording artists generated 60% of their sales outside the United States in 1993; by 1998 that figure was down to 40%. Rather than fold their tents, however, the four media transnationals that dominate the world's recorded-music market are busy establishing local subsidiaries in places like Brazil, where "people are totally committed to local music", in the words of a writer for a trade publication. Sony, again, has led the way in establishing distribution deals with independent music companies from around the world.

With hypercommercialism and growing corporate control comes an implicit political bias in media content. Consumerism, class inequality, and individualism tend to be taken as natural and even benevolent, whereas political activity, civic values, and anti-market activities are marginalized. The best journalism is pitched to the business class and suited to its needs and prejudices; with a few notable exceptions, the journalism reserved for the masses tends to be the sort of drivel provided by the media giants on their US television stations. In India, for example, influenced by the global media giants, "the revamped news media . . . now focus more on fashion designers and beauty queens than on the dark realities of a poor and violent country" (Mishra, 2000). This slant is often quite subtle. Indeed, the genius of the commercial-media system is the general lack of overt censorship. As George Orwell noted in his unpublished introduction to *Animal Farm*, censorship in free societies is infinitely more sophisticated and thorough than in dictatorships, because "unpopular ideas can be silenced, and inconvenient facts kept dark, without any need for an official ban."

Lacking any necessarily conspiratorial intent and acting in their own economic self-interest, media conglomerates exist simply to make money by selling light escapist entertainment. In the words of the late Emilio Azcarraga, the billionaire founder of Mexico's Televisa: "Mexico is a country of a modest, very fucked class, which will never stop being fucked. Television has the obligation to bring diversion to these people and remove them from their sad reality and difficult future." The combination of neoliberalism and corporate media culture tends to promote a deep and profound depoliticization. One need only look at the United States to see the logical endpoint (Perry, 2000). But depoliticization has its limits, as it invariably runs up against the fact that we live in a social world where politics have tremendous influence over the quality of our lives.

Finally, a word should be said about the Internet, the two-ton gorilla of global media and communications. The Internet is increasingly becoming a part of our media and telecommunications systems, and a genuine technological convergence is taking place. Accordingly, there has been a wave of mergers between traditional media and telecommunication firms and each of them with Internet and computer firms. Already companies like Microsoft, AOL-Time Warner, AT&T and Telefonica have become media powerhouses in their own right. It looks like the global media system is in the process of becoming a globally integrated, commercial communications system where six to a dozen "supercompanies" will rule the roost. The notion that the Internet would "set us free," and permit anyone to communicate effectively, hence undermining the monopoly power of the media giants, has not materialized. Although the Internet offers extraordinary promise in many regards, it alone cannot slay the power of the media giants. Indeed, no commercially viable media content site has been launched on the Internet, and it would be difficult to find an investor willing to bankroll any additional attempts. To the extent the Internet becomes part of the commercially viable media system, it looks to be under the thumb of the usual corporate suspects.

For much of the 1990s even those that were alarmed by the anti-democratic implications of the neoliberal global economy tended to be resigned to these developments. The power of capitalism and the profit motive was such that it would inexorably establish a world system based on world markets and unchecked capitals flows. Likewise, the globalization of the corporate media system was inexorable. As one Swedish journalist noted in 1997, "Unfortunately, the trends are very clear, moving in the wrong direction on virtually every score, and there is a desperate lack of public discussion of the long-term implications of current developments for democracy and accountability." It was presented as natural, as inexorable. And for those in power, those who benefited by the new regime, such thinking made their jobs vastly easier.

But, as I developed at the outset of this chapter, the truth is that there is nothing "natural" about neoliberal globalization. It requires extensive changes in government policies and an increased role for the state to encourage and protect certain types of activities. The massive and complex negotiations surrounding NAFTA and the WTO provide some idea of how unnatural and constructed the global neoliberal economy is. Or consider copyright, and what has come to be considered intellectual property. There is nothing natural about this. It is a government granted and enforced monopoly that prevents competition. It leads to higher prices and a shrinking of the marketplace of ideas, but it serves powerful commercial interests tremendously. In the United States, the corporate media lobby has managed to distort copyright so the very notions of the public domain or fair use – so important historically – have been all but obliterated. The US government leads the fight in global forums to see that the corporate friendly standards of copyright are extended across the planet and to cyperspace. The commitment to copyright monopolies, now granted for 95 years to corporations, as the *sine qua non* of the global economy shows its true commitment is to existing corporate power rather than to a mythological free market.

The traditional myth of the relationship of the state to the private sector in US media has become the neoliberal myth on a global scale. The myth now has become transparently a tool of propaganda. The Enron affair highlighted again how closely intertwined our government is with the largest private corporations. The widespread graft associated with neoliberal privatizations and deregulations – in telecommunication more than anywhere else – has augured in a wave of corruption of world historical proportions. If the market is God and public service in bunk, why on earth would anyone enter government, except to feather their own nest, by any means necessary? For those at the receiving end of neoliberal globalization – the bulk of humanity – the idea that people need to accept neoliberal globalization as a given is untenable. For those committed to democracy above neoliberalism, the struggle is to require informed public participation in government policy making. Specifically, in view of the importance of media, the struggle is to democratize communication policy making.

In February 2002 in New York City the World Economic Forum held its annual meeting. Meant to gather the leading visionaries and figures of global capitalism and government leaders eager to serve them, what was striking was the very high number of prominent media figures who participated in their panels. It was an indication of what a prominent role the global corporate media system plays in the new regime. Concurrently, several thousand miles to the south, in Porto Alegre, Brazil, the alternative World Social Forum met to pose an alternative view for the global political economy. A central theme there, as well, was media. Much of the attention of the tens of thousands of people from around the world who participated addressed the limitations of the corporate media status quo for democracy, the need for democratic media policy making, and the need to develop viable alternative non-commercial media as the basis of a just and humane society. The overriding spirit at the WEF was that economic and media policies are too important to be trusted to the common people; the attitude in Porto Alegre was the opposite. Indeed, there are indications that progressive political movements around the world are increasingly putting media issues on their political platforms. From Sweden to France and India to Australia, New Zealand and Canada, democratic, left-wing political parties and social movements are beginning to make structural media reform – breaking up the big companies, recharging non-profit and non-commercial broadcasting and media – a part of their agenda. They are even finding out that this sometimes can be a successful issue with voters.

There are no simple solutions to the question of how best to organize media and communication to promote a healthy economy and democratic values, just like there is no simple answer to how best to structure the global political economy. Moreover, it is clear that the two debates are very closely related, in view of the significance of media and communications to both capitalism and democracy. That is why it is imperative that the debates on this topic be widespread and held under the light of day. If we know one thing from history it is this: if self-interested parties make decisions in relative secrecy, the resulting policies will serve the interests primarily of those who made them. As the old saw goes, "If you're not at the table, you not part of the deal." Our job, as scholars, as citizens, as democrats, is to knock down the door and draw some more chairs up to the table. And when we sit at that table we have to be armed with the most accurate understanding of what is taking place and what is possible that we can generate. This is no time for a bogus mythology that masks the naked self-interest of the dominant parties.

References

Bianco, A. (2000) 'Deal time at Seagram', *Business Week*, 26 June, 60.

Brodesser, C. (2000) 'Sony's global gaze pays', *Variety*, 3–9 April, 13, 62.

Brooke, J. (2000) 'Canadian TV makes a move into papers', *New York Times*, 1 August, C1, C25.

Brown-Humes, C. (2000) 'Bonnier Scotland', *Financial Times*, 20 September, 9.

Business Weekly, (2000) 'Talk Show', 2 October, 12.

Cherney, E. (2000) 'Can West tightens its media grip', *Wall Street Journal*, 2 August, A17.

Cullison, A. (2000) 'Russia arrests president of big private media company', *Wall Street Journal*, 14 June, A21.

D'Alessandro, A. (2000) 'The top 125 worldwide', *Variety*, 24–30 January, 22.

Dickson, M. (2000) 'Gap between the rich and the poor is widening', *Financial Times*, 22 September, XXIV.

Duke, P.F. (2000a) 'House vote cracks China's Great Wall', *Variety*, 29 May–4 June, 10.

Duke, P.F. (2000b) 'Robinson explores Asian films for Sony', *Variety*, 28 August–3 September, 7, 128.

Elliott, S. (2000) 'Publicis plans to buy Saatchi for at least $1.5 Billion', *New York Times*, 20 June, C1, C8.

Foreman, L. (2000) 'Teuton tongues untied', *Variety*, 14–20 August, 39–40.

Goldsmith, C. (2000) 'BBC forms commercial internet unit; US firms to fake stake in subsidiary', *Wall Street Journal*, 23 August, B10.

Goldsmith, A. and Dawtrey, J. (2000) 'Murdoch: Sky's the limit', *Variety*, 28 August–3 September, 1, 130.

Gordon, M. (2000) 'A Russian press beholden to many', *New York Times*, 17 March, A10.

Grey, T. (2000) 'Promo effort key in France', *Variety*, 21–27 February, 30, 106.

Grover, R. and Siklos, R. (1999) 'Where old foes need each other', *Business Week*, 25 October, 114, 118.

Groves, D. (2000) 'Star connects dot-coms', *Variety*, 29 May–4 June, 63.

Guider, E. (2000) 'AFMA exports up 22% as global TV booms', *Variety*, 19–25 June, 14, 75.

Hansell, S. (2000) 'Murdoch sees satellites as way to keep News Corp. current', *New York Times*, 16 June, C7.

Hatfield, S. (2000) 'EU turning into battleground over more curbs on marketing', *Advertising Age*, 18 September, 60.

Hoag, C. (2000) 'Empire Building: The slow track', *Business Week*, 11 September, 126E3–126E4.

Jacob, R. (2000) 'Star is shooting towards interactive TV', *Financial Times*, 10–11 June, 11.

Kirkpatrick, D.D. (2000a) 'HarperCollins plans to buy a small British publisher', *New York Times*, 11 July, C6.

Kirkpatrick, D.D. (2000b) 'Not quite all-American, Bertelsmann is big on U.S.', *New York Times*, 3 September, section 3, 2.

Larsen, P.T. (2000) 'Little time for a commercial break', *Financial Times*, 25 August, 15.

Lyman, R. (2000) 'No trace of anti-Hollywood bias in French purchase of Universal", *New York Times*, 20 June, C12.

Mermigas, D. (2000a) 'International plays take media firms to next level', *Electronic Media*, 31 July, 22.

Mermigas, D. (2000b) 'Morgan Stanley Banks on Media', *Electronic Media*, 15 May, 17, 20.

Mishra, P. (2000) 'Yearning to be great, India loses its way', *New York Times*, 16 September, A27.

Molony, D. (1999) 'Utsumi's CEO think-tank to shake up ITU', *Communications Week International*, 4 October, 1, 74.

Perry, J. (2000) 'Shades of 1960 are superficial amid changes in electorate', *Wall Street Journal*, 14 September, A12.

Preston, J. (2000) 'Mexican TV, unshackled by reform, fights for viewers', *New York Times*, 7 June, A3.

Reed, S. (2000) 'A Media Star is Born', *Business Week*, 24 April, 136–137.

Rohwedder, C. (2000) 'Kirch tightens control over German broadcast assets', *Wall Street Journal*, 29 June, A18, A21.

Rooney, D. (2000) 'Ciao time for Italy', *Variety*, 19–25 June, 72.

Schechter, D. (2000) 'Long live chairman Levin!', Mediachannel.org. 5 July.

Stern, A. (2000a) 'EU questions Pubcaster aid", *Variety*, 22–28 May, 67.

Stern, A. (2000b) 'EU to change Pubcaster financial rules', *Variety*, 10–16 January, 105.

Stern, A. (2000c) 'Microsoft/Telewest deal faces high EC hurdles", *Variety*, 3–9 April, 79.

Sutter, M. (2000) 'Hicks, muse invests $1 bil in Latin American drive', *Variety*, 17–23 January, 70.

Swarns, R.L. (2000) 'Tightening control on media worry journalists in Angola', *New York Times*, 20 September, A8.

Teinowitz, R. and Linnett, I. (2000) 'Eye on mergers: Media behemoths up agency ante', *Advertising Age*, 8 May, 3, 105.

The Economist, (2000) 'Free to be Bad', 11 March, 44.

The Economist, (2000) 'Growing Up', 12 August, 57–58.

The Economist, (2000) 'Scardino's way', 5 August, 62.

The Economist, (2000) 'Star turn', 11 March, 67–68.

The Economist, (2000) 'Stopping the rot in public life', 16 September, 41–42.

Tomkins, R. (2000) 'Zenith spotlights advertising surge', *Financial Times*, 18 July, 21.

TV International (2000) 'US Cable channels tighten their grip on Latin American cable viewers', 12 June, 6.

Tyler, P.E. (2000) 'Russian media magnate reports Kremlin is trying to silence him', *New York Times*, 5 September, A12.

Wall Street Journal (2000) 'The World's 100 Largest Public Companies', 25 September, R24.

Wright, R. (2000) 'Hungary packs broadcasters with party names', *Financial Times*, 2 March, 7.

Global Institutions and the Democratization of Media

Seán Ó Siochrú

The media crossroads

We stand at crossroads in media and communications. At stake is the type of media environment we seek to inhabit, from local to global level, for ourselves and future generations. Formidable forces propel us down one route, the commercialization of activities and outputs, subsuming media and communication "products" under general market rules. The alternative route, currently much less prominent, is a road in which media are focused on fulfilling human needs and reinforcing human rights and aspirations, under a revised and invigorated structure of global governance.

The crossroads metaphor is apt. If we travel down the former route it becomes increasingly difficult to make our way back since each move is locked into place, ratchet-like, by powerful institutions with an armoury of enforcement mechanisms and sanctions at their disposal. But building an impetus to move down the path of human fulfilment will demand conscious and co-ordinated effort from civil society, international institutions and governments.

This chapter:

- Outlines the role of media in society, and why regulation has emerged everywhere.
- Reviews some of the main international bodies involved in regulating or governing media, with a brief glance at other actors on the global stage.
- Describes some relevant trends in media and communication governance globally.
- Describes two divergent avenues facing us, and where each might lead in the future.
- Concludes with a comment on the role of civil society.

Why regulate media?

The existence of institutions to govern media presupposes a need to regulate media, in ways that do not apply to other products of human labour. Yet the question is sometimes asked: *Do we need to regulate media at all?* Why not let the market decide what television, radio, newspapers, and the rest can offer, just as it does for other goods, with governments and institutions intervening solely to ensure a level playing pitch? Why are media products so special that we cannot let media enterprises get on with what they claim to do best – producing what people want, measured by what they will pay for? If this argument can be upheld at the national level, then at the international level it surely must apply, *mutatis mutandi*.

Media products *are* different, not least because they are more than mere consumer goods; in important respects they also "produce" us. Mass media and electronic media in today's highly differentiated and compartmentalized world are becoming the primary means through which people interact with each other, beyond their immediate everyday contacts. Our sense of belonging, of being part of a wider community, a culture, a nation, and a single human race, is increasingly "mediated through media". Beyond even an individual's relationship to society, the very mode in which society as a whole realizes its aspirations and fulfils its claims to offer freedom and democracy to its members, to support rational and fair legal, political and social institutions – its legitimacy in claiming to act in the best interests of people in general – all of these ideas and realities are represented to us and brought to us primarily by the media. They provide us with the raw material, often even the tools, to comprehend what our society is beyond our immediate experience, and ultimately to participate in that society and perhaps even to change it.

The notion of "media products" seems somehow too feeble to encompass the role they play in our lives. In listening to, watching, and reading media we do not just consume, we interact. We interact with other people, and through them with society in general. We interact with ourselves, sometimes unconsciously, with our sense of sharing a common culture, and sense of being a part of something beyond ourselves.

Thus virtually every society has developed two distinct ways to govern media, as a sector of economic activity and for their role in politics, society and culture. Each follows a separate rationale and is deployed in different configurations by different societies. The two are:

- Regulating the media as a sector of the economy, or *industry regulation*, similar to that of other economic sectors. In a market economy this usually involves regulating in the interests of people as *consumers* by preventing market dominance and sustaining competition, ensuring a legally secure foundation for instance for intellectual property rights (IPRS), allocating fairly public resources such as radio spectrum, and so forth.

- Regulating to sustain and strengthen the social, cultural and political role of media and communication or *societal regulation*. This is regulating in the interests of people as social, cultural and political actors, and includes the *regulation of content*, policing acceptable "outer limits" of specific content, based on social norms. This may involve everything from the support of public service media, to limits on advertising, to expanding public domain information, to universal service obligations, to content censorship.

Forms of regulation often come into conflict. Too strong an emphasis on regulation as an industry in a market economy may be at the expense of media's social or cultural roles. For instance, intellectual property rights by their nature involve a trade-off between the monopoly economic rights of content owners and public domain information available freely to all.

From a human rights perspective, societal regulation should have clear preference over industry regulation, in areas of conflict but also in terms of determining overall priorities. *Within* industry regulation, the rights of consumers should be preferred over the interests of industry, where they conflict but also in general. Unfortunately, as we shall see, in the current situation and trends precisely the inverse holds. The powerful countries, with a view to global dominance, promote corporate needs over those of people as "consumers" of media; and societal regulation, along with people's social, cultural and political needs in relation to media and communications, are given low priority or ignored altogether.

As the media globalize, questions of regulation are posed at the international level. As national boundaries of media are gradually relaxed, media and communications issues have generated their own international institutions or have become integrated into the activities of existing general purpose ones.

Global governance institutions and actors in media and communications

Four of the main international organizations involved in regulating and governing the media at global level are covered here. There are others, but the ITU, UNESCO, Internet Corporation for Assigned Names and Numbers (ICANN) and WTO stand out. Their responsibilities and powers are briefly outlined in the next section.

Media governance institutions

The International Telecommunication Union, founded in 1865 and the oldest of them, is responsible for the allocation of radio spectrum across borders, terrestrially and via satellite, for the purposes of telephony (mobile and fixed), data, television, radio and others. The use of spectrum is co-ordinated to prevent interference and border "spillover"; and slices of it are allocated to different uses and users. Since it is a scarce public resource, allocating it among users is an important and contentious issue internationally. The ITU also divides out the satellite orbital slots, including the valuable and scarce geo-stationary orbit.

A second major ITU function is in standardization for telecommunication networks. The standardization of equipment and of protocols can also be highly contentious since they are tied up with issues such as market control. A further activity has been to facilitate the so-called "accounting-rate" system, whereby telecommunication operators reimburse each other for the use of their networks in another country to complete calls. In net terms, many poorer countries have, for a number of reasons, benefited from these cross-payments, yielding sometimes significant amounts of foreign exchange. The ITU also is concerned with extending telecommunication to less industrialized countries, but has only very limited means by which to do so.

Thus the ITU has responsibility for several narrow but critical areas of strong interest to governments, corporations and civil society alike.

UNESCO, on the other hand, has much 'softer' responsibilities but they extend to many areas of social concern. It is important less for its formal powers and its capacity to enforce multilateral agreements, than as a forum for voluntary cooperation on (usually non-contentious but necessary) issues of mutual concern across a wide area, and to raise and debate issues of global import. UNESCO in its early decades was instrumental in many conventions, declarations and congresses, overseeing agreements on issues such as the exchange of audio-visual content for educational use, cross-border direct broadcasting satellite, and copyright exemptions for development purposes. In the late 1970s to mid 1980s it came to the fore as a debating arena for global communication issues, with the New World Information and Communication Order (NWICO).[1] Its fingers were badly burned on this, however, as cold world politics and entrenched positions of some of the major powers eventually led to the

---

1. There are many publications on this. For a recent retrospective review, see Vincent, Richard C., Kaarle Nordenstreng and Michael Traber (eds), 1999. *Towards Equity in Global Communication: MacBride Update.* Cresskill, NJ: Hampton.

defeat of voices calling for more open and democratic global media flows and structures. UNESCO has never fully recovered in terms of facilitating vibrant debate, and indeed the US has still not rejoined after leaving in the mid 1980s, believing, probably correctly, that it can wield more influence by remaining outside.

In 1995, the UNESCO-sponsored *World Commission on Culture and Development* put forward some significant proposals regarding media, raising the idea of a tax on the use of spectrum, the proceeds to be utilized for non-commercial programming for international distribution, and questioning the growing concentration of media ownership. However, it is probably indicative of UNESCO's broader constraints that these failed to be ratified, or even discussed, at the follow-up intergovernmental meeting in 1998. Nevertheless, it continues to support progressive media initiatives and to sponsor debate at a lower level.

The newcomer is ICANN.[2] Established in 1998, its main job is to manage the process of assigning names and numbers for the Internet, an issue that has gradually taken on huge commercial and legal significance. ICANN initially saw itself as primarily technical, but its management of the IP addresses and of the Domain Name System (DNS), which ultimately controls routing of Internet traffic, quickly moved into economic, political, social and even cultural domains.

It is interesting not just for what it does, but for how it does it. It was constituted as a non-profit private-sector corporation under Californian law, and designed to allow the US Department of Commerce to maintain ultimate control over the DNS (which it still does). This places it in the non-governmental sector. Its governance is still in transition, as yet not having attained stability, but the original decision to allow the election from at-large membership (i.e., Internet users who registered to the process) of five of the nineteen directors was reversed, and the current members is merely advisory. Although too fragile and structured to present a new model of governance, and with a very narrow mandate, it does point to the feasibility of different approaches.

Last and certainly not least is the WTO, which straddles some key areas of media and communications and is set to extend its mandate further.

---

2. ICANN is not alone in being dedicated to governing the Internet. The Internet Architecture Board (IAB) oversees technical development, and formed both the Internet Society (ISOC), a body of coordinating professionals, and the Internet Engineering Task Force (IETF), the accredited standards body. The World Intellectual Property Organization (WIPO), by agreement with ICANN, is a key body in resolving domain name disputes.

Although WIPO is an international UN agency set up to oversee intellectual property rights, the WTO (which is not a UN organization) decisively gained pre-eminence with the signing of the Trade Related Aspects of Intellectual Property Rights (TRIPS) Agreement in 1995. The WTO now has at its disposal some of the strongest policing and enforcement powers ever ceded to an intergovernmental body by governments, and it uses them extensively in copyright. The copyright industries, such as film, music, books, television and magazines, include the world's largest media corporations, and the WTO underwrites and enforces their rights in all TRIPS signatory countries. The WTO is also the forum in which these rights have become, on the one hand, narrower, retaining only the model used by wealthy countries, and on the other, deeper in terms of duration and breadth.

In telecommunication, the shift from monopoly national providers to competitive international supplies has brought the trade paradigm of the WTO to the fore. An area of interest here is universal service policies, by which governments can facilitate cross-subsidization from large business users and urban areas to domestic and small users and rural areas. The WTO agreement permits this only where they do not interfere unduly with competition – a vague formulation yet to be tested. The move to trade is also leading to the redundancy of the ITU's accounting-rate system, and to the net loss of foreign earnings for some of the poorest countries.

Finally, the WTO is active in the area of media products. For magazines, newspapers and other non-audio-visual media, countries are not allowed, on pain of strong financial or trading sanctions, to introduce barriers to market entry on the basis of protection of cultural integrity. An attempt was made in the Uruguay Round to lay down the same rules for film, video, television and audio-visual products, which failed due to European and other opposition. But this was back on the table at the Doha Round of Negotiations and also at Cancun. Unfortunately, nothing positive transpired.

These, then, are some of the individual institutional players. They are not, however, a power unto themselves.

Other actors

Intergovernmental organizations (ICANN being an odd one out) are ultimately subject to governments. In formal terms they exercise no more power than is (more or less voluntarily) ceded to them by governments. Yet not that all governments are equal – a range of pressures can be brought to bear by powerful governments to force others to cede their authority to a treaty or agency. The WTO, for instance, is regularly accused of being the arena for such strong-arm tactics. But governments in general remain the most powerful single set of actors.

Nevertheless when inter-governmental agreements are reached and ratified, they tend to take on a life of their own, and the central role of the administering agency in interpretation and implementation lands it in the driving seat. The agencies thus gradually carve out a sphere of influence, and must thus be considered as actors in their own right.

The global private sector, through multinational corporations and their well-funded associations and lobbying bodies, is also a major force in the international scene. Its avenues of influence extend everywhere, through some major governments who virtually identify the national interest with that of its corporations, to sitting on the arbitration boards of the WTO and recruiting their former senior officials, to concerted long-term lobbying of international agencies. In media and communication, as in other areas, the private sector does not always speak with one voice. The issue of copyright over downloaded pages on the Web pitted the content 'copyright' industries against the Internet and telecommunication industry, the former seeking to extend copyright to even temporarily downloaded pages. The latter won out in the end of the day, and the Web retains for the moment that aspect of public access.

Nor does the private sector always get its own way. Non-governmental, non-commercial organizations have enjoyed a special relationship with the UN system since its foundation. (Oddly, the ITU is an exception, and the WTO, which is not a part of the UN system, also closes out NGOs from any formal role.) This relationship has gradually expanded and taken on concrete forms in terms for instance of access to information and influencing the agendas. However, it is outside the institutions, through mobilization at major events and at other times, that civil society organizations are currently flexing their muscle and are staking a claim to be heard. In media issues and communication, civil society as a whole has so far been largely, and surprisingly, silent, viewing the media primarily as tools to promote their agendas, rather than as active and hugely influential agents in their own right. But this may be changing.

Influences and trends in governance

If the intent is to influence them, then media trends must be set in the wider context.

Dominating this context is the new phase of globalization characterized on the one hand by a diminishing role in certain respects of the nation state, coupled with the limited capacity of most UN multilateral agencies to cope with the expanded global governance tasks. Into the vacuum, one deliberately engineered by powerful nations, steps the liberalized industries, across commodity, services, information and communication technology sectors, with their own integral, exclusive, forms of 'governance' and control overseen by their favoured international institutions such as the WTO, G8 and OECD. UN agencies risk floundering in the wake of these unelected elites.

A simplified global institutional dynamic can be identified: UN multilateral organizations, with at least some claim to uphold balanced global development, are struggling against a trade and commercial paradigm based on private property and contractual rights driven largely by non-UN organizations, especially the WTO, and supported by more powerful governments and the interests of private capital. On the side of more balanced development is probably the majority of world governments, though unable to act in concert, as well as most of the UN agencies themselves in terms of their remit and secretariats, and civil society.

But the media industry is not only a lead sector in the rise of the trade paradigm; it provides many of the tools and instruments that drive it along. The media, and especially the cultural content industries, help open up new markets internationally through advertising and through the promotion of consumerist lifestyles in which entertainment is usually packaged. As tools, the pace of globalization would be almost inconceivable without telecommunications and information and communication technologies (ICTs) generally. It is because the media occupy this key double role that attempts to influence their course of development will always confront the larger forces of globalization.

As micro-expressions of these macro trends, a number of distinct, intertwining strands are likely to influence the future media landscape, among them the following.

First is the declining role of most governments and UN organizations in media and communication governance, and the ascendance of the trade paradigm. Six points stand out over the last decade or two:

- The transfer to the WTO of sovereign government power in the area of telecommunications and IPRs, and possibly in the future regarding audio-visual products and the capacity to protect cultural diversity and identity.
- The effective loss of IPRs by WIPO and its Conventions to the WTO and the consequent strengthening of trade and competition rules over human rights, and cultural and social considerations.
- The general decline of the ITU as the global governing body in telecommunications with much of its previous domain moving over to trade and market mechanisms.

- The inability of the multilateral organizations to agree on regulating foreign direct satellite broadcasting, and the consequent absence of regulation in the sector.
- The careful distancing of UNESCO from political issues and any debates casting doubt on the supremacy of the trade and market paradigm.
- The failure of the UN system to gain governance over the Internet, underlined by the creation of ICANN as a non-governmental and non-representative body that received its power directly from the US government.

Many of these are actively pursued by governments, belying any simple argument concerning the eclipse of the national state by some competing power – the loss of sovereignty to global market forces is seen by many as to their individual commercial benefit. Both the EU and US, for instance, anticipated and achieved huge benefits from the opening of telecommunication markets in less developed countries (for whom the long-term benefits are a lot less clear). However, the net effect is the loss of sovereign power of governments, and their transfer to selected multilateral organizations, most significantly the WTO.

Second is the related emergence of closed, quasi-governmental organizations controlled by the private sector, pushing market mechanisms to the fore in media and communications.

As we have seen, the private sector is already a major player, perhaps the most powerful, in the global arena. Yet it falls short of what is needed to achieve its ultimate ambition: freedom to operate when, where and how it likes in an unrestricted global marketplace for all media and communication products. The exclusion of the audio-visual sector from the WTO's Uruguay agreement (ironically because of differences between the US and the EU), and market barriers based on cultural preservation; the inability to buy and sell satellite slots and radio spectrum at will; continuing government ownership of some telecommunication networks and media, as well as universal service obligations; time-consuming negotiations in UN agencies; and other nuisances cramp their style and cost them profits. Their banner-waving governments began to reinforce existing closed, semi-secretive clubs such as the G8, OECD and World Economic Forum (Davos), and invited in the private sector. The concepts of the Global Information Infrastructure and the EU's Global Information Society were refined here, in close consultation with business and putting them firmly in the driving seat. Civil society and development issues travel in baggage class, offered amid much publicity some pilot projects and fine-sounding but ultimately self-serving plans to bridge the Digital Divide. Entirely new entities were constituted to represent business and patron governments, for instance the Global Business Dialogue on Electronic Commerce, and the Global Information Infrastructure Commission whose core objectives are to plot a future for governance in which business interests are permanently to the fore.

Nevertheless, the trend towards private sector governance faces an ongoing legitimacy deficit. Credible and durable governance structures are not yet in sight.

A third trend in media and communication is the tentative emergence of civil society influence, and the rise of "people's media".

Although civil society in the form of NGOs has long been recognized within the UN system, it was only within the Earth Summit in 1991 that they began to take on a more organized and collective role, moving on from individual consultations with The United Nations Economic and Social Council (ECOSOC) and specialized agencies. But it was because of NGO activity outside the UN system, at least formally, that the other players began to sit up and take notice. The success in opposing the Multilateral Agreement on Investment (MAI) initiative and the street demonstrations against the WTO, G8 and others moved civil society into a new category of actor on the global scene, the implications of which are still being played out. In media and communication, however, there has been little direct action, and only slightly more within the formal intergovernmental structures. The organization of civil society around media and communications can be seen in three strands.

First is the emergence of transnational advocacy and activist groups in media and communications concerned with the global trends and pushing for enhanced democracy and the right to communicate. These include the People Communication Charter, the Platform for Communication Rights, the World Association of Community Radio Broadcasters (AMARC), the World Association for Christian Communication (WACC), ALAI, Les Penelopes, PANOS Institute, Association for Progressive Communication (APC).[3] Second is the more frequent inclusion of a right to communicate or similar calls in the statements and goals of (non-media) umbrella NGO and civil society entities and events, for instance in the Civil Society Summit (Montreal December 1999) the World Social Forum in Porto Alegre in January 2001 and 2002.[4] This suggests that the issue is slowly but steadily gaining a profile across civil society as a whole. Third is the growth of community

---

3. See http://www.amarc.org, http://www.crisinfo.org, http://www.wacc.org, http://www.wacc.org/pcc, http://www.penelopes.org, http://www.apc.org, http://www.panos.org.

4. See http://www.forumsocialmundial.org.br for outcomes of WSF 2002.

or "people's media", in many countries across the world, motivated in large part by the need to provide an alterative to mainstream media and to democratize media structures and access.[5] These include public access and community access television, community and independent non-profit radio (many under the umbrella of AMARC), the global community networking movement, Indymedia Centres, as well as regional and global information services such as MediaChannel, WETV, FreeSpeech TV, Undercurrents and others which not only offer alternative media content but comment extensively on the media. There is also some evidence that these issues and actions are beginning to emerge in less industrialized countries, which suffer from some of the worst excesses of media globalization, and this augers well for the future.[6]

Their potential impact on global governance structures has yet to be tested. But the World Summit on the Information Society (WSIS) in December 2003 and again in December 2005, led by the ITU, will test the waters. Several groups have organized to broaden the WSIS agenda, and external events, to deal fully with issues of information and media, and to enable it to play a catalytic role in civil society organization in media and communications.[7] However, an enhanced role for civil society in global media governance would also raise issues of legitimacy and representation, just as it does in all sectors.

A fourth trend is a growing sophistication of less industrialized countries in relation to their role in multilateral organizations. Over the years, fewer industrialised countries have expressed concern at the imposition of external media content and structures, and the liberalization of the telecommunication and other communication sectors. Although their motivations varied, many drew on genuine concerns and an informed understanding of the long-term risks. The debates in and around UNESCO during the 1980s, with the Non-Aligned Movement playing a central role, raised for the first time in global debate a great variety of matters concerning media, the press, information and data flows, concentration of ownership, etc.[8] The virulent opposition of the US and the UK, which in part caused their departure from UNESCO, is an indication of the extent to which these regimes felt their interests threatened.

---

5. See http://www.devmedia.org for a composite list.

6. Community radio, in particular, is gaining momentum in countries such as Nepal, Mali, Nepal, and much of Latin America and the Caribbean.

7. See http://www.itu.int/wsis/ and http://www.geneva2003.org for official sites, and http://www.crisinfo.org for one civil society response.

8. See the MacBride Commission Report: *Many Voices, One World: Report by the International Commission for the Study of Communication Problems*, UNESCO 1980.

The decades since have been more muted: yet the issues have not gone away, but were eclipsed by more immediate and pressing needs. Often, media and communication issues were put in that basket of things that were, regretfully, to be traded off in the WTO, often with very little return. Some of the larger countries, such as Brazil and India have their own media sectors, and attempt to negotiate to carve out a niche for their own industries within the overall neoliberal paradigm.

Nevertheless, in some countries there is evidence that a more sophisticated, long-term, and strategic understanding of the role that media and communications can play, not just economically but also socially, politically and culturally, is emerging. For instance, South African President Mandela's refusal to simply accept what was offered at the G7 summit on the information society South Africa in 1996; the success of a group of west African countries in brokering a deal that kept copyright away from downloading from the Web;[9] and the more recent positions and actions of President Konaré of Mali in supporting radio and other media. These suggest a growing willingness to cooperate, between less industrialized countries but also with the more progressive industrialized ones, that has been absent for some time.

Two scenarios for the media future

We have trod a somewhat circuitous route in our exploration of global institutions and the democratization of media. Having positioned ourselves at a crossroads to the future of media and communications, we then posed the question of why media needed regulation and governance at all, and hence why institutions have sprung up nationally and globally to regulate them. This was followed by a description of the main governance institutions and what they do. A dynamic was introduced, in the form of some trends in media and communications that are likely to influence these institutions.

We now find ourselves back at the crossroads. Here we present two avenues down which we may move, each leading to a very different scenario. They are at opposite ends of a spectrum, but well within the

---

9. A proposal from a group of African countries enabled the software and telecommunication industries to defeat the efforts of the US, EU governments and the "copyright" industries to extend copyright to temporarily downloaded Web pages, at a WIPO conference in 1996. This *ad hoc* coalition of advanced industry and African countries will yield benefit to the latter only in the long-term. See Ó Siochrú and B. Girard (with Amy Mahan) (2002). *Global Media Governance: A Beginner's Guide.* Oxford: Rowman and Littlfield/UNRISD

bounds of possibility. Scenario 1 is based on the extrapolation of the commercially driven scenario to its ultimate, but still plausible, conclusion. Scenario 2 sees the democratic core of the current system revived and extended.

Scenario I: A dominant trade and liberalization paradigm

The first scenario envisages current dominant trends proceeding several steps forward. The main thrust is for the commercial and liberalization logic to permeate virtually the entire media and communication sphere, nationally and internationally, largely at the expense of social, cultural and political dimensions of the media. Multinational industry reigns, the UN system is gradually displaced by an ever more powerful WTO, and closed intergovernmental clubs of powerful governments and private sector become allies. It leads to a contraction of the public sphere and of human rights imperatives, and an extension of the private sphere and the economic rights of those that can afford to exercise them.

At the macro level, this would require the resolution of current struggles concerning for instance the WTO and Bretton Woods institutions in favour of the neoliberal approach, with little structural change and emerging governance needs settled in compliance with the market driven status quo.

For the media and communication sector, structural conditions and regulation of this scenario would include the following:

- Unimpeded global trade in media and cultural products, with no protection on the basis of cultural, social or environmental outcomes.
- A fully enforceable, and all-embracing, intellectual property regime that benefits owners most.
- The virtual elimination of universal service instruments in telecommunication, deemed to interfere with competition and the operation of the market.
- Heightened commercialization and looser regulation of radio, television and other mass media, and public service media compelled to compete in the market place.
- The commercialization of spectrum terrestrially and in space, sold to the highest bidder.
- The gradual extension of industry self-regulation in emerging media sub-sectors.

Were these trends to gain an inexorable momentum, other global stakeholders would face stark choices. The UN system would be forced to choose between accommodating itself to the new world order, and risking redundancy, being cash-strapped and lacking the internal capacity to devise and enforce an alternative development or human rights based agenda.

Less developed countries, similarly, would probably divide between a minority who object, and so are sidelined from the globalization process or perhaps suffer the full rigour of what they have already signed up to; and a majority who believe they have no option but to join in.

Civil society, realizing the dangers too late to mount an effective opposition, would find itself more or less excluded from this domain altogether, spectators as the global media circus rolls on.

The medium term outcomes of such a scenario may be as follows:

- The number of media channels and sources available grows, especially from international sources by direct satellite broadcast and other means.
- Within these, diversity of programme content diminishes and quality falls.
- Media ownership and content portfolios concentrate and centralize further.
- Public service media disappears or dwindles to a niche provider.
- Support measures for local, community and people's media disappear in the clamour for market sustainability.
- Public domain information shrinks, as lucrative parts are hived off to profit-making concerns.
- Infrastructure and new services in telecommunications grow, but are confined mainly to urban and business markets, leading to a greater disparities.

Brought to its (unlikely) ultimate conclusion, media and communications in a few decades could be expunged of all voices of dissent and criticism, an entire generation having grown up knowing little else, not just incapable of autonomous political action but unaware of the concept and practice; the gap between those with access to media and those without accentuating the already great economic inequalities; media content and information becoming the almost exclusive property of giant corporations, controlling creativity and diversity on the short rein of profit maximization. Most insidiously, the process slowly but surely transforms the very well-spring of ideas, people's creative capacities, in the end yielding a self-perpetuating cycle that stifles genuine diversity and is purged of all dissent and non-conformity.

The circle is complete; the end point feeds back to the beginning. A consistent and coherent pattern of domination impels media in a downward spiral to a new Information Dark Age.

Is this the brave new world we are irreversibly careering towards? Probably not, at least not the whole way.

The core weakness of this scenario is the legitimacy deficit it would generate. Current tensions would intensify, and the systematic roll out of this agenda through all media would require such an ever-growing abuse of power that it probably could not be sustained for long. The virtually complete subjugation of the public interest to commercial capital, although possible in individual countries and indeed approximated already in the US, would encounter sustained and deep resentment and opposition globally. Many governments, powerful and less so, would balk at the prospects of such explicitly one-sided development, and its long-term implications.

Thus a more credible future for this scenario would require the cooption of major civil society interests and of the some governments of less industrialized countries. This would in turn mean a series of concessions in non-core areas that would at least mitigate the outcomes. Nevertheless, finding ourselves even half down this route should be enough to frighten most ordinary people.

Scenario 2: Multilateral cooperation reborn

The second scenario represents a decisive shift in the other direction, reinvigorating the democratic core of the media and communication governance structures. A reformed and rejuvenated UN system, with mechanisms enabling the participation of civil society as well as governments, regains the upper hand in media and communication governance. It reinstates social, economic and cultural rights and the satisfaction of human needs as the core objective, and economic and political structures as means to deliver these. Social and cultural needs and equitable economic relations as objectives are elevated above the pursuit of any particular economic model as means.

This scenario would bring some significant regulatory and governance changes:

- A review of the rules of international trade in media products, with priority accorded to renewal of culture and to potential social risks; and a range of measures for citizens and governments to influence the impact of external media products, including advertising.
- Promotion of a range of measures for providing universal access to telecommunications and media, in rural and remote areas and among marginalized groups, even where these significantly impinge on the operation of market mechanisms.
- Support for global public service and development oriented media, perhaps through a multilateral agency, including ongoing funding

from a tax on commercial satellite use, on turnover of the media industries generally, or another similar source.

- Enforceable mechanisms to halt, indeed reverse, concentration of media ownership.
- An international agreement on media transmitted across borders that covers issues of content quality, diversity and independence, and freedom from political and other interference.
- Reformulation of intellectual property rights to ensure wider and quicker access to the public domain and to support development goals, while preserving the incentives for creativity and innovation in media content.
- The allocation of international spectrum, as a global public good, explicitly factoring in social, cultural and development needs of marginalized countries and groups, as well as public service and people's media, and dedicated spectrum at no or reduced cost.

Faced with such a panoply of checks and regulations, the transnational corporate sector in this scenario would find itself forced to roll back expectations and operate internationally for the first time within a regulated environment. Some global corporations might be obliged to split up. Profitability would probably suffer a temporary setback, until the sector reorganizes to the new rules of the game. Civil society, at least some less industrialized countries and marginalized groups in general, however, would see an expansion of media and communication opportunities, offered access they could hitherto only dream of, in terms of participating in media and promoting their diverse views, cultures and ideas.

Medium term outcomes may include the following:

- A significant rise in non-commercial media, with a mission specifically to contribute to a media environment that puts people at the centre, from local to global levels.
- The emergence of well-funded quality public service media globally and perhaps regionally, alongside the commercial sector.
- A reduction of advertising presence and impact, and of the need to maximize advertising revenues, resulting in the alleviation of commercial and consumerist pressures.
- The emergence of public communication spaces for informed democratic dialogue on issues of global concern, and perhaps of a global civil society.
- More equitable access to media services, including telecommunications, reducing the gap between wealthy and poor regions and groups.

Conceivably, such a scenario could become a realistic prospect, for instance, were it to be supported by a number of breakaway industrialized country governments, collaborating with a majority of less industrialized countries, and riding on the back of a wave of civil society lobbying and action at national and international levels.

Realistically, any shift at all in this direction would be (and is currently) opposed forcefully by the US and some other powerful countries, and by most of the institutions through which these countries cooperate, such as the G8, OECD and WTO. A break in these ranks would be an essential prerequisite. The private sector would use all possible means to oppose such trends. Global media owners in the past have not stopped short of explicitly deploying their media to protect and expand their private interests, and the threat in this case is probably strong enough to provoke an extreme reaction.

Such a radical shift would confront other problems. There are genuine concerns regarding the capacity of current multilateral governance structures to function democratically and effectively. Such a scenario would very quickly face its own crisis of legitimacy, given the generally unaccountable, relatively opaque nature of the UN system, and its composition almost entirely of governments. To be plausible and gain the level of support needed, a reconstructed UN system would need greater accountability and transparency and, most important, extended participation beyond governments to embrace other actors, especially civil society and the private sector.

Yet the full realization of Scenario 2 in the absence of a broader move to rethink global governance structures, and refocus them on human development, stretches credulity somewhat. A fully fledged Scenario 2 would require, in the sphere of media and communications, entirely new instruments, even agencies, setting the UN system on par with, or indeed above, the WTO in its capacity to enforce agreements; and counterbalancing the WTO trade focus with explicit consideration of social and cultural rights and other economic and sustainability objectives. This is likely only against the backdrop of a much wider movement to reinvent global governance. And a very broad, powerful and robust coalition indeed would be required to wage a sustained campaign to see this agenda through. It would undoubtedly have to incorporate civil society elements globally, especially in the industrialized countries, involve concerted action from many governments, and courageous stances from the UN system.

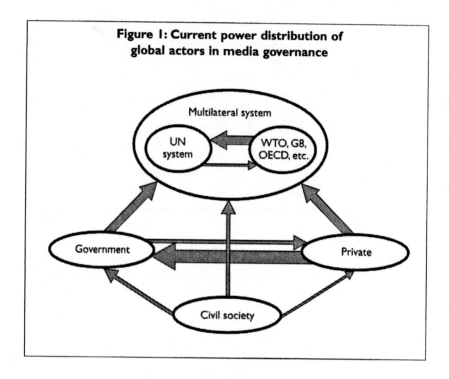

Figure 1: Current power distribution of global actors in media governance

Conclusion

At the risk of mechanical over-simplification, the power dynamics between the main global actors is sketched out on Figure 1 as it applies generally and to media and communication.

At present, the balance of power lies clearly with the private sector. Their direct influence on global governance is enormous, through lobbying and directly in non-UN entities. But their real grip on power is secured through powerful governments that identify their own interests with those of the private sector. Yet even these governments have individually relinquished much of their direct control over global corporations, pooled into multilateral agencies over which they hope they can maintain secure control.

Within the multilateral sphere, the UN system is losing out, both in formal powers and in imposing strategic direction, to the WTO and other informal organizations controlled by the wealthy countries.

Civil society has long had some limited influence on governments, and recently flexed its muscles in relation to the multilateral system. But it would be a mistake to overestimate its current strength and power base, especially in media and communication.

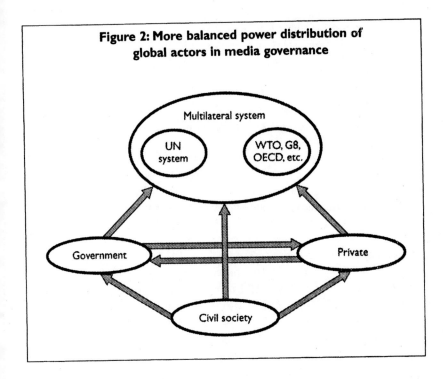

Figure 2: More balanced power distribution of global actors in media governance

Despite an apparent loss of sovereignty, governments still play a pivotal role because they still maintain formal control in most areas of governance. At the end of the day, what governments cede individually, they can take back collectively, or at least influence who benefits from the giving.

Of course, Figure 1 fails to differentiate between governments, and particularly between the wealthy and poorer ones. But no matter. The intent is to focus on the role of civil society and the need to work at several levels at once.

More balanced power relations from the perspective of civil society and human rights, and indicative of moving towards the second scenario discussed earlier, is represented on Figure 2.

From a strategic civil society view, this would mean acting in several ways at once.

First, sustained pressure would have to be brought on multilateral agencies, acting both within and outside the formal structures. The 'surprise' factors of recent years is likely in time to be replaced, or supplemented, by a 'long march through the institutions' influencing and lobbying at every step. Yet this can have little permanent impact if governments cannot also be persuaded to focus more on the human rights and civil society needs, and collectively begin to stand with them against private interests. Thus national level lobbying and interaction will be vital. At the same time, the private sector can also, though ultimately only to a limited extent, be directly influenced through consumer and shareholder action and by building a civil society enterprise sector of cooperative, fair-trade companies and the like.

Ultimately, this means coordinated civil society organization at these levels, for coordination and concertation in themes and timing will be vital if action is to be effective.

The schema above is generic enough to be applicable equally to achieving global human rights as to media and communications. Indeed, for better or worse, significant change is unlikely to come about in media and communication governance except in the context of a reappraisal of governance structures as a whole. Yet just as media and communications are at the forefront of recent and current trends towards the market-driven consumerist model of society, so could they form, if turned around, the spearhead of a new human rights based model. Storming the media and creating their own are often among the first actions of national revolutionaries. So too at global level, human rights activists could do worse than to concentrate early efforts on creating a new media for a new world, and progressive institutions on building a global media regulatory framework that puts the needs of the people first.

Intellectual Property Rights

Cees J. Hamelink

Everything belongs to he who makes good use of it.

André Gide

International rules for the protection of intellectual property rights (IPRs) find their origin in the 19th century. From its beginnings this protection has been inspired by three motives. The first motive was the notion that those who invested in the production of intellectual property should be guaranteed a financial remuneration. With the establishment of the first international treaties on intellectual property protection (the Paris Convention for the Protection of Industrial Property of 1883 and the Berne Convention for the Protection of Literary and Artistic Works of 1886) a monetary benefit for the creator was perceived as a necessary incentive to invest in innovation and creativity. During the 1928 revision of the Berne Convention the notion of moral rights was added to the entitlement to economic benefits. The introduction of the moral value of works recognized that they represent the intellectual personality of the author. Moral rights protect the creative work against modification without the creator's consent, protect the claim to authorship and the right of the author to decide whether a work will be published. Early on in the development of intellectual property rights it was also recognized that there is a public interest in the protection of intellectual property. As a common principle it was recognized that IPRs promote the innovation and progress in artistic, technological and scientific domains, and therefore benefit public welfare. The US Constitution, for example, articulates this as follows, "to promote the progress of science and the useful arts, by securing for limited time to authors and inventors the exclusive rights to their respective writings and discoveries". The protection of intellectual property rights is in fact a delicate balancing act between private economic interests, individual ownership, moral values, and public interest.

With the increasing economic significance of intellectual property, the global system of governance in this domain has moved away from moral and public interest dimensions and emphasizes in its actual practice mainly the economic interests of the owners of intellectual property. Today, such owners are by and large no longer individual authors and composers who create cultural products, but transnational corporate cultural producers. The individual authors, composers, and performers are low on the list of trade figures and as a result there is a trend towards IPR arrangements that favour institutional investment interests over individual producers.

The recent tendency to include intellectual property rights in global trade negotiations demonstrates the commercial thrust of the major actors. Copyright problems have become trade issues and the protection of the author has conceded place to the interests of traders and investors. This emphasis on corporate ownership interests implies a threat to the common good utilization of intellectual property and seriously upsets the balance between the private ownership claims of the producer and the claims to public benefits of the users. The balance between the interests of producers and users has always been under threat in the development of the IPR governance system, but it would seem that the currently emerging arrangements provide benefits neither to the individual creators, nor to the public at large.

Its key beneficiaries are the transnational media conglomerates for which the core business is content. Several of their recent mergers are in fact motivated by the desire to gain control over rights to contents such as are, for example, invested in film libraries or in collections of musical recordings.

German media tycoon Leo Kirch made much of his enormous fortune through the acquisition of rights to content. Kirch bought from United Artists/Warner Brothers the rights to some hundred successful American TV programmes, he holds rights to over 50,000 hours of such TV series as Baywatch and owns copyright to 16,000 film titles which he bought from Columbia Pictures, Paramount and Universal. He also acquired the Pay-TV rights to Disneyfilms. British music company EMI owns the copyright to over one million of the world's most popular songs.

Recent developments in digital technology, which open up unprecedented possibilities for free and easy access to and utilization of knowledge, have also rendered the professional production, reproduction and distribution of content vulnerable to grand scale piracy and made the content owners very concerned about their property rights and interested in the creation of a global enforceable legal regime for their protection.

Protecting intellectual property is however not without risks. The protection of intellectual property also restricts the access to knowledge since it defines knowledge as private property and tends to facilitate monopolistic practices. The granting of monopoly control over inventions may restrict their social utilization and reduce the potential public benefits. The principle of exclusive control over the exploitation of works someone has created can constitute an effective right to monopoly control which restricts the free flow of ideas and knowledge. In the current corporate battle against piracy it would seem that the key protagonists are in general more concerned about the protection of investments than about the moral integrity of creative works or the quality of cultural life in the world.

With the currently emerging IPR a few megacompanies become the global gatekeepers of the world's cultural heritage. At the same time the small individual or communal producers of literature, arts or music hardly benefit from international legal protection. Most of the collected money goes to a small percentage of creative people (some 90% goes to 10%) and most artists that produce intellectual property receive a minor portion of the collected funds (some 90% share 10%). Most of the money goes to star performers and bestselling authors. The media industry does not make money by creating cultural diversity as it gets its revenues primarily from blockbuster artists. If there was more variety on the music market, for example, the smaller and independent labels would become competitive to the transnational market leaders. Although this would fit into the conventional thinking about free markets, the industry in reality prefers consolidation over competition!

It becomes increasingly clear that the drive to protect media products against unauthorized reproduction leads to an increasing level of restrictions on reproduction for private purposes.

The leading musical recording companies that are part of large media conglomerates, such as Bertelsman, Sony, Vivendi, and Warner Music, battle against the downloading and sales of illegal CDs. They do this through sectoral organizations such as the International Federation of Phonograph Industries (IFPI). In many countries, however, such as China, people cannot buy CDs, DVDs or computer software as current IPRs make these items too expensive. As a result many Chinese resort to piracy. In many Western countries it remains a contested issue whether free downloading really damages sales. There are studies that show that Napster users (the peer-to-peer music sharing system that is now part of the Bertelsman empire) buy more CDs than other consumers (Jupiter research).

The prevailing system often works to the disadvantage of smaller parties in the market. The Recording Association of America has lobbied for a bill (effective 20 October 2002) that imposes a fee for all Webcasters that stream music to their audiences. The bill is to be retro-active from 1998. The law implies that the fee is based upon the numbers of listeners. The result will be that the fee exceeds the revenues for most Webcasters and they will be forced out of business. This is not a normal royalty fee which amounts to 3% of revenues. The same fee is not imposed for broadcast radio stations because the powerful National Association of Broadcasters stopped this.

An attempt to change the current system of IPR protection could begin with the critical analysis of its essential assumptions. These are that culture can be legitimately appropriated for private commercial purposes, that cultural works are original, that without protection there would no cultural production and that without royalties there would be no other sources of revenues. These assumptions are seriously flawed.

Culture cannot be privately owned so that access, use and adaptation can be commercially controlled. Cultural products are developed in dynamic social processes and are as such always the result of what predecessors have done and of collective efforts. Most creative work is in fact the re-ordering of already existing work. Intellectual production is typically a collective effort and it makes little sense to single out some few stakeholders as the only beneficiaries.

Against the claim that there would be no cultural production without adequate ownership protection, it can be argued that artists do in fact have other ways to make money than from royalties (live performances for example). Moreover, the argument is thinly based upon the expectation that cultural production is motivated by monetary interests and not primarily by the drive to create and innovate.

There are also strong arguments in favour of the abolition of the system of IPR protection.

- The system makes access too expensive and thus prohibitive for the world's majority!
- It stifles creativity because of its concentration on a limited number of star cultural producers. Once the IPR system has gone there will be space for a greater number and variety of creative artists.
- It poses a serious threat to the public domain. Increasingly freely available cultural products (which are in the public domain, meaning there are no longer copyrights claims against users, as in the case of works by Shakespeare or Mozart) are stored in digital format and deposited in electronic databanks. Such databank collections are entitled to copyright protection as a result of which public access is restricted.

As the likelihood of an abolition of the system of IPR protection is very slim indeed, given the enormous interests and powerful actors in the game, the international community should at a minimum try to perceive of intellectual property rights as basic human rights.

Intellectual property rights are recognized as human rights (Article 27:2 of the Universal Declaration of Human Rights) and this should shape the political framework for all parties involved: producers, distributors, artists, and consumers. If this was done then the context for the protection of intellectual property rights would be made up of: the right to full participation in cultural life for everyone; the right of affordable access to information for everyone; the recognition of moral rights of cultural producers; the rights of creative artists; the diversity of cultural production, and the protection of the public domain.

As human rights always imply responsibilities, it would make sense to follow Larry Lessig's proposal to add to "copyright" a "copyduty". As he writes, "We may well see the day when our students are taught not of "copyright" but of "copyduty" – the legal duty of copyright holders to assure public access".[1]

A human rights approach would give full meaning to the so-called "fair use" doctrine. In a general sense "fair use", which is an important provision on US copyright law, claims that the use of a copyrighted work for purposes like criticism, comment, new reporting, teaching or research should not be considered an infringement of copyright protection.

The fair use doctrine is under serious threat through the use of advanced technologies that allow rights-holders the control over access by third parties of works in digital form. The use of protective technologies (such as encryption, copy protection codes) strengthens the monopoly control of IPR owners. As consumers are likely to develop and apply circumvention technologies to undermine this control, the US administration and US motion picture industry effectively lobbied the WIPO to incorporate in the 1996 WIPO Copyright Treaty the following Article 13, "Contracting Parties shall provide legal protection and effective legal remedies against the circumvention of effective technological measures that are used by authors in connection with the exercise of their rights under this Treaty or the Berne Convention and that restricts acts, in respect of their works, which are not authorized by the authors concerned or permitted by law".

In the USA this provision was enacted in the 1998 Digital Millennium Copyright Act (DMCA) which went much further than the WIPO agreement. The DMCA prohibits the manufacture, sales, or import of technologies that can be used to circumvent protective technologies. This could make it impossible for people who buy perfectly legal items and want to make extra copies for private use (the extra CD or DVD in the car or second home, for example).

It may also become impossible to play copyrighted items – legally acquired – on different platforms (not the CD players but your PC).

---

1. Lessig, L. (1998), Life, Liberty, Copyright, *The Atlantic Monthly Unbound*, 10 September 1998.

The DeCSS case demonstrates where this could lead to. In 1999 Norwegian teenager Jon Johansen was arrested on the accusation of creating a circumvention technology to crack the protection code for DVDs. Contrary to most media publicity cracking the DVD encryption was not an individual effort, but was the effort of the MoRE group that authored DeCSS. This is a software application to decrypt DVD movies that can be used among others to play DVDs on Linux-operated computers. When the magazine Computer 2600 reported about this (and offered a link to the programme), the publisher was successfully sued by the Motion Picture Association of America.

In conclusion: the statement from André Gide that provided the motto for this article fits very well into a human rights IPR framework and it should provide guidance to the future of intellectual property rights.

Regional and Country Case Studies

Privatization: The Cost of Media Democratization in East and Central Europe?

Slavko Splichal

While the collapse of the socialist systems in the late 1980s formally reduced the complexity of the former "three-world" international structure, the world of "post-communism" continues to appear as a distinct entity, as did the "Second World" of communist countries earlier in the past century. Post-communism has been described as "a *suigeneris* system which is marked by some democratic practices, with stronger or weaker commitments to pluralism, and characterized by political and economic competition. At the same time, anti-democratic ideas and practices are also current" (Schöpflin, 1993: 63). This also applies to the transition processes emerging in the mass media that are closely linked to the main actors and controversies of social change and progress[1] in the region. Although post-communist countries share many common experiences, there are no less significant differences between them in terms of their political, economic and cultural positions. As Holmes (1997: 4) argues, there is now even "far less of a basically common blueprint than there was up to 1989." It is difficult to generalize the main tendencies in the development of the press and broadcasting during the last decade in countries as diverse as, for example, Russia and the Czech Republic, or Romania and Slovenia. Nevertheless, these countries experienced important changes in practical (political, economic, cultural) terms when compared with the former, more unified, systems. While several countries are moving towards the establishment of democratic political systems, others have hardly made any progress, and some of them have even

---

1. The term "progress" is used to denote the processes of social changes that occur not just at the level of political and social orientation, but – as the consequence of purposive, concentrated efforts – in fundamental elements of the power structure, particularly in the development of a political public sphere and political pluralism. See Habermas (1990).

regressed. Changes to their media systems remain an important political issue. Discussions on the future of the media are divided along party political lines and are related to the division of power among political actors. This process is seldom accompanied by a discussion – let alone systematic implementation – of the new media, such as the Internet, or has led to a radical departure – with the exception of processes related to the privatization of the media. During the early period of transition many East-Central European (ECE) countries saw a significant increase in the diversity of media ownership compared to the communist era, but the experience in recent years seems to be the opposite: an increased concentration of media ownership resembles the scenarios in Western Europe and the USA.

In the early 1990s, I had challenged the idea that the burial of authoritarian practices in the former socialist countries would automatically bring about the rise of democratic political and media systems (Splichal, 1994). My doubts were largely provoked by the fact that ECE societies were caught up in the imitation of West-European practices in economy and society rather than selectively adapting Western media practices and systems and applying them to the specific situations in East-Central Europe. As Habermas has argued, the peculiar characteristic of the democratic "revolutions of recuperation" in the ECE countries is a "total lack of ideas that are either innovative or orientated towards the future" (Habermas, 1990: 27). The changes in media systems suffered from the absence of both theoretical foundations and practical citizen participation. There were almost no forces setting up competitive models of social development. Imitative political and economic transformations across the region also endangered critical studies and new social movements as forces of democratization. Another major source of contemporary problems in the former socialist countries is certainly an "uncritical critique" of the recent (socialist) past, which is considered the *only* source and cause of all problems arising *after* the fall of the old system. Since the late 1980s, many prophets of democratic changes have believed that ECE countries had no other history than that of socialism. Although it is beyond doubt that limited economic, technical, and staff resources resulting from the "socialist times" hinder these countries from media restructuring and general progress, there are other impediments to the development of more democratic systems which go beyond the direct consequences of the former system. These include the broader historical, cultural and geographic environments as well as new, indigenous actions.

The media had, and still have, an important role in the historic battle for democracy and pluralism in the region. In a number of former socialist countries, the media (at least some of them) were agents of the revolutionary political changes of the 1980s. At the same time, in all ECE countries revolutionary changes in society were aimed at the transformation of the party- or state-owned media. In one way or another, all the central questions of transition of these societies pertain to the media: the role of the state and civil society, the question of democratic pluralism, problems of denationalization and privatization of the means of production, the quest for sovereignty and, of course, the liberalization of media systems.

In the 1990s, all countries in the region privatized the press and introduced a form of dual ("public – commercial") broadcasting system. Initially, this era was characterized by strong political dependence of the broadcasting sector on the new political elites. But radio and television soon took to the path of commercialization and content today is dominated by cheap studio programmes and talk shows, reruns and, particularly, increasing foreign (mainly US) entertainment. The withering away of the idea of the public sphere was caused by a combination of *internal commercial pressures* (e.g., technological underdevelopment, economic problems) and *external influences* (e.g., TV stations controlled or directly owned by transnational corporations). Compared with the situation before 1989, the media in East-Central Europe have certainly made significant gains in liberalization and pluralization. However, in contrast to the demonopolization of the state-owned media, which has made decisive progress, other fundamental prerequisites of media democratization – e.g., media diversity, access to the media, professionalization of journalism – are yet to become realities. While state-owned media monopolies were abolished everywhere, television and radio-transmitting facilities and the licensing of frequencies are still under direct government control, and the state-run postal systems often continue to exercise near-monopolies in the distribution of newspapers and magazines. Politicians in all countries tend to constrain journalistic freedom by using or introducing anti-defamation laws to penalize journalists for writing openly about public officials and institutions. In the former Soviet Union, Bulgaria, Romania, and several of the former Yugoslav republics, poor economic conditions, the lack of a developed advertising market, continuing monopolies (e.g., of press distribution) and a considerable degree of state control (with subsidies and content-based criteria for registration of newspapers) leave little room for truly independent newspapers. Democratization of the press is also impeded by slow progress in the professionalization of journalists, understood both in the sense of professional individual skills and competencies, and in the sense of collective professionalization, that is a prerequisite for journalists to perform a public service and to protect the autonomy of the profession.

Searching for a theory

Colin Sparks identified four specific theories aiming at the explanation of changes that took place in the ECE countries after 1989, which differ in how they conceptualize the old economic and political system, the nature of changes (primarily social or political), and the nature of economic and political systems emerging from the changes, ranging from structural continuity to discontinuity. (1) "Total transformation" theory conceptualizes the changes as both political and social revolutions that profoundly changed all levels of society – from a totalitarian communist system to the market economy and political democracy. (2) "Social (counter-) revolution" theory stresses the impetus revolutions gave to economic progress while political changes are seen as less significant. (3) "Political revolution" theory characterizes the changes as a transition from the state-capitalist to private capitalist system, without substantial changes in state power and ruling class. (4) The fourth set of "what-revolution?" theories argue that "the collapse of the communist regimes, although visibly dramatic, did not in the end constitute any serious transfer of political or social power, and thus cannot really be termed a 'revolution'" (Sparks, 1998: 78–92).

Beyond significant differences regarding the outcomes of revolutions (*What* has happened?), all the four theories in Sparks' typology neglect the process of transformation itself, i.e., *how* it happened, whereas the question of *why* the old system collapsed is almost superfluous after the decades of theoretical and empirical critiques of the inefficiency and untenability of the former political and economic system in the era of globalization of the late 20th century. The two opposing views present in the four theories that try to explain change in the ECE countries are *continuity versus discontinuity*. These correspond closely with two main (and antagonistic) processes of social *adaptation* identified by one of the prominent French sociologists of the nineteenth century, Gabriel Tarde, i.e., *accumulation* and *substitution*. Tarde's theory based on the theoretical triad consisting of *invention*,[2] *imitation*, and *opposition* seems to be particularly relevant for our discussion of the post-communist transformation of the media because, in *L'opinion et la foule* (1901/1961), Tarde also examines the relationship between the means available to achieve specific goals and conditions restricting social actions, and identifies communication

---

2. According to Tarde, invention or, as he also names it, adaptation and consequently human progress (i.e., the change of social conditions), result from oppositions; while at the same time "we see harmonious things which, by multiplying, come into conflict with one another" (1902/1969: 144).

(technology) as particularly important on both accounts. As a matter of fact, at the beginning of the 20th century, Albert Venn Dicey already applied Tarde's "laws of imitation" to explain social changes in Russia. (Dicey, 1905/1981: 4) has suggested that in "many Eastern countries, opinion . . . has for ages been, in general, hostile to change and favorable to the maintenance of inherited habits", and that in countries such as Russia, all the reforms have been performed without much deference to local opinion, but were rather guided exclusively by ideas imported from elsewhere.

In the effort to identify major tendencies in the transformation of media systems in East-Central Europe, the reality of imitation and a lack of innovation have attracted particular attention. Tarde's theory of imitation as a general law of development seems to offer a valid explanation of these (r)evolutionary changes because it transcends the division between dependency and diffusionist modernization theories. The former claim that the process of modernization in the world periphery of less developed countries is shaped (imitated) in such a way as to lead to their exploitation, and to the strengthening of the dominance of most developed nations. The latter believe all societies (not only less developed ones) borrow or imitate elements of other political and economic systems and cultures. Tarde's theory does not specify *in advance* the nature of imitation, but recognizes several forms of imitation that are related to innovation and opposition. In this sense, both dependency and diffusionist theories may be considered special forms of Tarde's general theory. Similarly, theories attempting specific explanations of the transition in the ECE countries, focusing either on continuity or discontinuity, actualize Tarde's ideas of accumulation and substitution as two specific innovative processes that are always combined with imitation.

Tarde pointed to a fundamental difference between two ways in which progress through imitation is effectuated, *substitution* and *accumulation*. The now ruling ECE progress is primarily unilateral (passive) imitation based on substitution. Changes are introduced through the substitution of former institutions,[3] and only exceptionally through accumulation. Such unilateral and (thus) uncritical imitation of democratic institutions developed in

---

3. This process can also be conceptualized with Tehranian's terms of "dissociation" and "assimilation", with dissociation denoting the reaction against the institutions of the former system, and assimilation the acceptation of external models of developments ("Westernization") – in contrast to "selective participation", which was, according to Tehranian, typical of some ECE countries such as Poland, Czechoslovakia and Yugoslavia, in the 1980s (Tehranian, 1990: 187–189).

Western democracies may also have non-democratic consequences. As Benjamin Barber (1992: 63) demonstrates, "importing free political parties, parliaments, and presses cannot establish a democratic civil society; imposing a free market may even have the opposite effect." Instead, Robert Dahl (1991: 15) suggests that the countries in transition to the inauguration of democratic institutions should "discriminate between the aspects of the mature democratic countries that are essential to democracy and those that are not only *not* essential to it but may be harmful."[4] Otherwise, an enduring imitation can establish a long lasting, even institutionalized dependency. Thus the conservative Austrian government, for example, officially proposed in January 2001 to the four ECE countries who expect to join the European Union by 2006 – Poland, Czech Republic, Hungary, and Slovenia – to form a sort of Central European "Commonwealth" with the leading role of Austria – an alliance clearly resembling the old-time Habsburg Austro-Hungarian Empire that perished in the First World War.

The extreme case of substitution is the process of *lustration* initiated – in more or less institutionalized form – in a number of ECE countries.[5] *Lustration* is the means of investigating and exposing those who participated in power during the former communist regimes in a number of the ECE countries including Poland, the Czech Republic and Bulgaria. However lustration literally tends to substitute the old power elite with a new one by a non-judicial practice of exposing those who participated in power in the former regimes (particularly former Party functionaries and

---

4. Of course, this is not a new idea. Bryce reports about Hamilton's remark in his letter to Montesquieu that "a government must be fitted to a nation as much as a coat to the individual; and consequently that what may be good at Philadelphia may be bad at Paris and ridiculous at Petersburg" (1888/1995: 1542n).

5. Poland was among the last of the former Warsaw Pact countries to confront the issue of investigating public officials for collaboration with the country's communist-era secret service, enacting its lustration law in 1997. In January 2000, a group of about thirty Polish journalists and public officials signed an appeal to the Parliament asking that the lustration law be extended to journalists, publishers and editors of large private media. The appeal resulted from a controversy over lustration between the leading daily newspapers *Gazeta Wyborcza* and *Zycie*. *Zycie* argued that lustration would be good for public opinion and journalism in general, while *Gazeta Wyborcza* contended that lustration would only be used arbitrarily as a weapon against critical journalists. We may speak of "tendencies" for changes not brought about by the purposive actions of specific groups, and "strategies" for changes that have resulted from such actions.

collaborators with the secret police) and barring them from public office in the newly established post-communist systems of government. The formal and certainly legitimate motive for lustration was to protect democracy from threats posed by the old regime, but in fact, newly emerging democracies were not at risk from representatives of the old regime.

The "cosmopolitan models a la Klaus, Balcerowicz and Sachs" in the economy (Zeleny, 1991: 4), advertised by many ECE governments, represent another example of imitation through substitution, that had no theoretical and practical value, but effectively cleared the way to the colonization of ECE economies. Another clear, perhaps even extreme, example of a pure substitution is the case of the "right to publish opinions", which became a constitutional right in the former Yugoslavia in 1963. In the 1980s, this right – together with the right of reply and the right of correction – were widely used by citizens and supported by editors (mostly in the press) as an instrument to achieve some degree of political autonomy. An important precedent occurred in a 1985 lawsuit when the Supreme Court of Slovenia ordered the main daily newspaper in Slovenia *Delo* to publish an article by a citizen criticizing a high political functionary. This case became a celebrated one for editors, journalists, and (critical) citizens. However, when in 1991 the Slovenian Ministry of Information proposed amendments to the former Law on Public Information adopted in 1985, it suggested that it was necessary "to cut out the provisions related to the publication of opinions" because "this citizens' right represented a great achievement of civilisation under the conditions of one-party system, but in a plural society and developed information market, such a citizens' right, or duty of the media, is an anachronism; the media will be forced to publish opinions important for the public primarily because of the pressure of competition." Some Western prophets of democracy regard even the internationally enacted citizens' *right to reply* as a repressive instrument in the new ECE democracies because it "could force papers to double in size, making printing and distribution costs soar" (e.g., Schmidt, 1996). Although such an argument is aimed at establishing free press not inhibited by authoritarian interference, it turns on another dogmatism by underestimating the tendencies of mental homogenization and monopolization inherent in a market-driven media system.

In other words, imitation through *accumulation*, which combines new and old desires, as Tarde would put it, rather than substitution should be the preferred option. Such a critical view is particularly needed not only because the extent and forms of privatization of the mass media in ECE exceed what has been practised in Western capitalism, but also, or even primarily because ECE countries are becoming a kind of experimental zone for those strategies of privatization initiated by Western media capital, but which are still held back by social responsibility doctrines in the West. A policy unwilling to restrict or oppose the operation of the free market in the media is clearly in favour of *corporate speech* rather than *free speech*; it is far from being a continuation of the ideas of the former democratic opposition in Eastern Europe. Jakubowicz (1992: 72) once said for Poland, "The results of the Solidarity revolution and the rule of post-Solidarity forces are almost the reverse of what was originally intended." A similar observation by Czech journalists was reported by Duncan and Rosenbaum (1999: 3), who indicated that "While Czech journalism did provide a forum for political debate in the 1990s, journalists perceive they had less influence on the government and society than they thought they would after the Velvet Revolution."

Imitation through substitution of a Western-type capitalism is also problematic because of immense *cultural* specificities (differences in traditions, lifestyles, national identities) that are certainly not known to, or understood by, those "irresponsible foreigners who do not distinguish between Mongolia and Slovenia" but were nevertheless invited by post-socialist governments to act as economic saviours Mencinger (1991: 25). In *political* and *economic* terms, ECE countries were often closer to developing than developed countries. Thus, the concepts and strategies, which may well apply in the developed market economies of the West, are not wholly or directly appropriate to the former socialist countries; in addition, there is a great variability in patterns of change in developed countries themselves. Japan, for example, is a typical case of successful accumulation rather than substitutional imitation of Western capitalism, with a significant economic role of the state and weak civil society Morishima (1990: 62). Accordingly, while discussing forms of ownership, Cui (1991: 65) confronts imitation with Tarde's fundamental principle – *innovation*, emphasizing that "when we think of reforming state ownership in existing socialism, we need not search for a single 'best' form of ownership and adopt it once and for all. The most important lesson of human progress is that the 'experimental space' for innovation should be kept open." That would imply that even state ownership might still be an efficient form of ownership in some sectors of the economy.

Imitative tendencies

Several structural tendencies or strategies[6] in the ECE countries may be identified that are, in different degrees, spread throughout the region and

---

6. We may speak of "tendencies" as long as changes are not brought about by purposive actions of specific groups, whereas "strategies" are based on such actions.

reflect the imitative nature of the new systems. Five property-related tendencies are particularly important for the development of new or future media systems: (1) renationalization, (2) denationalization and privatization, (3) commercialization, (4) inter- and transnationalization, which are usually (5) "cross-fertilized." These five imitative tendencies could be clustered into two broader groups: the first one is imitating the *"endogenous" past* whereas the rest of the tendencies imitate contemporary *exogenous environments*, primarily Western Europe and the USA.[7] The two groups of tendencies oppose each other, but this kind of opposition is not likely to cause any *innovation*; rather, it validates Tarde's idea that "when societies are in their uninventive phases, they are also uncritical" (Tarde, 1890/1969: 181). For example, not all forms of state intervention in the economy and society – as a typical opposition to the newly materialized free market principle – should be considered productive "innovations."

After decades of state-controlled media, it was largely believed that freedom of ownership and particularly private ownership would be the guarantor of democracy and free media. Privatization was seen as the only instrument that could reduce and possibly abolish state intervention in the media. In practice, however, the disentanglement of state property and its conversion into private property had been intensely party-political. The cumulative effects of the rise of a free market economy and a widespread economic underdevelopment in ECE countries do not stimulate "demonopolisation, differentiation, professionalisation of journalists and . . . democratisation," – the fundamental prerequisites for media change in the region Jakubowicz (1995: 67–68). The underdeveloped economy is impeding the deployment of new information and communication technologies for computer mediated communication and the Internet, i.e., in sectors left to private initiative and commercial interests like the denationalized press. Even the denationalization of broadcasting, which formally resulted in a dual broadcasting system, turned into a paradoxical negation of the development of public service media based on renationalization, privatization and transnationalization.

During the early post-communist period, one of the most significant characteristics of ownership changes in the press was the elimination of the previous dominant role of the state. Practically all newspapers and some local radio stations were privatized, and a number of new, privately

---

7.　I have, in the past referred to this imitative tendency or tendencies as a case of "Italianization", Splichal (1994). However, naming it after a specific nation is not the best solution because it indicates that, (1) it is peculiar to a nation (state) and (2) that the whole system is imitated rather than its specific characteristics. On the contrary, some of these characteristics are present in most capitalist systems, and not all of these are imitated in the ECE countries.

owned and commercially oriented radio and television stations were set up. East Central European countries have widely embraced liberal-pluralist economic and political models. Press freedom was equated with the right of private property, and the market was seen as the surest safeguard against state interference. But in practice, governments did not withdraw completely and the press throughout the region is still influenced by politics. Besides intervening through media and cultural policies, some degree of direct or latent state ownership is still found in many print media sectors. As Vartanova (1999) argues, "the long-standing authoritarian tradition of state pressures over the Russian media has marginalised the scope of market activities of independent newspapers or TV stations. In recent years state owned and Government run media have got a dominant position at the media market being increasingly used for getting political benefits, not revenues." For example, the first Slovenian post-communist government financed the establishment of a privately owned conservative daily, whose owners were primarily party officials. The licensing of new privately owned broadcasting stations was often much more a party-political decision resulting in the selection of the most politically "correct" or highest bidder rather than the result of (or at least attempts at) identifying the needs and interests of publics, e.g., through public hearings as practised in some Western countries. A case study that examines recent efforts by the Hungarian government to use public money to establish a right-centrist newspaper (Gálik and James, 1999) shows that the government advocates a "hybrid paternal-democratic model" Splichal (1994: 139) which overlays the existing commercial foundation. It is "paternal" in that the government on behalf of the people determines how these principles get put into practice, and "democratic" in that the principles do indeed demand public support for ideologically diverse media. Although the government's fundamental insistence that it is unacceptable to leave the allocation of informational resources to the market could lead to a more democratic reorganization, in practice this could result in the endorsement of media diversity by conservative media.

The media industry, which was supposed to be subject to regulation, has, in the countries in which it has acquired licenses for nation-wide broadcasting, e.g., in the Czech Republic), become a very powerful partner of political actors. In other countries, it remains under the (informal) control of political parties. In both cases, such "partnerships" have led to the marginalization of the autonomy and role of regulative bodies. It is also generally the case that the mass media are likely to provide support for the establishment, in general, and government, in particular, primarily to avoid informal or formal "inconveniences" related to licenses. The increase of mutual influence between political and economic establishments and the media does not allow for a liberal media market characterized by a diversified supply of newspapers and broadcast programming as "planned" by the new political forces in the period of political upheavals.

In order to retain control over national broadcasting – either a direct control by appointments of boards, directors and editors, or a more indirect control over the budget and other economic instruments (e.g., state advertising) – the new governments did not hesitate to use regulations and strategies of the former regimes in almost all countries in the region. Renationalization is the strategy of imitating the media policies of the former dominant (party-state) political power. Governments "justified" their essentially undemocratic control over the media with the argument that some of the old restrictions must be maintained until democratization could be successfully accomplished. "In particular," the argument went, "the media have to be controlled because they are not yet ready to act responsibly, as democracy requires" (Kovács and Whiting, 1995: 118). In some countries, as for example in some former Yugoslav republics, the broadcasting acts of the 1980s have been changed to (re)establish the control of the state over radio and television organizations typical of earlier periods of socialism. While in the former self-management oriented system, the right to participate in appointments to managing and editorial positions in the media was granted to media workers, the amended broadcasting acts in all Yugoslav republics have abolished this workers' right and made it a privilege of either the government (e.g., in Serbia, Vojvodina, Kosovo, Croatia) or the parliament (Bosnia and Herzegovina). Slovenia is the only country that retains this right although it was reinstated after a four year interruption in 1994.

The media have often been used as the battleground of party elites wanting to maximize their political power and to change the political map. Not surprisingly, broadcasting is still largely organized in accordance with the former "collectivist" ideology and the dominant role of the party-state, and its restructuring aimed at establishing a national, politicized and (quasi) commercial "public" broadcasting *subordinated to state authorities and party elites* rather than to public accountability. Political parties, parliaments or even governments usually act as the only representative of "the public", thus having the right, for example, to appoint both the board and directors and editors of state broadcasting companies. Although the new systems differ from the former ones in that these functions were transferred from the Communist Party to the democratically elected political parties and state organs, this does not change the fundamental dependence of the media on external political authorities, and the reduction of the public to the masses of passive consumers. All forms of broadcasting regulation in East-Central Europe are apparently borrowed from West-European countries. However, access to "public" broadcasting is either still severely limited to political elites in most countries of the region – in some countries only to those belonging to the ruling coalitions – or commercially based. Broadcasting councils as the main regulatory bodies are, as a rule, appointed by parliaments or (partly) even by governments. This also applies to supervisory bodies of public broadcasters. In both cases, civic associations, societies, and movements have no access to the institutional forms of media management and control.

Cross-fertilisation refers to the kind of "innovation" caused by the opposition between attempts at the denationalization of the media and the imitation of the traditional and modern Western (particularly Italian) party-political and media model: it blurs political, commercial and professional interests and dissolves the borders between the state, economy and civil society.[8] Since this innovation emerged in Western Europe much earlier, it cannot be considered anything more than a pure imitation in Eastern Europe. Unlike denationalization, which imitates the regulatory ideas of the former socialist system, "cross-fertilization" reflects media developments in Italy, particularly before the *partitocratic* political system crashed in 1992, but also more recent developments. Several characteristics of the old Italian media system, as described by (Mancini, 1991: 139), pertain to emerging post-communist systems: (1) The media are under state control, either directly, as in the case of public broadcasting, or indirectly through various forms of state-owned and/or economically supported press. (2) The degree of mass media partisanship is strong. Political parties are involved in editorial choices and the structure of the mass media. (3) Equally strong is the degree of integration of the media and political elites. For example, there is a strong professional mobility between the worlds of politics and journalism. (4) There is no consolidated and shared professional ethics among media professionals. In addition, post-socialist media are in a political environment similar to that in Italy of the 1980s (5) because of the instability of the political system, which represent a kind of "coalitional complex" consisting of a large number of parliamentary parties or single "great coalitions", essentially based on the division between pro- and anticommunist parties. (6) Like in the Italy of the 1990s, new political parties established in the 1990s in the ECE countries are not organized in the way traditional mass parties were. New

---

8. I used to name this imitative tendency/tendencies after Italy as "Italianization" (Splichal, 1994), but naming it after a nation is not the best resolution because it wrongly insinuates that (1) it is peculiar to a nation (state) and (2) that the whole system is imitated rather than its specific characteristics. On the contrary, some of these characteristics are present in most capitalist systems, and not all of them are imitated in the ECE countries.

parties resemble the structure and strategy of business corporations. In terms of corporate philosophy, there is no difference between managing a political party, a business corporation, or a television station or newspaper company. The "Italian model", characterised by the largely unregulated development of private television of Berlusconi, may serve as a warning not only because of its strict commercial orientation, which – as in other Western countries – challenged the traditional quality orientation of public television, but also because of its final de facto politicization, when Berlusconi's party won parliamentary elections in 1993 and 2001.

The former communist media systems were based on secondary content regulation (e.g., different forms of publication or information subsidies) that was expected to limit the flaws and "side effects" of media markets, although no true market actually existed. That was probably the main reason for the complete disappearance of secondary regulation during the reregulation period in the 1990s: it was considered a form of state intervention, like the former system. Consequently, even public media were not liberated from competition for (advertising) income; neither are they politically independent and protected against particularistic (political) interests. Mass media remain vulnerable to manipulation by political forces and, in addition, have become dependent on commercial corporations, resulting in limits to resources, variety, and autonomy. It is obvious that the media are not only instruments of democracy; they are no less effective as instruments of manipulation. The underdeveloped economy in the region is inhibiting the deployment of new information and communication technologies both in private and public sectors. Even the denationalization of broadcasting – which resulted in a dual broadcasting system – has rather paradoxically resulted in the negation of public service media.

As a consequence of such commercialization private publishers and broadcasters have, in the quest for readership, audiences, advertisers and profits, opted for packaged entertainment. Unfortunately, even public broadcasters have taken the same route (Negt and Kluge, 1973: 191), and have been forced to respond to the environment as business companies. For example, audience measurement has become the means of determining the value of programming and earning money for future productions; these companies are managed according to the same managing principles as any other company; and they are directly involved in transactions with private (foreign) suppliers of programmes and equipment, who are often in a monopoly position.

A kind of *paternal-commercial* media system is emerging, characterised by a tendency towards privatization and commercialization of the media (particularly the press) on the one hand, and by the maximization of political power over the media (television in particular) on the other. In many countries in the region, the lines between political and business interests have been blurred. The competition for consumers has led to competition for the latest news and this has made journalists vulnerable to political influences. Political influences affect the practice of journalism either directly by way of interviews and press conferences, or indirectly through "information subsidies" (making information available to journalists on a *quid pro quo* basis). Such influences lead to journalistic agenda setting, to the politicisation of attitudes and actions, and eventually to making journalism a subsidiary of *public relations*.

Since the development of capital-intensive media such as television heavily depends on the state of the economy, in many ECE countries it would have been impossible to improve newsprint and printing quality or modernise editorial offices. It had been argued, that in order to establish and equip radio and television stations, foreign investments were necessary. All countries in the region allowed their media markets to be accessible to foreign capital. Post-communist media became internationalized at five levels: reception, media content, funding, regulation and organisation, including foreign media ownership. Foreign investments and ownership led to a move away from the previously overpoliticized media and the direct influence of the state. These results are perhaps but not always dependent on contemporary party politics. In addition to foreign capital, there is an increased dependence on imports of Western managerial and professional practices in media operations and the diversification of media products, e.g., magazines, tabloids, and new types of programming.

Media internationalization and globalization may have opposing and controversial consequences: on the one hand the international circulation of cultural products, if adapted creatively by the local populations, may enrich national cultures. On the other hand, dependence on such products may lead to demise of local cultures. In the ECE countries the consequences of this process are predominantly negative, because all countries in the region remain "recipients", but not actors. In a number of countries in the region, for example Hungary, Poland, and Czech Republic, more than 50% of the national dailies are owned by foreign companies. Thus Fabris (1995) argues that the "Westification" of East-Central European media has fully progressed and there is a good chance that East-Central Europe will become a "supplemental engine for the Western European media industry." As Sparks (1991: 20) suggested, the processes of privatization and "colonization" of the East by the West could lead to "a stratified press in which the majority of the population will be effectively denied access to information about matters of public importance."

Conclusions

In the late 1980s and early 1990s, democratic changes in the ECE countries were expected to bring a higher degree of political participation and personal freedom, and the media were believed to contribute significantly to that process. In order to achieve these goals, the political and legal system had to be based on a clear separation of powers (legislative, executive, judicial), forms of control (political versus cultural), and between the state and civil society. In hindsight, given the previous regime, it was only to be expected that the state would be intolerant of the new, independent media. As the state is now the safeguard of civil society, it ought to establish a regulatory framework for the media to serve democracy. If the line between the political, economic, and public spheres is blurred, as is often the case in the ECE countries, a radical departure from the non-democratic practices of former regimes is not feasible. In fact, institutions of civil society and public opinion are still effectively marginalized, and access to the media is either limited to political elites – in some countries to the ruling coalitions – or to commercial powers. In some countries, the Church has taken over the role of the dominant partner of the state once reserved for the communist party. It has become a powerful economic force by its ownership of the media, thus substantially contributing to the non-transparency of the borderline between the state and civil society.

There is no doubt that the former centralized socialist economy based on state ownership was both *economically inefficient* and *inimical to democracy*. But it would also be mistaken to assume that private property and free marketplace are the only (or, at least, the best) alternatives in *both* respects. The question of an alternative to *laissez-faire* is particularly important for such vital activities in civil society as education, science, culture, and communication. There may be some serious doubts as to whether the *imitative nature* of the changes in the media sphere stimulates democratic transformations of societies, or if it remains an obstacle to the development of more democratic systems in the region. Imitation, if reciprocal and based on accumulation – an *active imitation* – may well lead to genuine changes and innovations. For example, the newly designed parliamentary political systems and the establishment of the private economic sector represent what one calls positive imitation in the ECE countries. In the field of the media, however, imitation has not only resulted in democratic progress but also in several negative consequences that could have been avoided if the changes were designed and planned. Although advocacy of any form of socialized markets and social ownership is regarded with suspicion in contemporary *laissez-faire* ECE, Blackburn (1991: 234) claims, that "the imposition of narrow commercial criteria menaces the integrity of civil society and hands the initiative to rapacious commercial interests" ought to, at least, be acknowledged.

In most countries in the region, the general success of the efforts during the last ten years to establish a truly democratic system is still rather limited. *Structural regulation* – media ownership, organisation, financing, management, control, procedures for licensing, rules for access – remains ineffective, since legal violators are often not prosecuted either for political reasons or for a general lack of personnel and technical means to enforce the respective laws. *Content regulation* (what content is permitted or required, and how it ought to be selected and presented in programming, including quotas) has not contributed to a higher quality of programming. Media products in the ECE countries today are certainly less politicized than under the communist regime, but they are becoming increasingly commercialized, and prone to the tendency towards "tabloidization".

Although there may be some serious doubts about concrete forms of legal regulation of media operations, it is clear that the introduction of the market economy and private media ownership alone or in combination with political (party) pluralism can either result in the expansion of, or reductions to, the democratic potential of the media. While the market is essentially a terrain for different policies and coalitions – based on different ideologies – media systems are established, maintained and eventually abolished by political decisions. Since media development requires an economic underpinning, a rich diversity of media can only exist in a prosperous economy within a market-based system. Whereas the absence of market competition makes the media politically dependent, the opposite does not hold true: a market economy cannot guarantee politically autonomous media. As a consequence, developments in the ECE countries have led to the establishment of a kind of "political capitalism" and created a system of "paternalist commercialism" in the media. This has exposed the ECE countries to the danger of becoming a kind of "twilight zone" of uncontrolled privatization – aided by deficiencies in the newly established legal systems that ignore the social responsibility of the media and citizens' rights and freedoms, and refuse to enforce sanctions against corporate law-breakers.

References

Barber, B.R. (1992) 'Jihad vs. McWorld', *The Atlantic Monthly*, March, 53–63.

Bryce, J. (1888/1995) *The American Commonwealth*, 2 Vols., Indianapolis: Liberty Fund.

Blackburn, R. (1991) 'Fin de siècle: Socialism after the crash', in R. Blackburn (ed.), *After the fall. The failure of communism and the future of socialism*, 173–249, London: Verso.

Cui, Z. (1991) 'Market incompleteness, innovation and reform: Commentary on Adam Przeworski's article', *Politics and Society*, 19, 1, 59–69.

Dahl, R.A. (1991) 'Transitions to democracy', in G. Szoboszlai (ed.), *Democracy and political transformation: Theories and east-central European realities*, 9–20, Budapest: Hungarian Political Science Association.

Dicey, A.V. (1905/1981) *Lectures on the relation between law and public opinion in England during the nineteenth century*. New Brunswick: Transaction Books.

Duncan, H. and Rosenbaum, J. (1999) 'When the watchdog sleeps: Perceptions of Czech journalists in the 1990s', paper presented at the EURICOM colloquium on media ownership and control in East-Central Europe, Piran, 8–10 April 1999.

Fabris, H.H. (1995) 'Westification?' in D. Paletz, K. Jakubowicz, and P. Novosel (eds.), *Glasnost and after: Media and change in Central and Eastern Europe*, 221–231, Cresskill, NJ: Hampton Press.

Gálik, M. and James B. (1999) 'Ownership and Control of the Hungarian Press', *Javnost – The Public*, 6, 2, 75–91.

Habermas, J. (1990) 'What does socialism mean today? The revolutions of recuperation and the need for new thinking', in R. Blackburn (ed.), *After the fall: The failure of communism and the future of socialism*, 25–46, London: Verso.

Holmes, L. (1997) *Post-communism: An introduction*, Cambridge: Polity Press.

Jakubowicz, K. (1992) 'From party propaganda to corporate speech? Polish journalism in search of a new identity', *Journal of Communication*, 42, 3, 64–73.

Jakubowicz, K. (1995) 'Television: What kind of continuity and change', *Javnost – The Public*, 2, 3, 61–80.

Kovács, I. and Whiting, G. (1995) 'Hungary', in D. Paletz, K. Jakubowicz, and P. Novosel (eds.), *Glasnost and after: Media and change in Central and Eastern Europe*, 97–127, Cresskill, NJ: Hampton Press.

Mancini, P. (1991) 'The public sphere and the use of news in a "Coalition" system of government', in P. Dahlgreen and C. Sparks (eds.), *Communication and Citizenship*, 137–154, London: Routledge.

Mencinger, J. (1991) 'Vlada, bobni, harmonike, zastave', *Delo*, 19 October, 25.

Morishima, M. (1990) 'Ideology and economic activity', *Current Sociology*, 38, 2–3, 51–77.

Negt, O. and Kluge A. (1973) *Öffentlichkeit und Erfahrung. Zur Organisationsanalyse von bürgerlicher und proletarischer Öffentlichkeit.* Frankfurt: Suhrkamp.

Schmidt, J. (1996) 'A media blizzard overwhelms Eastern Europe', *Nieman Reports,* Summer, 39–47.

Schöpflin, G. (1993) 'Post-communism: A profile', *Javnost–The Public,* 2, 1, 63–73.

Sparks, C. (1991) 'From state to market: What Eastern Europe inherits from the west', *Media Development,* 38, 3, 11–15.

Sparks, C. (1998) *Communism, capitalism and the media,* London: Sage.

Splichal, S. (1994) *Media beyond socialism. Theory and practice in East-Central Europe,* Boulder, Co: Westview.

Splichal, S. (2001) 'Imitative revolutions: Changes in the media and journalism in East-Central Europe', *Javnost – The Public* , 8, 4, 31–58.

Šmid, M. (1999) 'Testing ground for deregulated media in the Czech republic', paper presented at the EURICOM colloquium on media ownership and control in East-Central Europe, Piran, 8–10 April 1999.

Tarde, G. (1890/1969) 'The Laws of Imitation [from *Les lois de l'imitation]*', in T.N. Clark, (ed.), *On communication and social influence,* 177–191, Chicago: University of Chicago Press.

Tarde, G. (1901/1961) 'The Public and the crowd [*L'opinion et la foule]*', in T.N. Clark, (ed.), *On communication and social influence,* 277–318, Chicago: University of Chicago Press.

Tarde, G. (1902/1969) "Basic principles [from *Psychologie économique]*", in T.N. Clark (ed.), *On communication and social influence,* 143–148, Chicago: University of Chicago Press.

Tehranian, M. (1990) *Technologies of power,* Norwood, NJ: Ablex.

Vartanova, E. (1999) 'Russian media market vs. the authoritarian tradition of control over the Russian media', paper presented at the EURICOM colloquium on media ownership and control in East-Central Europe, Piran, 8–10 April1999.

Zeleny, M. (1991) 'Soumrak ceskoslovenskeho hospodarstvi', *Tvorba,* 11 September, 36–37, 3–6.

The Politics of the Media in the English-Speaking Caribbean

Hopeton S. Dunn

Introduction

The Caribbean and global media

The majority of emerging societies in the English-speaking Caribbean continue to face profound socio-political and economic challenges. As these countries negotiate the curves and turns of the 21st century, there is a critical need to reevaluate their journeys. This reevaluation has focused on the systems of cooperation and governance, judicial administration and law enforcement mechanisms, and of course, the traditional economic foundations on which the region has relied on for centuries. However, any resolution of these challenges cannot but deal with the many issues related to emerging technologies in media, telecommunications and information processing.

Girvan has called our attention to the vulnerabilities faced by sub-groups of small economies, including the Caribbean. "Their scale of production is a fraction of what obtains in the larger countries, so their unit costs of production are higher. Their infrastructure costs are higher because of the dis-economies of small scale. Productivity is low because of limited human and physical capital. And the lack of vertical integration in many of their industries will make it more difficult to satisfy the rules of origin of the FTAA" (Free Trade Area of the Americas) Girvan (2002: 10). However, in building a new regional cultural and information economy, size, though still important, should matter less and less. "Improved information and communication networks may be fundamentally altering the structure of markets." In the same vein, Melody has observed that advances in telecommunications, microelectronics and computing are "pushing back extensive geographical limits of markets to global dimensions . . ." (Melody 1996: 307).

At the heart of this process of revisioning popular empowerment and economic development is the relationship between the region's peoples and its systems of information, communication, cultural production and trade in services. In other words, the future, in an era characterized by economic globalization and technological convergence, largely depends on the region's capacity to link and manage its human creativity, natural beauty, media technology, information resources and telecommunication infrastructure. The challenge to building an integrated service economy may not be unique to the Caribbean. But in a region with limited and diminishing natural mineral resources, a sunset agricultural sector (dominated by sugarcane, bananas and citrus) and a weak manufacturing sector, the resolution of these difficult challenges cannot but be a priority concern.

In this chapter, I analyse the political economy of media and telecommunications – a crucial element of the wider project for regional economic and social reform in the region – by attempting to answer a number of interrelated questions: To what extent do historical patterns of ownership and control continue to fashion media and telecommunications systems in the Caribbean? What are some of the key power relations in the production, distribution and consumption of media and telecommunications? How are the media and information systems being redefined by emerging technological changes? How are the emerging new media and telecommunication services affecting traditional centres of ownership and control? And, what are some of the political, legislative and economic reforms that are needed to help restructure these relations in an era characterized by the increasing commodification of media products and audiences? These are some of the issues that have engaged our attention in the Caribbean.

In a region such as the Caribbean, which many regard as being, historically, among the most exposed to centuries of economic plunder by external interests, it will also be useful to examine the residual effects of colonialism on such important sectors as media, telecommunications and popular culture. At the same time, many of the territories in the region are on the verge of completing four decades of political independence. Even in this relatively brief period, the people of the Caribbean have begun to experience the social impact of "local" decision-making in media and communication institutions, while indigenous Caribbean cultural and artistic expressions have made their mark globally.

The Caribbean often denotes the diverse mix of peoples, cultures and activities linked to the many countries washed by, or bordering on, the Caribbean Sea. This includes territories with a predominant African, Indian or Amerindian population, with Anglophone, Francophone, Iberian, Dutch or other European colonial and linguistic heritages. These countries have a combined population of over 35 million people. Worrell argued that faced with this diversity and wide geographic spread, the Caribbean has tended, historically, to define itself in linguistic groups:

Language grouping has been reinforced by patterns of travel and migration, shared institutions, common traditions and initiatives for integration among Caribbean territories. There is very little travel between islands belonging to different language groups, their legal systems, political and social institutions vary, and attempts to unify the Caribbean have, up to the present, all taken place within language groups. Cultural links have tended along similar lines until recently, but modern telecommunications have led the Caribbean to uncover strong cultural affinities that transcend language barriers. (Worrell, 2001: 433).

While understanding the term Caribbean in this wider context, this chapter will focus mainly on the Anglophone territories, with Jamaica (2.6 million), the largest country by population, as a major case study that will be used to highlight the similarities and differences evident in the sub-region. This English-speaking segment of the Caribbean consists of over 6 million people living in a range of islands and mainland territories formerly colonized by Britain. Among them, Barbados (population 300,000) occupies a central location in the Eastern Caribbean where some 500,000 people occupy the archipelago. While some countries Trinidad and Tobago (1.4 million), Guyana (population 800,000) reflect a strong presence of East Indians in their population, the majority of people in the region trace their origins to Central and Western Africa. The European-led traffic in slaves resulted in the implantation within the Caribbean area of large numbers of people of African origin, who became the dominant ethnic and cultural group in the majority of these countries. Despite the passage of up to five hundred years since the start of this process of enslavement and displacement, there remain many important cultural and linguistic retentions from Africa, and to a lesser extent Asia, in the region. These traditions in combination with an enforced tutelage from Europe have contributed to the making of a diverse social and ethnic *mélange* in the Caribbean. This diversity has been reinforced by the indirect involvement of many more millions of Caribbean people who are themselves part of a Caribbean diaspora born of a strong history of migration.

Despite the establishment of the Caribbean Free Trade Area (CARIFTA) under the Treaty of Chaguaramas in 1973 as a precursor to the founding of the Caribbean Community and Common Market (CARICOM), Worrell observed that trading links within the Caribbean have remained weak. In spite of the free movement of media workers and broader professional talent within the region, there has only been limited trade in cultural products and media services. The tendency has been to look towards the United States for trade, investment, communication technology and content with a consequential impact on regional media, lifestyles and business.

Lent observed that in the period since political independence, the Caribbean has been inundated with a plethora of mainly American transnational corporations (TNCs). "By the mid-1980s, more than 1,723 branches of U.S. TNCs existed in the region, with another 2,000 in Puerto Rico. Additionally, 550 TNCs from other countries had offices in the Caribbean, including many of the world's largest corporations, such as 77 of the top 100 U.S. corporations and the three largest banks." He continues: "The strong presence of TNCs in the Caribbean has tied the economy and politics of each country to those of the large industrial nations, particularly the United States" (1991: 74). Economic liberalization and deregulation together fuelled the bid for global dominance and profit maximization by the new corporate information service providers. The major objectives of these corporate providers are to increase profits and through selling information and related services to high concentrations of easily accessible population groups capable of paying for these services. The media and communications are among the sectors in which external conglomerates have been highly influential in the region.

Both CNN and the BBC are standard bearers and maybe precursors in the region for a number of other global level conglomerates dominating worldwide media, information and entertainment services, which include the Disney Group, AOL-Time Warner (whose empire includes CNN), Viacom, Sony, Vivendi, News Corporation and Bertelsmann.

The vast resources of these information conglomerates often dwarf the economies of many underdeveloped countries, such as those in the Caribbean, whose inexperience at negotiating complex trade agreements often places them at a distinct disadvantage. Some developing countries feel threatened by the power of large corporations as they once did with their colonial masters. With the global homogenization of markets and restricted competition through mergers and corporate convergence, Caribbean countries are justifiably concerned with issues related to sovereignty and local control. Unregulated investment methods, intellectual property demands and the lack of real diversity in information and media production raise real questions that these countries will need to grapple with. In doing so, it is increasingly being recognized that the issues linking culture, development and globalization are far from settled ones.

Writing in 1995, I made the point that globalization was, perhaps uniquely, already a part of the experience of the Caribbean area for several centuries (Dunn, 1995: xiii). However, the resurgent processes of globalization over the last two decades are driven both by trade in global information and also by technological innovation. Converging techno-scientific innovations, including satellite technology, advances in microchip circuitry, revolutionized computing and enhanced systems of information storage and manipulation have each contributed to the acceleration of globalization in the region.

Media and telecommunication industries based on these innovations were typically single-country operations providing local audiences or users with basic services. In the Caribbean, these service providers were state-owned entities, that later, under the influence of International Monetary Fund (IMF), World Bank and more recently World Trade Organization (WTO) pressures, divested their operations to local business interests linked to transnational corporations, supported by governments of the global North. The first round of telecommunication divestments in Jamaica and Trinidad and Tobago, for example, was done under IMF conditionalities without due regard to the need for creating or safeguarding regulatory institutions in the "public interest" (Dunn, 1995b: 212).

A cautionary note on the dangers of unfettered liberalization was sounded by Arnold McIntyre, in an address to the Third Caribbean Media Conference in Guyana in May 2000. "Globalisation has been encouraged by the increasing influence of the policy prescription of economic liberalization, which has its origins in neo-liberal economic orthodoxy." He argued that development policy was prone to fashion, and observed that "(D)uring the 1950s and 1960s, when import substitution was in vogue, there was excessive optimism about what government interventions could achieve. Now that outward orientation is the norm, there is excessive faith in what openness can accomplish. A lot of that excessive faith comes from the remarkable convergence of views among policy makers and academics on the benefits of what has been defined as the 'Washington Consensus', the market oriented model or the neo-liberal approach to development policy" (McIntyre, 2000: 20).

Political economy as framework

Political economy provides a useful context within which to examine media and communication dynamics in the English speaking Caribbean. This approach is one that emphasizes power relationships, resource allocation and issues of justice and policy reform. It interrogates the systems of ownership and control and seeks to deepen understanding of the activities of the economic and political elites in their global and local interactions. As Mueller points out, the foundations of present-day political economy are located in the theoretical contributions of 18th and 19th century classical political and economic philosophy. "Classical political economy did not rigidly segregate economic and political phenomena. The relationship between the two was one of its central pre-occupations,

and it was the first to attempt to approach this relationship scientifically."
(Mueller, 1995: 460).

Consideration of historical context is also as important in present-day
analysis as it was in the early approaches to political economy. Classical
European theorists such as Ricardo, Malthus, Adam Smith, Mill and Marx
placed considerable emphasis on the stages of human development
through time, struggle and change as they contemplated the human
condition. Caribbean social scientists such as Beckford and Witter (1980),
Rodney (1971), Stone (1980, 1989), Girvan and Jefferson (1971), Thomas
(1988) and others also offered historically integrated analyses of regional
issues, combining the political, the economic and the social contexts. While
their work emanated from specific disciplines, their research and analyses
transcended the limits of unitary discourses. In this regard, Mueller
appropriately points out that in considering the policy issues of
communication, telecommunication, information technology and
development ". . . we do not need arbitrary fragmentation of the essential
problems of the information age into self-contained domains already
owned by other disciplines. It is the *synthetic or integrated* character of
political economy which makes it an attractive model for communication
scholars" (Mueller, 1995: 460).

Murdock and Golding's emphasis on a "critical political economy"
appears key to understanding regional media environments, historically
characterised by a strong government presence in the broadcast and
telecommunications sectors, weak regulatory structures and a dominance
of private capitalist investment in newspapers and publishing generally.
(Golding and Murdock, 1991). Mosco is among those who remind us of
the value of holistic analysis and the importance of taking account of the
totality of social relations. His concepts of "commodification" and
"spacialization" provide useful tools for analysis. His notion of
"structuration" in which social practice and processes are incorporated
into structural analyses remains an important contribution Mosco (1995).

Emerging patterns of media ownership in the Caribbean

Newspapers

The history of the media and telecommunication infrastructures in the
Caribbean is intertwined with the region's tryst with British colonialism.
Print media preceded the electronic networks by well over two centuries.
The first newspapers in Jamaica, for example, were established by British
settlers in 1716. Both Lent and Gordon, in their investigations into print

media ownership in the region, have conformed the correspondences between media ownership and the landowning settler elites (Lent, 1991; Gordon, 1999). There were many publications but few survived, the most prominent survivor being the *Gleaner* in Jamaica, which has been in continuous publication since 1834. In its close to one-hundred-and-seventy year history, the Gleaner Company has remained within the ownership of a succession of slave-owning and oligarchic families. It continues operations as the region's largest newspaper publishing group, functioning within the barony of the Clarke/Ashenheim families who have a history of large traditional landholdings, and with links to banking, building societies, radio broadcasting services and publishing.

According to Ken Gordon, the *Gleaner*, as a locally owned media institution, was unique in the late colonial period. "Lord Thompson's newspapers and the London-based Rediffusion Group used their financial muscle to establish newspaper and radio networks from Jamaica to Guyana – the only indigenously owned daily newspaper at that time being the *Gleaner* of Jamaica." Gordon, who himself emerged as one of the major regional owners of a multimedia network of Caribbean newspapers, television and radio services in the 1990s, was critical of the attitude and motivation of this early external media ownership. "Foreign owners had no more than an academic interest in press freedom, their concern was to make an attractive return on their investments" Gordon (1999: xi). It is ironic that similar concerns have been expressed about the motivation and business practices of some of the post-colonial regional entrepreneurs in traditional newspaper publications in the region.

Although there have been notable government-owned daily newspapers in the region, (*Jamaica Daily News, Guyana Chronicle*), that sector continues to be dominated by private capital. Among the other leading regional private sector newspaper publishers are Harold Hoyte's Nation Group from Barbados, the Ken-Gordon-founded Caribbean Communication Network (CCN) based in Trinidad and Tobago, the *Stabroek News* of Guyana and the *Jamaica Observer*, owned by Gordon "Butch" Stewart, operator of the expanding Sandals chain of Caribbean hotels and Chairman of Air Jamaica. Most of these newspapers operate online editions and websites, with the most well established being the Gleaner's Go-Jamaica site. The attempt by the larger regional newspapers to maintain Internet-based editions appears to be an investment in the as yet unproven possibility of revenues from an additional income stream. Online editions also provide channels for the companies to reach the disparate global Caribbean diaspora and are also the means by which online readers respond via published letters and comments. Caribbean newspapers have tended to reproduce the content of their printed versions onto their websites, without adopting the new techniques of electronic writing and publishing appropriate to the new medium.

Radio

When radio arrived in the mid 19th century, London was already exercising uncontested political control over the region and its nascent electronic media infrastructure. The early public radio communications facilities set up in Jamaica, for example, were meant to maintain the morale of the population and provide government information during the Second World War that began in 1939. The privately owned amateur radio station VP5PZ was acquired by the government and the new facility, renamed ZQI, became one of the region's earliest radio broadcasting services. In 1949, the colonial government sold the station to the British Rediffusion Group, which renamed it Radio Jamaica and Rediffusion Ltd. (RJR). This station, for a long time the leading radio broadcaster in the country, was taken out of foreign ownership in the mid 1970s by the government of Prime Minister Michael Manley, who distributed the shares to what were then called "people-based organizations". The radio service of the state-owned Jamaica Broadcasting Corporation was established under the regime of Michael Manley's father, Norman Manley in 1958–59.

Similar processes were underway in Trinidad and Tobago. In 1947, Broadcast Relay Services (Overseas) Ltd., London, was granted a franchise to operate the Trinidad Broadcasting System and this led, after independence, to government ownership of and involvement in radio and television broadcasting. The first radio station in Barbados started in 1934. It was called Radio Distribution and its signal was transmitted through a cable network built by retired British Commander Mansfield Robinson. Seventeen years later, it was bought by the Rediffusion Group in 1951 and named Barbados Rediffusion. It was acquired by local business interests in 1979.

Following independence in the 1960s and the influence of the movement for a New World Information and Communication Order (NWICO) in the 1970s, several regional governments nationalized local electronic media ownership. In Guyana, the government acquired the assets of Radio Demerara from Broadcast Relay Services (Overseas) Ltd. and combined the operation of this station with the Guyana Broadcasting Service to create the Guyana Broadcasting Corporation, in the late 1960s.

For over half a century, the British Broadcasting Corporation (BBC) has been a strong voice in the region, initially on short-wave radio. Later its newscasts from London began to be transmitted once or twice a day to national audiences via satellite to local radio networks, including those of the compatriot British Rediffusion Group within the region.

In the Windward Islands of the Eastern Caribbean, the BBC operated the Windward Islands Broadcasting Service (WIBS) between 1956 and 1971. This radio service, which was headquartered in Grenada, also served St Vincent and the Grenadines, St Lucia and Dominica. Many regarded it as a British colonial sounding post in an area of industrial unrest and political tensions related to the struggles for independence. Its demise, ostensibly for financial reasons, followed the irrevocable acceleration of the process of decolonization in that part of the region. The emerging small independent states established their own government-run radio stations, thereby creating the foundations on which the growing electronic media of the early 21st century is now being built.

In both these smaller and larger territories, BBC's radio news transmissions were complemented in the late 1990s by BBC World, the television service, which is beamed via satellite to the Caribbean from studios in the United States, and then conveyed locally by cable into millions of homes. In 2000, the BBC also applied to the Broadcasting Commission in Jamaica for a broadcasting licence to establish a local 24-hour FM transmitting radio service to be based in Kingston as part of a strengthening of British presence in Caribbean media at the start of a new century. The fact that similar applications were made by the BBC in other parts of the region and the world is a reflection of its continuing global strategy as well as its historical influence and reach into the countries of the British Commonwealth and even in the United States.

Over the last 40 years, and in contrast to its colonial past, radio has, to a large extent, become locally owned. It has been the sub-sector least penetrated by foreign ownership during the last decade. The establishment of a business model based on audience segmentation created successful broadcasting niches and stations such as the reggae-dedicated Irie FM Jamaica. Others like the University of the West Indies (UWI)-owned Radio Mona reaches another niche audience with mainly World Beat and European classical music within its educational programming format. And still others, such as Love FM, owned by a consortium of religious groupings, offers a predominantly gospel output. But the entry of locally based BBC FM services has marked a resurgence in external influence. Audience preference for local interactive talk radio and the growth of several community radio stations seem to indicate that even with new foreign players and the emergence of digital audio broadcasting (DAB), the medium of radio will remain strongly local and Caribbean in content and ownership.

Television

Ownership of television in the Caribbean is changing from strong public sector dominance to a combination of local private and international capital. In Dominica, a privately owned television service, Marpin, is successfully competing against the government run Dominica Broadcasting Corporation. And in Grenada, St Vincent as well as in Jamaica, private sector providers have begun to dominate following the divestment of state-run TV services. In Barbados, government continues to operate the Caribbean Broadcasting Corporation (CBC), while private sector operators have gained strength in the growing subscriber television market.

The chief competitor to the BBC in externally owned international television news output in the region is Cable News Network (CNN). This US transnational company is the primary source of news for subscriber television viewers, and, like that of the BBC, its content is increasingly being rebroadcast in major evening newscasts by local free-to-air TV companies throughout the region.

Television was introduced to the Caribbean in the 1960s. Trinidad and Tobago Television (TTT) was inaugurated in November 1962 and the Jamaica Broadcasting Corporation (JBC) was granted a licence to operate a television station in 1962 and began transmission in the following year. The Caribbean Broadcasting Corporation in Barbados started operation in 1964 as the island's first TV station and in 1971 became the first post-independent Caribbean station to transmit in colour. These stations were all government-owned and part of an emerging region-wide post-independence pattern of electronic media ownership that is now undergoing significant change.

The influence of neoliberal ideas on media policy along with the financial difficulties faced by many of these state-run broadcasting enterprises have resulted in either closure or private competition for many of these one-time broadcasting monopolies. The JBC ceased operation in 1997 after 38 years of operation. Its television service and one of its radio subsidiaries were divested to its old competitor Radio Jamaica, and promises of a new public service broadcasting entity have not materialized as yet. However, a state-owned video production and educational facility, the Creative Production and Training Centre (CPTC), has assumed some aspects of the role of a public service provider by establishing the cable channel Creative Television (CTV) in December 2001 that transmits a wide range of exclusively local programmes from its archives and new or commissioned productions.

The Caribbean television sector continues as a site of struggle both in terms of ownership and content. Without policy planning, regulation and private investments, indigenous regional interests are in danger of making large concessions to external corporate investors and programmes providers.

Geopolitics of imported content

Throughout the history of electronic broadcasting in the region, questions related to the origin of content have arisen, especially in the case of television. The proximity and dominance of the United States to this English-speaking region has meant easy access to US media products. As a result, much of the television output has been dominated by imported content. The relatively low cost of foreign materials encouraged stations to purchase overseas-produced sitcoms, game shows and news programmes to fill airtime.

Despite some current national and regional efforts to localize some segments of broadcast schedules, "the enticements that cable systems, satellite relays and overspills, and videocassettes provide in the way of inexpensive, easily accessible foreign programming are . . . overwhelming." (Lent, 1991: 83). Since the middle of the 1970s, the main delivery system for foreign content flowing into the region has been direct broadcasting satellites, especially in the Northern Caribbean where the signal over-spill from US domestic satellites has been substantial.

In Jamaica, the initial growth and popularity of satellite (dish) receivers (almost 50,000 by the end of 1997) fell away (reduced to 25,000 in 2000) in the face of increased use of cable TV, a cheaper way of receiving multiple channels of external and local programming. Cable TV has grown exponentially, from an estimated 137,000 subscribers in 1996 to 283,000 subscribers in the year 2000 in the sub-region's largest single market. There were over 129,000 VCRs in 1984 but this number has now been significantly reduced, as a consequence of Cable TV. Despite continuing issues of accountability for some programmes, the cable sector has undergone a transformation from its "illegal" beginnings, to a regulated industry consisting of 46 licenced operators in 2002. Some of these cable companies have also been awarded licences as Internet Service Providers (ISPs) with the capacity to deliver multiple services to local subscribers, using a single cable network.

Although a third of the cable operating companies also provide local community channels, the net effect of the growth of the cable sector is an increase in the volume of foreign content available on television in Jamaica and the region. This was already a concern two decades ago, well before the entry of cable. According to (Brown, 1987), the imported portion of TV programmes rose by 1% each year between 1976–1986 in Jamaica

(JBC), Barbados (CBC), Trinidad and Tobago (TTT) and Antigua (ABS). (Brown, 1987: 12).

Table 1: Growth in imported television content in the Caribbean

Country	Average imported content, 1976–1986 (%)
Barbados	92
Antigua	91
Trinidad and Tobago	89
Jamaica	76

Source: Müllerleile (1996)

This trend, indicated in Tables 1 and 2, has not significantly altered in the last two decades. Although several new television stations have been established in the 1980s and 1990s, many still substantially rely on externally produced content.

Table 2: Growth in imported television content in Jamaica

TV station	Foreign content, 1999 (%)
JBC	76
CVM	78
Love TV	92

Source: The Broadcasting Commission, 'Survey of Jamaican Indigenous Programming' (1999)

These statistics reflect the ongoing challenge to continued and increased production of local programmes. In a global environment characterized by fluidity in both capital flows and cultural interchanges, the Caribbean will have to adapt to the pressures of globalization without surrendering its own role and unique identity within the regional and global mix. However, the academic prognoses of the imminent demise or "synchronization" of cultural identities have not yet been confirmed despite the region being a classic "victim" of "cultural imperialism". Cultural resistance in the Caribbean continues to be strong. Reggae music along with its indigenous inspirational source of Rastafari remains a strong local and international cultural force, with the BBC, no less, declaring the widely acclaimed Bob Marley song "One Love" the global anthem of the past century. Similarly, Caribbean lifestyles, languages, cuisine and other forms of expression such as soca music and the pan instrument continue to grow in regional and global influence. It can to some extent even be claimed that Jamaica and the Caribbean have achieved what one of its cultural icons, Louise Bennett, in an earlier era, described poetically as "Colonization in Reverse":

> What a joyful news, Miss Mattie,
> I feel like me heart gwine burs
> Jamaica people colonizin
> Englan in reverse. . . (Bennett, 1986: 32)

The celebration of this prospect is also reflected in the attitude of Caribbean people to the game of Test Cricket, something that another regional writer, CLR James has described as extending "Beyond a Boundary", into the arenas of society and politics. The recent ill-fated attempt on cable television by black American would-be seer "Miss Cleo" to affect a Jamaican accent as a means of wooing clients, also reflects the attractiveness of diversity and resistance in a region that continues to face external pressures and challenges to its cultural expressions, media institutions and audiences.

Endangered regional media ventures: CBU, CANA, CMC

The leading cooperative ventures in media are encountering grave struggles for survival in the face of the changing global environment. Private sector, and to a lesser extent public sector, media leaders, belonging to the Caribbean Broadcasting Union (CBU), appear to be in crisis. Based in Barbados, the CBU was founded in 1970 by 14 state-owned radio stations located in 13 countries. Private media owners are now the dominant group in the CBU. As a non-governmental agency, the CBU claims to represent broadcasters from the English-, Spanish-, French- and Dutch-speaking Caribbean. But its primary market remains in the English-speaking region.

With the assistance of UNESCO, the CBU acquired satellite transmission facilities and sought to promote the sharing of technical know-how and live region-wide coverage of major events such as cricket, the Commonwealth Games, Pan-American Games, CARICOM Heads of Government Conferences, national elections, among other events. It was also mandated to implement daily news exchanges among its members.

The CBU also assumed responsibilities for technical in-service training of media personnel and maintenance of professional standards. But its stewardship has been found wanting and its future viability is in doubt.

Full members of the Caribbean Broadcasting Union include: Anguilla, Aruba, Antigua, Bahamas, Barbados, Belize, Bermuda, Curacao, Dominica, Grenada, Guyana, Jamaica, Montserrat, St. Kitts, St. Lucia, St. Vincent and the Grenadines, Suriname, Trinidad and Tobago, and the Turks and Caicos Islands. Associate members include several media organizations in Canada, Cuba, France, Germany, The Netherlands, Tortola, Jamaica, Trinidad, the United Kingdom, the United States, and the U.S. Virgin Islands.

Despite its impressive range of duties, the CBU has encountered acute problems related to financing and management. It has remained dependent on UNESCO and other grant funding for several decades. The situation worsened in early 2002, when its attempt to combine some of its operations with those of the Caribbean News Agency (CANA) led to the collapse of the merged business entity called the Caribbean Media Corporation (CMC). Despite an historical arms length relationship from governments, the CMC/CANA collapse in 2002 led leaders of the CBU to the doorsteps of regional governments asking for a bailout. However, the millions of US dollars required to resuscitate the entities were not forthcoming as, rather ironically, the governments demanded evidence of improved business practices, including credible business plans and projections. Even without the complications of government control, the CMC/CANA Enterprise was also threatened from the outset by internal contradictions among its members, many of whom saw the joint company as a mere service unit for growth of their own private empires. A closer examination of the news agency side of the enterprise provides further insights into its contradictions.

The CANA came into being following a 1967 conference of Commonwealth Caribbean Heads of Government. This group unanimously approved a resolution calling for the establishment of a regional news agency. After a series of detailed UNESCO feasibility studies CANA was born in 1976 and assumed control of the Caribbean office of Reuters News Agency in Barbados. It continued to rely on Reuters for international news, while providing that British agency with Caribbean regional news feeds. It was the primary source of regional news coverage, particularly for newspapers and radio stations. However, not all members paid up regularly for its services, and some felt that CANA's growth would be at the expense of their private enterprise. As a result, many of CANA's major bills went unpaid and when it collapsed in 2001, over 50 members of staff were sent home without salaries or redundancy payments.

Table 3: Members of the Caribbean News Agency

Newspapers	Broadcasting Enterprises
Jamaica Gleaner	Radio Jamaica
The Trinidad Express	Television Jamaica (formerly JBC)
The Trinidad Guardian	The Caribbean Broadcasting Corporation
The Barbados Advocate	(Barbados)
	Barbados Rediffusion
	Trinidad and Tobago Television
	Antilles Radio Corporation (Montserrat)
	The Trinidad Broadcasting Company
	The National Broadcasting Service
	(Trinidad)

Source: CANA

CANA was the main supplier of regional news from the Caribbean, information and analysis to virtually all major newspapers, radio and TV systems in the English Caribbean. The suspension of its service continues to be keenly felt throughout the region and beyond. Its subscriber base includes Reuters News Agency, the BBC, the German News Agency (DPA) and a variety of companies, international organizations and diplomatic offices that keep abreast of developments in the Caribbean. Following meetings of CARICOM heads of government and information ministers, efforts continue to refloat CANA.

Part of the challenge is to reform the entities to take better account of competition from new media such as the Internet and from larger news conglomerates with regional coverage, such as the BBC and CNN. Another key task is to effectively consolidate the multiple agencies (CANA/CMC/CBU) into a single regional information and multimedia establishment. The restructuring of CANA/CMC also requires a new approach to ownership and management. Only radical reform that frees it from the limiting controls of some self-interested part owners and to give it greater business autonomy will spell a secure future. The new integrated entity will also have to take on board improved management, less reliance on grant funding and government subventions as well as adopt a wider geographical remit to better service information requirements beyond the region.

Challenge and change in
Caribbean cinema and film

Traditional cinema in the Caribbean is an example of both the crisis and the process of successful readjustment and transformation taking is currently taking place. Mark Wilson writes that in multiethnic Trinidad and Tobago, "there were 56 cinemas" in 1986. Six years later it was "down to 16, 15 more than most of the smaller islands." He has observed that "what was The Roxy in Port of Spain is now a Pizza Hut. . . The Ascot in Woodbrook and the Superstar on Abercromby Street are evangelical churches. Others have been converted to supermarkets and parking lots. The art deco De Luxe just off the Savannah in Port of Spain is still there, a little shabby in places, but with plenty of personality. . . but it doesn't show movies regularly anymore" Wilson (2002: 52).

In the Caribbean, as in many other parts of the world, the traditional medium of cinema is being overtaken by a range of alternative sources of visual entertainment. The emergence of the VCR, video rental stores as well as cable television has given audiences greater content opportunities via renting a movie or Cable TV. While for a minority the big silver screen still holds the allure of a romantic or relaxing social night out, for the majority of movie watchers in the Caribbean, the cinema as we know it is certainly no longer the most attractive screen in town. "There are plenty other ways to catch a movie." explains Wilson. "In Trinidad and Barbados, television in the 1980s meant a single rather drab state-owned channel. Now there's cable and satellite-based Direct TV with dozens of channels and the possibility of a couple of hundred before long. Guyana still has 18 cinemas but there are also 17 TV channels, mostly re-broadcasting US programming, with local news, chat shows and a thick scatter of Bollywood. The Barbados phone book lists 34 places to rent a video or a DVD" (Wilson, 2002: 53).

In Kingston, Jamaica, alone, six cinemas have closed down over the last ten years, all within a few miles of each other in the city centre. The spaces once occupied by The State, Regal, Rialto, Odeon, Cinema One Drive In and Cinema Two Drive In have now been occupied by a department store, an evangelical church, a bus terminus and a dramatic arts centre. New multiscreen cinema operations have also sprung up in two shopping centres, and an old large-auditorium movie-house which had been damaged by fire has been redesigned into a five-screened multiplex. A single firm, Palace Amusement Company, owns all the six major cinema complexes in operation in Jamaica.

At the same time, there have been attempts to invest in local cinema production. The region had gained confidence from the enormous success of local classics produced in the 1970s: *The Harder they Come* and *Smile*

Orange, both of which received excellent reviews and cinema screenings internationally. In Jamaica alone, in the succeeding two decades, there have been a further 10 locally directed films, some of which have experienced box office success. The movies *Dancehall Queen* and *Third World Cop* successfully ran for several weeks in local cinemas and enjoyed modest success in some cities in the United States and the UK with large Caribbean populations.

Other productions such as *Milk and Honey* and the screen adaptation of the theatre production *Two Can Play* enjoyed some success on international television. Many of these were produced with the proverbial shoestring budget. Movies such as *Children of Babylon*, *Klash*, *Rockers* and more recently *Goat Head* contributed to the net experience of the region in movie production. Elsewhere in the Caribbean, full-length movies have also been attempted with limited success. However it is in television productions by such companies as Banyan Productions in Trinidad and Tobago, and MediaMix and the CPTC in Jamaica that we observe sustained efforts to create alternative local television programmes, including local soap operas such as *Royal Palm Estate*.

It is clear that in the area of cinema, and within the local production sector, technological changes have affected the structure of these cultural industries. Audiences have responded positively to new ways of exhibiting visual productions and to a crop of locally directed films, documentaries and TV dramas. The cinema sector has contracted, but survives because it has adapted its delivery methods to the changing environment. The use of multiple screens at a single venue offers greater choice to cinema goers and allows for more dynamic marketing to compete with video and with multiple TV home channels. While lower socio-economic groups tend to favour the less expensive video outlets, the cinema has moved up-town. This innovation of the multiplex, which emerged as a US response to contracting audiences, now offers a lifeline to local cinema providers and has given a boost to big-screen productions from Hollywood that remain the main source of box-office hits in the region.

Emerging trends in Caribbean telecommunications

There are many commonalities evident in the growth and development of Caribbean media that are reflected in the changing regional telecommunication systems.

As with the electronic media, telecommunications in the English-speaking Caribbean region developed as part of the infrastructure of colonial control (see Barty-King, 1979 and Dunn, 1991). The telecommunication segment of a converging regional information industry continues to be dominated by the British transnational company Cable and Wireless

(C&W). However, as emerging innovations reduce operational costs for telecommunication service delivery, and public opposition to monopoly control has increased, this dominance is under increasing challenge and change. Whereas the company was the monopoly operator of telecommunications in 14 Caribbean territories in the year 2000, many of these countries, including Jamaica, Barbados, St. Lucia and Grenada have moved to introduce new competitive policies and new competitive service providers. But initially, this has been confined to the mobile services, particularly cellular telephony.

Table 4 sets out the continued extensive C&W ownership of operating companies in the Caribbean in April 2002, despite the atmosphere of change pervading the entire region.

In seven territories the company held 100% ownership of the integrated local and overseas telecommunication firms. In these territories, five of which are remaining British colonies, C&W is a monopoly in both ownership and total service provision. These include St. Vincent, St. Lucia, Montserrat, the Cayman Islands, the British Virgin Islands, Anguilla and Turks and Caicos islands.

In four other countries, C&W is the majority shareholder in dominant telecommunication network operating companies. These are Barbados, Jamaica, Dominica and Grenada. These are among the larger and more lucrative Caribbean markets for the company, particularly in Jamaica where Cable and Wireless Jamaica Limited is the largest of the region's operating companies.

In Antigua/Barbuda, C&W operates the overseas carrier, while the domestic telephone company is locally owned and operated by government. In Trinidad and Tobago, the company has an overall minority equity position in Telecommunication Services of Trinidad and Tobago (TSTT). While the Trinidad and Tobago government holds a majority 51% of the company, C&W continues to carry out executive management of the integrated operating company. In St. Kitts, C&W owns 51% to the minority block of 49% local ownership.

In Jamaica, as well as in St. Lucia, C&W also owns the main wired network and has full control of teleport facilities: Jamaica Digiport International in Montego Bay and the St. Lucia Teleport in Castries. Additional C&W enterprises in Antigua, St. Kitts, St. Lucia, St. Vincent and Jamaica operate mobile, cellular and boatphone services, some coordinated out of Antigua by Cable and Wireless Cellular Limited. Since 1999, the situation in Jamaica has been changing with the entry of three competitors in the cellular market. The Irish-owned firm Mossel entered the Jamaican cellular market in 2001, and after being operational for a year claimed over 50% of the cellular customer base, eroding C&W

Table 4: C&W ownership levels in Caribbean

Territory/Operator	Telecommunications companies	
	% C&W	% Local
C&W Anguilla	100	0
C&W Antigua/Barbuda (Overseas)	100	0
APUA - Antigua/ Barbuda (Domestic)	0	100
C&W Barbados	81	19
C&W British Virgin Islands	100	0
C&W Cayman Islands	100	0
C&W Dominica	80	20
C&W Grenada	70	30
C&W Jamaica	82	18
Jamaica Digiport Int.	100	0
C&W Montserrat Unit	100	0
C&W St. Kitts/Nevis	51	49
C&W St. Lucia	100	0
C&W St. Vincent/Grenadines	100	0
TSTT Trinidad and Tobago	49	51
C&W Turks and Caicos	100	0

Source: Compiled by H.S. Dunn, CARIMAC, UWI, from Company Records, April 2002

dominance in this sub-segment of the market and relieving strong pent-up demand (*Sunday Herald*, April 7, 2002: B1). The American firm Centennial also joined in the competition and there was the prospect of a fourth cellular operating company starting operations in 2003. Enactment of the Telecommunications Act 2000 to replace the obsolete 1898 Telephone Act provided the framework for the transition, overseen by the regulatory Office of Utilities Regulation (OUR) and the Jamaica Telecommunications Advisory Council (JTAC) at the Ministry of Industry, Commerce and Technology.

In Barbados, where C&W owns Digital Information Systems Limited (providers of specialized services in computer sales and information technology, including consultancy and training), changes have also been introduced to set the stage for competition.

The transnational company's dominance in the region, though diminishing, also extends to control of the main pan-Caribbean telecommunication arteries, such as the Digital Eastern Caribbean Fibre System (DECFS), which links countries in the Eastern Caribbean. The DECFS is also the main cable backbone linking the eastern region with the rest of the global wired telecommunication infrastructure. This fibre optic network replaced the old Digital Eastern Caribbean Microwave System, and the regional troposcatter system which the company also owned. The Trans-Caribbean System (TCS), linking the northern Caribbean islands of Jamaica and Hispaniola with Florida in the north and the DECFS in the south, is also part owned by Cable and Wireless West Indies Limited, in association with AT&T. The dominance of C&W control also extends to most of the region's satellite uplink and downlink facilities and Cable and Wireless has occasionally contested in court the right of new entrants in Jamaica and Dominica, to use very small aperture terminal transmitting systems (VSATs) for voice telephony. Nonetheless, this regional monolith is being successfully challenged by new entrants, and as a result, ownership in the market has begun to diversify. As competition is not co-terminus with good service and low cost, it is too early to estimate the real merits or futility of this process of liberalization.

However, governments throughout the region are only now beginning to come to terms with the profound and explosive implications of many of their earlier telecommunication policy decisions such as allowing monopoly control over the networks. Many have recognized that this critical sector of future development must benefit from multiple operators and a competitive framework. Despite the changes being introduced, it is necessary that policy-makers in the region do not regard competition as an end in itself but as the means to lower prices and to stimulate urban and rural development using telecommunications. Strengthening of regulatory institutions, improved regional cooperation in policy formulation, fiscal accountability for returns from the industry as well as legal reforms remain critical. Decisions relating to new technology applications, capital investment, intra-regional linkages, interconnectivity and development of universal access to the global information infrastructure are important functions of a strengthened regulatory regime. The experience of the last 15 years, according to Melody, "has convinced most observers that effective regulation must be an essential component of the new telecom structure if industry reform is to succeed" (Melody, 1997: 3)

The pressure for reform of monopoly control in the Caribbean region has, in part, come from demands for change in the wider global community. The World Trade Organization secured commitments for liberalization of telelcommunications under the Uruguay Round. In the

United States, the Federal Communications Commission (FCC), has been avidly pursuing a policy of rate rebalancing with its telecommunication counterparts globally, which resulted in reduced international telephone rates through more competitive business practices. Jamaica, the leading telecommunication market in the English-speaking Caribbean, introduced a phased programme of reform which culminated in fiscal year 2002–2003 with the complete opening up of the local and international markets to competition. The new transitional Telecommunications Act 2000, which replaced the Telephone Act of 1893, is under further review as the policy environment develops. The new policy direction, under the guidance of the Office of Utilities Regulation and the Telecommunications Advisory Council, declares that "It will be the policy of government to use telecommunications technology to enhance education, health and national security. No private monopoly will be entertained in this area." (Telecoms Policy Framework, 1998).

In embarking on market reform and other changes, it is important that the remarks of Melody ought not be ignored. "The significant changes in the role of the market that are taking place in telecom internationally are not founded simply upon ideological shifts and a new found faith in the so-called free market. Nor are they a directly determined response to the dictates of new technologies. Rather, the inherited monopoly institutions (public or private) have had great difficulty adapting to changing economic, political and social conditions, of which changing technology is only a part. Monopolies operating in a protected, stable environment are not well suited to adapt to a new and increasingly diversified and dynamic market place" (Melody, 1997: 3).

The Internet, new media and the Caribbean

Less that 5% of the population in the English-speaking Caribbean own or have access to the Internet. In that respect the region is not alone and is similar to large sections of the global South and certain communities in the North that are not yet active commuters on the new superhighway of digital multimedia information flows. In Jamaica, 17 existing Internet service providers were joined in mid 2002 by others who started as cable television providers. They are part of a new group of licencees empowered under the phased reform process of the Telecommunications Act 2000. In addition to home-based Internet services, a number of Internet kiosks were established throughout the region, along with Internet service centres in schools, libraries and post offices.

The Organization of American States (OAS) and the University sector together played a crucial role in the establishment of the Internet in the Caribbean. In 1991, the OAS invited representatives from the English-speaking Caribbean, Suriname and Guyana to a meeting in Puerto Rico to discuss the linking of the Caribbean to the Internet, through the establishment of nodes, which would be connected to the main US backbone. The University of the West Indies (UWI), University of Technology, UTECH (formerly CAST) and the Jamaican Scientific Research Council (SRC) were among those from the region represented at this meeting.

The first phase of the plan involved establishing nodes in each territory, to provide basic email service by dial-up to the University of Puerto Rico. Mona Information Systems Unit (MISU), a UWI company, provided Jamaica's first Internet connection in September 1991. The company obtained a 256 Kbps link to the Internet backbone. After setting up a server, it started out with a few dozen UWI-based users, whose numbers expanded rapidly. The university set up its own network with a supercomputer. By the end of 1993, the system had grown to the point where MISU had to go back to the OAS for help to establish full connectivity. In November 1993, MISU applied to the then overseas telecommunication provider JAMINTEL for an international leased circuit, which was made available in August 1994. Using this 64 Kbps, MISU linked up to an Internet node in Maryland, USA. In September 1994, UWI established its own website and students and staff were able to obtain general email accounts. MISU also provided non-commercial connectivity to 20–30 schools and private institutions in the formative years of the system in the region.

In Jamaica, this pioneering system was later joined by commercial service providers, initially by the main telecommunication network provider, and later by Infochan. Many others followed suit as the business and academic elites in Jamaica and the region became exposed and involved in the new globe-spanning networks. Other early providers of the service include Colis, Jamaica Online, KasNet, WorldTelenet, N5, Cybervale, APC Systems, JM.Net, JamWeb and Netcomm Jamaica. While some companies have merged and others have restructured ISP out of their business plans, several of the early providers remain in business alongside new entrants offering a range of services, including website design and hosting.

The Internet is now part of the business tool of many companies, particularly those involved in real estate, car rental, tourism and regional and global trade. The service generated several legal battles in the region, as C&W sought to restrict use of VSATS and voice over the Internet, claiming breaches of its exclusivity. For example, in Dominica in mid 1999, C&W disconnected Marpin's subscribers because of that company's use of a VSAT. The courts however declared that Marpin was entitled to compensation, and that C&W's 25-year monopoly was unconstitutional and violated the freedom of expression of Dominicans. In August, the litigation over the use of the VSAT was settled out of court. There were similar court battles by Infochannel Limited and Cable and Wireless Jamaica Limited, but these were later settled in August 1999. As a result, Infochan was given permission to operate services. The decision taken in Dominica had an important beneficial effect for Infochan's settlement in Jamaica.

Media companies and the small business sector were among those who were relatively slow in adopting the new Internet technology, although its corporate use in firms of varying sizes and types is now more widespread, particularly for email.

Conclusion

Changes in the technological and political environments do not just create difficulties for traditional operators but also spawn opportunities for new entrants, whether in telecommunications, new media or related cultural industries. Global-level innovations in information technology and digital media have created the potential for new owners and new hybrid systems. Cable and Wireless is emblematic of other traditional Caribbean companies, whether government-owned, private or run as part of transnational conglomerates, that have been subject to new conditions. The resulting deconstruction and in some cases reconstruction can lead to a new lease of life, or alternatively, result in terminal decline. Many government-owned and some traditional private media entities are now in crisis, generated in part by a slow rate of technology adoption, limited internal restructuring and ineffective institutional reforms. Some also face a shortage of financial resources, a dearth of innovative media management personnel and an insufficiently acute vision of alternative business models.

After a crucial period of inertia and resistance, some of the long established media houses and telecommunication providers have begun to respond by grafting into their operations new technological offshoots including websites and Internet-based portals. However, it is proving difficult to teach old dogs new tricks, so to speak. In developing and introducing these new offshoots, many of these companies simply replicate traditional production formats or reproduce imported content which they had become accustomed to using in their traditional operations. The challenge to this old approach from upstart companies involves greater emphasis on indigenous or repurposed content and on even more innovative use of emerging technologies.

While the cinema sector, for example, is seeking creative solutions to the challenge of change, other local and regional media operations have failed to do so, or to make the necessary transitions in the increasingly globalized neoliberal environments in the Caribbean. The fate of the Jamaica Broadcasting Corporation in Kingston and the Caribbean Media Corporation in Bridgetown, Barbados, are examples of the difficulties being encountered by different conventional entities in coping with changes in the industry characterized by the commodification of media products and audiences. In the case of the Jamaica Broadcasting Corporation, the station racked up large deficits in its financial operation, leading to its eventual removal as a recipient of an annual grant from the government. The JBC was shut down in late 1997, and its TV service divested for less than its market value to its competitor, RJR Group. This decision, however, led to the demise of the country's only public service broadcasting facility and to the rule of the market.

Part of the JBC's problem was that it failed to take advantage of its monopoly position in TV broadcasting nor did it compete with emerging cable television industry. Its operations were also hampered with a conflicting mandate. While it was on the one hand asked to provide public service programming, it was on the other asked to operate a fully-fledged commercial operation to fund its day-to-day operations. Like many other hybrid broadcasting operations, it failed to ride the proverbial horse "both ways".

The Regional Caribbean Media Corporation, the business arm of the Caribbean Broadcasting Union and the Caribbean News Agency, was shut down in early 2002 for lack of resources. The overlap of functions, inexperienced management and internal conflict over its role and funding led to the collapse of the CMC at a time when many regional media outlets as well as audiences had developed other electronic means of receiving regional information, including from online sources. The gap in the region's information infrastructure continues to be felt. CANA, which went down with CMC, represented an important organized source of professionally compiled regional news packages. Having taken over in 1976 from the British agency Reuters, CANA was invested with high hopes of providing regional news for the region by the region. But the limited scope of the English speaking Caribbean market, and insufficient reach into the wider Caribbean and global markets eventually contributed to its demise.

The failure to rapidly adopt the most advanced technologies and to respond to the needs of a changing market impacted negatively on the CMC. Despite efforts aimed at resuscitating the CMC, it will require large sums of new capital resources and a new vision capable of eliminating its internally contradictory and cumbersome management structures. The revitalized CANA/CMC service or any successor entity would also need to take a more aggressive approach to marketing Caribbean content in the global community. Greater use of the Internet and other new digital and multimedia technologies would be required to accomplish viability in the global distribution of a wider range of products, including news, features, financial data, music, and other non-traditional cultural products and services within and outside of the region.

While some national stations, regional broadcasting operations and traditional cinema monoliths are facing an uncertain future or even collapse, community level players and operators of new media in the Caribbean are in a growth phase. These emerging grassroots, community and Internet-based entities are engaging the historically dominant media and telecommunication establishments in a sharp struggle for audiences, subscribers and influence within the region.

New media businesses are also being built around popular cultural forms such as local music, roots theatre, community radio as well as local cable channels that offer live content and Internet services. Such community outlets and live local media channels help to fragment audiences, disperse advertising resources and alter the demographic and financial patterns of media and telecommunication operations.

As fragile new competitors in a regional and global market known for consuming weak dot.coms, the new entrants will have to pay attention to customer service, innovative ideas and strengthened management. This is especially the case if they are to survive the possible resurgence of traditional local players, as well as the externally based global conglomerates such as the BBC, AT&T and CNN. The future economic development of the region will depend in part on the success of the challenge, continued resistance to cultural incorporation, and creativity in the design and application of new communication technologies by both the more mature and the newly emerging regional enterprises.

References

Barty-King, H. (1979) *Girdle round the earth: The story of cable and wireless*, London: Heinemann.

Beckford, G. and Witter, M. (1980) *Small garden bitter weed*, Kingston: Maroon Publishing House.

Bennett, L. (1986) 'Colonizin in reverse', poem in Burnett P., *Caribbean verse in English*, London: Penguin.

Broadcasting Commission (1999) 'Survey of Jamaican indigenous programming', unpublished report, Kingston.

Brown, A. (1987) 'TV programming trends in the anglophone Caribbean: The 1980s', a report to UNESCO, Kingston.

Boyd-Barrett, O. and Newbold, C. (1996) *Approaches to media: A reader*, London: Edward Arnold.

Curran, J. and Gurevitch, M. (eds.) (1991) *Mass media and society*, London: Edward Arnold.

Dunn, H.S. (1995a) *Globalization, communication and Caribbean identity*, Kingston: Ian Randle Publishers, and New York: St Martin Press.

Dunn, H.S. (1995b) 'Caribbean telecommunications policy: Fashioned by debt, dependency and underdevelopment', in *Media, culture and society*, London: Sage.

Dunn, H.S. (1991) 'Telecommunications and underdevelopment: A policy analysis of the historical role of cable and wireless in the Caribbean', Ph.D. thesis, London: City University.

Girvan, N. (2002) 'The FTAA – A Caribbean perspective', text of an address to the conference on Caribbean and Canadian NGO's perspectives on the FTAA, Ottawa, 21–23 February, 2002.

Girvan, N. and Jefferson, O. (eds.) (1971) *Readings in the political economy of the Caribbean*, Trinidad and Tobago: New World Group.

Golding, P. and Murdock, G. (1991) 'Culture, communication and political economy', in Curran, J. and Gurevitch, M. (eds.), *Mass media and society*, 70–92, London: Edward Arnold.

Graham, A. and Davis, G. (1997) *Broadcasting, society and policy in the multimedia age*, Luton, England: Luton Press and John Libby Media.

Gordon, K. (1999) *Getting it write: Winning Caribbean press freedom*, Kingston: Ian Randle Publishers.

Hamelink, C. (1983) *Cultural autonomy in global communications*, New York and London: Longman.

Lent, J, and Sussman, G. (eds.) (1991) *Transnational communications*, California: Sage Publications.

Market Research Services Limited (2000) 'Print and electronic all media survey', Kingston: MRSL.

McIntyre, A. (2000) 'Globalization and strategic alliances', in *Caribbean communications and globalization: Perils, potentials and prospects*, proceedings of the 3rd Caribbean media conference, 5–7 May 2000, Georgetown, Guyana; UNESCO, Kingston, 19–21.

Melody, W.H. (ed.) (1997) *Telecom reform: Principles, policies and regulatory practices*, Denmark: Den Private Ingeniorfond.

Melody, W.H. (1996) 'The strategic value of policy research in the information economy', in Dutton, H. (ed.), *Information and communication technologies: Visions and realities*, 303–318, Oxford: Oxford University Press.

Ministry of Commerce and Technology (1998) 'Telecommunications policy framework', unpublished document, October 1998, Kingston: Government of Jamaica.

Mosco, V. (1995), 'The political economy tradition of communication research', in Boyd-Barrett, O. and Newbold, C. (1996), *Approaches to media: A reader*, London: Arnold.

Mueller, M. (1995) "Why communications policy is passing 'Mass Communication' by: Political economy as the missing link", CSMC, *Review and Criticism*, December 1995, 457–472.

Müllerleile, C. (1996) *CARICOM integration: Process and hurdles. A European view*, Kingston: Kingston Publishers Limited.

Rodney, W. (1971) *How Europe underdeveloped Africa*, Dar es Salaam, Tanzania: TPH Limited.

Schiller, H.I. (1971) 'The International Commercialization of Broadcasting', in Schiller H.I. *Mass communication and American empire*, 94–103, Boston: Beacon Press.

Stone, C. (1989) *Politics versus economics: The 1989 elections in Jamaica*, Kingston: Heinemann Publishing (Caribbean) Limited.

Stone, C. (1980) *Democracy and clientalism in Jamaica*, Kingston: Transaction Books.

Sunday Herald (2002) 'Digicel grabs greater market share', Kingston: Herald Newspaper, 7–13 April, 1B.

Surlin, S.H. and Soderlund, W.C. (eds.) (1990) *Mass media and the Caribbean*, New York: Gordon and Breach.

Thomas, C.Y. (1988) *The poor and the powerless: Economic policy and change in the Caribbean*, London: Latin American Bureau.

Wilson, M. (2002) 'The glory days are coming back: Cinema in the Caribbean', in *Caribbean beat*, BWIA, Port of Spain, Trinidad and Tobago, No 54 March/April 2002.

Worrell, D. (2001) 'Economic integration with unequal partners: The Caribbean and North America', in Hall, K.O. (ed.), *The Caribbean community: Beyond survival*, 427-472, Kingston: Ian Randle Publishers.

The Political Economy of Media in Southern Africa, 1990–2001

William Heuva, Keyan Tomaselli

and Ruth Teer-Tomaselli

Globalization is one of the most over-used terms and least understood phenomenon in contemporary social theory. The confusion is all the more prevalent since globalization always appears Janus-faced: as both an economic and a cultural phenomenon.

While there is a great deal of debate – much of it contradictory – there is nevertheless a recognition of the central role played by the media and communication infrastructure in the process.[1] In part, this is due to the dual nature of communications as an economic player in its own right, and as an enabler of economic development, nationally and transnationally, as well as the site of cultural production and dissemination.

Changed political and ideological climate

The post-Cold War free market economy has been driven by a neoliberal ideology, which advocates the liberalization of political and economic institutions. One result has been the emergence of multiparty political systems and the consolidation of free markets in many parts of the developing world, not least in southern Africa. In southern Africa, as in much of the world, the erstwhile public services and parastatal providers of communication infrastructure and content – the broadcasters and the telecommunication companies – were traditionally under the control of governments. Under the new climate of neoliberalism, state control is

---

1. The former Secretary-General of the International Telecommunication Union (ITU), Dr. Pekka Tarjanne, noted in a statement reported in *Telecommunication in Africa* that the information/communication sectors generated revenues of US$1.43 trillion, or 5.9% of the world's global domestic product. Thus, for every US$1,000 earned and spent by the world in 1995, US$59 was created directly, or indirectly, by this sector.

being replaced in large part by market control. This chapter will explore some of the major developments that have contributed to the restructuring of media, telecommunication and other communication networks within the southern African region.

What is globalization?

In the light of the confusion around terminology and theory, a few thoughts on the nature of globalization are in order. The global is dialectically connected to the local, and our concern with both "globalization" and "localization" reflects an attempt to conceptualize boundaries, delimitations, connections and interconnections. Globalization and concomitantly localization, are both economic and cultural phenomena. In this chapter, we are more concerned with the economic aspects of the process, although fully cognizant that the flow of capital and the changing nature of ownership and control have significant cultural consequences.

The period of "late capitalism" has been marked by a number of notable trends, most significantly, a general movement towards neoliberal economies and interdependence between national economies on a global scale. Globalization does not happen in a uniform manner, but affects nation states differentially. This uneven impact illustrates the continuity of historical processes, although in some cases the impact of globalization has been distinct. The unequal power relationships between the large, industrial nations of what used to be called the "centre" and the smaller nations at the "periphery", which was a characteristic feature of economic relationships during the colonial era, remain. At the same time, at a regional level, there are also asymmetries of power, with some of the larger countries playing the part of regional, or even sub-regional "hubs". (Robertson, 1992: 174). We argue that an integrated economy, within an inter-continental or more localized regional domain, exhibits aspects of both dependent and "independent" globalization.

Globalization "penetrates" local economies in at least three separate but interrelated ways. The process normally starts with a "state-led configuration of financial and economic sectors" and their "alignment with international monetary agencies". This is followed closely by "a 'liberalization' of trade and monetary policies which encourage private sector investment, (and the) exchange (of) business alliances across national boundaries". Finally, there is a restructuring of state owned assets to bring them into line with the demands of neoliberal economic imperatives (Robertson, 1992: 174). Financial sustainability and profitability become the watch-words and key objectives, rivalling others including universal access, diversity and cultural specificity. This, in turn, has led to the increasing "commercialization" of services previously provided by the state, including most notably communication services such as broadcasting and telecommunications. Typically, much of the responsibility for providing these services has been shifted to private suppliers. Some private enterprises were set up originally as public utilities and later sold to the "market", and certainly, both "public" and "private" enterprises tend to operate increasingly under a similar logic.

Globalization, as an economic phenomenon, is centuries old. In its "modern" guise however, it can be traced to the Bretton Woods meeting of 1944 where the economic reconstruction of Europe following the Second World War was considered. The International Bank for Reconstruction and Development, better known as the World Bank (WB), the International Monetary Fund (IMF) and the General Agreement on Tariffs and Trade (GATT) were created at this time. It was agreed that the World Bank would provide credit, the IMF would regulate global monetary exchange, and that GATT would liberalize trade. While the initial target for intervention was Western Europe, this was extended to the entire 'Third World' by US President Truman's Point Four Program, the equivalent of the Marshall Plan. Summarized briefly, the Plan was based on four propositions: first, the US would support the UN to strengthen its ability to enforce decisions; second, the US would continue its work in vitalizing the world economy; third, the US would "Strengthen freedom-loving peoples around the world against the evils of aggression"; and fourth, the US would "embark on a new program of modernization and capital investment" (Truman, 1949 quoted in Melkote and Steeves, 2001: 51).

The end of the "Soviet Threat" saw the reduction of aid to Africa from the West, but this was balanced out by support for new markets and increased economic assistance to the emerging Eastern European states. In order to attract investments from the West, African countries had to open up their economies as trade increasingly replaced aid to the continent. In the intervening years, both the IMF and the World Bank advocated economic "structural adjustment programmes" (SAPS), a shift in emphasis from "development planning and active commanding role of states to devaluation, deregulation, liberalisation and privatisation" (Buthelezi, 2000: 197). This has been a part of the core strategies of the World Bank and the IMF in their bid to promote private foreign investment and profit making opportunities for multinationals.

The "trilemma" of delivery

In the 1990s, the supply of telecommunication services by the industrialized countries was frequently far in excess of domestic needs, resulting in surplus capacity, technologies, expertise and capital. This was particularly so before the collapse of the information and telecommunication sectors in the early months of the year 2000. Thus it was in the interests of developed countries to explore markets in the less industrialized countries. These countries, in turn, were relatively or even chronically under-serviced in the areas of communication technology, but were faced with a contradictory set of imperatives. At one level, these countries were in a perfect position to absorb technical transfers, particularly if they were accompanied by significant capital investments. However, less developed countries face serious choices, not the least of which is the reluctance to relinquish control of strategic national assets and infrastructure to an foreign power. Some countries in the less developed world remained locked in a dissociation phase of developmental strategy, preferring to "go it alone". An example of this approach is Zimbabwe, a point to which we will return later to in the chapter. Yet without foreign investment, most countries are not in a position to develop local links to the "international superhighway", a required point of entry to international/global trade. A third contradiction is the need to provide affordable access to universal service for the local population. The latter is seldom a profitable enterprise, since the return on investment in producing a communication grid to a geographically dispersed, economically poor population with little or no disposable income is not seen as a glowing investment opportunity.

This then is the classic "trilemma" for developing countries in the provision of communication infrastructure: the need to accelerate service delivery through attracting foreign investment, while at the same time working towards universal service, often for little economic return, and at the same time attempting to retain a measure of national sovereignty.

Multilateral trade agreements

Powerful trading blocs replaced military blocs after the Cold War. These trading blocs redefined international trade through global and regional, bilateral and multilateral agreements. One such instrument with the potential to influence the media and communication sectors is the World Trade Organization (WTO). The WTO operates through trade-related aspects of intellectual property rights (TRIPS),[2] trade-related investment

---

2. TRIPS (Trade Related Intellectual Property Agreement) has forced developing countries to pay more attention to policing copyright violations. Countries that do not enforce this agreement are faced with sanctions. South Africa faced sanctions following threats from the Washington-based International Anti-Counterfeiting Coalition (IACC) which claimed that 75% of the computer market consisted of pirate products (*Mail & Guardian*, April 26–May 3, 2001: 6).

measures (TRIMS) and trade in services (TIS). Together with the IMF and World Bank's Structural Adjustment Programmes (SAPs) these three provisions/agreements are important instruments that continue to influence and direct the restructuring of the media and communication sector in the southern African region.

Initially, the Uruguay Round of GATT only dealt with enhanced or valued added telecommunication services (such as cellular or mobile telephones, email and online information services). In 1993, enhanced services were incorporated under Annex X to the Uruguay Round. Fifty-four nations acceded to this agreement that was enacted on 1 January 1995. The agreement was extended to cover basic telecommunication services and a second agreement, the Basic Service Agreement, signed by 69 countries on the 15 February 1997, came into operation on 5 February 1998. Not only are basic services more lucrative, there was also the need for new markets in the context of market saturation in the developed world. This agreement provides for market access and promotes fair treatment of suppliers of telecommunication services in second countries. It guarantees foreign investments in telecommunication services and facilities and the adoption of the "pro-competitive regulatory principles" that is essential to ensure free market access.[3] Technically, WTO commitments apply to many countries, to countries that have not made a formal commitment, even those that have not ratified the WTO treaty. The WTO commands about 85% of the global telecommunications sector (Cowhey and Klimenko, 1999). However, countries within the Southern African Development Community (SADC)[4] have committed themselves to these agreements. The commitments include the nature and pace of telecommunication restructuring as well as expectations related to the how and when of the restructuring processes.

---

3. See WTO Agreements at: http://www.wto.org.
4. The SADC consists of South Africa, Zimbabwe, Botswana, Namibia, Lesotho, Swaziland, Tanzania, Zambia, Mauritius, Democratic Republic of Congo, Angola, and Mozambique, with a population close to 200 million. South Africa, a leading economic and political power in the region, took the lead by committing itself to end its monopoly in telecommunications and to introduce a second operator by 2003 in public-switched, facilities-based services including voice, data transmission, telex, facsimile, private leased circuits and satellite-based services. It also committed itself to a duopoly in the supply of mobile cellular telephony. It did not limit the number of suppliers in paging, personal radio communication and trunked radio systems. However, South Africa limited foreign investment in its telecommunication suppliers to 30%. It has promised to liberalize resale services between 2000 and 2003. South Africa has committed itself to the Reference Paper on regulatory principles. See WTO's Telecommunication Services: Commitments and Exemptions at http://www.wto.org.

The WTO agreements have influenced contemporary telecommunication structures in the developing world in general and in southern Africa in particular. While the process of liberalization in the region began in the early 1990s, the WTO negotiations and agreements led to the consolidation of this trend.

Even before 1995, African governments had adopted a framework for telecommunication infrastructure development; approved measures to harness and apply information and communication technology, and decided to work towards the construction of a sustainable African Information Society Initiative (AISI) by 2010. The objective was to restructure telecommunications by expanding its infrastructure. Some countries set up national committees to coordinate the transformation of their countries into "information societies".[5]

It is instructive to revisit the initial position adopted by developing countries to understand the reasons for acquiring new communication technologies and the type and direction of restructuring. Developing countries, for the first time, articulated their desire for acquiring new communication technologies at the Information Society and Development Conference (ISAD) hosted by the G8 countries in South Africa in May 1996. The objective of the conference was to explain the benefits of the emerging information society to developing countries and to induce them to join the emerging global information society (Sergeants, 1996). However, while the developing countries were not against this in principle, they wanted to acquire the new communication technologies at their own pace, on their own terms and according to their own specific needs. The conference not only succeeded in highlighting the differences between the developed and the developing countries, but also in resolving them. It concluded a "compromise" but changed the original position of the developing countries. This had a tremendous impact on the future direction of the restructuring of the communication sector in the developing countries including those of the SADC region.

Initially the divergent positions were presented as follows: the industrialized countries were keen to access the "huge, untapped and attractive markets" of developing countries. To achieve this they needed the cooperation of the developing countries. The latter had to open their

---

5. Namibia, for instance, hosted two conferences in 1998 and 1999, under its National Information and Communication Initiative (NICI) involving stakeholders. The conferences submitted recommendations to the government. The government, however, has assigned a private computer company to formulate a policy on the information society in Namibia.

economic institutions through processes of deregulation, commercialization, liberalization, privatization and internationalization[6] in order to attract "international investors" (Richardson, 1996: 11). But the developing countries presented a different perspective. Their initial position placed people not profits at the centre of restructuring of their communication sectors. They wanted their governments (not the markets) to be at the centre of telecommunication restructuring. This was supposedly to guarantee "universal service/access", as they felt that an information society without "universal service" was not desirable. The conference struck a compromise. In Richardson's words (1996: 12):

> The ISAD conference shows that there is a clear need for international support for public/private partnership projects in a number of domains aimed at helping to build a truly global information society. The developing world has unique needs and challenges and also special skills and experiences in addressing these issues.

SADC protocol on telecommunications

One of the internal dynamics that influenced the restructuring process was the adoption of the SADC Protocol on Transport, Communication and Meteorology. The protocol itself was drafted with external expertize and funding from USAID. Article 10 deals with telecommunications. SADC member states took advantage of "opportunities" provided by new technologies to enhance the provision of telecommunication services. To this effect the protocol is geared towards the establishment of national telecommunication networks providing reliable, effective and affordable services. It obliges member states to harmonize their telecommunication policies, restructure their systems, create conducive environments for investment, develop universal service goals and encourage local (national) and regional participation. It also calls for the establishment of "autonomous, independent and national regulators" (SADC Protocol of Transport, Communication and Meteorology: 45–50 in SATCC Annual Report, 1998). The SADC countries also adopted a Model Telecommunications Policy and Regulatory frameworks, which is the guide supposedly to be used by member states in designing their (national) policies and regulations.[7]

---

6. See Mosco (1996) for a discussion on liberalization, commercialization, privatization and internationalization.
7. See the Southern Africa Transport and Communications Commission Annual Report, 1998.

Reconfiguration of regional interests

Globalization and localization are not inimical, but are synergistic aspects of the same process. As noted earlier, developing countries, including those in the SADC region, are faced with the need to develop their own technological infrastructure while ensuring a measure of autonomy and self-determination. Resistance can take the form of insularity, adopted for instance by Zimbabwe's refusal to entertain foreign ownership at any level within the broadcasting sector. Another approach has been to embrace globalization, but to do so on local terms. The most common tactic has been one of aggressive localization, as "the need to maintain local or national control over the processes and pace of change" (De Kock, 1997: 6). Here, localization is seen in terms of a local reaction to external forces of globalization. In the area of communications, localization has resulted in the expansion of markets and communication grids at both local and regional level.

Regionalization can thus be seen on two levels: as localization writ large, and as globalization writ small. The two processes work together dialectically as thesis and antithesis (Gillespie, 1998). In other words, regionalism can be seen as a quasi-global force. Regional responses can either damage or help others in adjacent areas. Positive examples include the establishment of cooperative ventures within the SADC area. Negative examples include predatory moves into other territories that undermine the viability or cultural integrity of national institutions. Cross-border localization has its own pitfalls because it can be perceived as a form of localized globalization (Conradie 2001: 73).

Liberalization and privatization of the African communication sector has led to a new form of "regionalization". The concept is used very loosely to emphasize the process of internationalization (see Mosco, 1996) on the continent, that is characterized by cross-border partnerships in the communication sector. Regionalization in this context, is seen as form of localization, that is dialectically aligned to, rather than opposed to globalization. This process involves cross-border ownership and teaming arrangements in the media and communication sectors. It can be traced to the beginning of the 1990s, if not earlier, but has not enjoyed attention in the academic literature on "transformations". We do not intend to assess the scope and depth of regionalization in this chapter but will merely highlight its constitutive trends.

As a result of the liberalization discussed earlier, the SADC media market has attracted media operators from other developing countries, especially from the newly industrializing countries (NICs) such as Malaysia, a process that has boosted South-South trade and cooperation. More importantly, liberalization has boosted regionalization within SADC and the broader African context. Media companies have established and consolidated new regional partnerships and alliances. Cross-border expansion initially involved stronger economies moving into weaker ones, but of late joint ventures have been established within small economies. This was demonstrated by the Namibian independent public payphone operator Tele2, owned by among others a hawkers association, which teamed up with Botswana residents and opened a subsidiary in Gaberone to provide payphone services (Botswana *Daily News*, 10 October 2001; *MISA Updates*, October 2001). Different countries have specific requirements in terms of the proportion of shares to be awarded to the strategic partner. In some countries foreign companies are not normally allowed to own 100% of shares or full ownership in the media sector. In Namibia foreign interests in the media are limited to less than 50%, while Zimbabwe prohibits foreign ownership in broadcasting (MISA, Broadcasting Update, April 200: 6).[8] South Africa limits foreign ownership in broadcasting to 20% (*The Star*, 20 March 2001 and *MISA Broadcasting Update*, April 2001), but it worked towards licensing a second fixed line operator in 2002. The 2001 telecommunication policy dropped the 49% limit initially placed on foreign ownership of fixed line operations (*MISA Telecom Update*, August 2001).

An example of a stronger economy entering into a dependent one is that of South African companies entering the Namibian communication sector (radio and television) through partnerships with local companies. Dagbreek Electroniese Media (Daybreak Electronic Media) teamed up with Cosmos Namibia Limited to set up Cosmos Radio in which the South African company has a 49% stake (*Die Republikein 2000*, 9 May 2000: 9). There are other South African interests in Namibian commercial radio such as Radio Wave (see Kandjii, 2000).[9] In television M-Net teamed up with Kalahari Holdings (fully owned by the ruling party, Swapo) in setting up Multi-Choice Namibia. Swapo has a 51% stake in this venture, and M-Net the remainder. Another South African company has stakes in the direct-to-air television station, Desert Entertainment (where South African and US companies jointly own 49%). There is also a 49% South African ownership in rebroadcasting pay television station called A-TV (*The Namibian*, 4 June 2001).

8. The Zimbabwean Broadcasting Act Services (2001) passed by Parliament on 4 April 2001 seeks state consolidation of broadcasting. It prevents political parties from owning and running broadcast media, force operators to air at least 75% of local content, prohibits foreign ownership/investments in broadcasting, and compels operators to devote one hour a week to government policies.

9. Ownership/investment in broadcasting, and compels operators to devote one hour a week to government for airing its policies.

In Malawi, a South African black empowerment group, Union Alliance Media (UAM), bought shares in Capital Radio Malawi. The deal will lead to the setting up of a youth radio station in Malawi, the YFM (*Misa Broadcasting Updates*, January 2001). In the spirit of regional (and South-South) cooperation, the Government of the Democratic of Congo (DRC) invited Telecom Namibia to help with the reconstruction of its telecommunication infrastructure (*The Namibian*, 28 August 2001: 5). The South African cellular operator MTN and the Zimbabwean Econet entered the Nigerian and Ugandan mobile telephone markets. The Saudi Arabian company, Saudi Ogre, which entered the market in November 2001, owns 60% of Cell C, South Africa's third cellular operator. South Africa cellular operator Vodacom entered Lesotho and Tanzania[10] in partnerships with two local shareholders to form Vodacom Tanzania Limited, paying US$1 million in licence fees (*MISA, Telecom Update*, July 2000). It also set up Vodacom Lesotho Limited. MTN opened a subsidiary in Swaziland, by establishing Swazi MTN.

One of the examples of how global conglomerates have entered regional markets through partnerships with local (national) and regional companies is represented by Warner Brothers International Television. This international group together with Midi Television co-owns eTV. Warner Brothers International Television has 12% shares in this venture, while the rest is owned by Mineworkers Investment Company (MIC), an investment arm of the Cosatu-affiliate National Union of Mineworkers (NUM). An example of "forced privatization" is found in Mozambique where the country was put under pressure through the SAPS to reprivatize its film and video industry (*MISA Telecom Update*, July 2000). An independent company Promarte Entertainment teamed up with a strategic partner, Investment Company, and acquired ten cinema houses from the government (*MISA Broadcasting Update*, December 2000: 2).

Foreign investment from the developed countries into the regional communication sector is represented by German capital, notably Siemens and Deutsche Telecom. The latter entered the Mozambican mobile market through a partnership with the local telecommunication parastatal, TDM. It now co-owns the country's cellular operator M-Cell (*MISA Telecom Update*, December 2000). Siemens, through its subsidiaries, has become one of the major suppliers of equipment and infrastructure for a GSM mobile network in about 18 countries in Africa, including the SADC. Siemens Telecommunications, owned by Siemens South Africa, won a US$35 million contract from Vodacom Tanzania to roll out the second phase of its operations, the largest in the country (Tanzania). Vodacom

---

10. Tanzania has other cellular operators including Tritel and Morbitel.

Tanzania was established in August 2000, but within a period of less than a year it overtook the two existing cellular operators, Mobitel and Tritel (*Independent Business Report*, 25 May 2001: 4). Siemens also provided equipment and infrastructure to Zimbabwe (signed US$45 million contract with the state-owned Net One) and Lesotho (*MISA Telecom Update*, July 2000). Siemens has subsidiaries and operations in Tanzania, Mozambique, Zimbabwe, Namibia and Botswana, apart from South Africa. About 50% of its revenues from the southern African region comes from telecommunications, such as network infrastructure and cellphones (Sukazi, 2001).

Regulatory authorities and commissions

The idea of "independent" regulatory bodies has taken root in the sub-region (SADC) and by 2001 almost all the member states had regulatory bodies in place. Thirty-three African states had "independent" regulatory authorities at the beginning of 2001, while nine were in the process of setting up their regulators (*Sunday Times Business Times*, 4 November 2001: 19). Two types of regulatory bodies ("authorities" and "commissions") have emerged, determined by the state's perception of convergence. We distinguish between regulatory bodies that belong to states anticipating immediate convergence and therefore set up measures to regulate both broadcasting and telecommunications on the one hand, and those countries that have separate regulatory bodies, one for broadcasting and the other for telecommunications. The first category is represented by the Namibia Communications Commission (NCC) and the Independent Communication Authority of South Africa (ICASA). In the second category are bodies that regulate broadcasting only, such as the Tanzania Broadcasting Commission (TBC) and Broadcasting Authority of Zimbabwe (BAZ), and those that solely regulate telecommunications, like the Tanzania Communications Commission (TCC) and the Botswana Telecommunications Authority (BTA). The "independence" of these bodies has been contested by regional media rights organizations such as MISA. If checks and balances and transparency are not built into the regulatory policies, regulatory bodies face the danger of being captured by the state or by capital (or by an alliance of both).

Telecommunications: Opening markets and extending services

Southern African states liberalized their erstwhile broadcasting and telecommunication monopolies in two ways: in the enhanced (value-added) telecommunication market, liberalization has led to the opening up of opportunities for public, private and community operators. In the area of basic services, the strategy has been one of "managed" or partial privatization through the establishment of "strategic partnerships" between state monopolies and business interests (national, regional and/or global). Normally, partial privatization has resulted through the public listing of a certain number of shares in the state-owned telecommunication monopolies and on the basis of the selection of a private partner.

Basic service

The situation in southern Africa is dictated by the WTO agreement on "basic telecommunications services". Almost all the SADC member countries have committed themselves (formally or otherwise) to the privatization of this sector. According to *Telecom Africa 2001*'s statistics, by the beginning of 2001 eighteen African states had privatized (fully or partially) their national operators, while 22 others were in the process of doing so (*Sunday Times Business Times*, 4 November 2001: 19). Various forms of privatization are evident. We can distinguish privatization involving the selling of a relatively small proportion of about 30% shares (i.e., South Africa, Malawi, etc.) from the selling of larger amount of shares such as 70% (i.e., Lesotho) in the state monopoly to private enterprises. Some countries are yet to make public equity percentages, although they have, in principle, committed to privatization.

Namibia, for instance, commercialized its telecommunication sector in 1992 and created a state-owned company called Telecom Namibia, 100% owned by the state and run on business principles. In 1999 the government adopted a telecommunication policy and regulatory framework that arguably sought to balance public and commercial interests in the telecommunication sector. The state plans to continue regulating the basic service as it intends to open this market on a "restricted basis" (Republic of Namibia, 1999). While Namibia has committed to open its basic services by 2004, the government is under pressure from business to hasten this process, because of skyrocketing tariffs in long distance calls that is ascribed to a poorly functioning state monopoly.[11] However, the basic service is regarded as strategic and the government has therefore given the state-owned Telecom Namibia time (until 2004) to expand its infrastructure in order to increase universal access, while at the same time balance its tariffs in order to "price itself competitively", before competition is introduced (Republic of Namibia, 1999: 16).

---

11. The business community has argued that competition would reduce telephone costs. See Duddy, J. (2000) 'Telecommunications policy: Stakeholders demand swift action' *Die Republikien 2000* (The Market Place), May 27, 1999, 1–2.

Tanzania has sold 35% shares in the state-owned Tanzanian Telecommunications Company Limited (TTCL) to a consortium comprising a German (Detecom) and a Dutch (MSI) company, called the Detecom/MSI, to the tune of US$120 million (*MISA Telecom Update*, July 2000). South Africa had also privatized 30% of shares in its public telecommunications monopoly, Telkom, by selling this to foreign interests in line with its commitments to the WTO. The US-based SBC Communications and Telekom Malaysia Berhad share another 30%.

Enhanced or value-added (Internet and cellular services)

The Internet has not only taken root but has overtaken fixed lines in terms of growth. According to ITU figures released at the Telecom Africa 2001 there were 25 million cellular subscribers compared to 5 million fixed telephone lines in Africa in 2001. By the end of 2001 cellular subscriptions reached 30 million. This growth is ascribed to the introduction of prepaid services, as more than 80% of subscribers are on the prepaid system. (*Independent Business Report*, 12 November 2001, p1 and *Independent Business Report*, 13 November 2001, p7).[12] This sector has enjoyed progressive liberalization from the start, long before Annex X to the Uruguay Round paved the way for liberalization of enhanced or of value added telecommunication services. In fact the Internet has come to southern Africa as a private and independent activity from government.[13] Globally it has been associated with democratic forms of communication before its eventual privatization and subsequent co-option by global capitalism. In Namibia the Internet was initiated by a non-profit Internet Service Provider (ISP), the Namibian Internet Development Foundation, (Namidef) during the first part of the mid-1990s. This ISP was launched by academics and professionals and provided services to schools, government offices and UN agencies in Windhoek, through a line leased from the Namibian and South African telecommunication operators. The success of Namidef was undermined by the rapid emergence of commercial ISPs with access to colossal finances and the latest infrastructure.

The national telecommunication operators (state-owned monopolies) are increasingly diversifying their services and vertically integrating their operations. Many national operators have turned to providing enhanced

---

12. *Independent Business Report*, 12 November 2001, p1 and *Independent Business Report*, 13 November 2001, p.7).

13. See UNESCO's World Communication and Information Report, 1999–2000, Part Three, Chapter 13: 180–196.

(cellular and Internet) services to the dismay of private ISPs.[14] This is arguably contributing to mixed telecommunication systems. The SADC states have also set up strategic partnerships in the value added telecommunication market. The state-owned basic telecommunication monopoly, Telecom Namibia teamed up with Swedish companies (Telia International and Swede Fund) to launch Mobile Telephone Company (MTC), the country's first cellular operator in 2001. Telecom Namibia owns 51% shares in MTC, while the Swedish companies own 49%.[15] This example illustrates a form of internationalization,[16] a process undertaken by many state-owned companies in the region. In another form of vertical integration Telecom Namibia established in 2000 an ISP called 'iWay'.[17]

The Malawi Telecommunication Limited (MTL) operates an Internet service provider called Malawinet, while the Botswana Telecommunications Corporation operates Bosnet (an Internet service provider established in 1999). Zimbabwe was one of the last countries in the region to split its former telecommunications and post monopoly during the middle of 2001, after enacting a new telecommunication legislation in September 2000. Under this arrangement the former monopoly is divided among Zimpost (post services), Net One (cellular operator) and Tele One (a fixed line operator) (*MISA Telecom Update*, 18 July 2001).

The cellular phone industry has recorded spectacular success in the region. One such success story has been the Zimbabwe-based Econent. Econet has become one of the continent's major cellular operators.[18] The other major operators are South Africa, MTN and Vodacom and Egypt's Orascom Telecom. These four operators have changed the face of mobile

---

14. See for instance an article by Kaira, C. 'ISPs lash out at state's control of cyber space', *The Namibia Economist*, 9 November 2001.

15. Karlson, R. and Renstrom, L. (1995) 'Cellular phones in Namibia: A case study of an internationalisation process' unpublished MA thesis, Mid-Sweden University.

16. In the context of the SADC, this process has involved the formation of "strategic partnerships" between state-owned monopolies and international companies. For a detailed discussion, see Mosco, V. (1996) *The Political Economy of Communication: Rethinking and Renewal*, London, New Delhi, Thousand Oaks: Sage Publications.

17. Angula, C. 'New ISP shows Namibia iWay', *The Namibian*, 30 November 2000: 10.

18. Econet Wireless Limited, which has been Zimbabwe's leading cellular operator, is part of the international company Econet Wireless Holding incorporated in the United Kingdom. The holding company has stakes in telecommunication sectors in Nigeria, Lesotho, United Kingdom and South Africa (*MISA Telecom Update*, 18 July 2001).

telecommunications in Africa, though their footprints are confined to cities and national road routes. Econent has grown very fast. Within the first 20 months of its establishment Econet grew by 2000% and became the second largest firm on the Zimbabwe Stock Exchange. In 2000 Econet was the largest among 32 companies in sub-Saharan Africa (*MISA Telecom Update*, July 2000).

Basic telecommunication service providers?

Liberalization has created new forms of vertical and horizontal integration in telecommunications. A consequence of this are moves by transport and electricity companies to provide telecommunication services. In South Africa, Transtel and Esi-Tel, the telecommunication arms of the transport and electricity utilities (Transnet and Eskom respectively), supply telecommunication services to their parent bodies. These companies have also ventured into supplying telecommunication services to countries outside of South Africa. Transtel provides telecommunication and information technology related services to companies in about 15 African countries. This includes the provision of a virtual private network for Zambia's central bank, satellite communications for Nigeria and Zimbabwean banks and the telecommunication company of Congo (ONPT). Transtel was also targeting the Middle East in 2001 and won a contract to upgrade communications for the Saudi railway. In 2001, it considered taking a stake in Mount Kenya, a consortium bidding for 49% of Telkom Kenya (*Independent Business Report*, Tuesday February 27, 2001: 7).

Namibia's electricity utility, Nampower, plans to apply for the country's second fixed line (basic service) telecommunication operator's licence, when this market is opened for competition in 2004 at the latest.[19] Nampower has also over the years supplied communications services, over its power lines, using a SCADA system. This parastatal had operated a well-oiled communication system that linked a number of points (stations and sub-stations) along its main power lines stretching thousands of kilometres. This system was upgraded and fibre-optic lines were installed along power lines. The new system provides better telecommunication capacity than the conventional copper lines because fibre optic carries a much higher load of information at a much higher speed. The content-capacity of new fibre-optic lines is often far in excess of company requirements and this is why Nampower is considering offering

---

19. Namibia committed itself to the privatization of its fixed line operations in 2004 although the government is under pressure from the private sector to implement this process earlier.

telecommunication services to the whole country. Its facility roll out covers almost the entire country unlike Telecom Namibia that does not reach the far-flung areas (*The Namibia Economist*, 19 October 2001: 1).[20] This unutilized capacity has spurred Nampower to enter the basic telecommunications sector.

The Media Institute of Southern Africa (MISA)

One of the key institutions that advocate a liberal ideology of the press is the Media Institute of Southern Africa (MISA).[21] Since its establishment, MISA has campaigned vigorously for press freedom and the plurality of the press, which comprise basic tenets of the philosophy of liberal media.

MISA was established in response to the UNESCO-sponsored Windhoek Declaration of 1991 and was mandated by concerned journalists in the region to implement decisions adopted under the Declaration in the SADC region.[22] The original 1991 Windhoek Declaration was confined to the press, although it carried a caveat in Paragraph 17 which recommended that another meeting be convened to address independent and plural broadcasting in the region. This meeting was held a decade later. MISA took the lead in launching campaigns that propagated the liberalization of the airwaves. These campaigns created a general awareness and realization about public ownership of the airwaves and the need for their management in the public's interest. The Zambian Independent Media Association (ZIMA), in response to this campaign, drafted broadcasting policy and regulatory regimes at a workshop on 20 December 2000 and submitted them to government for consideration and implementation (*MISA Broadcasting Updates*, January 2001).

New Charter of the Windhoek Declaration (2001)

The Windhoek Charter on broadcasting and telecommunications was adopted at the 10th anniversary of the Windhoek Declaration. It seeks to expand the focus beyond the press-centric confines of the 1991

---

20. Craign, A. (2001) 'Nampower vs. Telecom', *The Namibian Economist*, 19 October 2001: 1.

21. MISA is not the only institution that is involved in campaigning for press freedom and plurality in the region. There are other organizations including South Africa's Freedom of Expression Institute. MISA has a regional focus and is present in all SADC member states.

22. UNESCO did not establish MISA. Journalists concerned with press freedom are the ones who pushed for the establishment of this institute.

Declaration. It is committed to the consolidation of media freedom through extending the right to communicate and of access to telephone, email, Internet and other new forms of the media. It seeks to ensure diversity in both the broadcasting and the telecommunication sectors through the establishment of mixed services (public, private/commercial and community) in broadcasting and telecommunication sectors. The Charter embraces the promotion of community-controlled information and communication technology (ICT) centres specifically in poor and marginalized areas.

Moreover, the Charter calls for the establishment of independent regulatory authorities free from political and economic imperatives; a transparent process in appointing members of the regulatory authorities; and an open and transparent process of frequency allocation and their equitable distribution among the above-mentioned three tier broadcasting system. While conceived within the dominant neoliberal ideology driven by commercial interests of international organizations and multinationals, the Charter seeks to negotiate public interest (democratic) clauses within this broader framework. In Part I, paragraph 7 on General Regulatory Issues the Charter urges governments to "promote an economic environment that facilitates the development of independent productions and broadcasting". Paragraph 2 of Part IV on Telecommunications and Convergence calls for the promotion of the "goals of universal service and access" through the adoption of access clauses within privatization and liberalization processes (*MISA Broadcasting Update*, May 2001).

In what amounts to democratic communication discourse the Charter in Part II on Public Broadcasting calls for the transformation of the state broadcasters into public service broadcasters accountable to all strata of society through independent boards that serve the public interest. It also calls for an equitable "non-discriminatory" and easy access to transmission facilities used by public service broadcasters.

Changes to the structure of broadcasting in the region

A new mixed broadcasting system is being consolidated in the region as more commercial and community-broadcasting stations are licensed, in addition to the existing state/public broadcasting stations. It is interesting to note that the emerging mixed media systems reflect the type of economic systems that has emerged in the SADC region during the 1990s. The mixed economic system (which is basically a capitalist one) accommodates public, private, joint public-private, cooperatives, etc. The rationale of mixed economic ownership is now being extended to the communication sector as it is increasingly gaining economic importance, surpassing many of the traditional economic activities. The rationale of mixed economy has been used to defend the participation of the state in print media (*The* [Tanzanian] *Guardian*, 16 November 2001; *Mail & Guardian*, 2 - 8 November 2001: 16; SADC Protocol on Culture, Information and Sport, 2001).

Like the government press, the state broadcasting system refuses to die. It has continued its dominance in many parts of the region despite the enormous challenge posed by the emerging commercial system, and financial constraints resulting from SAPS. Politicians, especially the ruling party elite, refuse to confer control to professional broadcasters and to appoint independent board members. The state broadcaster is very crucial for the survival of the political elite, because it is the medium for the government (party in power) to propagate its policies. South Africa is one of the few examples in the region to operate a public service broadcaster relatively free from political influence, although this system is increasingly coming under the sway of commerce.

While remaining firmly under the control of the state, most of the national (state and/or public) broadcasters rely partially on commercial activities, such as advertising for income, because many are faced with budget cuts.[23] Zimbabwe plans to commercialize its national broadcaster. It has, to this effect, gazetted a new bill, the Broadcasting Commercialization Bill, that will split the Zimbabwe Broadcasting Corporation (ZBC) into two separate companies. Both institutions will be run on business principles. One company will operate radio and television services, while the other will concentrate on signal distribution services. It is expected that the two new companies will be run on profit making principles and will remain independent of state ownership and state subsidies (*MISA Broadcasting Update*, late November 2001).

Most governments in the region, with the exception of South Africa, have continued to exert almost monopoly control over the public, or more correctly, the state broadcaster, despite the processes of transformation currently unfolding in the region. The Namibian example is an example of "transformation as control". Namibia at its independence in 1990 transformed the former *South* West African Broadcasting Corporation (SWABC) into a new organization called the Namibian Broadcasting Corporation (NBC), in a process that entailed a bit more than a mere change to its name. Prior to 1994, The SWABC was run on the same

---

23. The cut in the budgets of public broadcasters are related to SAP directions that are anti-subsidy. This has not only negatively affected the operations of state and public service broadcasters, it has also presented politicians with a dilemma – cutting of funding to their megaphones!

principles as its mentor, the former South African Broadcasting Corporation (SABC). The revamped corporation, the NBC, retained much of the organizational and operational logic of the former SWABC. It remained a parastatal (state-owned enterprise), established by an Act of parliament, the Namibian Broadcasting Act, 1991, (Act No. 9 of 1991). It remained under political authority, under the Ministry of Foreign Affairs, Information and Broadcasting, which handpicks its governing body, the Board of Directors. The Cabinet must approve its board members.[24]

Research needs to establish the neutrality of the so-called "independent" boards and regulatory authorities/commissions in the region and beyond. It would be interesting to find out how different interests are represented by such boards and authorities.

The Namibian government was one of the first countries in the region to liberalize the airwaves soon after independence in 1990. It adopted an Information Policy suited to a mixed media system. In 1992 the government created a regulatory body, the Namibian Communications Commission (NCC) to regulate the new entrants (community and commercial broadcasters) in the field of broadcasting. The NCC also regulates the telecommunication sector, but the national broadcaster, the NBC, does not fall under the jurisdiction of the NCC. It is regulated by its enabling Act (No. 9 of 1991) Heuva (2000).

Zimbabwe remains one of the last of the countries in the region to liberalize its broadcasting system. For the better part of its post-independence period, broadcasting was dominated by the state-owned Zimbabwe Broadcasting Corporation (ZBC). It needed a legal challenge to the dominance of the ZBC to change the system. Section 27 of the ZBC Act gave the corporation "exclusive right" to operate broadcasting services. A small station, Capital Radio, challenged this and the court declared on 22 September 2000, that section 27 was unconstitutional. This decision threw broadcasting in Zimbabwe into turmoil. The state intervened through presidential interim measures, followed by the adoption of the new broadcasting legislation, the Broadcasting Services Act, that was enacted on 4 April 2001. This Act bans foreign investment

---

24. Generally the NBC has enjoyed a close relation to the State House (the President's Office in Namibia) and to the Cabinet as many of its day to day problems related to budgetary constraints, salary hikes, strike threats, board-management conflicts, etc. are solved by these two institutions rather than by the Chamber of the Board of Directors (see *The Namibian*, 21 September 2001). The cancellation of a radio programme called the 'Prime Minister's Question Time' was referred to the ruling Party's Politburo and the Cabinet (See Hamata, M. 'NBC's silencing of PM angers SWAPO body'. *The Namibian*, 19 November 2001).

in broadcasting. It also bans political parties from owning and running broadcasting media, but more importantly, the Act compels independent broadcasting operators (commercial, church and community) to devote one hour per week to government policies (*MISA Broadcasting Updates*, April 2001: 6).

While the emergence of radio dates back to the 1920s, television is relatively new. South Africa began broadcasting in 1976, Tanzania in 1994, Botswana in 2000 and Malawi in 1998 (Bourgault, 1995). The national broadcasters set up an umbrella body, the Southern African Broadcasting Association (SABA), with its Head Office in Windhoek, with the primary objective of coordinating the activities of public broadcasters under its umbrella. SABA has urged SADC member states to implement independent regulatory bodies to ensure editorial independence. However, SABA has not been very successful in these demands, partly because its members continue to depend on state funding.

Conclusion

The transformation and restructuring of communication systems in the region is driven by economic imperatives, despite the rhetoric of universal access that have accompanied these processes. Moreover, partnerships between state and capital have increased, while media rights groups and other actors in civil society continue to be locked out of major restructuring decisions. This can lead to the marginalization of important democratic (public interest) issues in the emerging (restructured) media and communication systems. There is therefore a need to lobby for a balance between commercial and non-commercial imperatives in the emerging media systems. Attempts at balancing these conflicting interests should be included in the transformation and restructuring processes, as proposed by the 2001 Windhoek Charter. Moreover, discussions of this should start at the policy level. This will only be possible if a broad spectrum of views and perspectives are given access to, and contribute to, policymaking processes. Without the benefit of such provisions, the emerging media systems are bound to remain irrelevant to the majority of the SADC region.

References

Bourgault, L.M. (1995) *Mass media in Sub-Saharan Africa*, Bloomington and Indianopolis: Indiana University Press.

Buthelezi, S. (2000) 'Globalisation and the process of democratisation in Southern Africa', in Nabudere, D.W. *Globalisation and the post-colonial state*, Harare, Zimbabwe: AAPS Books.

Conradie, D.P. (2001) 'Reactions to globalisation by the television industry in post-apartheid South Africa', *Communicatio*, 27, 2, 70–83, (University of South Africa.)

Cowhey, P. and Klimenko, M.M. (1999) The WTO agreement and telecommunications policy reforms, A draft report for the World Bank, Washington, DC: World Bank.

De Kock, P. (1997) 'Globalisation: Investigating the process', *Politeria,* 15, 2, 15–21, (University of Pretoria).

Gillespie, P. (1998) 'Answer to globalisation is Europeanisation', Online article in *The Irish Times on Web*, accessed from http://www.irish-ties/paper/wldrev1.html.

Heuva, W. (2000) 'A decade of broadcasting in independent Namibia', Working Paper, No. 6, 2000, Switzerland: Basler Bibliographien.

Kandjii, K. (2000) 'De-regulation of the Namibian broadcasting industry: Challenges and contradictions', unpublished paper presented at the political economy of the media in Southern Africa seminar, University of Natal, Durban, 24–29 April, 2000.

Manoim, I. (2000) 'Wiring up African news', *Daily Mail & Guardian*, 22 February 2000.

Melkote, S.R. and Steeves, H.L. (2001) *Communication for development in the Third World: Theory and practice for empowerment*, New Delhi: Sage.

Mosco, V. (1996) *The political economy of communication: Rethinking and renewal*, London: Sage.

Richardson, W. (ed.) (1996) 'Telecommunications and the information revolution', *Telecommunications in Africa*, May/June 1996.

Robertson, R. (1992) *Globalisation*, London: Sage.

Republic of Namibia, (1999) *Telecommunications Policy and Regulatory Framework for Namibia*, Windhoek: Government Publications.

Sergeants, M. (1996) 'A Different Kind of Revolution?', *Telecommunications in Africa*, May/June 1996.

Southern African Development Community (SADC) (1998). *Southern African Transport and Communication Commission (SATCC) Annual Report 1998.*

Sukazi, N. (2001) 'Siemens to pursue empowerment trail further', *Business Report*, Wednesday, 21 November, p4.

Tipoteh, T.N. (2000) 'Globalisation and development', in Nabudere, D.W. *Globalisation and the post-colonial African state*, Harare, Zimbabwe: AAPS Books.

Media Ownership and Control in Africa in the Age of Globalization

Francis B. Nyamnjoh

Introduction

Current debates on media ownership and control are informed by, and largely focused on, the effects of globalization and neoliberalism on media scenarios the world over. Almost everywhere, old patterns are giving way to new configurations at a phenomenal pace. National, state-owned, public service media systems are yielding to commercial media characterized by increasing concentration of ownership and control through takeovers, mergers, and globalization. Propelled by "the incessant pursuit of profit" global media entrepreneurs are lobbying for the total "relaxation or elimination of barriers to commercial exploitation of media and to concentrated media ownership" (McChesney, 2001: 1–4). According to Robert McChesney, who has written extensively in this area, the trend is towards the creation of global oligopolies. The guiding logic of media firms is one of "get very big very quickly, or get swallowed up by someone else". Firms, he argues, "must become larger and diversified to reduce risk and enhance profit-making opportunities, and they must straddle the globe so as to never be outflanked by competitors." Not only is the traditional idea of public service radio and television fast becoming outmoded, calls by concerned countries for some ground rules to protect cultural diversity by keeping culture out of the control of the World Trade Organization (WTO) have simply been greeted with the rhetoric of free flows. What is more, the corporate media are in a particularly powerful position to "get their way with politicians", given their ability to "use their domination of the news media in a self-serving way" (McChesney, 2001: 3–9). As Thomas and Lee (1998: 2) observed, "Global media corporations . . . enjoy an enormous leeway to negotiate and protect interests from the vantage of prior monopoly positions. Bill Gates, Rupert Murdoch and the owners of Time-Warner do not have to bend over backwards to strike deals. It is generally the case that they decide and the world follows suit."

This implies that the global media corporations are not all about "unregulated flows" of the world's cultural diversity. They perpetuate a "deeply and starkly inegalitarian" process (Golding and Harris, 1997: 7) that favours a privileged minority as it compounds the impoverishment of the majority through closures and containment. The objective of the corporate media operators is to control not only global markets, but also global consciousness, by encouraging "the emergence of a small number of monopoly concerns which command a disproportionate share" of the global market (McChesney, 1998, 2001; Murdock, 1994; Thomas and Lee, 1994). As Murdock argues, "the new media mogul empires" are "empires of image and of the imagination" in that "They mobilise a proliferating array of communications technologies to deliver a plurality of cultural products across a widening range of geographical territories and social spaces, and are directed from the centre by proprietors who rule their domains with shifting mixtures of autocracy, paternalism and charisma" (Murdock, 1994: 3). The tendency is to mistake plurality for diversity, oblivious of the possibility that an appearance of plenty could well conceal a poverty of perspectives (Murdock, 1994: 5).

This literally leaves ordinary consumers at the mercy of the "Mcdonaldized", standardized or routinized news, information and entertainment burgers served them in the interest of profit by the global corporate media. Because the global media system "advances corporate and commercial interests and values and denigrates or ignores that which cannot be incorporated into its mission", content becomes uniform, regardless of whether shareholders are Japanese or French, or whether corporate headquarters is in New York, Germany or Sydney. This is hardly surprising since the media prefer passive, depoliticized, unthinking consumers to those who question the "light escapist entertainment" menu presented to them (McChesney, 1998: 7). In this regard, "the basic split is not between nation-states, but between the rich and the poor, across national borders" (McChesney, 1998: 6; 2001: 13). However, the fact remains that the investors, advertisers and affluent consumers whose interests global media represent, are concentrated in the developed world. This is not the case in Africa where only an elite minority are involved. This chapter seeks to place Africa in relation to this global trend, and to discuss the crystallization of resistance to victimhood.

Ownership and control trends in Africa

In September 1997, a three-day workshop on Media ownership and control in West and Central Africa was held in Cameroon. Funded by WACC and initially scheduled to take place at the University of Buea where I taught and headed the Department of Sociology and Anthropology, the workshop was moved to Yaounde at the last minute, because the Vice Chancellor of the University of Buea, Dr Dorothy L. Njeuma, had given the background paper a second reading. In her memorandum of disapproval to me through my Dean, she wrote, inter alia:

> It will be recalled that the initial title of the workshop was Communication and the Globalization of Poverty. In his response dated 3 July 1997 to the observations which we made relating to the need to observe instructions requiring prior authorisation from the Presidency of the Republic for International meetings and the apparent contradiction in the subject of the workshop, Dr. Nyamnjoh underlines that the workshop would be a purely academic exercise and that the new title is a sub-theme of the initial subject.
>
> We regret to inform you that the background paper on Media Ownership and Control as contained in document No. 0111/75-4/UB/SOC of 24 March 1997 carries sensitive political overtones which are inappropriate for the University of Buea to be seen to promote at this particular time. The slant given in the paper is also at variance with the view presented by WACC on the factors which they perceive as contributing to the globalization of poverty; the WACC document faults rich nations, international financial institutions and communication transnationals for the spread of poverty (cf. WACC Programme for 1997–2001).
>
> In these circumstances, we regret that we cannot give approval for the University of Buea to host the workshop on Media Ownership and Control [. . . .][1]

The background paper in question was what I had submitted to WACC for funding, and what she objected to were the following paragraphs:

> A look at the literature and research on media and mass communication in Africa prior to 1990, reveals a tendency towards centralised broadcast systems and a highly repressed private press. At independence, governments almost everywhere opted for the rigid highly centralised colonial model to the freer and more accessible metropolitan one, of which as colonies they experienced next to nothing, and which was transferred just a little before or after independence, in order to fill the gap left by removal of colonial control. There is little evidence of autonomy from government control, and governments have waited till the pro-democracy clamours of the 1990s to contemplate weakening their monopoly of radio and television, and curbing their stranglehold on the press. Commercial or non-state-owned radios like Africa No.1 of Gabon, radio SYD in Gambia, radio

---

1. Memorandum No. 0708/75-4/UB/W000 dated 16-07-97 from The Vice Chancellor to the Dean, Faculty of Social and management Sciences, University of Buea.

ELWA in Liberia and Trans-World Radio in Swaziland, were rare intrusions in a continuous spread of state dominance.

In opting for state ownership and control, these governments sought to justify why mass communication needed to be controlled. They claimed that centralism was necessary for successful nation-building. Government ownership and control was justified as being less wasteful of the limited resources, and as guaranteeing the political stability badly needed for rapid development. Generally, they claimed that once their countries have become more mature and stable, they would loosen their hold over the media.

As development becomes more and more illusive and disillusionment at the grassroots widespread, the question arises whether government ownership and control of the media is an answer to the problem of people-centred development communication in Africa. On the other hand, a cursory look at private initiative in the domain, points to commercialisation and globalization, resulting in polarisation and marginalisation of peoples and societies. A fact that shows that private ownership and control does not necessarily guarantee media of public service. Thus the question: What form of media ownership and control can best promote public interest, civil society and democracy in Africa?

The question of ownership and control is all the more relevant in Africa today, given the multiple crises the continent is undergoing. Africa has been plunged, since the mid-1980s into a series of political, social and economic crises. These were compounded by the clamour for democratisation following the collapse of the Berlin Wall. As attention and money are turned to Eastern Europe by Africa's traditional partners, the continent, in desperation, has accentuated its dependence on the financial institutions of the West for assistance in solving these problems.

A direct consequence of this has been increased involvement by the World Bank and its allied institutions in the internal affairs of African countries, through the imposition of Structural Adjustment Programmes (SAP). The growing consensus is that these foreign-induced economic policies only exacerbate the polarisation of peoples and the globalization of poverty; the free-market economic order having ignored such key issues as the quality of life, the plurality of cultures, and environmental protection.

Issues of media ownership and control must be debated and resolved, if the globalization of poverty consequent from current models of ownership and control of communication technologies, institutions and practitioners, be curbed or reversed.

The Vice Chancellor's claim that "the WACC document faults rich nations, international financial institutions and communication transnationals for the spread of poverty", is basically true. But it tells only part of the story, one that absolves the state and government she represents of all responsibility. This points to the dangers of communication scholars, non-governmental organizations (NGOs) and media activists being caught up with the challenges posed by globalization and neoliberalism in media ownership and control, to the point of trivializing or ignoring the traditional hurdles to freedom of expression posed by the highhandedness of governments and their acolytes. African governments are all too eager to capitalize upon any concessions or oversights on the part of their critics, to divert attention from their own excesses vis-à-vis the media and freedom of expression.

In Cameroon and most of Africa the threats to a free, open and participatory media system and society emanate from repressive governments as by the interests of rich nations, international financial institutions and communication multinationals. Given the weakness of African states in relation to the latter collection of interests, and given their peripheral position in the global economy and politics, their exercise of power is directed towards controlling their own populations. What neoliberalism wants of them, as governments, are national and regional policies in tune with the needs of capital; policies that minimize countervailing traditions, customs and expectations. Once they have guaranteed global capital the stability, security and protection from labour that it needs, African governments need not do more than embrace the rhetoric of liberal democracy and the tokenism of its freedoms. And once they have opened up passively to the unregulated flow of global news and entertainment media, they can control local political media content unpoliced by the gendarmes of free information flow. All capital really needs of them is not so much a guarantee of democracy as a dictatorship to ensure that labour and national interests are kept subservient to the interests and power of business. Often, it is understood, though not openly stated, that they need not go beyond lip service to democracy, since no one seriously believes that it is possible for African states or governments to be both tolerant of the demands of global capital and to the needs of their own citizens.

Nowhere is this partnership and collusion better illustrated than in the relationship between African governments and the World Bank and the International Monetary Fund (IMF). Both institutions have preferred the rhetoric of "uncritical and idealized models of liberal democracy, the market and civil society" (Berman, 1998: 307), to the reality of even an imperfect democracy. Keen to see their neoliberal projects through, the World Bank and IMF have readily provided support for acquiescing states and governments in order to neutralize opposition to their unpopular structural adjustment related loan conditionalities. In this way, instead of helping bring about democracy the way its proponents would like to think and make believe, structural adjustment has had highly repressive and authoritarian political consequences; exogenously induced, it has had to repress popular opinion and rely on authoritarian regimes for its implementation, thereby thwarting democratization. Its negative economic, social and political effects are believed to have been responsible for popular appeals for political reform (Gibbon, et al. 1992; Mkandawire, 1996; Mkandawire and Olukoshi, 1995; Mkandawire and Soludo, 1999). The polarization of power and wealth produced by such neoliberal structures and global capitalism makes democratic rule at peripheries like Africa virtually impossible, as global capitalism needs autocratic powers to be able to penetrate the peripheries with its inequalities (Amin, 1997a: 22). Globalization and so-called free and accessible media have not significantly corrected, in practice, this centre–periphery logic as far as Africa is concerned (Amin, 1997b). If anything, it has rendered democracy irrelevant universally, and particularly so in relation to Africa (Ake, 2000: 29–32).

This perspective explains both economic underdevelopment and stalling democracy essentially in terms of the assimilation and exclusion logic of global capitalism, according to which only the handful of power and economic elite in Africa stand to benefit from its internalization and reproduction. The implications of this situation is a world where globalization does not amount to the homogenization of entitlements and recognition, but rather to an intensification of hierarchies and inequalities among individuals, groups and regions. One can therefore not afford to be insensitive to the hierarchies of inequalities that make of globalization less a process of flows than closures, compression than inflation, enhancement than depletion for most in the world.

Mindful of this, it should surprise few that the mediascape in Africa at the age of globalization is one of continuity rather than change. Despite the winds of liberalization of the late 1980s and early1990s, it is still very common in many countries to charge journalists simply for making statements that bring any state official into disrepute. Equally frowned upon are journalists asking national or foreign dignitaries questions that are perceived as embarrassing by government. Decades of dictatorship seem to have instituted a perennial fear in officials, even the most highly placed, of the administrative axe from above. The over-centralized systems of most states make people who are experts in their domains reticent to give information to journalists. Although governments may proclaim democracy and freedom of information as is currently fashionable, in practice most do not hesitate to sanction even a Cabinet minister who makes an un-cleared statement on a burning issue. This restricts access to government-held information for journalists in general and those of the private press in particular. Some governments, by practice, do not usually invite journalists belonging to the private press to official ceremonies, or as part of government missions within or abroad. So these journalists write about government as outsiders, which accounts for some of the inaccuracies that slip through in reports, and for the general attitude of scepticism vis-à-vis any information volunteered by government through official channels. There are African governments that encourage and trust foreign rather than local journalists.

Over the years governments have effectively controlled the press by encouraging a culture of one-dimensionalism and by using repressive legal frameworks. An examination of most legal frameworks in Africa, even after the liberalizations of the 1990s, reveals a craving to control that leaves little doubt of lawmakers perceiving journalists as potential troublemakers who must be policed. The tendency is for new laws to grant freedom in principle while providing, often by administrative nexus, the curtailment of press freedom in practice. Although strongest in francophone Africa, this use of derogable and claw back measures by the state to limit the right of expression and press freedom is common throughout the continent. Lush (1998) discusses how Southern African governments have continued to use "out-moded legislation inherited from their one-party and colonial predecessors" to criminalize dissent and numb the critical instincts of the press. Even the Nigerian press, often presented as the most vibrant and critical, has had to struggle with a battery of laws which the Nigerian Union of Journalists "considers to be inimical to journalism or press practice in general and a disincentive to the development of the profession" (Oloyede, 1996: 55–71). In South Africa where the first liberation was only achieved in 1994, the press is yet to break free of its past record of black debasement. Although the end of apartheid has led to some degree of black ownership and partnership in the press, this has not necessarily made the newspapers more representative of South African society. Newspapers are yet to develop a more comprehensive news formula that articulates mainstream black interests and aspirations. Although much has changed within an extremely short space of time, there is a lot that remains to be changed. The press continue to practice exclusion even as it preaches inclusion.

Although certain aspects of draconian press laws of the colonial period, the one-party era and military regimes have generally been replaced by new provisions that are relatively more tolerant of opposition views and of criticisms since the 1990s, the selective application of the law, together with the use of extra-legal measures, have been to the detriment of the critical private press, making it very difficult for the latter to have the professional independence it needs (M'Bayo et al. 2000). Such control occasions self-censorship by the press that has proved far more restrictive to critical journalism than any pressure by political powers. These developments have led to a crisis of credibility of the press in many countries. Whenever stories break which portray the government in a bad light, people tend to rely on the foreign broadcast media for the truth.

Indeed, "the access that foreign journalists have to the corridors of power in many African capitals is the envy of their African counterparts – and yet another indication of the imbalance of credibility on the continent" (Onadipe, 1998: 263). It also raises questions of an epistemological nature about reportage on Africa, for consumption not only by European and North American audiences but also by Africans, based on Western representations that do not exclude preconceptions, prejudices and misinformation.

This situation of political control has only been aggravated by the resilient economic, technical and professional difficulties facing the press in nearly all countries. Rigid control means that few serious local investors (never mind the global moguls or oligopolies) have found the press in Africa an attractive option. Hence, financial difficulties have compounded the problems of news gathering and news production, and made newspapers in most countries even less credible as they stretch and strain to produce every single edition. Even the official press has not always escaped financial difficulties. An obvious consequence of this situation is lack of research and background in most news stories, while the electronic media have simply been pushed into the arms of global news and entertainment radio and television corporations for cheap alternatives to locally produced programmes. In some countries, there is simply no means to encourage specialized reporting, and journalists are compelled to be "jacks of all trades" and "masters of none". Another result is the dearth of trained and experienced personnel. Most newspapers have a skeletal staff, and some are virtually a one-person affair. This is especially the case since the 1990s when greater tolerance of press freedom attracted opportunists who saw in the press an opportunity for self-enrichment and the pursuit of other ambitions. Because of such constraints, between 1960 and 1990, the press lost much of its dynamism, vibrancy and credibility of the colonial era. Almost everywhere until recently, only governments have afforded to operate daily newspapers, with the advantage of being able to shape public opinion on a daily basis both by the print and state-owned electronic media which they are reluctant to privatize or to make truly public service in character and content. Forces critical of government have often had to wait for the weekly or monthly publications to express their views, no matter how urgent.

Despite such persistent government control, it is worth reiterating that even though the continent is yet to attract big capital investments by the global oligopolies of the media world, there has been significant opening up to private capital and initiative almost everywhere since the 1990s. The current democratic process in Africa has brought with it not only multipartyism, but also a sort of media pluralism. In almost every country, the number of private newspapers has increased dramatically following the clamour for more representative forms of democracy in the early 1990s. Private FM radio and television stations have mushroomed almost everywhere, with international broadcasters such as the BBC and RFI now readily available locally on FM stations in certain capital cities. The entire continent is experiencing a boom in private, local or commercial radio stations and satellite television. Malawi launched its first national television station in January 1999 and Botswana did the same in July 2000. On their part, Lesotho and Swaziland have mobilized a South African commercial broadcaster – M-Net, to provide a pseudo-national television system that broadcasts mostly foreign programmes from South Africa and the West.[2]

South Africa in particular has not only reformed the South African Broadcasting Corporation (SABC) that served as the mouthpiece of apartheid into the early 1990s (Teer-Tomaselli and Tomaselli, 1996), but has also opened up to satellite television in a big way. A subscription satellite television service M-Net, operational since 1986 and owned by a consortium of South African newspaper publishers, has rapidly spread its tentacles throughout the continent, and together with Multi-Choice (a subscriber management company whose Digital Satellite Television – DSTV – offers over 23 satellite television channels and 48 audio channels) and Canal Horizon of France virtually dominate the satellite entertainment television scenario. M-Net and Multi-Choice specialize in routinized, standardized, McDonaldized international sport and entertainment, which they serve to every subscriber on the continent, regardless of region, nationality or cultural preferences, an approach that has occasioned renewed criticisms of Western cultural imperialism through South African media. Apart from increasing its local programming content, and bringing a bit of the rainbow composition of South Africa to reflect on its on-air presentations, M-Net has done little to alter its positioning in the new South Africa (Teer-Tomaselli, 2001). Transformation, Tomaselli and Dunn (2001: 3) point out, should mean more than a mere shift in discourses and demographics; it should entail a change in structures and ethos, something yet to be reflected in the mediascape of the new South Africa.

South Africa has also witnessed an explosion in community radio stations, with more than one hundred licences granted, of which some 80 stations were actually on the air on a daily basis in 1998. It is estimated that there will be over 200 community radio stations in the near future. Although according to veteran community broadcaster Zane Ibrahim of Bush Radio Cape Town, a proliferation of stations is not necessarily a

---

2. For an idea of the changing media ownership and control scenarios in West, Central and Southern Africa, see *Media Development*, Vol. 65, 4, 1998 and 68, 4, 2001.

good thing, as likely to benefit most "are the 'consultants' and the many new broadcast equipment supply companies" who are both more interested in "laughing all the way to the bank" than in serving any community interest. He is equally critical of government involvement with community radio as such involvement can only be detrimental to "communities not overly friendly with the ruling party of the day" (Ibrahim, 1999: 15). This admission by a veteran of community radio calls for a reassessment of the tendency by analysts to mistake labels for realities by uncritically accepting as "empowering", everything that passes for "community media".

If the private press and private broadcast media of Africa are often independent and critical of government, they have not always succeeded in displaying a similar attitude vis-à-vis the opposition or other pressure groups and lobbies (M'Bayo et al. 2000). This position is usually informed by the mistaken assumption that what is anti-government is necessarily pro-public interest. The consequence has been that, instead of seeking to curb intolerance, fanaticism, or extremism of all kinds, some of these media have actually fuelled them. Examples abound of newspapers throughout the continent that have served as mouthpieces for divisive forces, often reproducing calls to murder, destruction and hatred. Radio Mille Collines of Rwanda stands as an example of the use of broadcasting for extreme, partisan politics. Evident from discussions of the relationship between the media and democratization in a multiparty context is the inadequate attention given to the quality of democracy needed and the quality and role of the media that should foster such democracy. Almost everywhere liberal democratic assumptions have been made about the media and their role in democratization and society, with little regard to the histories, cultures and sociologies of African societies nor to the type of democracy desired by Africans. Difficulties and contradictions of the media in action must be understood not only as failures, but also and more importantly, as pointers to the very inadequacies of the democratic model under which democratization in Africa has been sought.

This modest opening up to, and involvement of, private capital and initiative in the media, could be termed *change* in media ownership in Africa. But control remains largely with government (in terms of laws regulating media ownership and operation), or with transnational producers of global news and entertainment content on which the continent's media rely heavily. In other words, the media in Africa are effectively controlled by government and capital, who are both keen to feed the public with nothing subversive to their interests and power. Thus, if the growing concern in the world is how to mobilize forces to curb or resist the growing concentrated ownership of the media in the service of neoliberalism, in Africa there is the added concern of mobilizing forces to resist government repression and highhandedness to or through the media. Such mobilization must be undertaken with the understanding that African governments are in a predicament: compelled by the World Bank, IMF, WTO and other institutions of neoliberalism to facilitate the penetration of their markets by multinational capital on the one hand, and on the other hand having to face up to the rising expectations and growing disillusionment of their own populations.

Resisting victimhood in Africa

In a context like the above in which Africans find themselves – peripheral to global trends and subjected to the highhandedness and repression of their own governments, it is easy to slip into meta-narratives that celebrate victimhood. While there is genuine reason to be pessimistic and cynical, there is often, at a closer look, reason to be hopeful as well. However repressive a government is and however profound the spiral silence induced by standardized and routinized global media menus, few are ever completely mystified or wholly duped. In other word, there is always room for initiative or agency at individual or group level to challenge domination, exploitation and the globalization of poverty. Histories of struggle in Africa are full of examples in this connection. It is therefore important always to explore how people at the margins of power and wealth strive to survive. People always find creative ways of making ends meet and of keeping hope alive in a hopeless world. My contention here is that Africans have found myriad ways of participating as active agents in national life and global socio-economic processes, their victimhood notwithstanding.

Far from giving up in the face of rigid colonial repression for example, threatened African nationalists eager to communicate their liberation agenda among themselves and with the African masses adopted various strategies, including the following: they published despite the restrictions placed on them by the colonial administration; they used the underground press – pamphlets, tracts, and word-of-mouth, alternative channels of communication such as the grapevine, political rumour, caricature and derision, and indigenous media as substitutes or supplements to the press. These strategies were as useful in the Algerian revolution as they were in the radical nationalism of Cameroon's Union des Populations du Cameroun party, both against brutal French colonialism and racism. Frantz Fanon, as a member of the Services de Presse du Front de Liberation Nationale in Tunis, was able to take advantage of *El Moudjahid* whose articles were not bylined, to disseminate his revolutionary ideas on colonialism in Algeria and Africa. Thanks to such excessive control and creative responses, the press in Africa has since colonial times shared many characteristics with rumour and political derision, including identification with certain values, beliefs and outlooks commonly held by ordinary Africans, some of which may appear bizarre and highly implausible to Western reporters and readers (Ellis, 2000).

Thus faced with post-colonial repression in the 1970s and 1980s, Africans easily drew inspiration from the more muted forms of criticism of colonial times. Excessive control of conventional channels of communication greatly accounted for the popularity and importance of Radio Trottoir (Pavement Radio in Anglophone Africa (Ellis, 1989) or Rádio Boca a boca in Lusophone Africa (Seibert, 1999)) in the continent. Wherever it has been studied, Radio Trottoir has proved itself the perfect medium of communicating dissent and discussing the powerful in unflattering terms. In Togo (Ellis, 1993; Toulabor, 1981), Zaire (Diamani, 1995; Nlandu-Tsasa, 1997), Sao Tomé and Príncipe (Seibert, 1999: 389–403), Cameroon (Mbembe, 1992, 1997; Monga, 1997; Nyamnjoh, 1999), Nigeria (Medubi, 2000; Sekoni, 1997), and elsewhere in Africa (Ellis, 1989), Radio Trottoir has proved effective not only as a vehicle for popular and informal discussion of power and current affairs by urbanites in particular (Ellis, 1989), but also as a counter-power: the "poor-man's bomb" (Mbembe, 1997: 157) or the "weapons of the powerless" (Toulabor, 1981: 69) in the face of government's arbitrariness, water cannons, tear gas and guns. Usually in the form of "anecdotical gossip", Radio Trottoir serves the poor as "a phenomenon of revenge and a rebuttal of censorship" (Yoka cited in Devisch, 1995: 623) against "the totalitarian discourse of the Party-State", often through the display of "an extraordinary verbal creativity" (Devisch, 1995: 623–624).

In his provisional notes on the post-colony, Mbembe argues that political derision or humour directed at the autocrat is an attempt by ordinary folks to present the powerful as ordinary mortals with the same appetites and nature like any other person. "Hence the image of, say, the President's anus is not of something out of this world – though to people's great amusement the official line may treat it as such; instead, people consider it as it really is, capable of defecating like any commoner's." Through ridicule, Mbembe argues, ordinary people can tame, shut up and render powerless state power. The autocrat thus stripped of his aura or magic, becomes domesticated – a mere idol, a familiar friend or a member of the family as much for the ruled as for the rulers (Mbembe, 1992: 8–9).

As the most distinctive feature of Radio Trottoir, rumour defines itself in opposition to official discourse, which it challenges and seeks to replace. The same is true of political cartooning in general, which could be described as the sketched or caricatured version of rumour about the high and mighty in society. Both political rumour and cartooning, it could be argued, are ways of cushioning the hardness of the crushing and stifling official discourse, which monopolizes the public sphere, often claiming to be the sole bearer of truth. They are an unequivocal confirmation of the truism that withholding relevant information from the public results in desperate attempts by the public to invent that information, and that such inventions are seldom a flattering mirror of the status quo.

Today not only has Radio Trottoir and political derision become more open and more daring, but cartooning has joined the bandwagon of political commentary and satire. The situation of cartoonists has changed remarkably; caricatures of presidents and their ministers are not uncommon in the press. In Nigerian newspapers, *The Guardian* and *The Times* for example, cartoons depict political leaders and the military, their partners in power, in very stereotypical fashion. Associated with the Nigerian politician in cartoons are such words as: "rigger, thug, area boy, hidden agenda", lexemes which imply "a cheating, deceitful, crooked, and corrupt individuality, and emphasize the politician's lack of morals and ignorance and contempt for justice and fairplay." Through such cartooning, the politicians are stereotyped as "completely selfish, self-centred, and self-indulgent, lacking in any altruistic thought, action, or motive", and being completely at variance with those they purport to serve. The military, in general, are depicted to be forceful, disdainful of propriety, indifferent to established rules and regulations, and as having "a tendency towards absolutism and totalitarian control" (Medubi, 2000:200-205). This shows that the cartoonists and the ordinary Nigerians and Africans who appreciate their art, "can see beyond the mask of veil of deception worn by the people in power" (Sekoni, 1997: 143).

In relation to neoliberalism and the globalization of poverty, Africans have been equally creative in their responses, despite their perceived passivism and victimhood. Like other anti-neoliberal forces in the world, African activists have taken advantage of the new information and communication technologies (e.g., Internet) to mobilize and strategize against the multinational corporations and the uncritical support they receive from African governments. Prominent African activists such as Dennis Brutus, Trevor Ngwane and Fatima Meer of South Africa are leading members of the anti-globalization coalition that has given WTO a tough time in recent meetings. A recent victory by popular forces against giant pharmaceutical companies in South Africa in connection with the production of affordable generic versions of AIDS drugs locally, is equally significant. In general, formal and informal networks of various kinds are taking advantage of the Internet to push ahead their agenda in situations where the conventional media continue to blunt aspirations for creative diversity. True, the Internet is not free from the logic of domination and appropriation typical of neoliberalism, but it clearly offers marginalized voices an opportunity for real alternatives, if well harnessed. Although connectivity in Africa is lowest compared to other regions of the world (Jensen, 2000), Africa's cultural values of solidarity, interconnectedness and interdependence (Nyamnjoh, 2000) makes it possible for others to access the Internet and its opportunities without necessarily being connected themselves. In many situations, it suffices for a single individual to be connected for whole groups and communities to benefit. The individual in question acts as a relay point (or communication node) linking other individuals and communities in myriad ways, and bringing hope to others who otherwise would be dismissed as not belonging. The same is true of other technologies such as the cellphone: diasporic Africans or migrants collectively supply a free phone to someone in a village whom they can call to give and receive messages from family and friends. Because the tam tam remains relevant, even as the Internet and the cellphone are adopted (Ras-Work, 1998), Africans are able to make the best of all worlds in a context where surviving has long ceased to be a matter of course. All of these creative responses imply that it is hardly the end of the story to acknowledge disempowerment and marginalization in Africa, for in process, and often veiled or subtle, are countervailing forces in the service of hope. Ordinary Africans have refused to celebrate victimhood.

References

Ake, C. (2000) *The feasibility of democracy in Africa*, Dakar: Codesria.

Amin, S. (1997a) 'Reflections on the international system', in Golding, P. and Harris, P. (eds) *Beyond cultural imperialism: Globalization, communication and the new international order*, 10–24, London: Sage.

Amin, S. (1997b) 'L'Afrique et le développement', *Jeune Afrique Economie*, 3 Février 1997, 234, 36–43.

Berman, F.B. (1998) 'Ethnicity, patronage and the African state: The politics of uncivil nationalism', *African Affairs*, 97, 388, 305–341.

Devisch, R. (1995) 'Frenzy, violence, and ethical renewal in Kinshasa', *Public Culture*, 7, 3, 593–629.

Diamani, J.P. (1995) 'L'Humour politique au phare du Zaire', *Politique Africaine*, 58, Juin, 151–157.

Ellis, S. (1989) 'Tuning in to pavement radio', *African Affairs*, 88, 352, 321–330.

Ellis, S. (1993) 'Rumour and Power in Togo', *Africa* 63, 4, 462–475.

Ellis, S. (2000) 'Reporting Africa', *Current History* 99, 637, 221–226.

Gibbon, P. Bangura, Y. and Ofstad, A. (eds.) (1992) *Authoritarianism, democracy and adjustment: The politics of economic reform in Africa*, Uppsala: Nordiska Afrikainstitutet.

Golding, P. and Harris, P. (eds.) (1997) *Beyond cultural imperialism: Globalization, communication and the new international order*, London: Sage.

Ibrahim, Z. (1999) 'What does 'Community' mean for community radio? Reality check', *Rhodes Journalism Review*, December, 15.

Jensen, M. (2000) 'Making the connection: Africa and the Internet', *Current History*, 99, 637, 215–220.

Lent, J.A. (1997) 'Rebirth of cartooning in the South', *Media Development*, 64, 4, 3–7.

Lush, D. (1998) 'The role of the African media in the promotion of democracy and human rights', in Kayizzi-Mungerwa, S., Olukoshi, A.O., Wohlgemuth, L., (ed.), *Towards a new partnership with Africa: Challenges and opportunities*, 42–65, Uppsala: Nordiska Afrikainstitutet.

M'Bayo, R.T., Onwumechili, C., and Nwanko, N.R., (eds) (2000) *Press and politics in Africa*, New York: The Edwin Mellen Press.

Mbembe, A. (1992) 'Provisional Notes on the Postcolony', *Africa*, 62, 1, 3–37.

Mbembe, A. (1997) 'The "Thing" and its double in Cameroonian cartoons', in Karin Barber (ed.), *Readings in African popular culture*, 151–163, Oxford: James Currey.

McChesney, R.W. (1998) 'The political economy of global media', *Media Development*, 65, 4, 3–8.

McChesney, R.W. (2001) 'Global media, neoliberalism, and imperialism', *Monthly Review* 52, 10, <accessed from http://www.monthlyreview.org/301rwm.htm.>

Medubi, O. (2000) 'Leadership stereotypes and lexical choices: An example of Nigerian cartoons', *International Journal of Comic Art*, 2,1, 198–206.

Mkandawire, T. (1996) 'Economic policy-making and the consolidation of democratic institutions in Africa', in Havnevik, K. and van Arkadie, B. (eds.), *Domination or dialogue: Experiences and prospects for African development cooperation*, Uppsala: Nordiska Afrikainstitutet.

Mkandawire, T. and Olukoshi, A. (eds.) (1995) *Between liberalisation and repression: The politics of structural adjustment in Africa*, Dakar: Codesria Books.

Mkandawire, T. and Soludo, C.C. (1999) *Our continent, our future: African perspectives on structural adjustment*, Dakar, Asmara: Codesria/IDRC/Africa World Press.

Monga, C. (1997) 'Cartoons in Cameroon: Anger and political derision under monocracy', in Anyidoho, Kofi (ed.) *The word behind bars and the paradox of exile*, 146–169, Evanston, Illinois: North Western University Press.

Murdock, G. (1994) 'The new mogul empires: Media concentration and control in the age of divergence', *Media Development*, 61, 4, 3–6.

Nlandu-Tsasa, C. (1997) *La Rumeur au Zaire de Mobutu: Radio-trottoir à Kinshasa*, Paris: L'Harmattan.

Nyamnjoh, F.B. (1999) 'Press cartoons and politics in Cameroon', *International Journal of Comic Art*, 1, 2, 171–190.

Nyamnjoh, F.B. (2000) 'A cultural foundation for communication reconciliation', *Media Development*, 67, 4, 36–39.

Oloyede, B. (1996) *Press freedom in Nigeria: A critical analysis of salient issues*, Abeokut: Kunle Alayande Printing & Publishing Company.

Onadipe, A. (1998) 'The media in Africa: In the eye of the storm', *West Africa*, 4186, 262–265.

Ras-Work, T. (1998) *Tam tam to Internet: Telecoms in Africa*, Johannesburg: Betam Communications & Mafube Publishing.

Seibert, G. (1999) *Comrades, clients and cousins: Colonialism, socialism and democratization in Sao Tomé and Príncipe*, Leiden: Leiden University Press.

Sekoni, R. (1997) 'Politics & urban folklore in Nigeria', in Karin Barber (ed.), *Readings in African popular culture*, 142–146, Oxford: James Currey.

Teer-Tomaselli, R. (2001) 'Transformation, nation-building and the South African media, 1993–1999', in Tomaselli, K. and Dunn, H. (eds.), *Media, democracy and renewal in Southern Africa*, Denver: International Academic Publishers.

Thomas, N.P. and Lee, P. (1994) 'Editorial: Public communication-superhighway or one-way street', *Media Development*, 61, 4, 2.

Thomas, N.P. and Lee, P. (1998) 'Editorial', *Media Development*, 65, 4, 2.

Toulabor, C.M. (1981) 'Jeu de mots, Jeu de vilains', *Politique Africaine*, 1, 3, Septembre, 55–71.

Media and Neoliberalism in Latin America

Ana Fiol

There are several Latin Americas. As different as nations as far apart as Honduras and Uruguay, or as close as Chile and Bolivia, can be. But from a small nation can come a grand poet, Rubén Dario, and from very large countries, very small dictators: Pinochet, Videla . . . Despite all this, there are features that unite us. The Spanish language. People of mixed race. A shared culture that refuses nationalist pigeon-holes: Martí, Neruda, Borges, Orozco, Niemeyer, Carlos Gardel and Agustín Lara. And a difficult, steep and determined struggle for freedom.

Carlos Fuentes[1]

Introduction: The Latin American experience of neoliberalism

In Latin America the concept of neoliberalism has many meanings. It is simultaneously description and prescription and, as with all prescriptions, its normative framework defines a field of battle. Its daily use – by critical academics, popular activists, and alternative media[2] – reveals its many facets. Neoliberalism describes both the profound transformation of productivity structures in Latin America during the last 20 years and the radical changes in social classes, institutions and culture.

---

1. This quotation is from the contemporary Mexican writer Carlos Fuentes. *La Jornada*, May 2001.
2. Alternative media are non-profit and grassroots media. In Latin America they refer to "popular radio", which was an important development on 1960s and 1970s and which is now in decline; and the publications of community and non-profit political organizations; and more recently partisan or anti-hegemonic websites. In this category I include local commercial media (in towns, provinces and regions) which, although they are part of networks whose main offices are in the national capitals, retain a certain amount of editorial independence.

Neoliberalism, understood as an ensemble of economic policies negotiated by Latin American governments – both dictatorships and elected governments following the "democratization" of the 1980s – with the International Monetary Fund (IMF), World Bank and Washington, is an expression of a new and different phase in the political, military and economic relationship of Latin America with the USA.[3]

In any case, neoliberalism refers to the consequences of the creation of a new correlation of class forces in the region, the main outcome of an attack on workers' participation in the gross national product (GNP), the destruction of national productive sectors (and directed towards the internal market) and the monopolistic concentration of land (and seeds).

To contain the growing discontent of social movements, which are the organized fraction of the 260 million old and new poor, the state re-militarizes with the consequent destruction of civil liberties.

Neoliberalism, I shall argue, is about the reorganization of regional power elites as a new transnational class. With this reorganization begins a new phase in the organization of the state and the institutions of representative democracy. It is a change that, in the words of Slavko Splichal,[4] affects "the institutions which '(re)present' public opinion in

---

3. Petras, J. and Veltmeyer, H. (2001) *Globalization unmasked: Imperialism in the 21st century*, New York: Zed Books. Summarized as follows: 'Through trial and error, improvisation and deliberate intervention, USA has come to fashion a complex and coherent regional strategy that operates on three mutually reinforcing and interrelated levels:

   (i) Through the imposition of an economic policy.

   (ii) As a military strategy, which is integrally related to the free market ideology, that can be organized as: [a] narco-intervention, as in Colombia, Peru and Bolivia (Plan Colombia and its extension Plan Andino), [b] "low-intensity warfare" against social movements in Central America, [c] direct, large-scale intervention as occurred in Grenada, Panama and via Contras in Nicaragua and [d] routinized, bureaucratic and ideological work to prevent, repress or suppress popular upheavals in the rest of the region, and finally

   (iii) A political strategy, which involves the promotion of electoral regimes in the interstices of its economic policy and law and order/repressive/military framework. The existence of these tightly restricted civilian governments and the parliaments, parties and political processes (and oligopolistic media corporations) that accompany them, serves or attempts to demobilize opposition social movements ("they endanger democracy"), to co-opt "progressive intellectuals" ("we have to ensure democratic governability"), and to restrict political agendas ("there are no alternatives to Neo-liberalism").'

4. Splichal, S. (2001) *Public opinion and democracy. Vox Populi - Vox Dei?* New Jersey: Hampton Press. Splichal, S. (2002) 'The principle of publicity, public use of reason and social control', *Media, Culture and Society*, 1, 24, 5–26.

modern societies": the political parties, parliaments, elections and mass media. In very general terms, we can say that traditional political parties are disintegrating, politicians are being co-opted by the right's free market programme and the parliamentary left is waning. Politics is lining up with, and serves, the new economic order and is losing all capacity for directing the civil life of the majority. In the words of Latin American scholars, politics is "disappearing". Parliaments are losing power in the face of ever more powerful Executives and the use of the Presidential Executive Decree in the region is becoming commonplace. The level of corruption among politicians and businessmen is a function of the private businesses carried out with public or state assets during the period of privatization.[5]

A new power elite is consolidating itself. It comprises a handful of local and regional businessmen, a caste of high officials in the central banks, the judiciary and the military, a large part of elected politicians, representatives of foreign transnational corporations (TNCs) and officials of the IMF and World Bank.

As we shall see later, the mainstream media (press, radio and television) took an active part in this process of structural reform. They acted to speak up for and to legitimize the good of changing the economic model and its new rules of the game. At the same time, they were direct beneficiaries of new cross-ownership legislation, the privatization of state-owned terrestrial television networks, the deregulation of the cable and satellite television business, the privatization of telecommunication systems and fundamentally the liberalization of foreign investment in media operations.

This process of transnational capitalist integration and dramatic technological development strengthened the worst authoritarian trends of what today are regional multimedia giants.

The national media markets diversified (e.g., with the first expansion of cable TV and the falling cost of radio broadcasting and publishing technologies) and almost simultaneously became concentrated. Small and independent media disappeared, taken over by the large groupings, both regional and foreign, or were expelled from the market. The large newspapers in the capital cities bought up the provincial newspapers, forming compact national chains that were later incorporated into multimedia groups. The disappearance of local economic sectors and

---

5. Joseph Stiglitz, former World Bank Chief Economist and winner of the Nobel Prize in 2001, stated that Step One in a "structuring agreement" between the World Bank and the Third World countries is always privatisation, which Stiglitz said could more accurately be called "Briberization". "You could see their eyes widen at the prospect of 10% commissions paid to Swiss bank accounts for simply shaving a few billion off the sale price of national assets". See http://www.gregpalast.com originally published for *The Observer*, London.

economic concentration intensified advertising budget concentration into a few media operations (generally working out of Miami). Multimedia expanded their financial alliances with foreign banks and their links to key sectors of national economies such as mining, airports, telecommunications, etc.

As a result of the past 20 years of liberal reform of the Latin American media system, a group of business families continues to dominate – after the best fashion of the well-known propaganda model of Chomsky and Herman[6] – the production of published political opinion.

There is growing consensus among critical academics and social activists concerning present-day media corporations. Multimedia in Latin America have become autonomous institutions in the board game of national politics, with their own business and class interests, which are reflected in their editorial policies and the way they run their businesses.

The historical defeat of nationalist and Marxist social movements

In my view, an economic and cultural swing to the right of such magnitude could only be constructed and consolidated on the basis of a series of successive defeats inflicted on the nationalist and Marxist politics and movements in Latin America. These movements challenged US hegemony, approximately from 1930 to 1970, and spread the social successes of the workers, a fruit of industrialization. In order to quash popular resistance, the dictatorships, which ran from 1973 to 1990, carried out selective assassinations to remove the leaders of popular organizations and even mass killings such as the 30,000 "disappeared" in Argentina and the Mayan genocide in Guatemala.

From 1982 onwards the elected governments continued and increased neoliberal reforms. The social protest provoked by the structural adjustment policies of the IMF/World Bank were countered by invoking *l'État penal*,[7] by means of the extensively documented practices of funding paramilitary structures and the systematic elimination of social leaders

---

6. Herman, E. and Chomsky, N. (1994) *Manufacturing consent: The political economy of the mass media*, London: Vintage. Herman, E. (2000) 'The Propaganda Model: A retrospective', *Journalism Studies*, 1, 101–12. Klaebn, J. (2002) 'A critical review and assessment of Herman and Chomsky's "Propaganda Model"', *European Journal of Communication*, 17, 2, 147–182.

7. I am using the heuristic notion advanced by Pierre Bourdieu and Loic Wacquant and referring to the USA's state apparatuses. See Bourdieu, P. and Wacquant, L. (2001) 'Neoliberal newspeak: Notes on the new planetary vulgate', *Radical Philosophy*, 108.

and human rights activists. All the elected governments that followed the dictatorships granted legal amnesty to the military. Today, in a climate of immunity from prosecution, serious human rights violations against social movements and human rights leaders are on the rise throughout Latin America. Torture, disappearances, and summary executions are becoming all too familiar in the region.

Despite everything, Latin America started the third millennium with powerful classist social movements, whose interests, ideas and policies are in open contradiction with capitalist globalization. The Movement of Landless Peasants in Brazil is an organization with a social base of three million people whose policy is to occupy the *haciendas* (farm lands). The Landless "located", that is to say gave cultivable land to, half a million people during the last few years.

In March 2000 the Zapatistas marched through six Mexican states and spoke on behalf of 26 indigenous peoples. They took a Bill to the National Congress, proposing recognition of their right to land, language and dignity. The exultant arrival of the march of "the earth-coloured people" in Mexico City's "Zócalo" (central square) had so many repercussions both inside and outside the country that Televisa was finally obliged to cover it. However, President Fox remained unmoved. The native people are still awaiting legal sanction that they are Mexican.

CONAIE, the powerful organization of indigenous peoples in Ecuador, backed two assaults on power. On 5 February 1997 a popular uprising toppled the government of President Bucaram; similarly, on 21 January 2000, an alliance of peasants and army rank and file toppled the government of President Mahuad.

Indigenous organizations in Paraguay and Chile, the movement of coca growers, students and debtors in Bolivia, the organizations of pickets in Argentina (and following the crisis of December 2001, urban "people's assemblies") and the Bolivarian Revolution Centres in Venezuela, the controversial FARC and ELC in Colombia are all growing.

In Latin America the objective conditions for socialism were never as clear as today and never were its cultural and political means further away. Never before were inequalities so acute or the contradictions in the economic system so obvious. More importantly, never before were social movements so numerous and at the same time so impotent when it comes to influencing state policies. In other words, despite the existence of massive social forces, these organizations have had little concrete impact on the state's economic decisions. Studying the reasons and consequences of this paradox goes a long way beyond the scope of this article.

However, the evidence allows us to conjecture a confrontation driven by conflicting class interests between the mainstream Latin American media and the social movements. This antagonism would have direct consequences on the public representation of social movements and as a result on their chances of political success. On the other hand, this article will suggest that the role – the political will – of Latin American governments has been central to the neoliberal spiral, contrary to opinions in vogue that identify Latin American states and governments as victims of uncontrollable globalising forces.

I shall now review the change that took place during the dictatorships from populist state with authoritarian features to neoliberal authoritarian state and the role of the media during these historical stages. I shall then point out some key characteristics of the post-1990s media scenario in Latin America. Finally, I shall focus on the economic integration of Mexico with the USA as expressed by the North American Free Trade Agreement (NAFTA) of 1994 – the same type of neoliberal integration that the USA and 34 Latin American governments will extend throughout the region in 2005, when the Free Trade Agreement of the Americas (FTAA-Alca) comes into force.

From populist state to revolution

In the 1930s Latin America confronted a world economic crisis beginning with the imposition of import substitution industrialisation policies (ISI). Substitution was, however, very relative, since it was always necessary to import machinery for production, technology, know-how and consumer goods. Added to this, from the 1950s with development policies that culminated in the launch of the Alliance for Progress in 1961, denationalisation of economies accelerated due to massive penetration by multinational companies.

The system of two social classes, peasants and landowners, that had prevailed until the 1930s became more complex. The ISI contributed to a growing working class, a small middle class of skilled workers, civil servants and professionals, and an industrial middle class.

Latin American audiences grew enormously during this process of urbanization and expansion of literacy and the welfare state, principally in Mexico, Brazil, Argentina, Venezuela and Colombia. Expansion of the cultural industries took place, the creation of popular genres and the consequent creation of a media constructed public sphere. In the 1930s and 1940s radio and radio-theatre spread, precursor of the "telenovela" (soap opera); the genre originated in the "cordel literature" of Brazil and the newspaper serials of the River Plate region.

The cinema boom of the 1940s and 1950s in Mexico and Argentina turned Mexican cinema into the first regional industry to export successfully to the rest of Latin America. Black urban music from Brazil – the samba; bossa nova and the "tropicalia" musical movement – by means of radio and LP records dominated the Brazilian market in the 1960s and was exported throughout Latin America.

In the 1960s, one in three books in Spanish published throughout the world were published in Buenos Aires, contributing to a boom without precedent in the publishing industry. Brazil's O Globo Group and Mexico's Televisa developed strong audio-visual sectors and became exporters of telenovelas to other Latin American countries and elsewhere and, in the case of Mexico, to a wealthy Spanish-speaking market in the USA.

Armand Mattelart (1990) has shown that "broadcasting institutionalisation" in Latin America can be understood as a system in which broadcasting was in private hands in a market economy under authoritarian governments. This meant that the years of Brazilian dictatorship "would be the worst years of state violence Brazil would live through – and those in which her television industry took off; two decades later, it would be the biggest market in Latin America."[8]

Moreover, as he points out in his book *Mapping World Communications: War, Progress, Culture* (1994): "To assure a minimum of consensus for a political project that was forced to resort to coercion and police control, state power had to call on the commercial machinery of mass culture, the product of a society in which public opinion is a recognized actor in the public sphere."[9] Until recently, Mexico had a 70-year-old single-party regime, and during many years of rule by the Partido Revolucionario Institucional (PRI) – Institutional Revolutionary Party – the media were, for the most part, fully integrated into the power structure.[10]

During this period, the mass media were central to what Benedict Anderson (1991) describes as "official nationalism":[11] compulsory state-controlled primary education, state-organized propaganda, official rewriting of history and militarism. Television was a functional tool, as was radio at first, in bringing about social integration within national states, as Canclini (1989), Martín-Barbero (1987) and Pasquali (1967), among others, have established.[12]

---

8. Mattelart, A. (1990) *Carnival of images: Brazilian television fiction*, London: Sage.

9. Mattelart, A. (1994) *Mapping world communications: War, progress, culture*, London, Minneapolis: University of Minnesota Press.

10. Hallin, D. (2000) 'Media, political power and democratisation in Mexico', in Curran, J. and Park, M. (eds.) *De-westernising media studies*, London: Routledge.

11. Anderson, B. (1991) *Imagined communities*. London: Verso.

12. Canclini, N.G. (1989) *Culturas Híbridas: Estrategias para entrar y salir de la Modernidad*, Mexico: Grijalbo. Martín Barbero, J.(1987) *De los medios a las mediaciones: Comunicación, cultura y hegemonía*, Barcelona: G. Gilli. Pasquali, A. (1967) *El aparato singular: un día de televisión en Caracas*, Caracas: Universidad Central de Venezuela.

The populist state was the unstable product of the class alliance between national middle classes, organized workers, the church and nationalist militaries. It originated in the need for the industrial middle class to gain the support of the workers and, to a lesser extent, of the peasants in order to contain the commercial and land-owning oligarchy. This class alliance in favour of the state can be seen in the Mexican PRI (the Cardenas governments of 1930 and 1940), in the national-populist regime of Getulio Vargas in Brazil (1964–85) and in the Perón (1946–55 and 1973) and Frondizi governments in Argentina, among others. These regimes promoted the development of national industry under protective trade barriers and initiated a wide movement of nationalization of industries and strategic resources.

In the 1950s Jacobo Arbenz, President of Guatemala, expropriated the land owned by United Fruit and redistributed it to the peasants, provoking a successful coup d'état led by the CIA. In 1952 a nationalist revolution took place in Bolivia, which cannot be explained without reference to the Miners' Radio Movement that forged part of its social base and gained strength during the revolution.

In Peru, the nationalist military regimes of Velazco Alvarado (1968–75) and General Bermudez (1975–80) made radical social changes in favour of the popular classes and the peasants and produced one of the greatest transformations in media structure and legislation in the region. Luis Ramiro Beltrán (1988) explained that Velazco Alvarado nationalized and integrated the state media and approved strict regulations for privately owned media. He set up institutions to promote and produce social programming; approved legislation that strengthened the state's role in telecommunications; and limited involvement of private and foreign capital. In 1974 newspapers based in Lima were expropriated with the ultimate aim of giving them to different social organizations such as peasant leagues or workers' unions, inaugurating what came to be known as an era of social ownership, neither public nor private, of the media. Similar experiments, although not so radical, took place in Chile – after 1938 with the founding of the Popular Front – and in Venezuela in 1974.

With the Cuban revolution of 1959, the socialist government of Salvador Allende (1970–73) in Chile, and the Sandinista revolution in Nicaragua in 1979 (which won the elections in 1984), a strongly revolutionary period began that covered the whole of Latin America. The parliamentary left, popular movements, sectors of the church oriented towards liberation theology, urban and rural Marxist guerrillas pushed for the imposition of direct controls on the transnational corporations (TNCs). Regulations on employing nationals, control of foreign exchange, investment and repatriation of profits became widespread. Governments applied national communication policies: they subsidized the film industry, protected the publishing industry and offered broadcasting industries the use of state telecommunications and satellites,[13] as well as giving them a large amount of government advertising.

It was the age of the New World Information and Communication Order (NWICO), challenging inequalities in the flow of information. Cultural dependency theory informed debates that began with the 1976 San José Meeting in Costa Rica and culminated in the MacBride Report in 1980.

The dictatorships

In 1978 Armand Mattelart described how the dictatorships of the 1970s were creating a state for the multinationals.[14] The National Security Doctrine[15] gave South American juntas and land-owning oligarchies of Central America adequate rationalization for the real process. The 1970s saw the contradiction sharpen between the transnational character of the economic structure and the national character of the political structure. Only the fraction of the middle class (the industrial and commercial bourgeoisie) that was connected to foreign capital could adapt to the new economic dynamics and the struggle intensified between two modes of accumulation, that is to say, between the model of big international monopoly capital and the old model based on the national market.

A new class of wealthy business operators and bankers turned to the armed forces and TNCs to suppress labour laws, controls placed on their capital and all the measures taken to redistribute productive resources such as wages or land.

Military dictatorships were the response to the institutional tension between the economic structure and political organization. We can say that the two main aims of the dictatorships were, on the one hand, to modify basic state structures and, on the other, to discipline the workers and stop the left.

With the overthrow of Allende by Pinochet in 1973 there began the systematic application of neoliberal reforms: capital mobility, deregulation, fiscal austerity, trade liberalization and privatizsation. The neoliberal reforms concentrated riches, dismantled half a century of state regulations

---

13. The best documented cases are those of the Brazilian state telephony company, EMBRATEL and O Globo; and the state satellite system Morelos and Televisa.

14. Mattelart, A. and Siegelaub, S. (eds.) (1979). *Communication and class struggle, Volume 1, capitalism, imperialism*, London: IG/International Media Research Centre.

15. The names given to the ideology that justifies the coordination of the Cold War in Latin America, led by the USA.

and lowered the cost of labour. Legislation was enacted to maintain the payment of foreign debts and to decrease corporate wages and taxes. Indiscriminate opening up of national economies led to an inundation of cheap imports. As a result, provincial and regional economic sectors broke up.[16]

The concentration of production resources and consequent polarization of society led to a new and deeper class division. On the one side was the middle class, dominated by a handful of super-rich billionaires linked to global capital and a small cluster of export-oriented multinational corporations.[17] On the other side was the growing mass of impoverished, exploited and marginalized workers and peasants in the burgeoning informal sector of the region's economy, stripped of social rights and protective labour legislation. This change in production structures had

---

16. By 1982, up to $257 billion of loans were extended to governments and the private sector in Latin America, particularly in Brazil, Mexico and Argentina, which accounted for over 50% of the accumulated Third World debt. Over the course of the 1980s, the accumulated external debt in the region grew from $257 billion to $452 billion, despite total *annual* interest payments of $170 billion. According to data from Sistema Económico Latinoamericano (SELA), in 2002 the debt represented 201% of the total of Latin American exports and 39% of gross regional product. Its value almost doubled in the decade from 1990 to 2000, when it increased from $452 to $750 billion. According to SELA, every inhabitant of Latin America owes $1.550 at birth.

Over the course of the 1990s the flow of direct investment increased 223% worldwide, but in Latin America the rate of increase was close to 600%. Brazil, Mexico and Argentina accounted for 62% of this FDI, and Chile, Colombia and Peru accounted for another 26%. Most of this FDI was used to purchase the assets of privatized public enterprises and private enterprises, with little capital formation involved. By 1999 over 33 of the top 100 Latin American corporations had fallen victim to foreign investors.

As officially reported by ECLA (Economic Commission for Latin America, UN), the rate and magnitude of profit repatriation was $157 billion from 1996 to 1998 alone. Between 1982 and 1992 the payments of royalties and licensee fees totalled over $1.3 billion, but throughout the 1990s they exceeded a billion dollars a year. Petras and Veltmeyer (2001) pp 77–82.

17. Many sources have confirmed that within the framework of neoliberal policies implemented in the 1980s, a major context for the formation of the new Latin American billionaires was provided by the large-scale privatization of state enterprises undertaken by governments. These new billionaires, and the thousands of mere millionaires formed by and within the economic reform

direct social consequences in terms of labour force migration, falling wage levels, massive increases in unemployment, and unprecedented declines in overall living standards.[18]

The concentration of social production resources in the hands of the super rich and upper classes (between 15% and 20% of the population) can be seen in the two following examples.

In 1975 in Argentina the ratio of income between the top and bottom fifths of income earners was 8:1. By 1991 this gap had doubled and by 1997 it was a staggering 25:1. In Brazil the top 10% of income earners received 44 times more income than the bottom.

During the past 20 years the number of rural and urban poor, people previously or newly excluded from work, land, education and health, has multiplied. They represent a growing legion of inhabitants of *barrios* in Mexico, *favelas* in Brazil, and *villas miseria* in Argentina (all words for large clusters of dwellings that suffer from varying degrees of degradation). In Chile under the Allende government, workers had an almost 60% share of the GNP; by 1989 it had fallen to 19%, one of the lowest in the world. In the 1970s the percentage of wages to national income was 40.9% in Argentina, 34.4% in Ecuador, 37.7% in Mexico and 40% in Peru. By 1989 the percentages had fallen to 24.9% in Argentina, 16% in Ecuador, 28.4% in Mexico and 25.8% in Peru. The figure for Peru fell to 16.8% in 1992 and in Argentina, following the debt default crisis of December 2001, workers returned to levels before the Perón government of the 1950s.[19]

---

politically well-represented elite, connected to the local political establishment as well as to the circuits of international capital. On the consolidation of a new transnational class, see: Sklair, L. and Robbins, P. (2002) 'Global capitalism and major corporations from the Third World', *Third World Quarterly*, 23, 1, 81–1000. Sklair, L. (2001) *The transational capitalist class,* Oxford: Blackwell. Petras, J. and Veltmeyer, H. (2001) *Globalization unmasked: Imperialism in the 21st century,* London: Zed Books. Rahman Embong, A. (2000) 'Globalisation and transational class relations: Some problems of conceptualisation', *Third World Quarterly*, 21, 6, 989–1000. The 2002 list of billionaires in Forbes shows 25 Latin American billionaires, among them Ricardo Salinas Pliego, owner of TV Azteca and Emilio Alcárraga, owner of Televisa.

18. According to the International Labour Organization, in 2001 unemployment remains endemic throughout the region, and about 85% of new jobs created in the past decade were in the 'informal' sector, euphemism for cheap labour without rights. Like the rest of the world Latin America is witnessing the trend toward less labour-intensive industry; therefore about 90% of new jobs created in the formal sector belong to the middle classes oriented service sector.

Throughout this process, as many studies have amply demonstrated, the dominant media organizations fervently supported the military coups, applauded IMF economic programmes and silenced dictatorship atrocities (Beltrán and Fox, 1980; Fox, 1988; Mattelart, 1979; Portales, 1981).[20]

El Mercurio in Chile has often been cited as the prototypical case of a newspaper closely identified with authoritarianism, given its open support for the 1973 coup and the Pinochet dictatorship. Brazilian daily newspapers generally accepted official censorship, while the Globo network assumed the role of the government's principal supporter. The Argentine media kept quiet about state-sponsored crimes. Examples of this include the media's proclamation "We are right and humane" during President Carter's human rights mission to Argentina in 1978 and the media's diligent work as the voice of the government during the Malvinas/Falkland war of 1982.

The decade of the 1980s

During the 1980s elected governments had to confront the results of the technological innovations applied to mass communications. A new cultural era began. It was the time of satellite television and video cassette recorders (VCRs), which thwarted authoritarian efforts to control citizens' access to news.

It was also during this decade that political activity and free elections returned to the region with longstanding Washington/IMF "free market economy" pressures and negative economic growth. The lost decade, as it is called, began with the debt crisis of 1982 and ended (?) with the four-year deluge of privatization (1989–93) when most of the privatizations were agreed.

As Martín-Barbero puts it: ". . . in the 'lost decade', of the eighties the only industry that developed in Latin America was communication. The number of television stations multiplied – from 205 in 1970 to 1,459 in 1988; Brazil and Mexico acquired their own satellites; radio and television

---

19. ECLAC/CEPAL (1999) *Growth, employment, and Equity: The impact of the economic reforms in Latin America and the Caribbean*, Quito, Ecuador: CEPAL. Vetmeyer, H. (1997) *Neoliberalism and class conflict in Latin America*, Basingstoke: Macmillan.

20. Fox, E. (ed.) (1988) *Media and politics in Latin America: The struggle for democracy*, London: Sage. Beltran, L. and Fox, E. (1980) *Comunicación dominada: Los Estados Unidos en los Medios de America Latina*, Mexico: Nueva Imagen. Portales, D. (1981) *Poder Económico y Libertad de Expresión: La industria de la comunicación chilena en la democracia y el autoritarismo*, Mexico: ILET/Nueva Imagen. Mattelart, A. (1979) *Multinational corporations and the control of culture: The ideological apparatuses of imperialism*, Brighton: Harvester.

opened world links via satellite; computer, satellite and cable TV networks were set up; regional television channels were established."[21]

For the first time, politicians made use of mass television and intensive and "scientific" use of advertising for election campaigns. Alan García in Peru, Raúl Alfonsín in Argentina, Tancredo Neves in Brazil in the early 1980s, the Chilean plebiscite on Pinochet's continued presidency in 1988, all have in common a new and central actor in national politics: television.[22]

The mass audience in Latin America only became possible since the 1970s as the cost of TV sets dropped and the geographical coverage and the number of stations increased. And only since the 1980s have people had the opportunity to vote. Previous elections were in the 1960s and early 1970s (in the Brazilian case, more than 20 years earlier, and in the Chilean one, 15). In the 1980s a new relationship between politicians and the media began to take shape.

The culturally vibrant 1980s were the decade of the return to democracy in the South Cone and a decade of popular upheaval and revolution in Central America. Human rights groups that had started life fighting against dictatorships combined with new forms of struggle and social expression. The struggle for indigenous rights became organized and social movements arose that would play a leading role in resistance to globalization in the 1990s: the Landless in Brazil, the Zapatistas in Mexico, the CONAIE in Ecuador, the coca growers in Bolivia, workers' pickets in Argentina, etc.

The post-dictatorship period was characterized by struggles for democracy, the neoliberal offensive of the New Right of Ronald Reagan and Margaret Thatcher, and a technological explosion and media expansion that made total public awareness possible. But for the forces of popular protest, however, the 1980s were a backward step in the face of the advance of neoliberalism.

The 1990s

Between 1989 and 1990 Colombian President Virgilio Barco, Brazilian President Fernando Collor de Mello, and President Fujimori's regime in

---

21. Barbero, J. (1997) 'Cultural boundaries: Identity and communication in Latin America', *Media Development*, 1, 64.
22. The impact of television on politics and on political competitiveness was the theme of extended research at the time. See Skidmore, T. (ed.) (1993) *Television, politics and the transition to democracy in Latin America*, Baltimore and London: John Hopkins University Press.

Peru, among others, signed agreements with the World Bank, the IMF and the Inter-American Development Bank[23] to implement austerity measures and to auction state-owned enterprises.

Of all the regimes in South America, the government of Carlos Menem in Argentina (1989–99) typified the most extreme case of adopting the neoliberal economic directives of the US-IMF without questioning their implications. For Menem's government, the items at the top of the deregulation and privatization agenda were communications and transport, including the enormous state-run telephone company, ENTEL.

The National Congress never debated any of these reforms. In other words the government of President Menem embarked on the most radical transformation of telecommunications, media systems and the cultural industries without the involvement of society in the deliberations ad negotiations. The sole exception was the law protecting the film industry. The mainstream media were totally uncritical of the process and, in fact, Grupo Clarín, Telefé, and the Eurnekian Media Group directly benefited from privatization and deregulation.

During the 1988 presidential election in Mexico, the left-wing candidate Cuauhtémoc Cárdenas was robbed of victory due to a mysterious computer breakdown – an excuse frequently used in Latin America! In 1989 the "victor", President Salinas de Gortari, signalled his intention to abolish nearly all the tariffs and requirements for import licences. To ease the restrictions on foreign investments further, Salinas started the programme that sold off the huge state-owned telecommunications conglomerate, the television industry known today as TV Azteca, state-run banks, mines and food distribution.

Latin American elected governments rely on the time-proven tactics of dangling economic carrots in front of media organizations in the expectation of receiving favourable coverage or silencing critical reporting. For example, in 1992 in Argentina the axing of a critical TV report on the building of a multimillion dollar airstrip inside President Menem's home property in La Rioja province was the result of government pressure. There has been no way to press the Argentine judiciary to investigate this case, or many others, despite the fact that Eduardo Eurnekian, head of the conglomerate that owned the station where the report was scheduled for broadcast, was favoured in the privatization of Argentina's main airports.

---

23. Inter-American Development Bank was established in 1959 to fund "development projects"; in 2001 IDB had authorized capital for $101 billion and offices in 26 countries.

Silvio Waisbord states that in Colombia, analysts concluded that those media groups that supported President Ernesto Samper when the scandal about pouring drug monies into politics exploded during the 1994 election campaign, were rewarded with the privatization of two television channels.[24] Moreover, those broadcasters that criticized the President did not have their licences renewed.

In this way the multimedia groups of today consolidated their power. Two anecdotes go to show the new, unregulated and unaccountable autonomy of the mainstream Latin American media. The first took place when Alberto Fujimori assumed the presidency of Peru, for the third time, in 2000. From 1990 to 2000 Fujimori's government was a dictatorship. His second-in-command, Vladimiro Montesinos, turned out to be an arms trafficker with strong links to the CIA. Fujimori dissolved the National Congress and during his term of office serious and systematic violations of human rights deserved international condemnation.

When Fujimori took up government again *for the third time*, after suspected fraudulent elections, popular demonstrations took place in the streets of Lima. For several hours a furious crowd destroyed public buildings, set up barricades and demanded the immediate resignation of the President and his Cabinet. While that popular fury raged through the streets, the media broadcast the presidential inauguration ceremony without saying a single word or showing a single image of what was happening beneath the windows of the National Congress. Eventually, Fujimori was dismissed from office and exiled himself to Japan.

The second anecdote comes from April 2002 when US oil interests allied to the Chamber of Commerce of Venezuela, promoted a coup d'état against the elected government of populist President Hugo Chávez. Venezuela is the fourth largest provider of oil to the USA (Mexico is the fifth). The Venezuelan oil industry is the only state-owned one left in Latin America and Venezuela is a member of OPEC.

The attitude of the Venezuelan media before, during and after the failed coup d'état, which lasted just 24 hours, reminded analysts of the attitude of the Chilean media during the overthrow of Salvador Allende. The press and privately owned radio and television stations actively colluded in the coup and celebrated the brief presidency of Alberto Carmona – president of the Chamber of Commerce – which he assumed with the immediate blessing of the US State Department, the IMF and the European Community, presided by Jose Maria Aznar.

---

24. Waisbord, S. (2000) 'Media in South America: Between the rock of the state and the hard place of the market', in Curran, J. and Park, M. (eds.) *De-Westernising Media Studies*, London: Routledge.

The contemporary media scenario

Latin America has at least four second-rank global firms, each of which dominates its national market and is expanding regionally and globally: Televisa (Mexico), the Globo Group (Brazil), the Venevisión Cisneros Group (Venezuela) and the Clarín Group (Argentina). The region has a formidable media system. There are an estimated 570 terrestrial channels currently broadcasting in the countries of Latin America and the Caribbean, of which 64 are state-oriented and cultural and educational in scope. Privately owned media largely predominate. In all, the average annual budget for private stations is barely 6% of the budget of commercial stations. Today, in every country with the exception of Ecuador and Paraguay, a small state broadcasting sector exists whose audience share in 1990 – prior to privatization and deregulation – was 3.7% radio and 5.2% television, including the Caribbean.[25]

It is estimated that digital television will reach some 5.3 million households and the cable market more than 30 million households by 2005. The cable industry is concentrated in Mexico, Argentina and Chile. In Mexico it accounts for 10% of a market of 17 million households in total. In Argentina 51% of the 10 million households with television are connected to cable TV. In recent years the Latin American market has offered good returns. In 1995 overall investment in pay-TV amounted to $684 million.[26]

Media corporations have established centralized structures, integrated production with distribution in terrestrial, cable and satellite networks, and have extended businesses to key sectors of national and regional economies previously unrelated to media, thus creating structures with multiple financial linkages. They have integrated traditional producers of TV content and telenovelas into new media carriers – monopolizing every distribution channel or "technological window": terrestrial, cable and satellite TV, telecommunications and the Internet.

There are multiple agreements among domestic, regional and global companies. They have arranged co-production deals and joined in common cable and satellite ventures, for example, joint ventures to distribute programming like Sky and Galaxy (satellite TV), and to produce programming like Univisión and Telemundo, which are networks for the US Hispanic market.

25. According to Roncagliolo, R. (1999) 'Las Industrias Culturales en la Viodeosfera Latinoamericana', in Canclini, N.G. and Moneta, C. (eds.), *Las industrias culturales en la integración latinoamericana*, Buenos Aires: Eudeba.

26. Sinclair, J. (1999) *Latin American television: A global view*, New York: Oxford University Press.

Miami, Florida, has emerged as the media capital of Latin America. Most Latin cable and satellite channels have their headquarters there and Latin American advertising is co-ordinated there. The big, regional TV advertising market is concentrated in a few media corporations. Latin America has a media environment that is crudely advertising-driven, with few regulations on what can or cannot be advertised. Networks have consistently used programmes to promote consumer products, from Coca-Cola to cigarettes, adverts for toys within children's programmes and drinks. Colgate Palmolive is the long-standing example of prime time sponsorship. "Merchandizing" is integrated into a narrative either directly by actors advertising a product or through product placement, when an item appears "in shot" (Tufte, 2000).[27]

Unequal development and concentration are reproduced both within countries and the region itself. For example, Ciespal's Media Inventory for 1993 shows that in that year Brazil and Mexico had more than 50% of newspapers and broadcasting stations on the sub-continent.[28] Octavio Getino (1998) points out that between 1930 and 1990 some 10,000 films were produced in the region.[29] Just three countries produced 90% of this total: Mexico (46%), Brazil (24%) and Argentina (19%).

Latin America continues to be a *net importer* of TV programming. Even Mexico, where 47% of the exports of the Ibero-American audio-visual industry were concentrated in 1998 (that is to say, including Spain), that same year had a deficit of $22.7 million in its TV balance of trade alone. In 1998, 87% of imports in TV products to Latin America came from the USA.[30]

The following are some data concerning the Brazilian TV market, about Rede Globo and the Televisa, Venevisión and Clarín groups.

Brazil and Mexico

Brazil's Globo network generated $2.2 billion in 1996. Not only is this media empire integrated horizontally and vertically, it also has interests in financing, banking, food, agriculture, mining, real estate, telecommunications, insurance and the electronics industry. Rede Globo has nine terrestrial television networks and attracts 68% of national viewers and

27. Tufte, T. (2000) *Living with the rubbish queen: Telenovelas, culture and modernity in Brazil*, Luton: University of Luton Press.

28. *Inventario de Medios de Ciespal* (1993), Quito, Ecuador: Ciespal.

29. Getino, O. (1998) 'El mercado audiovisual latinoamericano', *Voces y Culturas, Revista de Comunicación*, 13, 9–23.

30. *Comunicación* (2001) Estudios Venezolanos de comunicación. Segundo Semestre, 114.

75% of all advertising. It controls 70% of the pay-per-view market and owns numerous cable channels. The Marinho family owns the Globo network and also controls newspapers, paperback publishing, radio stations, Som Livre, Globo Multimedia, Globo Video, Globo Disk, and has shares in mobile telephony.

Globo exports television programming to nearly 60 nations, with Portugal being the primary customer outside Latin America. It formed an alliance with AT&T and Brazil's largest private bank (Bradesco) to bid for the privatization of Brazil's telephone system. Between 1994 and 1996 Brazil had the world's fastest growing pay TV market. Globo also set up several channels for the Sky Brazil service of Sky Latin America.

Brazil is the biggest single market in the region and has the sixth largest music market in the world. The Brazilian media market has a two-tier structure, with Globo occupying the dominant position and a second tier of smaller companies engaged in oligopolistic competition.[31]

Six private networks with national coverage exist, with 138 affiliated groups controlling 668 TV and radio stations and newspapers. The second largest group after Globo is Rede STB, which controls 200 companies producing magazines, guides, telephone directories, records, CD-Roms, electronic games, online services, videos by cable, MMDS and satellite. The other groups are Rede Record, Rede Bandeirantes, Rede TV! and Rede CTN.[32]

In Mexico, Televisa (1996 sales: $1.2 billion) is the leading media conglomerate and leading producer and exporter of Spanish-language programmes in the region. The original licensee first merged to form Telesistema Mexico in 1955, and then merged with a competitor to form Televisa in 1972. That was the position until 1993 when the Mexican government privatized part of its network to form TV Azteca.

In 1995 Televisa controlled 75% of the Mexican market, with four major national networks, 200 regional channels, and its cable distribution service, Cablevision, established in 1966. Televisa also owns several radios, 80 newspapers and two major football teams. In 1995 television absorbed 75% of all commercial investment, or $820 million. Like TV Globo, Televisa has become a vector for the culture industry with an audience share outside peak hours of more than 80%. Televisa's production power is considerable. It has vertically integrated production with distribution. By the late 1970s, more than 80% of programmes were produced

---

31. Sinclair, J., Jacka, E. and Cunningham, S., (eds.) (1996) *New patterns in global television: Peripheral Vision*, Oxford: Oxford University Press.

32. *Os donos da mídia* (2001) EPCOM Instituto de Estudos e Pesquisas em Comicacao, Porto Alegre: EPCOM.

domestically and in 1991 its companies produced 45,000 hours of programming and exported more than 36,000 to 52 countries. Televisa's *telenovelas*, the Latin American television product par excellence, are exported to over 100 countries and in 1995 accounted for 85% of Televisa's $71 million programme exports. The dubbed programmes are especially popular in East and Central Europe, China, India and Turkey.[33]

Yet Televisa is not satisfied with being the pre-eminent Spanish language media conglomerate in the world. Currently it is producing low-budget English-language programming for US audiences and broadcasting them from a series of stations along Mexico's northern border.

Venezuela and Argentina

The Cisneros Group in Venezuela, with sales of $3.2 billion in 1995, is an industrial conglomerate that moved aggressively into media. It is the primary partner of Direct TV Galaxy in Latin America and it has media and telecommunication joint ventures with Motorola, Microsoft, AT&T, BellSouth, Televisa and Hearst. Cisneros owns television stations in Venezuela, Trinidad and Chile, and is a partner in a Spanish-owned digital joint venture. "We want to be a very large force in Latin America," the CEO of Cisneros said, "and throughout the hemisphere."[34]

In Argentina, privatization led to the formation of a virtual duopoly: Grupo Clarín and CEI-TISA. Citicorp Equity Investments (CEI) owns two of the four main terrestrial television channels (Canal 9 and 11), as well as cable and telecommunications enterprises. Clarín and CEI-TISA control four of the five terrestrial channels in Buenos Aires and 95% of cable customers.

Grupo Clarín, which made a total of $1.2 billion in 1996, owns the highly influential daily newspaper *Clarín*. The Grupo Clarín controls interests in regional newspapers, the principal AM and FM radio stations, over-the-air and cable television (Clarín is also the biggest producer of TV content), a news agency, news print production, and also collaborates with foreign groups in satellite television. For example, Clarín is a partner of the news network TeleNoticias and has teamed up with Globo to

---

33. *UNESCO World Communication Report* (1997). Fox, E. (1997) *Latin American broadcasting: From tango to telenovela*, Luton: Luton Press.

34. Quoted in Herman, E. and McChesney, R. (1997) *The global media: The new missionaries of global capitalism*, London: Cassell. The sales figures for 1996 for Televisa, Globo, Venevisión and Clarín also come from Herman and McChesney (1997).

develop Brazilian cable-TV systems and with TCI to develop Chilean cable systems.[35]

The neoliberal integration model: NAFTA and FTAA-ALCA

Since 1994 the North American Free Trade Agreement (NAFTA) has regulated a commercial bloc made up of the USA, Canada and Mexico, with a population of 370 million and combined economic production of approximately $6 trillion (in 1997). Despite its title, NAFTA was not primarily concerned with free trade. By 1990 tariff and even non-tariff barriers to USA-Mexico trade were very low. NAFTA was primarily concerned with investment, competition, government procurement, telecommunications and financial services. The most troubling aspect of NAFTA was the inclusion of extensive new rights for multinational corporations. These same radical investor protections were at the core of the Multilateral Agreement on Investments (MAI).

NAFTA has opened up Mexico to US investment in significant ways: through the banking system, US banks and security firms can invest in Mexican banks and insurance industries; through the oil business (but not the oil fields); and through 49% of foreign investment in media operations and distribution services (cable and satellite TV).

The NAFTA section on cultural industries emphasized copyright and intellectual property rights. Canada already had a set of laws comparable with those in the USA. In anticipation of NAFTA, in 1991 Mexico passed significant changes in its copyright laws and in 1993 modified its Constitution to allow up to 49% of foreign investment in media. One of the main aims of enforcing copyright is to reduce piracy, which is an extended and serious business in Latin America.

Hernán Galperin is right to express the relationship with the metaphor "NAFTA regulates the exchange between David and Goliath."[36] In 1993 the volume of export revenues from the cultural industries was: for the USA in films and TV content, $7 billion; for Canada $280 million; and for Televisa $20 million.

NAFTA was set up on the neoliberal principle of capital mobility and an immobile labour force, combining an ever cheaper labour force with ever more modern technology. This enabled large US manufacturers (and

---

35. See Albornoz, L., (ed.) (2000) *Al Fin Solos ... La nueva television del Mercosur.* Buenos Aires: Ediciones La Crujía.

36. Galperin, H. (1999) Cultural industries policy in regional trade agreements: The cases of Nafta, the European Union and Mercosur, *Media, Culture and Society,* 21, 627–648. London: Sage.

certain Mexican enterprises) to exploit low paid but highly skilled Mexican labour and thus lose millions of jobs for American workers. The treaty contains no legal protections for workers nor any measures to protect the environment.

Between 1963 and 1981 the proportion of Mexicans living below the poverty line went down from 77.5% to 48.5%. But from 1982 until 1992 under pro-market reforms, it rose again to 66%. During the period from 1994 to 2001 the median wage of Mexican workers plummeted by 22.75%. Eight million Mexican families dropped from the middle class into poverty as US and Canadian giants gobbled up Mexico's manufacturing and retailing enterprises.[37]

Unprotected by the state, Mexican film production fell from 122 films in 1988 to seven in 1998.[38] The economic integration that NAFTA consolidated between the USA and Mexico reserved to the Mexican state the role of provider of a cheap and disciplined labour force. This situation has been characterized in recent literature[39] as "unequal" or "asymmetrical", but it has not been studied as an imperialist and classist policy whose continuation and extension is the Free Trade Agreement of the Americas (FTAA-ALCA). This treaty would extend NAFTA to the rest of continent's countries, with the exception of Cuba. If brought to completion, it would represent the largest trade bloc in the world, with a combined GDP of $11 trillion, 40% of world production and a population of 800 million.

In April 2001, under the Bush administration, the Third Summit of the Americas took place in Quebec, Canada, attended by 34 heads of state. Cuba was excluded. The Summit decided that the FTAA-ALCA would come into force in 2005. The negotiations are secret and participation is selective. No representative of non-profit media organizations has been allowed to attend the discussions.

---

37. Viera, C. (2001) 'FTAA: A prison for Latin America?' *Third World Resurgence*, 129–130 May/June. McMurtry, J. (2001) *The cancer state of capitalism*, London: Pluto. Skidmore, T. and Smith, H. (1997) *Modern Latin America*, fourth edition, New York Oxford: Oxford University Press.

38. Thussu, D. (2000) *International communication: Continuity and change*, London: Arnold. However, the calamitous situation of Mexican cinema did not prevent the international success of the film *Amores Perros* in 2002.

39. McAnany, E. and Wilkinson, K., (eds.) (1996) *Mass media and free trade. NAFTA and the cultural industries*, Austin: University of Texas Press. Canclini, G.N. and Moneta, C. (eds.) (1999) *Las industrias culturales en la integración latinoamericana*, Buenos Aires: Eudeba. Schiller, D. and Mosco, V., (eds.) (2001) *Continental order? Integrating North America for cybercapitalism*, Lanham, MD: Rowman and Littlefield.

The FTAA-ALCA has led to enormous popular resistance throughout Latin America and this active and increasingly organized opposition will be taken up below.

Some final thoughts

In 1843 Marx defined critical theory as "the self-clarification of the struggles and wishes of the age". Thus, a critical theory establishes its research programme and its conceptual framework with an eye to the aims and activities of those oppositional social movements with which it identifies in a partisan way, although not uncritically. If struggles contesting economic and political exclusion in Latin America figured among the most significant of a given age and geographical location, then a critical theory for that time would, among other things, aim at shedding light on the character and bases of such exclusion/subordination.[40]

The categories of political theory – democracy, public sphere and public opinion, civil society and citizenship – used to frame, think about and understand the relationship between media, governments and societies mask the inequalities of the present-day because they hide the class nature of the public sphere. If the concept of the public sphere is to retain its critical sense, one must focus on who is allowed in and who is kicked out, and this is the result of social struggles and power relations, which are the domain of political economy.

Resistance

The huge popular front against the FTAA-ALCA brings together social movements, trade unions and non-profit media organizations from the Río Grande to Tierra del Fuego. Predictably it includes opposition from President Chávez and President Castro, but also from Brazilian President Fernando Henrique Cardozo, who is no longer exactly socialist. This is because Cardozo is defending the regional development strategy that could be steered by the Common Market of the South (Mercosur). The FTAA-ALCA aims at breaking down the resistance of Brazil, the most powerful nation in Latin America, to the kind of integration with the USA that NAFTA consolidated between the USA and Mexico.

---

40. Fraser, N. (1986) 'What is critical about critical theory?' in Benhabib, S. and Cornell, D. (eds.) *Feminism as a critique: On the politics of gender,* London: Polity Press. I take up concepts used by this feminist author in the context of her discussion of the critical theory of Jürgen Habermas.

Brazil has developed high levels of social awareness about the need to reform its media. For example, as a result of a coordinated struggle by journalists' unions, university students and various civil organizations (ten years that are remembered as "the cable TV war"), new legislation was enacted in 1995. The law reserves cable TV station and broadcast time for civil institutions, trade unions and some popular organizations. However, without state financing, the system is dying and a good part of its provisions were never implemented.

The social and political movements of Latin America want democratic control of the social resources that the state gave to the transnational corporations and international financial institutions. Moreover, the social movements want to regulate the multimedia conglomerates and reorient their editorial policies. They know that for this the historical balance between social forces has to do an about turn.

The small hope of these few pages is that Latin American scholars and intellectuals can rediscover the lost link between thinkers and social movements. That relationship that, as Antonio Gramsci taught, combines theories with political actions and with time leads to social change.

Communications and the Crisis: From Neoliberal to Authoritarian Development?*

Dan Schiller

With the global economy's downward spiral into stagnation, and the renewal of a forthright US imperialism via the war on Iraq, the world fell into obvious crisis.[1] It is not well-enough appreciated, however, that as this crisis deepened, it intertwined in profound ways with communications and information.

Roughly from 1970 onwards, as political-economic elites impressed a refined and expanded capital logic upon a technologically dynamic communication system, a neoliberal model of what I call "digital capitalism"[2] was erected. This complex initiative required and rested upon radical institutional transformations. US authorities relaxed or withdrew welfarist regulatory restrictions on communication systems and services, thereby prodding the sector to adopt a more fully corporate-commercial, and, a transnational, increasingly structure; they expedited a rapid expansion of the system of commercial advertising; and they adumbrated and helped to enforce ever-more draconian intellectual property rights. China's embrace of the market and the fall of Soviet socialism gave powerful boosts to efforts by US agencies to deepen and broaden the capital accumulation process by opening up communications and information to market forces.

The neoliberal regime that acceded to global dominance in turn galvanized a process of unprecedented – though deeply uneven – network

---

* This chapter borrows from Dan Schiller, 'Digital Capitalism: A Status Report on the Corporate Commonwealth of Information', in Angharad Valdivia (ed.) *Blackwell Companion to Media Studies*, Cambridge: Blackwell, in press.

1. For a premonition, see Hobsbawm (1994): 416–22.
2. Schiller (1999); Schiller (2001).

modernization, and turned this networking project into the leading hub of the global political economy. However, beginning with the Asian financial meltdown of 1997–98, this neoliberalism began to exhibit significant institutional stress. As "new economy" speculation careened to a halt, and the pundits shifted from "long boom" to "burst bubble", digital capitalism's difficulties compounded. But these problems only became fully apparent after the attacks of 11 September 2001, when a spiraling economic slowdown which extended into digital capitalism's leading sector prompted a recrudescent national security state to try to reframe the historical project of digital capitalism in prospectively sweeping authoritarian terms. The success of this multifaceted initiative remained profoundly uncertain as of 2003. However, the present essay suggests that in responding to the crisis, the stewards of the political economy were attempting to shift digital capitalism into a new and ominous phase.

My discussion begins with the technological revolution in communications.

The technological revolution in communications

Consider the much-vaunted technological revolution in communications, itself fuelled by two powerful engines of the US political economy – military spending and consumerism. Beginning around 1975, the traditional media (and analog broadcasting in the VHF and UHF bands, in particular) were supplemented in rapid succession by new media systems and distribution channels. Some findings from a Spring 2000 study by the Pew Research Center for People and the Press:

- 79% of Americans had cable or satellite TV
- 59% had home computers.
- 53% had mobile phones.
- 29% logged on to the Internet on a typical day.
- 16% had DVD players.[3]

A year later, still more Americans went online, possessed mobile phones, and used DVD players.[4] To these new fixtures of cultural practice, one might add millions of fax machines, MP3 music players, digital assistants, video- and computer-game consoles, highspeed Internet access hook-ups, and other devices.

---

3. Kohut (2000): A25.
4. Berman (2001): B1.

Each of these characteristically privatized new media had been propelled forward by a burst of particularistic innovation but – more fundamentally – each also is prospectively linked to a more general transformation. A growing portion of human experience may be objectified and represented, with varying verisimilitude, in digital form – "the esperanto of 1s and 0s" as Davis and Stack[5] call the process. Digitization has proved compelling owing to commanding economic and strategic advantages: capaciousness, flexibility, security, and accuracy in processes of signal reproduction, storage and transmission. Digital signal coding also enhances efficiency by accommodating increased reliance on machine perception and handling of information.[6] But the process of digitization, and the networks to which it is increasingly tied, are nowhere close to being fully actualized.

Proliferating new media and the evolution toward a versatile but still half-formed highspeed, or broadband, digital operating environment, however, have already massively disrupted and destabilized what had been discrete, largely oligopolized, media markets. A leading response, examined below, was for corporations both to develop and exploit new advertising platforms, and to push for proprietary controls over increasingly diffuse works of intellectual property. But this dual endeavour itself dovetailed with a more general corporate objective: to gain leverage over the character and pace of the ongoing technical transition, both for digital variants of individual media systems and services, and general-purpose digital delivery infrastructures. Everything from computer operating system software to Internet addresses, and from digital music formats and television broadcasting standards to interconnection rules thus came under intense strategic scrutiny by a suddenly (and unstably) enlarged throng of self-interested actors. Most of the limelight was garnered by discrete corporate alliances and sometimes bitter turf fights over the terms on which digitization would proceed. But the decisive issue was whether this colossal technical transformation would be *generally* coopted.

The technical skills needed to produce for the emerging digital media were not yet by any means comprehensively monopolized by capital. Indeed, the declining cost of digital audio-visual production and the extraordinary capabilities of the open Internet for rapid, widespread and cheap distribution unfolded novel and important avenues of creative expression to individuals and groups long denied access to production for the corporate-commercial media. Military planners and intelligence analysts thus were quick to take note of the use of network resources by

---

5. Davis and Stack (1997): 128.
6. Davis and Stack (1997): 128, 124-25.

Zapatistas in Mexico in 1994, and by anti-globalization advocates mobilizing in the late 1990s against the World Trade Organization (WTO).[7] As the US undertook to wage war in Afghanistan, moreover, access via email and the Web to critical information produced by domestic and international sources continued to frustrate US government attempts to impose comprehensive information control. (*Le Monde diplomatique*, probably the world's leading journal of critical opinion, indeed reported a 25% increase in circulation for its English-language Internet edition.[8])

But we should also remember that the Internet was, first and foremost, a US creation – and that US political-economic interests continue to possess considerable ability to shape, or reshape, the new medium to suit their purposes. Alongside the integration of Internet systems and services within giant corporations, the rapid build-up of multimedia conglomerates thus signalled big capital's intention to canalize the digitization process on behalf of its own narrow concern for profit.

Bulking up: Emerging multimedia conglomerates

US media owners – purveyors to the world's single largest national media market, itself a vital stepping-stone to global cultural distribution – faced both challenges and opportunities. On the one hand, as audiences migrated away from prevailing free-to-air broadcast services, the predominant mass-market, or "broad-reach", model of media practice eroded. Unless owners could extend their control to a succession of individual new media, and lay prospective claim to key segments of the emerging digital environment, the access to audiences that they afforded to advertisers – and, therefore, also their own profitability – would be endangered. Media owners who successfully amassed control over these new distribution systems, and moved to unite them with existing and new programming assets, on the other hand, would be capable of inflicting punishing new pressures on rivals. Significant cross-media conglomeration, of course, already existed. However, a much-vaunted trend toward "media convergence" supplied rhetorical cover for an industry-wide scramble to attain comprehensive control over what had been more discrete media sub-sectors.

Obstructing this movement toward expanded conglomeration were significant legal and regulatory curbs, a legacy of the earlier 20th century, when an ascendant US liberalism still felt the need to make (limited) room for domestic social welfare. A political campaign to eliminate these constraints was launched.

---

7. Arquilla and Ronfeldt (2001).
8. *Le Monde diplomatique* (2001).

Through the 1980s and 1990s, US government authorities, both Republicans and Democrats, lent full-throated support to corporate-commercial media expansion. Continuing "liberalization" of media markets was the result, as existing governmental restrictions on cross-media ownership and concentration of ownership within individual media were swept aside. Capital flooded into the communications industry. In an epic buy-out binge, a torrent of multibillion dollar mergers and acquisitions flowed through the sector.

The size and scope of enterprise were, accordingly, dramatically enlarged. In 1982, the largest US media company was the American Broadcasting Company, claiming (current dollar) revenue of $2.5 billion;[9] in 2001, the largest US media company was AOL-Time Warner, with revenue projected to reach some $39 billion that year.[10] Passage of the Telecommunications Act of 1996[11] was a milestone. During just the first quarter of 1999, for example, $500 billion worth of US-based media, entertainment and telecommunication deals were announced.[12]

The change was not merely quantitative. The assets of the huge conglomerates under construction encompassed everything from television networks, film and television programme producers, broadcast station and cable groups, to billboards, satellite services, print publishers, recorded music companies, live-entertainment venues, professional sports teams, video game creators, and theme parks, to – most recently – interactive Web services. As broadcast news organizations were enfolded, while even the largest newspaper chains were forced to give up pride of place within the greater communications industry, already inadequate news coverage – especially of foreign affairs[13] – was slashed, and slashed again. For the general audience, market-driven journalism and celebrity reporting replaced much of what had remained of informed comment.[14]

Further relaxation of ownership restrictions and operating constraints on communications industry markets continued to constitute the dominant trend. In keeping with suggestions that the Bush Administration was poised to authorize "sweeping consolidation" across both broadcasting and telecommunications,[15] a well-placed executive and former Federal

---

9. *Advertising Age* (2000)
10. Grimes (2001): 15.
11. Hundt (2000).
12. Aufderheide (1999): 91; Mermigas (1999): 34.
13. Front-page space accorded to international news in ten medium and large newspapers, according to University of Maryland journalism professor Carl Sessions Stepp, declined from 20% in 1963 to 5% in 1999. Campbell (2001): 15A.
14. Schiller, (1986): 19–36; McManus, (1994); Kimball (1994); McChesney (2000).
15. Legg Mason report quoted in Koerner (2001): 41.

Communications Commission (FCC) chief of staff predicted "that practically every major telecommunications restriction will be lifted."[16] The Department of Justice, by settling a major antitrust case on terms highly favourable to Microsoft, licensed the software company to renew its aggressive efforts to develop interactive and other new service markets.[17] And, at the FCC, cable system and broadcast station ownership limits and service requirements, restrictions on cross-media ownership of newspapers and television stations, controls over the terms on which major telephone companies may furnish Internet access and services, limits on how much wireless spectrum may be owned by an individual company, barriers to consolidation between local and long-distance tele-communications, were all being renegotiated, as US government authorities helped enact a grotesque and deeply damaging parody of the concept of freedom of expression.

The business and economic consequences are already evident. Today's media conglomerates can and do track consumers across once discrete media frontiers, sell them a range of services directly, and offer major advertisers access to multiple media platforms on which to stage sales effort. These leaders' revenue streams, in other words, have been diversified, and increasingly embrace not only advertising sales, but also service subscriptions and other direct fees and charges. Viacom, which owns the CBS and UPN television networks, the Infinity radio chain, and MTV, Nickelodeon and other cable networks, still obtains only around half of its revenue from advertising – making it, surprisingly, among the *most* reliant of the media conglomerates on this income source.[18] AOL-Time Warner, in contrast, garners less than one-quarter of its revenues from advertising,[19] while Vivendi-Universal, which owns huge non-media businesses (prior to planned divestment of media assets during 2003) generates less than 5% of its sales from advertising.[20]

The political and ideological consequences of concentrated and vertical media ownership were vividly displayed in the aftermath of 11 September when a handful of gigantic media conglomerates placed its centralized image-making capability pretty much at the disposal of the national security state.[21] Significantly, however, anti-corporate media mobilization

---

16. Blair Levin, managing director at Legg Mason, in *Knowledge@Wharton* (2001).
17. Buckman, Tam and Mangalindan (2001): A1, A10; Labaton with Lohr (2001): C1, C6; Spiegel (2001): 12.
18. Peers and Flint (2001): B15; Witcher (2001): A13.
19. Balnaves, Donald and Donald (2001): 63; Schiesel (2001b): C8.
20. Carreyrou (2001): A21; Schiesel (2001c): C8.
21. Saunders (2001); Beatty and Cummings (2001): A10; Stanley (2001): B2; Haider (2001).

in the United States also grew, as hundreds of thousands of emails and letters flooded into the FCC, protesting – so far, fruitlessly – its proposals to loosen ownership restrictions.

Let us turn now to the other side of the US communication industry coin: telecommunications.

The new order in telecommunications

The project of modernizing US telecommunications has been almost violent. To understand this process, indeed, we must situate the US political economy within a wider global context. The dramatically altered circumstances of the 1990s – not only the continuing enlargement of the defining unit of contemporary enterprise, the transnational corporation, but also the collapse of Soviet socialism, coupled with China's embrace of the capitalist market – created space for a secular increase in overall foreign direct investment. A spectacular continuing surge in cross-border corporate mergers and acquisitions ensued: the value of completed cross-border buyouts rose from less than $100 billion in 1987 to $1.14 trillion (current dollars) in 2000.[22] Underway was a reorganization of ownership that is remaking nationally integrated markets and production systems into "a global market for goods and services and . . . an international production system, complemented by an increasingly global market for firms."[23] This ongoing process – which might be called "reactionary modernization" – both relied upon and largely motivated a concurrent rush of corporate-led innovation around networks.

Accelerated network development initially evolved within the post-war US domestic market. By elevating the precepts of liberalization of commercial market entry, and rapid buildouts of specialized systems and services aimed at privileged user-groups, US policymakers empowered a few thousand giant corporations and their affiliated managerial and technical strata, as well as a burgeoning group of high-tech network system and service suppliers.

Because large business users of telecommunications were mostly transnational companies, however, during the 1980s the US model once again began to be generalized.[24] With some internecine jostling, the World Bank, the International Monetary Fund, the International Tele-communication Union, and other organizations all enrolled in the liberalization effort. As US power groups' confidence increased, bilateral

---

22. United Nations Conference on Trade and Development (UNCTAD) (2000), (2001): Table 1.1, p.10; Quinlan (2001): 24.

23. UNCTAD (2000): xx.

24. Schiller (1982).

negotiations, US trade law, and encompassing multilateral initiatives were pursued. Under the sign of neoliberalism, the institutional basis of world telecommunications was transformed.

There really is no historical precedent for the overhaul of world telecommunications that has taken place. Between 1984 and July 1999, within a broader context of state-asset sell-offs, there occurred around $244 billion worth of privatizations of state-owned systems.[25] As a result, of the 189 members of the International Telecommunication Union, by 1999 almost half (90) had wholly or partially privatized their existing telecommunication operators, 18 completely. Of the remaining non-privatized operators, more than 30 planned to privatize.

The process of privatization itself was characteristically structured to ease market entry by transnational carriers.[26] The World Trade Organization Basic Telecommunications Agreement, forged in 1997, helped harmonize national operating frameworks, subjecting some 70 signatories to binding commitments enforced by a multilateral dispute settlement process, and thereby established more uniformly liberal market access to network equipment and services worldwide.[27] By early 2000, 25 countries had pledged to allow majority foreign-owned carriers seeking to furnish international voice service using their own wholly owned and controlled networks.[28]

Domestically integrated networks run by national flag carriers thus began to be superceded in scope and function by transnational systems. The result was to grant license to carriers and business users to assimilate networks as desired into a vast and growing range of business processes, though one characteristically associated with prosaic needs such as payroll accounting, employment relations, inventory, sales, marketing, research and development, and so on. By revolutionizing network systems and services, large corporations thus acquired new freedom of manoeuver in their attempts both to reintegrate the market system on a broadened, supranational basis, and to deepen it by developing information as a commodity.

Huge outlays were needed to provision digital capitalism with this central production base and control structure: transnationally organized networks, employing a lengthening list of media including wireless, telephone lines, cable television systems, fibre optics, satellites, and the

---

25. One report claimed that "more than $1 trillion" in state assets were sold to private investors through the late 1990s. Dreazen and Caffrrey (2001): A1.
26. U.S. Federal Communications Commission (2000): 6.
27. Barshefsky (1999): 6; Blouin (2000): 135–142.
28. U.S. Federal Communications Commission (2000): 6.

software-defined means for network access, operation, and management. Through the 1990s, moreover, the financial markets seemingly answered every call for capital by existing and would-be suppliers. As a bevy of entrepreneurs obtained the cheap debt financing they sought to build vast new networks, often employing Internet and related technologies, existing giants such as AT&T reacted by joining the stampede. Rival network operators each spent many billions of dollars a year building systems to link office complexes throughout central cities. Corporate network users based in every economic sector put out additional billions on the tangle of hardware and software they needed to enlarge and modernize their burgeoning proprietary systems.

It is now widely accepted that network-related investment functioned as the pivot of the late 1990s' US economic boom.[29] Here, in the most highly developed core of global capitalism, between 1995 and 2000, investment by US companies in information technology, including telecommunication and networking equipment, reportedly totalled a spectacular $1.4 trillion.[30]

The result was a sudden, stunning enlargement of information-carrying capacity, albeit principally on profitable, high-density traffic routes and, with explosive suddenness, for Internet systems and services. Most of the 39 million miles of fibre optic cable circuitry laid in the United States over the last two decades of the 20th century was installed between 1996 and 2000.[31] Especially but not only on US trans-Atlantic and trans-Pacific routes, new submarine cable systems added unprecedented increments to available network capacity.[32]

But the revelry occasioned for a few years in the business press by corporate-led telecommunication initiatives soon turned into something far less salutary. The real effects of networking the market system, it appeared, would be as contradictory as the political economy to which these systems themselves are hardwired. As a result, George Gilder's vaunted "telecosm," with its promise of "infinite bandwidth", now looks as much like a graveyard as a cornucopia.

Burgeoning transnational network systems steeply accelerated the speed and volume of largely unregulated international finance capital flows, some implications of which became painfully evident during the Asian financial crisis of 1997–98. The devastation of New York's World Trade Center hit hard not simply owing to the loss of life, or even because

29. Oliner and Sichel (2000); Wellenius, Primo Braga and Qiang (2000): 639, 642.
30. London (2001): 21.
31. Blumenstein (2001) A1, A 8; Ramstad and Stringer (2001): A1.
32. TeleGeography (2001).

one of the most potent symbols of American might collapsed before world television audiences, but because the attacks crippled 3.5 million private data lines for corporate customers, including some 20% of the data lines serving the New York Stock Exchange.[33] Attendant vulnerabilities afflicted the auto industry and other innovators of just-in-time inventory systems when, following the 11 September attacks, cross-border trucking and air transport were delayed and disrupted.

Even before the attacks, what had been glowingly referred to as "virtuous circles of investment" in networks had turned out to be anything but benign. As market entry policies were relaxed, specialized services aimed at corporate users were intensively cultivated, and system-development conformed ever more closely to corporate preferences. In the US, as national priorities shifted from roads, airports, power plants and bridges to telecommunication networks, these existing infrastructures deteriorated[34], and the hectic pace and giant scale of disruptive telecommunication network buildouts contributed to this erosion. Corporate ownership and performance norms were generalized, and profits made to flow disproportionately to investors rather other interests, while the existing – often very limited – social welfare character of the telecommunication industry was undercut. In what had been a heavily unionized industry, collective bargaining rights were typically withheld from employees working to build and service newly deregulated network systems; and layoffs as a byproduct of competition became standard practice.[35] Quality of service, now more comprehensively tied to the ability to pay, declined for many households.[36] Cheats and scams – overbilling of calling card users, illegally transferring long-distance accounts to new carriers, charging telephone users for services they do not order – became standard practice throughout large portions of the now-deregulated industry.[37] Far more important than any of this, at least from the rarified perspective of Wall Street, was that the intense bout of network investment ironically came to destabilize the accumulation process which previously it had propelled.

Stoked by investment bankers, and beguiled by business plans that forecast uninterrupted exponential growth of Internet traffic, tele-communication carriers took on gargantuan debt to finance their network

33. Pristin (2001): A12; Young and Solomon (2001): B7; Young and Berman (2001): A1, A8.
34. Alonso-Zaldivar (2001): A9.
35. Katz (1997).
36. Roycroft and Garcia-Murrilo (2000): 947, 965–66.
37. Schiesel (2001a): A1, C4.

modernization and expansion projects. Newly founded US communication carriers were carrying a total of $74 billion in debt by late 2000, requiring an annual interest expense of about $7 billion;[38] and AT&T's debt alone reached a high of perhaps $62 billion (late 2000), contributing to a spiral of destabilization that threatened this blue-chip company's very survival.[39] During 2001, all told, some $250 billion of telecommunication industry debt (mostly bonds), a share of which bore rapidly declining ratings, needed to be refinanced.[40]

A handful of analysts began to worry that the scale of debt-financed, frequently duplicative system-building might be outpacing demand by the late 1990s[41] when "private-line" circuit prices were dropping sharply, a process that has continued unabated since.[42] But Wall Street analysts imperturbably forecast continued profit growth, and investment capital continued to pour into the industry. In consequence, by one account a mere 2.6% of US long-distance network capacity was actually in use in early 2001.[43] Comparable overcapacity was apparent in transoceanic submarine cable systems, where "each new Atlantic cable adds as much bandwidth as all the previous infrastructure put together."[44]

During Fall 2000, amid the rapid decline of technology stocks, telecommunication industry executives began to reckon with the glut that market liberalization had induced. The ensuing debacle dwarfed the near-concurrent rout of the dot-coms. There commenced a drum-roll of competitive rate-cutting, network investment pullbacks, precipitous stock-price drop-offs, huge financial losses, employee layoffs, asset sales, business reorganizations, and bankruptcies. Telecommunication industry bonds, widely classed as sub-investment grade ("junk") offerings, comprised as much as one-third of the entire junk-bond market by 2001.[45] And job losses in the technology sector dominated by networks constituted 41% of the 650,000 jobs eliminated in the US between 1 January and 31 May 2001.[46] Broadband system development in the United States momentarily threatened to slow, as leading telecommunication companies and cable system operators pared capital spending projects.

38. Malik (2001): 66–68.
39. Rosenbush (2001): 88; Rosenbush, Grover and Haddad (2001): 52.
40. Curwen (2001): 92; "Moody's Says It May Downgrade Ratings Of Telecom Firms (2001): B6; Silverman (2001): 25.
41. Keefe and Batt (1997) in Katz (1997): 68-9.
42. Galbi (2001): Table 2, 143; Table 1, 142; Table 4, 146 ; TeleGeography (2001).
43. Blumenstein (2001): A1, A 8.
44. Roberts: (2001a): 10
45. Stempel (2001): C4.
46. Pham (2001): C1, C8.

All this had been accomplished under the sign of neoliberalism; but the ultimate costs of the industry's competitive network-building binge remained uncertain. As technology spending by business users and the carriers that sought to serve them slackened, the newfound centrality of that investment within the global economy ensured that the decline's repercussions ramified outward.[47] Because networking provided an increasingly general platform for new cycles of capital accumulation, it was likewise notably implicated in a resurgence of economic stagnation.

While onetime US FCC chairman Reed Hundt sought to insist that the network-building boom he helped along "will benefit the entire economy for years to come,"[48] at present, such arguments carry little weight. The stock market value of the world's telecommunication sector, including operators and equipment manufacturers, fell by $3.8 trillion between its peak (of $6.3 trillion) in March 2000, and September 2001 – far outstripping the combined losses on all of Asia's stock exchanges during the Asian financial crisis of the late 1990s ($813 billion).[49] With Japan, the world's second-largest domestic economy, undergoing a sweeping deflationary spiral, and deflation showing signs of encompassing Europe and the United States as well, the world economy had entered precarious straits. As of 7 September 2001, central bankers not surprisingly remained worried that, as the *Financial Times* reported, the debacle in telecommunications "could still destabilise the global financial system."[50]

Four days later, policymakers were presented with an opportunity to craft a new, "post-neoliberal", response to the crisis in telecommunications and, indeed, to try to reorganize the information sector in general.

Conclusion: Toward authoritarianism?

As many analysts have claimed, the 11 September attacks provided cover under the guise of homeland security for US leaders to force a realignment of global power relations, so as to grant qualitatively greater primacy to US interests. By invading and occupying Iraq, they signalled to the world that the terms of access to the strategic oil resource increasingly would be subject to US determination. At the same time, US

---

47. Blumenstein (2001): A1, A8; Hamilton (2001): A1, A13. In one estimate, overall US investment in information technology was set to fall during 2002 for the first time ever (by 2% compared with annual increases routinely totalled 20% during the late 1990s) – to a spectacular $798 billion. Feder (2001): C3.
48. McKinsey (2001).
49. Roberts (2001b): 10.
50. Roberts (2001a): 9.

leaders cast about for means with which to revive the faltering global economy, an economy which centred increasingly around information and communications. In this context, although "competition" remained US policy orthodoxy, the *laissez-faire* rhetoric of neoliberalism began to erode: an economist in the *Financial Times* even observed that "the capitalist fundamentalists' unswerving faith in the redeeming power of the market has proved to be a dangerous illusion."[51] Often explicitly declaring a need to fuse public and private power, in keeping with a longstanding structural trend, though one that the rhetoric of neoliberalism had tended to obscure, major corporations and state agencies instead worked together in an unfolding campaign of topdown preparations and proposals.

What, we may ask, distinguishes this ongoing anti-democratic mobilization from prior authoritarian experiments following the First and Second World Wars. In my judgment, the answer is to be sought in the fact that this corporate-state endeavour exhibits not a lessening of engagement with digital capitalism's leading sector, but a concerted intensification – often, on a global scale.[52]

Emergency US legislation escalated attacks on citizens' civil liberties; while, by presidential decree, non-nationals faced military tribunals without constitutional protection. These measures struck hard at what had passed for liberal democracy; provided sustenance for ready emulation by authoritarians elsewhere; and themselves possessed important supranational ramifications. They also focused in a newly comprehensive fashion on network systems and applications. Because around four-fifths of Internet access points in Asia, Africa and South America continued to be connected through US cities, for example, the "USA Patriot Act's" grant of temporary(?) prosecutorial powers to state agencies bid fair to expand US jurisdiction extraterritorially; computer security expert Mark Rasch termed this "a massive expansion of US sovereignty": "we're criminalizing anything that happens over the Internet because traffic passes through the United States . . . we will impose our values on anything that happens anywhere in the world provided it passes through our borders."[53]

Building on prior "soft power" initiatives, there rolled forth propaganda via "public diplomacy," jet aircraft-based broadcasts to Afghanistan, expanded Voice of America programming to the Middle East, and a summary termination by AT&T and British Telecom of international telecommunications and financial services offered by Barakat, a Somali

---

51. Beck (2001): 15.
52. For one premonition, see Committee on the Internet in the Evolving Information Infrastructure (2001): 81.
53. In Hopper (2001).

organization that stood accused by the US of financing al-Qaeda.[54] Covert and not-so-covert "infowar" tactics, refined a decade ago against Saddam Hussein and thence in Bosnia-Hercegovina, proliferated anew – first in Afghanistan and then in Iraq. Pursuing "global information dominance", the US transformed enemy information "assets" into prime military targets.[55] Relentless propaganda in the United States itself hammered home to the domestic population that what was branded the "Attack on America" posed an urgent need to "modify" traditional freedoms.

In the space created by war mobilization, numerous other topdown initiatives foregrounded information and communications. Bush Administration officials planned to erect a data network that would link federal, state and local health officials against bioterrorism.[56] This would be built, of course, by corporate network builders, whose sagging revenues would, thus it was hoped, be reinflated. Not to be outdone in their enthusiasm for a new round of militarized Keynesianism, on the other hand, the Silicon Valley companies that had been raised on Defense Department contracts – from Oracle, which originated in a CIA project, to Lockheed Martin, TRW, General Dynamics and Raytheon – stormed into Washington in search of new cost-plus contracts.[57] Possible establishment of what was termed "a secure new government communications network separate from the Internet that would be less vulnerable to attack" constituted a comparable move, of material interest to these and other faltering network equipment and software vendors.[58] Banks and police agencies considered a new information-sharing agreement "that could give authorities unprecedented ability to track terrorists using the US financial system . . ."[59] The "Infragard" program, commencing in 1996 but massively boosted after 11 September offered an apparently even more ambitious and systematic partnership between the FBI and 8,300 companies to share confidential information about threats to cyber- and other infrastructure.[60] Building on Clinton-era initiatives, President Bush's Critical Infrastructure Protection Board, and Office of Homeland Security, finally, constituted quasi-military agencies deliberately resistant to public oversight, whose responsibilities increasingly encompassed telecommunications.[61] On grounds of national

---

54. Rogers (2001): A24; Turner (2001): 9.
55. Denning (1999): 3-9; Romero (2001): C1; Kilibarda (2001).
56. Dreazen (2001): A4.
57. Thurm (2001): B6.
58. Mitchell (2001a): B7.
59. Beckett (2001): A2.
60. "Companies become eyes, ears for FBI" (2003).
61. Oremland (2001a), (2001b); McGuire (2001); Williams (2001): A10.

security, thus, the Bush Administration hoped "to limit the public's access to information that private companies voluntarily provide to the government about critical infrastructure systems . . ."[62] These and other efforts lent themselves both to an attempted reorganization of global power relations, and to the more centrally coordinated corporate-state planning that has become a key hallmark of late capitalism.

Will the political-economic leadership succeed in stabilizing the informationalized political economy on an altered basis? The situation remains fluid and complex, and there exists some countervailing tendencies. In addition to an invigorated grassroots anti-corporate media campaign, disagreements and cross-pressures within the US policymaking establishment have also broken out.[63] Highly significant as well is that the Bush Administration's unilateralism in prosecuting foreign policy alienated not only world public opinion, but also key allies. As the war on Afghanistan was succeeded by war on Iraq, tepid support by German and French leaders for the US gave way to real opposition. This dissensus, the most marked for half a century, of course contained vital self-interested elements. But it also showed real signs of spilling over into the economic realm, for example, in World Trade Organization negotiations, at a time of deepening economic stagnation. All these factors rendered the situation fluid and unpredictable.

In any case, the paramount question lay elsewhere: would conditions in the centre of global capitalism be conducive to a revival of democracy or, rather, would they spawn democracy's authoritarian antithesis?

---

62. Mitchell (2001b): B9.
63. Thus one-time Nixon speechwriter and *New York Times* columnist William Safire protested the "dictatorial power" being claimed by the Bush Administration. Safire (2001): A31.

References

AdvertisingAge (2000) '100 leading media companies by net revenue', S2.

Alonso-Zaldivar, Ricardo (2001) 'Nation's infrastructure crumbling, report says', *Los Angeles Times* (hereafter LAT) 8 March: A9.

Arquilla, John, and David Ronfeldt (2001) *Networks and netwars: The future of terror, crime, and militancy.* Santa Monica: Rand Corporation.

Aufderheide, Patricia (1999) *Communications policy and the public interest: The Telecommunications Act of 1996.* New York: Guilford.

Balnaves, Mark, James Donald and Stephanie Hemelryk Donald (2001) *Penguin atlas of media and information.* New York: Penguin.

Barshefsky, Charlene (1999) 'Electronic commerce: Trade policy in a borderless world', The Woodrow Wilson Center, Washington, D.C., 29 July.

Beatty, Sally, and Jeanne Cummings (2001) 'Networks hear from Bush on use of al Qaeda footage,' *Wall Street Journal* (hereafter *WSJ*) 11 October: A10.

Beck, Ulrich (2001) 'Globalisation's Chernobyl', *Financial Times* (hereafter *FT*) 6 November: 15.

Beckett, Paul (2001) 'Big banks, U.S. weigh pooling data on terror,' *WSJ* 26 November: A2.

Berman, Dennis K. (2001) 'Survey suggests access to Internet reduces time spent watching TV', *WSJ* 29 November: B1.

Blouin, Chantal (2000) 'The WTO agreement on basic telecommunications: A Reevaluation', *Telecommunications Policy* 24: 135–142.

Blumenstein, Rebecca (2001) 'How the fiber barons plunged the nation into a telecom glut', *WSJ* 18 June: A1, A8.

Buckman, Rebecca, Pui-Wing Tam and Mylene Mangalindan (2001) 'As rivals retrench, Microsoft muscles in on their home turf', *WSJ* 20 November: A1, A10.

Campbell, Don (2001) 'Suddenly, foreign news trumps local chatter', *USA Today* 16 October: 15A.

Carreyrou, John (2001) 'Vivendi posts strong earnings in third reriod, stands by targets', *WSJ* 31 October: A21.

Committee on the Internet in the Evolving Information Infrastructure (2001) *Computer Science and Telecommunications Board, National Research Council, The Internet's coming of age.* Washington, D.C.: National Academy Press.

"Companies become eyes, ears for FBI," *News-Gazette* (Champaign, Illinois), 23 June 2003: A1, A6.

Curwen, Peter (2001) 'Buddy, can you spare a billion?' *Info* 3 (1), February: 92.

Davis, Jim, and Michael Stack (1997) 'The digital advantage', in Jim Davis, Thomas Hirschl and Michael Stack, (eds.), *Cutting edge.* London: Verso: 121–44.

Denning, Dorothy E. (1999) *Information warfare and security.* Reading: Addison-Wesley.

Dreazen, Yochi J. (2001) 'Ridge plans health-data network to defend against bioterrorism', *WSJ* 28 November: A4.

Dreazen, Yochi and Andrew Caffrrey (2001) 'Now, public works seem too precious for the free market', *WSJ* 19 November: A1.

Feder, Barnaby J. (2001) 'Less information technology spending seen', *NYT* 29 October: C3.

Galbi, Douglas A. (2001) "Growth in the 'new economy': US bandwidth use and pricing across the 1990s", *Telecommunications Policy* 25: 142–6.

Grimes, Christopher (2001) 'Terrorist attacks hit AOL forecast', *FT* 25 September: 15.

Haider, Masood (2001) 'Pentagon blocks news pictures to media', retrieved at http://www.dawn.com/2001/10/20/top14.htm.

Hamilton, Walter (2001) 'Corporate tech spending helped set stage for slump', *LAT* 14 March: A1, A13.

Hobsbawm, Eric (1994) *The age of extremes*. New York: Pantheon.

Hopper, D. Ian (2001) 'New law lets U.S. nab foreign hackers', Associated Press, 22 November.

Hundt, Jr., Reed (2000) *You say you want a revolution*. New Haven: Yale University Press.

Katz, Harry C. (1997) *Telecommunications restructuring and employment relations worldwide*. Ithaca: Cornell.

Keefe, Jeffrey H. and Rosemary Batt (1997) 'United States', in Katz (1997): 31–88.

Kilibarda, Konstantin (2001) 'Militarizing the media monopoly, at http://www. infowarmonitor.netmodules.php?op=modload&name=Sections&file= index&req=viewarticle&artid=15&page=1.

Kimball, Penn (1994) *Downsizing the news: Network cutbacks in the nation's capital*. Washington, D.C.: Woodrow Wilson Center Press.

Knowledge@Wharton (2001) 'Behind the telecom meltdown', CNET News.com, 25 October. Retrieved 26 October 2001 at http://news.cnet.com/news/0-1004-202-7647580-0.html.

Koerner, Brendan I. (2001) 'Losing signal', *Mother Jones* September/October: 37–44.

Kohut, Andrew (2000) 'America the connected', *New York Times* (hereafter NYT) 23 June: A25.

Labaton, Stephen with Steve Lohr (2001) 'States weigh going it alone in legal battle with Microsoft', *NYT* 5 November: C1, C6.

Le Monde diplomatique (2001) http://english@Monde-diplomatique.fr, 'A changed world and a special offer', 12 November.

London, Simon (2001) 'High-tech rally sparks new crash fear', *FT* 28 November: 21.

Malik, Om (2001) 'Wrong number', *Red Herring* 16 January: 66-68.

McChesney, Robert W. (2000) *Rich media, poor democracy*. Urbana: University of Illinois Press.

McGuire, David (2001) 'Bush lays out cyber-protection plan', Washtech.com, 17 October.

McKinsey, (2001) 'Weathering the telecom storm', McKinsey Quarterly Special to CNET News.com, 3 October. Retrieved at http://news.cnet.com/news/0-1004-201-7387853-0.html?tag=prntfr.

McManus, John H. (1994) *Market-driven journalism: Let the citizen beware?* Thousand Oaks: Sage Publications.

Mermigas, Diane (1999) 'How companies deal with the Net', *Electronic Media* 19 April: 34.

Mitchell, Alison (2001a) 'To forestall a "Digital Pearl Harbor", U.S. looks to system separate from Internet', *NYT* 17 November: B7.

Mitchell, Alison (2001b) 'Limits sought on access to company data', *NYT* 28 November: B9.

'Moody's says it may downgrade ratings of telecom firms', (2001) *WSJ* 5 October: B6.

Oliner, S.D. and D.E. Sichel (2000) 'The resurgence of growth in the late 1990s: Is information technology the story?' Working paper, May. Retrieved at http://www.federalreserve.gov/pubs/feds/2000/200020pap.pdf.

Oremland, Ryan (2001a) 'Gilmore stresses need for improved coordination on infrastructure protection', *TR Daily* 17 October.

Oremland, Ryan (2001b) 'White House said to back "narrow" exemption for critical infrastructure', *TR Daily* 18 October.

Peers, Martin, and Joe Flint (2001) 'Media executives diverge on ad outlook', *WSJ* 3 October: B15.

Pham, Alex (2001) 'Nortel forecasts $19.2-billion loss, sets more job cuts', *Los Angeles Times* 16 June: C1, C8.

Pristin, Terry (2001) 'Phone service improves, but many are still without power in Lower Manhattan', *NYT* 14 September: A12.

Quinlan, Joseph (2001) 'No stopping the global M&A train', *FT* 12 November: 24.

Ramstad, Evan, and Kortney Stringer (2001) 'In race to lay fiber, telecom firms wreak havoc on city streets', *WSJ* 27 February: A1.

Roberts, Dan (2001a) 'Glorious hopes on a trillion-dollar scrapheap', *FT* 5 September: 10.

Roberts, Dan (2001b) 'The tangled legacy of a derailed revolution', *FT* 7 September: 9.

Rogers, David 2001 'U.S. dials up radio network to reach young Muslims', *WSJ* 27 November: A24.

Romero, Simon (2001) 'Telecommunications entrepreneur with a colorful resume', *NYT* 26 November: C1.

Rosenbush, Steve (2001) 'Armstrong's last stand', *Business Week* 5 February: 88.

Rosenbush, Steve, Ron Grover and Charles Haddad (2001) 'Hits a $5 billion wall', *Business Week* 15 October: 52.

Roycroft, Trevor R. and Martha Garcia-Murrilo (2000) 'Trouble reports as an indicator of service quality: The influence of competition, technology, and regulation', *Telecommunications Policy* 24: 947–66.

Safire, William (2001) 'Seizing dictatorial power', *NYT* 15 November: A31.

Saunders, Doug. 2001. 'Hollywood goes to bat for nation', *Toronto Globe and Mail* 19 October.

Schiesel, Seth (2001a) 'For some who use calling cards, the number is 1-800-BEWARE', *NYT* 15 February: A1, C4.

Schiesel, Seth (2001b) 'AOL, blaming terrorist attacks, says it will fall far short of its goals', *NYT* 25 September: C8.

Schiesel, Seth (2001c) 'Vivendi of France reports a strong financial quarter', *NYT* 31 October: C8.

Schiller, Dan (1982) *Telematics and government*. Norwood: Ablex.

Schiller, Dan (1986) 'Transformations of news in the U.S. information market', in P. Golding, G. Murdock and P. Schlesinger, (eds.), *Communicating politics: Mass communications and the political process*. Leicester: Leicester University Press: 19–36.

Schiller, Dan (1999) *Digital capitalism: Networking the global market system*. Cambridge: MIT Press.

Schiller, Dan (2001) 'World communications in today's age of capital', *Emergences* 11 (1): 51–68.

Silverman, Gary (2001) 'Review features telecoms loans', *FT* 8 October: 25.

Spiegel, Peter (2001) 'Outsider at the windows', *FT* 30 November: 12.

Stanley, Alessandra (2001) 'President is using TV show and the public in combination to combat terrorism', *NYT* 11 October: B2.

Stempel, Jonathan (2001). 'Falling telecom issues lead new slump in junk bonds', *LAT* 5 April: C4.

TeleGeography (2001) *International bandwidth 2001*. Washington, D.C. TeleGeography, Inc.

Thurm, Scott (2001) 'Silicon Valley returns to its roots in government work', *WSJ* 22 October: B6.

Turner, Mark (2001) 'Barakat has plug pulled on telecoms', *FT* 16 November: 9.

United Nations Conference on Trade and Development (2000) *World investment report 2000: Cross-border mergers and acquisitions and development*. New York: United Nations.

United Nations Conference on Trade and Development (2001) *World investment report 2001: Promoting linkages*. New York: United Nations.

US Federal Communications Commission (2000) International Bureau, Report on international telecommunications markets 1999 update, prepared for Senator Ernest F. Hollings, Committee on Commerce, Science and Transportation, U.S. Senate, 14 January.

Wellenius, Bjorn, Carlos Alberto Primo Braga and Christine Zhen-Wei Qiang (2000) 'Investment and growth of the information infrastructure: Summary results of a global survey', *Telecommunications Policy* 24: 637–42.

Williams, Krissah (2001) 'U.S. seeks to build secure online network', *Washington Post* 11 October: A10.

Witcher, S. Karene (2001) 'News Corp., in upbeat outlook, expects rebound in U.S. earnings', *WSJ* 12 October: A13.

Young, Shawn and Dennis K. Berman (2001) 'Trade Center attack shows vulnerability of telecom network', *WSJ* 19 October: A1, A8.

Young, Shawn and Deborah Solomon (2001) 'Verizon effectively rebuilds network for NYSE', *WSJ* 18 September: B7.

The State, the Market, and Media Control in China

Yuezhi Zhao

The Chinese media system has undergone an unprecedented transformation in the reform era that began in the late 1970s. While the Party state continues to exercise tight control, and is gradually modernizing its controlling mechanisms, market forces have permeated and transformed every aspect of the media system. Through a series of overlapping processes of accommodation, appropriation, state-engineered market consolidation, and selective incorporation of private and foreign media capital, Party state power is increasingly converging with the power of capital in the Chinese media. This fusion of Party state and market power has created a media system that serves the interests of the country's political and economic elite, while suppressing and marginalizing opposing and alternative voices. This chapter provides an overview of the evolving structure of media ownership and control and its implications for popular expression in China.

Modernization and the changing parameters of media control

Despite a quarter century of economic and social liberalization, and the apparent erosion of centralized control by market forces, the Party state still plays a formidable role in the Chinese media system. Evidently, the Party state's propaganda content changed as the objective shifted from a utopian one of raising people's consciousness to a more pragmatic one of promoting its own legitimacy (He, 2000a; Zhao, 1998). The Party's traditional regime of proactive and retroactive control, exercised primarily under the directives of the Party's powerful Propaganda Department, remains. This regime of control encompasses the imprisonment of journalists, the closure and forced reorganization of media outlets, editorial censorship, the imposition of an official line, or "the size of the mouth" (*kuojing*) in media reporting of major events, regular media monitoring by a specialized team of Party elders, the appointment of key management personnel in major media outlets, and the maintenance of ad hoc rules regarding media operations, or "propaganda disciplines" (*xuanchuan jilu*). For example, a crucial 1953 rule that forbids Party organs from criticizing the Party committee to which they are affiliated still applies, and remains a key instrument that keeps the media under the control of Party committees at various levels. Simultaneously, as part of the modernization and refurbishment of the Chinese state, media control and news management is being subjected to "processes of secularisation, formalization, and regularization" (Lee, 2000). Such processes involve the creation of new institutions, regulatory regimes, and deployment of modern media management practices that include:

- The establishment of state media and publicity management institutions. The State Press and Publications Administration (SPPA), established in 1987, is responsible for licensing, overall planning, regulation, and market discipline of the Chinese print media. The State Council Information Office (SCIO), modelled after the press offices of Western governments, is the de facto external arm of the Party Propaganda Department and manages media messages concerning China on the international stage. To coordinate control and strengthen state direction over the content of the Internet, a new unit, the Internet Information Management Bureau, was added to the SCIO in early 2000. The rhetoric of separating Party and state functions has little impact on the actual operations of these two critical state organs, as their operations are subordinate to the Party's Propaganda Department, which, as part of the Party's effort to update its own image, has been renamed the Party's Publicity Department in its English translation.

- The promulgation of media rules and regulations as a way to institutionalize and regularize media control. In abstract, the Chinese constitution affirms the right of Chinese citizens to freedom of speech. However, a whole series of laws, regulations, and often, rules and circulars from relevant Party and state agencies, serve to limit this right. The Party's Propaganda Department, for example, collected as many as 69 such media and cultural industry related rules and regulations issued by various government departments between 1996 and 1997 alone (Policy and Regulation Research Office, 1998). Topics ranged from the establishment of media outlets to censorship details, from the implementation of annual reviews for media outlets to the regulation of press credentials for journalists, and from the amount of financial penalties to be applied to publishers for various violations, to the minimum circulation figures of a newspaper. The regime of

Internet regulation is both expansive and draconian, with laws and policies aiming at controlling every aspect of Internet operations. The year 2000 alone, for example, witnessed the promulgation of six major regulations aiming at Internet content control, ranging from legislation enacted by the National People's Congress, regulations issued by the State Council and the Ministry of Information Industry (Ang, 2003; Cheng, 2003). These highly arbitrary and piecemeal responses to rising problems of media control are not always enforced; nevertheless, they represent the Party state's effort to make media control more acceptable by virtue of its predictability.

- The incorporation of modern Western media management techniques. The Tiananmen Square debacle in 1989, in which the Party state was completely upstaged by protesting students and the international media in the battle over media images and public legitimacy, undermined the last bit of the Party's confidence in the self-evident nature of its truth and its traditional approach to media control. The art of public relations, first adopted by Chinese businesses, is being adapted to serve the state's propaganda objectives. "Leadership image design" has become a new topic for applied media research. Public opinion polls, once condemned as a "bourgeoisie" practice, have been strategically incorporated into media management and media reporting (Zhang, Yong, 2000; Zhao, 2003). Similarly, proactive news reporting in cases of negative events is aimed at turning the Party state into a primary definer in a media world in which simple suppression no longer works: when an explosion occurred in Tiananmen Square on 15 February, 2000, the state media and the state controlled website http://www.china.org.cn quickly reported the incident and described the perpetrator as a "mentally ill" individual to deflect foreign media reports about the politically motivated nature of the suicide explosion (Wang and Zhang, 2000: 27–28).

- In an era of media explosion, "passive censorship", which aims at limiting the impact of oppositional ideas on a small elite circle by neglect, is adopted as a more practical form of ideological control. In the past, due in part to the Party's self-righteous impulse of maintaining ideological purity, and its self-proclaimed status as the monopoly holder of truth, the Party would typically organize a public critique of ideas deemed "incorrect". As part of the "no debate" decree imposed by Deng Xiaoping (that is, the Party does not engage in ideological debates regarding the political nature of the reform) and the Party leadership's own increasing cynicism over the effectiveness of its propaganda efforts, the Party realized that public criticism of oppositional and deviant ideas often has the reverse impact of rendering publicity to these ideas. These days, when a problematic book slips through the censorship system and appears in the market, authorities quickly and quietly try to stop the distribution of the work, but do not use the mass media to give adverse publicity to the book. Consequently, as Geremie Barmé (1998) observed, although controversial books have been published over the past few years, their reception is often limited to a small urban intellectual elite.

Of course, control is never total. In the 1980s, an unruly media system, staffed by liberal-minded journalists, played a crucial role in the 1989 student movement. As the leadership was engaging in a divisive power struggle during the height of the student movement, the Party's chain of command over the media system temporarily broke down. Journalists seized this opportunity to provide sympathetic coverage of the demonstrations, and mobilized support for the student movement. In the 1990s, the wide spread of the *Falun Gong* belief system, which had been condemned by the Party as anti-modern, anti-science heresy, was a slap in the face of the Party's attempt to maintain ideological and cultural control, and its topdown drive to build a "socialist spiritual civilization". The proliferation of commercial printing facilities and the availability of cheap video and audio reproduction technologies led to the flourishing of underground media production and distribution channels. Even state-sponsored publishing houses, driven by the commercial imperative, participated in the publication of *Falun Gong* material. The Internet, of course, has been instrumental both in spreading *Falun Gong* messages and in sustaining the group's transnational networking activities and media activism in the face of massive state repression (Zhao, 2003a).

Moreover, censorship is no longer a simple black and white issue in contemporary China. While the political elite may agree on the censorship of certain information and ideas vis-à-vis the general public, there may be divisive views within its own ranks. Censorship is always deeply implicated in elite power struggles. Indeed, the publication of certain news and views can serve as an effective bargaining chip in intra-Party policy and power struggles. Initial censorship and subsequent openness in media reporting of the spread of Severe Acute Respiratory Syndrome (SARS) in Spring 2003, for example, is implicated in power struggles inside the Party state, more specifically in the intricate politics and protracted process of power transition between the so-called "Third Generation" and "Fourth Generation" leaderships centred around Jiang Zemin and Hu Jintao respectively. In cases relating to the elite political debates, censorship is increasingly "more a matter of negotiation than negation" (Barmé, 1998: 258).

Finally, the introduction of Western-style media formats, such as live phone-in talk shows, not to mention the satellite and Internet technologies, have also created new problems for media control and put constant pressures on the Party to keep up (Lynch, 1999; Zhao, 1998). For example, although state broadcasting guidelines require the use of time delay devices in live talk show programs, only 50% of 695 provincial radio talk shows and 30% of 43 television talk shows were equipped with such devices in 1999 (Tian, 2000: 3). Even China Central Television (CCTV), the most tightly controlled television outlet in the country, has been lax in turning on its imported time delay device. On 16 October 1999, a "subversive" individual was able to seize the opportunity as a phone-in participant in a non-political weekend talk show programme and shout a "reactionary slogan" to a national audience (Tian, 2000: 4). The event shocked the Politburo, exposed the broadcasting system's weakness in management, and led to a series of efforts at strengthening control over broadcasting.

Nevertheless, the consequences of overt political control are profound. In addition to the major post-1989 political purge that saw the closure of liberal media outlets and the removal of outspoken journalists from their jobs, smaller-scale "surgical" operations have continued. The late 1990s, for example, witnessed the closure and major reorganization of a number of elite liberal journals, including the *Orient*, the *Way*, and the *Streets*, and the removal of chief editors at the country's two most outspoken popular newspapers, the *Beijing Youth News* and the *Nanfang Weekend*, for various violations of the Party's "propaganda disciplines". Although it is possible that Hu Jintao's new leadership may eventually support a more open media system, such a change is by no means certain, even if Hu is able to consolidate his leadership soon. Jiang Zemin's refusal to transfer the command of military power to the new generation of leaders underscores the unfinished nature of this power transition at this point. The ramifications for the media system have been immediate. While there have been some signs of change in the media, including a reduction in broadcasting minutes devoted to the ritualistic display of political power by national leaders at CCTV prime time news, and openness in media reporting of the SARS outbreak after the initial cover-up, blunt political crackdown remains the order of the day. The Nanfang Daily Press Group became the first victim of political censorship under Hu Jintao's new leadership when one of its subsidiaries, *21 Shiji Shijie Baodao*, was shut down in March 2003 after it published an interview with a senior Party intellectual who called for greater political openness. By June 2003, another newspaper, the *Beijing Xinbao*, had also been shut down, after it printed an essay criticizing the National People's Congress, China's parliament, for its rubber stamp status (Associate Press, 2003).

Liberal media outlets, however, are no longer the only casualties of Party censorship in China. As the Party increasingly colludes with domestic and international capital, and "is moving to reposition itself as a de facto right-wing dictatorship" (Gilley, 2001: 18), leftist ideas and publications have also become the overt targets of Party censorship. A quarter century of economic reforms have profoundly changed the Party's political orientations. While Deng Xiaoping sanctioned capitalist-style economic reforms by adopting pragmatism and prohibiting ideological debates on the exact political nature of the reforms, his successor Jiang Zemin supervised a series of major political and ideological changes after Deng's death in 1997. These ranged from recognizing private business as an important component of the socialist economy in China's state constitution, to repositioning capitalists and the newly enriched managerial and professional strata as the de facto advanced productive and cultural forces that the Party represents, and to bringing capitalists to the Party itself. Consequently, as Bruce Gilley has observed, the Party now "looks more and more like the right-wing authoritarianism of a Suharto of Indonesia or a Franco of Spain than anything Marx might have dreamt up" (2001: 19). Indeed, the leadership was so afraid of critiques of "capitalist restoration", and charges about its betrayal of its avowed core constituency of Chinese farmers and workers, that it forced the closure of the Marxist theoretical journal, *Zhenli de Zhuiqiu* (The Search for Truth), after it spoke out against the rightward drift of the Party in Summer 2001. For the same reason, Chinese critics of globalization – covering a wide ideological spectrum ranging from unreconstructed Maoists to anti-American nationalists, old-fashioned bureaucrats and protectionists, to neo-Marxist academics, and admirers of globalization protesters in the West – have been marginalized (Zhao, 2003). As the *Guardian* observed, these critics "get little coverage in the official media, and are not asked to express their views in the columns of newspapers that hail the 'courage' and 'foresight' of a 'great nation' that has decided to 'join the powerful torrent of world economic evolution'" (Bobin, 2002).

In short, although officially sanctioned anti-corruption stories have become popular media fare since the mid-1990s and created a sense of openness in the media (Zhao, 2000a), the media still observe strict guidelines in their coverage of major domestic and international events – from China's WTO entry (Zhao, 2003) and the NATO bombing of the Chinese embassy in Belgrade in 1999, to the reporting of the SARS outbreak in early 2003. Of course, it is almost unimaginable for the domestic news media to report on the numerous incidents of protests by overtaxed farmers and laid off state enterprise workers and uncompensated pensioners. Such protests, some violent and with thousands in attendance, took place throughout the country regularly throughout the 1990s. Ordinary Chinese who provided details of these protests to the Chinese National People's Congress, and the international media have received jail sentences as long as ten years (Zhang, 1999). This is arguably one of the biggest censored political stories in China in the past decade. Since political stability has been the overriding concern of the central leadership, and the possibility of leftist criticisms reaching the disenfranchised farmers and workers to form a formidable political opposition remains a potential, this is no small accomplishment.

Winners and losers in media commercialization

Concurrent with the fortification and modernization of media control and right wing drift in media censorship is the rapid commercialization of Party-controlled state media. Media commercialization is part and parcel of a broad state-directed transformation of the Chinese political economy from state socialism to "socialism with Chinese characteristics", or more appropriately, capitalism with Chinese characteristics. On the one hand, an expanding market economy fuelled a media boom and created the material conditions for the establishment of market-oriented media outlets. On the other hand, the overburdened state, with a declining share of the national gross domestic product (GDP), actively pushed existing media organizations to the market with the severance of direct subsidies and the provision for financial incentives, including tax breaks, performance-based salary supplements, and operational freedoms. Although commercialism has taken many extreme forms in the local media in the 1990s, it is important to note that the process started in 1978, at the very top of the media system, with the introduction of a for-profit accounting system by the *People's Daily* and several other national newspapers. Since then, especially with the suppression of the media democratization movement in 1989, and Deng's call for accelerated capitalistic developments in 1992, a commercial revolution has swept every corner of the Chinese media industry. The economic basis of the Chinese media has been effectively transformed from a system based on state subsidies to one based on advertisement subsidies (Zhao, 2000b).

In the 1980s and early 1990s, there were initial hesitations and lingering leftist concerns about the capitalistic nature of a market-supported media system. The energy for media commercialization came as much from state planners from above as from economic self-interest of media organizations and journalists from below. By the mid-1990s, however, media commercialization had became a more explicit state policy, promoted from above as a "law of motion" in newspaper publishing, and enforced through "thought liberation" sessions and media restructuring campaigns organized from above (Zhao, 2000b: 13–14). The State Press and Publications Administration (SPPA), in its "Plans for the Development of the Press and Publication Industries in Year 2000 and Year 2010". for example, stipulated that "newspapers must raise the percentage of advertisement revenue in its total revenue from an average of 60% in 1996 to 70% by 2000, and 80% by 2010" (SPPA, PRC, 2000: 57). This is both a market-driven and state-planned media economy.

The replacement of state subsidies with advertisement revenues, of course, is not simply a business matter. Advertisement is itself a form of propaganda. It not only influences media content, but shapes media structure as a "de facto" licensing authority (Curran, 1981). The dual compulsions of state control and market imperative have significantly transformed the content and structure of the Chinese media. Commercial propaganda rivals, if not replaces, political propaganda as the dominant form of mobilization speech. The appropriation of Maoist political slogans by the advertisement industry, demonstrated vividly by Barmé (1999), is thus not surprising. Though Maoist political propaganda and current commercial propaganda differ in content, there are similarities in the structure and ideological consequences of both discourses. Maoist political propaganda promotes the cult of political personality; commercial speech cultivates commodity fetishism. Maoism instructs the politicized subject of a socialist state to dedicate his or her transient life to the transcendental cause of "serving the people", while commercial speech directs the all-consuming subject to devote his or her limited life to the unlimited world of wealth accumulation and personal consumption. In an era of state-mandated consumerism, to consume is to be politically correct. Communist symbols and icons such as "East Is Red" and "Red Flag" have all become brand names for consumer products, and the Cultural Revolution has become just another popular decorating motif in dining and entertainment establishments. Even Mao's famous slogan "To Carry the Revolution to the End" has been appropriated by consumer magazines to promote new lines of jeans or cosmetics: "To Carry the Jeans to the End" declared the cover of the inaugural issue of the *China City Fashion*, launched in November 2000 as yet another trendy magazine catering to the urban white collar female market. The oft-noted tendency of "demobilized liberalization" (Lee, 2000: 560), which describes the transformation of the Chinese media from being an instrument of political mobilization and socialist indoctrination during the Maoist era to economic modernization and image management in the reform era, must be complemented with an understanding of the new role of advertisement in the intensified mobilization of consumerist desires and impulses. If Mao aimed to perpetuate the regime through "continuous revolution" and ongoing political mobilization through the media, the current regime survives upon political demobilization, particularly the containment of grassroots protests and the prevention of communicative linkages and formation of new social movements among disenfranchised social groups.

In addition to advertisements, commercial propaganda, the promotion of businesses, entrepreneurs, products and services, has become regular media fare, and another means by which media institutions and individual journalists accelerate the initial capital accumulation process. Those who can afford to hire public relations agents and image consultants to shape media messages, and to provide journalists with cash bribes, have the power to gain media access. Furthermore, given the official nature of the Chinese media, commercial propaganda becomes conflated with political propaganda and assumes the discursive power of the latter. A story about a successful business is simultaneously a story about the success of the Party's economic reform programme and its ideology of openness. A story about a star entrepreneur, in the Party's traditional journalistic discourse of "role model" reporting, confers enormous political and social capital to that individual, who in turn translates this power into economic power (Zhao, 1998). The following description, by Lui Yong, a reporter at the *Yangcheng Evening News*, captured the rising symbolic power of the economic elite in the media:

> Like other sectors, mass media organizations entered a rapid process of commercialisation in the 1990s. The hottest topics are no longer the sentiments of young poets and would be young poets, nor layoffs, unemployment, rural migrants, and other mundane stories. The protagonists of the stories have shifted to big shots and bosses, getting rich and gold rush. With commercialisation and the shift toward business, literature and the masses have become rapidly marginalized (2000: 302).

At the structural level, the shift to business subsidy through advertisement to media firms has been mainly responsible for the relative decline of the traditional monolithic national and provincial Party organs, and the rise of urban mass appeal newspapers (the "evening papers" in the 1980s and early 1990s and the "metro papers" in the mid and late 1990s) and broadcast channels. The same process has also been largely responsible for the proliferation of specialized business and consumer media outlets, and the marginalization of media outlets catering to social groups who are in the majority in numbers, but marginal in their political and economic power: workers, farmers, and poor women. Behind this process of "uneven liberalization" of the media that has created "new winners and losers" (Chen and Lee, 1997; Wu, 2000), therefore, is the (re)allocation of discursive power in an increasingly stratified Chinese society. The proliferation of newspapers specialized in stock analysis, elite business magazines and the availability of Chinese versions of Western consumer magazines such as *Elle* and *Esquire* (selling for 20 yuan per issue in the late 1990s, the equivalent of one day's salary for an unskilled labourer), is as much the unfolding of some abstract principle of media liberalization as a concrete manifestation of the class orientation of the media system.

It is often said that the Party maintains tight political control, but is loose in non-political business and lifestyle areas. For this reason, the Chinese media system is often seen as bifurcated and schizophrenic (He, 2000b; Lee, 2000). However, it can be argued that the persistence of control in the political domain, and liberalization in the economic and lifestyle spheres, are two sides of the same coin that serve the interests of the political and economic elite. The suppression of news about farmer and worker protests goes hand in hand with liberalization in business reporting, and the proliferation of glossy consumer and lifestyle publications. Although a capitalist economy may serve as a necessary precondition for liberal democracy, in the case of China, the suppression and containment of the voices of workers, farmers, and other groups that are disenfranchised from the very process of capitalist development have gone hand in hand with the consolidation of a capitalistic economy, rapid social polarization, and the creation of a privileged urban consumer class.

This, of course, does not mean that workers, farmers, and other disenfranchised social and cultural groups had a voice in the media system during the Maoist era. China was never a classless egalitarian society – as Maoist ideology seemed to have implied. Under Mao, the ruling elite and the urban minority enjoyed the relative economic security of state socialism while the rural population lived in a state of virtual apartheid. It was mainly the grain-growing peasants, not the urban population, who starved to death during the policy-induced famine following the Great Leap Forward of 1958. Although the publication of "scar literature" about the sufferings of the urban-based bureaucratic and cultural elite, and the critique of the so-called "egalitarianism" under Mao was part of the media's ideological mobilization that paved the way for economic reforms in the late 1970s, there has been no official recognition of the massive famine that took nearly 30 million lives, and few of China's established media gatekeepers and symbol producers have shown outrage.

Post-Mao reforms started with some promise for genuine democratization in Chinese society and in the media system. It is worthwhile to note in this context that although the *Worker's Daily*, the organ of the official trade union, the All China Federation of Workers, was established in 1949, the *Farmer's Daily* and the *China Women's News*, two national newspapers established in the name of the two largest social groups, but were generally seen in elite media circles by the late 1990s as marginal papers because of their weak political and financial clout, were not created during the Maoist period. Rather, they were established, and flourished, during the relatively politically open period of the 1980s. They were founded not on the orders of the Party's Propaganda Department for the purpose of ideological indoctrination, but by individuals with a social commitment to these groups and are the fruits of the general process of societal democratization during that period. Although these papers have never had the autonomy to speak freely, they have tried to speak out for their respective constituents, and as Guoguang Wu noted, they can be more courageous than strict Party and government organs in voicing different opinions (2000: 54). Their relative decline in the 1990s, both in circulation and in relative institutional power, was a result of not only overt political intervention, but also economic marginalization as these papers were not desirable advertisement vehicles. This is a clear sign of the class and gender bias of a market-based media system.

State mandated recentralization and the consolidation of party media capital

The unique aspect of Chinese media transformation is that, rather than creating a new institutional structure, market relations have been adopted and contained by the existing Party-controlled media structure. Thus, the market-oriented transformation of the Chinese news media occurred within the orbit of the Party state (Zhao, 2000b). In the newspaper sector, the licensing system, enforced by the SPPA, has ensured the Party's control over the press structure during the process of commercialization. No newspaper can be set up as an independent business. All prospective newspaper enterprises must be registered under a recognized institutional publisher or sponsor that includes Party committees, government bureaucracies, mass organizations, and other institutions of above county-level official standing. Among these authorized publishers, only Party committees, presumably capable of standing above different social groups and representing the "general interest" of the population, can publish general interest papers. All other publishers must confine their papers either to a special social group (women, youth, workers, and so forth) or to an area of specialization (business, sports, culture, health, and so forth).

Consequently, although there seem to be clear "winners and losers" in the media market with the rise of mass appeal papers and the decline of national and provincial Party organs, as far as the Party state is concerned, this development is not a zero-sum power game. Since the established Party organs and national, provincial and municipal Party committees have exclusive rights to enter the mass appeal media market, mass appeal papers are typically owned and controlled by core Party organs, which are in turn controlled by Party committees at various levels. The "evening papers", or the general interest social and entertainment oriented afternoon daily tabloids, were mostly published/revived in the 1980s and early 1990s by major provincial and municipal Party committees as second papers intended for the urban family, or by provincial and municipal Party organs as their urban subsidiaries. For example, the Guangdong provincial Party committee published the official organ, the *Nanfang Daily*, and the mass appeal afternoon paper, the *Yangcheng Evening News*. The "metro papers", which flourished by the mid-1990s and found a niche market between the official Party organs and the evening papers, are all subsidiaries of provincial Party organs. An example is the *Nanfang Daily*'s *Nanfang Metro News*, a mass appeal urban daily aimed at readers in the Guangzhou metropolitan area. While the market imperative makes mass appeal papers less overtly propagandist and more outspoken on social issues, they have limited institutional and editorial autonomy. Their rise underscores the market-based symbolic power of the urban middle class within the Party's hegemonic framework.

Still, by the mid-1990s, the decentralization, fragmentation, and socialization of the media market had become a concern for the central Party authorities. In the newspaper sector, although the Party-controlled mass appeal sector has been a political and market success, many bureaucratic and trade papers within the governmental and societal sectors are limited in circulation, and rely heavily on office subscriptions and direct financial subsidies from their institutional sponsors. Functioning as propaganda outlets for their sponsoring government bodies, and a means by which government bureaucracies extract subscription fees from subordinate units, these papers are the products of "bureaucratic capitalism", a particular form of state capitalism that involves the use of political power and official influence for pecuniary gain by bureaucratic units through capitalist or quasi-capitalist economic activities (Meisner, 1996: 301). They undermined the circulation and advertising base of central and provincial Party organs, inflicting heavy financial burdens on grassroots Party state units with forced subscriptions, and created "political troubles" by breaking the Party's political and moral codes, going beyond state-prescribed areas of specialization, or illegally contracting out editorial spaces and selling press cards to unauthorized groups and individuals operating outside the orbit of the Party state.

Similar structural problems in the broadcasting sector had also become apparent by the mid-1990s. At the eve of the economic reforms in the late 1970s, broadcasting provision was centralized at the national and provincial levels, while municipal and county governments relayed central and provincial programmes. The central state, incapable of providing the huge financial investments necessary for increased national television coverage, decentralized broadcasting provisions and allowed municipal and county governments to mobilize their own resources to build full-scale radio and television stations in a crucial 1983 policy (Guo, 1991: 186–94). This led to a proliferation of local radio and television stations. Simultaneously, provincial stations began to set up market-oriented subsidiary channels in the late 1980s to capitalize on an expanding urban advertisement market and an increasing television audience. The spread of cable technology in the late 1980s and early 1990s created yet another wave of television station multiplication at the provincial and municipal levels. By the mid-1990s, China had boasted of a total of 3,125 television stations (Liu, 2000: 269). Although all these stations were owned by the government at various levels, they operated as financially independent units, were highly profit-oriented, and often in direct competition with each other for programming and advertisements. In another important development, most provinces had sent their main television channel through the satellite-cable technological configuration to a national audience by the mid-1990s. The availability of more than 20 provincial satellite channels and a whole range of local channels in ordinary cable households completely changed the Chinese television scene, and challenged the monopoly of China Central Television in the national television market.

Within the general framework of public ownership, governments at various levels exercised de facto proprietary rights over their affiliated media operations, with direct financial stakes in these operations. Moreover, the personal incomes of employees were closely linked to their profitability. The profit motive is a driving force, and competition between media outlets affiliated with various Party state units is intense. For many broadcasting stations, especially those at the municipal and county levels with little in-house production capacity, the most profitable means is to broadcast imported shows beyond the state-set quotas, or even pirated foreign, Hong Kong and Taiwanese entertainment shows. Similarly, the live talk show became a favoured format because it is both low budget and popular among the audiences. Local stations rush to offer these types of programmes despite the fact that many are without necessary state-set programming production capacities, including the required time-delay equipment and a well-trained and politically reliable host who can maintain "correct guidance to public opinion".

In short, by the mid-1990s, market fragmentation and intense competition between media outlets owned by various levels of the Party state bureaucracy had undermined central Party organs and the central state's propaganda objectives. The process also created an industry structure where local bureaucratic and financial interests overrode the market rationality of the central Party state as the ultimate owner and manager of state media capital. There is a lack of scale economy, and, in the words of one central broadcast official, "too much duplication of efforts at the local level. When a tree falls on the bank of the West Lake, six television crews would show up and shoot the same scene. What a waste of resources!" (personal interview, 12 December 2000, Beijing)

Consequently, the conglomerate as a business organization form became the state's favoured vehicle for achieving the optimal integration of political control and market efficiency in the media industries. This, of course, does not mean that the Party state deliberately pursued such a strategy at the very beginning of the reform process, which after all has been an uncharted course. In fact, press conglomerates grew out of strict economic concerns in the late 1980s. In order to help major newspapers achieve financial independence, the Party allowed them to publish market-oriented subsidiaries and turn their non-editorial supporting departments into profit-making businesses. By the mid-1990s, however, media mergers and conglomeration were pursued as a state policy, with both political and market considerations. In the press sector, the *Guangzhou Daily*, the Guangzhou Municipal Party Committee organ that has managed to successfully expand into the urban middle class market, and operate extensive subsidiary publications and businesses in other areas, was selected as a pilot press conglomerate in January 1996. Since being conferred the official status of a "social press conglomerate", the Guangzhou Daily Group streamlined its organizational structure, strengthened the editorial control (for example, instead of having one daily editorial meeting, the group now has two meetings), upgraded newsroom facilities, and built an extensive distribution system both inside and outside the Guangzhou area. It quickly expanded its number of subsidiary publications, boosted the circulation of the flagship paper, and increased its overall profitability and financial strength. By 1998, with revenue at 1.72 billion yuan ($207 million) and profit at 349 million yuan ($42 million), the group had become one of Guangzhou's top 10 state enterprises and a major economic powerhouse in the region (Zhao, 2000b: 16). Officially under the control of the Guangzhou Municipal Party Committee, the enterprise is now vigorously competing with two other local press conglomerates, the Nanfang Daily Group and the Yangcheng Evening News Group, both under the control of the Guangdong provincial Party committee. Together, these three press conglomerates dominate the Guangzhou newspaper market with five general- interest daily newspapers catering to different markets, and a whole range of specialized niche publications.

The *Guangzhou Daily* experience was analysed by the central authorities and promoted in other parts of the country. The principal purpose of press conglomeration, agreed upon by the SPPA and the China Newspaper Association, was to "enable Party organs to consolidate a powerful economic base through the market mechanism and ensure the better fulfilment of the Party's propaganda objectives" (Tan, 1997: 254). In Shanghai, the municipal government single-handedly arranged the merger of two long established news organizations, the lucrative mass-oriented afternoon tabloid *Xinmin Evening News* and the more upscale and less profitable *Wenhui News*, to form the Wenhui-Xinmin Group in 1998. This created a highly rationalized duopoly press structure in China's biggest metropolis: while political and business-related newspapers were consolidated under the Liberation Daily Group, which is the official municipal Party organ, culture and lifestyle publications were grouped under the *Wenhui-Xinmin* folder. In most provinces, a press conglomerate is typically established on the basis of a traditional Party organ. At the central level, the Xinhua News Agency already operates as a vertically integrated, multimedia and multi-business conglomerate, with its wire service, audio-visual news service, daily newspapers, magazines, publishing house, advertisement, public relations, and other businesses. In addition to the *People's Daily*, which, like the Xinhua News Agency, has long been run as a conglomerate (although without the official sanction of such a status), two other centrally-controlled newspapers, the *Guangming Daily* and the *Economic Daily*, focusing on culture and the economy respectively, were also officially given the status of a "socialist press group".

The Party's most shrewd media conglomerate managers are positioning themselves as captains of state capital. The *Guangzhou Daily*'s now disgraced Director and Chief Editor Li Yuanjiang, for example, pointed out that conglomeration is a necessary strategy for better management of state assets, and for more effective use of press profits. Li also saw conglomeration as a means of press control and shared the Party's objective in merging smaller non-Party papers and minimizing their influence– "China's current press structure is not yet rationalized. . . . If these small publications rather lacking in social and economic benefits were merged with powerful press groups under leading Party organs, [this] would help to administer the publication markets" (*Zhongguo Jizhe*, 1996: 16). It is perhaps indicative of the unaccountable nature of Chinese media power that Li, a rising star of the commercialized Party press system, ended up using the Guangzhou Daily group to amass personal fortunes and pursue a lavish lifestyle, and was eventually exposed by Party authorities as a corrupted press baron.

As part of the strategy to consolidate Chinese media capital under major Party organs, the state announced a policy aimed at transforming, merging, and eliminating the more than 800 newspapers within the state bureaucratic sector in 1999. These papers were forced to either achieve complete financial autonomy or merge with central and provincial Party organs. They faced closure if their circulation was below 30,000 and if authorized central and provincial Party organs were unwilling to take them over. As a result of this policy, central and provincial Party organs were provided with an unprecedented opportunity to absorb press assets from the bureaucratic sector, and to expand their market reach. If Party-controlled press expansion allowed major Party organs to expand into the mass appeal market, the 1999 state-mandated "enclosure movement" allowed major Party organs to turn obscure industry and trade papers into lifestyle papers for every possibly profitable market niche. After 20 years of Party controlled commercialization and market rationalization, the press system remains dominated by central and provincial Party organs in structure. The crucial difference, however, is that these are no longer simple state-subsidized and single-minded propaganda sheets, but rather market-oriented press conglomerates with elite, mass appeal, niche market publications, and other business operations.

By the late 1990s, the broadcasting sector had also adopted corporatization and conglomeration as the focus of reform. The target was to consolidate radio, television, educational television, and cable operations under one corporate structure at the central and provincial levels, and to strengthen the vertical power of these corporations over municipal and county-level broadcasting operations. This inevitably undermined local bureaucratic interests, but central authorities were determined to push forward the process. The merger mania in the Western media market and the pressure of globalization, together with increasing domestic competition posed by an aggressive telecommunication industry, which has been increasingly encroaching into the cable broadcasting territory in the name of technological convergence, provided further rationales for the consolidation of the broadcasting industry. "Using administrative measures to integrate, using market measures to operate", was how a high-level official summarized the state's broadcasting reform strategy (personal interview, December 12, 2000, Beijing). Although the local-level broadcasting operations, which have their own political and financial imperatives to remain relatively autonomous, have resisted recentralization and some strong municipal broadcasters have managed to maintain their relatively autonomous status, many have no choice but to turn themselves into branch operations of broadcasting conglomerates at the higher administrative level.

The first pilot broadcast conglomerate was officially established on the basis of the Wuxi Broadcasting Bureau in June 1999. Under the new corporate structure, previously separate broadcasting operations – four radio channels and six over the air and cable television channels, were brought under one corporate structure. Programme production was completely centralized, allowing a single news centre to handle the production of news for all six over the air and cable television channels. At the same time, the government's broadcasting management functions were totally absorbed into the corporate structure. In December 2000, the first provincial-level broadcasting conglomerate was officially launched in Hunan Province. In January 2001, Zhejiang Province announced the merger of three previously separated provincial-level television stations, the Zhejiang Television, the Zhejiang Cable Television, and the Zhejiang Educational Television. The congregated provincial network runs one comprehensive channel, and five other channels specializing in urban life, business, science and education, arts and entertainment, and health and sports. This was described as the first step towards the establishment of a provincial broadcasting conglomerate (Zhang, Le, 2000: 5). Other provinces soon followed suit, making 2001 the year of state-engineered market consolidation in the history of Chinese broadcasting. In April 2001, Shanghai announced the formation of the Shanghai Culture and Broadcasting Group, a massive state conglomerate that monopolizes all aspects of Shanghai's broadcasting, film, and major cultural operations. The year of broadcasting corporatization and conglomeration reached its climax when, on 6 December 2001, just a week before China officially signed onto the WTO, the state announced the establishment of the China Radio, Film, & Television Group, a mega state media conglomerate that combined the resources of China Central Television, China National Radio, China Radio International, and China Film Group Corporation, which is the country's largest film producer and monopoly importer of films and related Internet and broadcasting production and distribution operations. With more than 20,000 employees and total fixed assets of 21.4 billion yuan (US$2.4 billion), the combined company has been widely saluted by state officials and the media alike as the Chinese broadcasting industry's "No 1 Aircraft Carrier", an industry champion ready to face the challenges of transnational media corporations in the post-WTO international competition. By mid-January 2002, China boasted 47 consolidated media groups, including 26 newspaper groups, eight broadcasting groups, six publishing companies, four distribution companies and three movie groups (Li, 2002).

China's newly established media conglomerates are part and parcel of "socialism with Chinese characteristics". Their status and future fortune are inextricably linked with the evolving structure of the Chinese political system, particularly the fate of China's one party system. Currently, these conglomerates are defined in nature and law as "cause-oriented enterprises" (shiye) that focus on the production of public goods and services, rather than purely profit-oriented businesses (qiye). They are not officially incorporated as independent businesses, but are managed as profit-oriented business and expected to rationalize production and take advantage of economies of scale. Instead of registering with the state's industrial and commercial administrations as independent businesses, they are directly affiliated with Party authorities at various levels. Senior editorial and management personnel are appointed by, and accountable to, their affiliated provincial and municipal Party committees.

The most crucial issue, however, is the exact ownership status of these media conglomerates. Do they belong to the Chinese state or do they belong to the Communist Party? Although the Communist Party effectively dominates the Chinese state, these are two separate legal entities in the context of a modern state. The Communist Party is not only fully aware of this distinction but also taking pro-active steps to secure its own interests in the event that it loses state power or is forced to share state power with other parties. In a secret document jointly issued by the Central Party Propaganda Department, the State Administration for Radio, Film, and Television (SARFT), and the SPPA in August 2002 (known as Document No. 17 in Chinese media policy circles), the Party claimed proprietary rights over these media conglomerates (Hu, 2003). According to this document, China's media conglomerates are owned by the Propaganda Departments of the Communist Party at various levels, while state agencies such as the SARFT, the SPPA, and their counterparts at local levels are Party delegated administrators of these media conglomerates. This explicit ownership claim by the Party is explosive in China (thus the secret nature of the document). Although the Party has always controlled the media, there has been a common assumption among Chinese media administrators, media practitioners, as well as media analysts that it is the Chinese state, rather than the Communist Party, that has ownership rights over the media. With its secret ownership claim, the Party has not only asserted its ownership rights over major Chinese media outlets, but also effectively separated media ownership rights from media management responsibilities. Within this framework, the Party has proprietary rights over the media, while agencies of the Chinese state are the Party's appointed media managers. By secretly "privatizing" key Chinese media assets, the Party is strategically positioning itself as the entrenched dominant owner of the Chinese media system. This secret claim has no practical consequences for media policy and media practice at the present. In the long run, whether this claim will be materialized or not in legal terms ultimately hinges upon the future fortune of the Communist Party in Chinese politics. As one Chinese media insider puts it in a confidential interview (October, 2002), the Communist Party's aggressive move can be seen as a sign of its strategic retreat. That is, it is possible that the Party is preparing for the eventual liberalization of media ownership and the ending of its monopolistic operation of the media. It is envisioning a media system in which Party owned media co-exist with media outlets owned by Chinese state capital, private capital, and transnational capital.

For now, the Party is determined to overcome existing bureaucratic barriers that have served to limit the further expansion of its media conglomerates across geographical boundaries, administrative hierarchies, and media sectors. According to Xu Guangchun, Deputy Chief of the Party Propaganda Department and Director of the SARFT, China's media conglomerates have to model themselves after Western multimedia conglomerates that know no regional boundaries and bureaucratic hierarchies (Xu, 2000, October: 10). Xu's words have been cautiously turned into policy. In November 2001, Party state authorities announced that newspaper organizations currently operating within the confines of one province were allowed to expand into other provinces and broadcasting organizations would be allowed to expand into the print media, although newspaper conglomerates were not allowed to expand into broadcasting (Chan, 2001). Although the actual implementation of such a policy requires the overcoming of deep entrenched bureaucratic interests and administrative barriers, the announcement of such a policy intention itself is significant. At the same time, the Party state is posited to step up its campaign to curb the bureaucratic press sector by forcing existing bureaucratic newspapers and journals, with the exception of core Party organs, to end their official affiliations and transfer their management rights to corporate entities ("China News Reform," 2003). Such a move, of course, is consistent with the Party state's overall economic strategy of "grabbing the big and letting go (i.e., privatizing) the small" in reforming state-owned enterprises. Nevertheless, the task of nurturing large-scale Party media industrial champions remains formidable. The China Radio,

Film and Television Group, the so-called broadcasting industry "aircraft carrier", for example, is simply not in the same league with major transnational media conglomerates in size and market power.

Negotiated liberalization: Private and foreign capital in the media

If the Party is turning itself into the biggest media capitalist by building media conglomerates and secretly claiming proprietary rights over them, Wang Changtian, the thirty-something owner of a Beijing-based private television production studio, aims to grow his operations into China's Time-Warner, while AOL-Time Warner, together with other multimedia transnational media conglomerates, had pushed hard to enter the Chinese media market. Although private and foreign forms of ownership are still prohibited in the Chinese media industry as a matter of general policy, they have gradually taken hold at the margins of the Chinese media system. Several cases had tested the boundaries in new forms of media ownership.

One controversial case involving the status of private sector involvement in media production centred on Wang Changtian, a former producer with Beijing Television, and his Beijing Light Television Production Company. With a beginning in selling programme consultation reports and low-budget documentary programmes to state television outlets, Wang's company has grown overnight with the launch of a Chinese version of *Entertainment Tonight* called the *China Entertainment Report*, in July 1999. By mid-2000, the company had become a multi-million business, with a weekly output of 10 hours of original programming in five programme packages. These programmes were syndicated to hundreds of local television stations, including the influential Beijing Television Station, and reached an audience of more than 350 million (Wang, 2000: 21). Although Wang's company managed to secure a business licence from the Beijing government's business bureau, its political status is still precarious: officially, no private business is permitted to engage in television news and feature programme production. Wang is politically very careful, and consciously limits his programmes to the entertainment field. Under the company's current status, to be explicitly political, not to mention politically incorrect, is to commit business suicide. The company does not have an official link to the Party state's information control chain of command, although Beijing Television, Wang's former employer, serves as a de facto link. Even so, Wang has run into trouble with the authorities. The problem is not so much with the content of his programmes, but with names such as *China Entertainment Report*, *World Entertainment Report*, and *China Network Report*. How dare a private television studio claim the name "China"? Only the state-owned media outlets, especially CCTV, have the discursive power to speak on behalf of China. How dare a private television production studio use the term "report" in a country where news reports are the exclusive right of state-authorized media operations? Wang was ordered by the authorities to change the names before 5 December 2000. He had no choice but to follow the order. Being a private owner of media production facilities is no protection from state interference in media production.

Wang, of course, is not alone. As many as 317 private television production studios participated in the 2000 Beijing International Television Week, and 88 of these were from Beijing alone (Duan and Kuan, 2000). These companies have grown out of an increasing demand for popular programming by local stations and the growing popularity of a reformist argument for the separation of broadcast, or program exhibition, from production in state television. Wang's dream is eventually to turn his production studio into a multi-media conglomerate. Although the Party tolerates the existence of private television product studios, it is not willing to accept a policy of separating program exhibition and production. As Xu Guangchun puts it, while it is acceptable to socialize production in some areas, the right to propaganda, which includes the right to produce, to broadcast, and to secure audience reach, must be kept firmly in the hands of the Party. Broadcast stations should never give up their production right, or "there will be big time problems at crucial moments" (11 September 2000).

The second area of contest involves property rights in the printing press. Although the Party state continues to prohibit state-owned businesses and private capital from entering the core media business, there are many de facto cases of collaboration between the Party and state entities that have monopoly access to publication licences, and businesses and private individuals with funds to invest in newspapers and periodicals (Huang, 2000; Liu 2000; Zhou, 2002). These publications are more explicit than the state-owned and advertisement-supported media in their orientation towards the urban middle class. *The China Business* (*Zhongguo Jingyingbao*), a Beijing-based weekly, has been such an operation. Although the Industrial Economy Research Institute of the Chinese Academy of Social Sciences has been its official publisher, the paper's initial investment came from its founding editors. Over the years, the paper, with its pro-middle class stand and in-depth business analysis, has become a popular item at the Beijing newsstands. Its consumer and lifestyle subsidiary, the *Fine Goods Shopping Guide*, a biweekly paper that unabashedly celebrates consumerism, achieved even more spectacular market success. The small initial investments by private individuals have quickly grown into a multi-million business. Who has property rights over these newspapers? The state-authorized institutional publisher that did not invest a single penny or the editors who provided the initial capital? In a decision on property rights over these two papers, the Ministry of Finance, the SPPA, and the State Council Administrative Affairs Bureau summarily affirmed the property rights of the state over the editors. According to the decision, all capital accumulated by the Chinese press, including publications with initial financial inputs by businesses and individuals, belongs to the state. The logic behind this argument is that state regulations do not acknowledge any entity other than the authorized publisher, which is always a state agency, as the legitimate investor. Instead of having the status of investors, businesses and individuals providing the initial funds for the establishment of a newspaper should be treated either as donors or loaners. According to Wang Guoqing, an official of the SPPA's newspaper bureau, this decision is applicable to similar situations in the entire press (*Baokan Guangli*, 2000: 8).

While private capital is financing media through the backdoor, Party state-media is broadening its capital base through the stock market. Once Party state-media outlets are operated as for-profit businesses and media managers are charged with the responsibility of accumulating state capital through the media, it becomes a logical step to subject the state-media to the logic of the stock market. This is precisely the practice of the Hunan Broadcasting Bureau, an upstart in the Chinese television industry. Since the late 1990s, Hunan-originated, Hong Kong or Taiwan inspired entertainment television – from variety shows to dating games to television series about the Qing emperors and empresses, with names such as *The Grand Happiness Camp, The Earnest Entertainment Vanguard, Dating Roses*, and *Lucky 99*, – has swept the whole country, rivalled CCTV in advertising revenue, and led to the proliferation of imitation shows by other television stations. The popularity of Hunan television reveals a simple truth to a Chinese television industry that has not fully discarded its traditional Party propaganda mentality: uplifting light entertainment is the safest and fastest means to accumulate capital. At a time of massive social and cultural dislocation, manifested by the rise of the *Falun Gong* movement and worker and farmer protests, entertainment television serves as an important mass diversion. Like advertising, it is another new form of "mobilization speech". It is not a coincidence that Hunan TV's flagship show, *The Grand Happiness Camp* is modelled after a Hong Kong television show entitled *Total Mobilization for Joyfulness*. With its commercial success, the Hunan Broadcasting Bureau listed parts of its businesses on the Shenzhen Stock Market in 1999. This is an unprecedented move in the Chinese media industry. As one of China's last monopoly businesses, a broadcasting share is a sure bet at the stock market. Within one year, the Hunan Broadcasting Bureau had raised 400 million yuan through the stock market, which it used to invest in even more entertainment, business, sports and leisure programming (Liu, 2000: 265).

Although the central authorities subsequently issued a circular banning stock listing by other media outlets in September 1999, the SARFT endorsed Hunan Broadcasting as a pioneer in broadcasting reform by holding a special on-location conference to discuss the topic of broadcasting corporatization and conglomeration (Ya, 2000: 6). Shanghai and Beijing broadcasting authorities have both established their own stock market listed companies with the approval of high-level state authorities, while other media operations have attracted outside capital indirectly through creative company structures. With increasing pressures to further capitalize state media operations, by early 2002 the state had reversed its September 1999 decree by allowing non-media state companies and other Chinese institutional investors to invest in Chinese media groups after these groups had been transformed into shareholding companies ("Chinese media," 2002). Although these investors would still be prohibited from holding controlling stakes and from making management and operational decisions and it is unlikely that the state will allow a rush of media companies selling shares in the stock market, the capitalization of Party state media through the stock market has become an indisputable state-sanctioned development. In short, the capitalization of the Chinese media has evolved from advertising financing to stock market financing. Chinese media capital is now participating in the general circulation of capital through the stock market. The entrance of non-media capital in the media sector will inevitably tighten the grip of the logic of capital on the operations of the Chinese media in general.

Compared with domestic Chinese non-media capital and private capital, transnational media capital has been in a relatively stronger position to negotiate with the Chinese Party state for market entry. As "the largest jewel in the Asian media crown" (Herman and McChesney, 1997: 68), China holds a perpetual allure for international media capital. Despite state regulations that prohibit foreign ownership in the Chinese media, there are significant exceptions with central authorities much in control over the terms and areas of foreign entry. In the print media, areas of operation for foreign capital have included publications in technical information for China's rising information elite and consumer and lifestyle magazines for the affluent urban middle class (Zhao, 2003b). The most significant foreign investor in the Chinese press has been the Boston-based information technology publisher, the International Data Group (IDG). As the *South China MorningPost* put it, the joint venture between IDG and the Chinese government is "arguably one of the quietest foreign investor success stories in the mainland" (Mitchell, 2000). Despite the Chinese state's long standing ban on foreign capital in the Chinese media sector, the *China Computerworld*, the Chinese version of the IDG's worldwide weekly publication, launched in 1980, was in fact the first Sino-US joint venture business. Today, *China Computerworld* is the most voluminous computer newspaper in the world. It sells 10,000 pages of advertisement a year and is among China's highest advertisement revenue earning newspapers, rivalling mass circulation papers in Beijing, Guangzhou and Shanghai. With the *China Computerworld* as the flagship, the IDG's publishing empire in China encompassed twenty-two titles in 2000. Among these are highly influential and popular titles such as the *Network World*, the *PC World China*, the *CEO & CIO World*, and the *Home PC World*. More recently, many other foreign publishers have managed to publish Chinese editions of their lifestyle and consumer magazines through advertising management and copyright collaboration agreements: *Cosmopolitan*, *Esquire*, *Popular Mechanics*, *Motor China*, *Electronics Products China*, *Elle*, *Madame Figaro*, the list goes on.

In the broadcasting sector, Phoenix TV, a Hong Kong based satellite television joint venture between Rupert Murdoch's Star TV, Liu Changle, an overseas Chinese entrepreneur well connected to the Chinese state, and the Bank of China, claimed to reach 44.98 million households in China, or 15.9% of total Chinese television households in the late 1990s (China Mainland Market Research Co, 1998). Similar to readers of foreign-brand Chinese publications, the Phoenix audience in China is no ordinary audience. Although state regulations prohibit the reception of foreign satellite television by private households, the Chinese elite has not been constrained by such regulations. According to state regulations, Chinese hotels that rank three stars and above, and luxurious apartment complexes catering to foreigners and affluent domestic customers are allowed to install satellite dishes to receive foreign satellite transmissions. In addition, major government departments, media, academic, and financial institutions are allowed to install their own satellite receiving dishes. Since most of these institutions have internal cable television systems that wire their offices and living quarters, residents in these exclusive neighbourhoods conveniently end up receiving Phoenix TV. Compared with the average Chinese television audience, Phoenix viewers are characterized by "three highs and one low" – high official rank, high income, high education level, and low age (Zhao, 2003b). Indeed, in the words of the *Wall Street Journal*, "Phoenix's stylish shows are a must-see for a growing middle class fed on, and fed up with, a diet of state-run television" (Chang, 1999).

With their continuing demonstration of willingness to please the Chinese leadership, from dropping the BBC World Service from Star TV's China service to the termination of a contract to publish former British Governor Chris Patten's critical book on China, and the public statement by James Murdoch that *Falun Gong* is indeed a dangerous cult, a position that happens to be in line with that of the Chinese authorities, the Murdochs have made themselves acceptable business partners for the Chinese state. This sets a model for other transnational media conglomerates, all of which have much to gain in the Chinese media market. Time-Warner enhanced the international status of the Chinese Party state by sponsoring the Fortune Forum in Shanghai in late September 1999, on the eve of the Party's celebration of its 50th year in power in China. Disney learnt a hard lesson in the Chinese market in the late 1990s when its release of *Kundun*, a movie about Tibet's Dalai Lama, led the Chinese state to impose a two-year ban on the release of all its films in China. Instead of trying to crack the Chinese media market in a high-profile way and focusing on content provision, Bertelsmann, the Germany-based transnational media conglomerate, has been quietly expanding its distribution system in China since 1994 through the establishment of its book club in Shanghai, which sold books, tapes, and compact discs. By 2001, Bertelsmann had achieved a total sale of 100 million yuan (US$12.1 million) in the Chinese market and planned to launch two magazines in China (Meng, 2001). In short, although the scope of transnational media operations in China remains limited, and profitability is by no means guaranteed, as McChesney (1999) has noted, the marriage between transnational media capital and the Chinese state has been less difficult than many people had assumed.

The collective will and the political power of transnational media capital were brought to bear through major Western states in China's WTO concession agreements. The US-based transnational media capital, in particular, mounted a major lobby effort in the US-China WTO negotiations. Although China did not open up direct foreign investment in its core media operations, transnational media secured significant market entry gains, including increased film import quotas, reduced tariffs on Chinese audio-visual imports, the opening up of China's consumer markets for audio-visual products to foreign distributors, and permission for foreign ownership in movie theatres and Internet operations (Zhao and Schiller, 2001). In late 2001, AOL-Time Warner and News Corporation achieved major breakthroughs in their long pursuit of the Chinese broadcasting market by securing cable-landing rights for their respective satellite television operations. The Chinese state, however, limited the access of these two companies to the Guangdong market alone, a province which due to its proximity to Hong Kong has already had considerable exposure to outside broadcasting. It also managed to get Time Warner and News Corporation to carry China Central Television's overseas English broadcasting channel in selected US cable markets.

The Chinese Party state, in short, is carefully negotiating terms for the entry and operation of non-media state capital, private capital, and foreign capital in the media market. While it is determined to maintain control over the core areas of news production, it is gradually accommodating domestic and international capital in other areas of media operation, including the production of entertainment, business, consumer, and technical information, and the financing and distributing ends of the Chinese media system – from advertising management to print media distribution, audio-visual product retailing, cinema exhibition, and book readership clubs. The same strategy has also been applied to the newest communications medium, the Internet. As Shanthi Kalathil (2000) has observed, in addition to a whole series of overt control mechanisms – firewalls, chat-room monitoring, jailing of website operators, shutting down of Internet cafes, the establishment of draconian content regulations and cyber police squads – the Chinese state has taken the carrot-and-stick approach in its dealings with domestic and foreign Internet capital, and it has achieved some success in information control on the Internet (see also Hachigian, 2001; Qiu, 1999).

Such a development, of course, is not unique in China. Private capital and authoritarian states have long sustained clientelist relationships in many media systems in Southern Europe and Latin America (Hallin and Papathanassopoulos, 2000), as well as in many Asian countries. Similarly, the market-entry stories of IDG and News Corporation suggested that the Chinese state and foreign capital seemed to have been able to strike "win-win" deals during the process. Zaharom Nain's observation on the relationship between transnational media corporations and the Malaysian state provides another illustrative example: "Rather than engaging in battle with the state, these multinationals so far appear to have been given the red carpet treatment and have become firm allies of the state; a regime which is in a position to bargain favourably (for its own interest, that is), hence maintaining its hegemony, while at the same time, helping the multinationals to maintain theirs internationally" (Nain, 1996: 62). If the dominant power in Malaysia, a market much smaller than the Chinese market, and presumably one that has less bargaining power with international capital, seems able to bargain favourably with international capital for its own interests, there is good reason to believe that the Chinese state can do no worse.

Conclusion

China's once state-subsidized and Party-controlled propaganda organs are rapidly transforming themselves into advertisement-based and market-driven capitalistic media enterprises under Party ownership. The Party is modernizing its media control regime, incorporating the market mechanism in its media operations, and consolidating media capital through top-down administrative orders. It is also carefully accommodating private and foreign media capital, while limiting their areas of operation and trying to politically contain them through the carrot-and-stick strategy. As a result of this transformation, the Chinese media system is increasingly becoming a platform for profit-making, while speaking in the voice of the ruling Party elite and the rising business and urban middle classes, who are the domestic and international capital's most wanted audiences. A reconstituted power bloc, consisting of bureaucratic capitalists of a transformed Party state, a business elite, and a growing urban middle class that has more in common with their counterparts in other countries than with disenfranchised workers and farmers inside China, and transnational capitalists and their operatives, effectively call the shots in the Party-controlled and market-oriented Chinese media.

Although much has been said about the democratizing impulses of China's raising middle class, the marginalization of issues of concern to the lower classes, in particular, the suppression of news about worker and farmer protests, may be as much in the interest of the Party state elite as in the interest of the business and the urban middle classes. As Robison and Goodman (1996) have argued, while there are many conflicts between the state and Asia's rising business and middle classes, any simple juxtaposition of the new rich and the state as inherently hostile is an inadequate basis for analysis. As the skills and purchasing power of the middle class become more essential to informational capitalism, "the state and capital are increasingly driven to accommodate this social force, whether it be within a conservatism that offers stability and protection, or a liberalism that offers more direct participation in the process of government" (Robison and Goodman, 1996: 11). In light of a global economic slowdown, mounting social pressures, growing class divisions, and the haunting ghost of the Cultural Revolution's radical politics, the Chinese power bloc is opting for political conservatism, while institutionalizing new forms of collusion and mutual cooptation. The Party's latest incorporation of private business owners, high-tech innovators, and managers in foreign businesses into its ranks is a clear sign of this trend. "We're the vested interest now . . . . We don't like change, we don't like chaos" (Chu, 2001), this statement, made by Xu Lei, a 29-

year-old employee at a foreign consulting firm in Beijing, may be read as the political manifesto of the middle class in reformed China. Just as the Party is unlikely to relinquish control, China's middle class, including media managers and journalists, have much to gain from a stable political environment, China's further integration with the global economy, and effective containment of protesting workers, farmers, and other disenfranchised groups such as the *Falun Gong*. Although it is possible that they may use the media to mobilize support for political reform, their newly gained market power and their increased economic and social isolation from the low classes and their increased materialism are likely to make them a "silent partner" (Kemenade, 1998: 401) of the Party in sustaining the current market-oriented, Party-dominated media system. They may dislike the Party, abhor official corruption, and harbour more liberal views; but they are also likely to ally themselves with the pro-market faction of the Party in marginalizing the voices of both the left and the radical right, while mediating the voices of other social groups in the name of building a strong and powerful China (Zhao, 2000b: 22).

Thus, on the one hand, the media continue to serve as sites of elite political struggles. With the decline of overt ideology-driven media campaigns, selective exposure of official corruption may become an increasingly common means of media involvement in elite power struggles. The press's exposure of former Premier and current National People's Congress Chairman Li Peng's nepotism in late 2001, involving problematic business operations by Li's wife and his sons, for example, is believed to be implicated in top level power struggles leading to the 16th Party Congress in late 2002 (Manthorpe, 2002; Shi, 2002). Widely seen as the man responsible for giving the formal order to send troops to suppress the Tiananmen Square demonstrators in 1989 and as a communist old guard who has grave misgivings about economic reforms, Li is the most hated Party leader in the eyes of the country's business and media elite. The exposure of a financial scandal involving one of Li's sons during an intense succession struggle, with or without the instructions of his political rivals, plays into elite power politics. The punishments of the author and the editor responsible for the exposure and Li's wife's public defence of her family in the media underscored the point that the ruling elite has a very high stake in media politics. On the other hand, the media continue to act as a means of popular containment by marginalizing the voices of the disenfranchised groups and ignoring their rally cries. While political censorship matters, it is by no means clear that, even if let alone, journalists would not stay away from news about social unrests out of concern for social stability. The issue of media openness and control in China must be understood within the context of elite and popular politics and reconstituted class and power relations.

Moreover, with the deepening of market relations and the increasing penetration of the capital logic in the Chinese media system, Party control and the inherent social biases of the market may be mutually reinforced. Far from being inherently antithetical to Party propaganda, China's commercialized media system may have helped to moderate opposition by marginalizing radical perspectives and issues of concern to groups that do not constitute media advertisers "most needed consumers", namely the small political and economic elite and the mostly urban middle class (Zhao and Schiller, 2001). Just like the commercial media in the West, market-oriented Chinese media outlets tend to stay away from politics and are disinclined to report domestic social conflicts. Mass entertainment, the mobilization of consumption, and stock analysis are politically safe and financially more rewarding. The current wave of state engineered market consolidation and the further penetration of capital logic into the Chinese media system will probably amplify the inherent social biases of a market-driven media system.

Similarly, given their market priorities and their increased stakes in the Chinese market, the democratizing effects of transnational media capital in China cannot be simply assumed. The sympathetic coverage of student demonstrations by foreign media outlets in 1989 was crucial for the spread of the movement. But the situation is very different now. On the Chinese side, regime protesters and English-speaking students and intellectuals in Beijing and other major urban centres are no longer media savvy. Instead, current social contestations often involve disenfranchised farmers and workers engaged in localized and dispersed struggles in the provinces, to which foreign journalists do not have easy access. Moreover, instead of invoking abstract liberal principles of freedom and democracy, which resonate well with the ideological scripts of Western journalists, today's regime protesters' more specific and mundane claims do not sound as heroic as the 1989 students, and are not necessarily compatible with the ideological framework of Western journalists. For their part, today's CBS, ABC, NBC, and CNN are different from yesteryear's CBS, ABC, NBC, and CNN. When Dan Rather reported from Tiananmen Square in 1989, he was not working for the media conglomerate Viacom. Nor was ABC part of Disney and CNN part of AOL-Time Warner. Now all the major US television networks have become subsidies of media conglomerates with business interests in China. After a decade of foreign investment in the 1990s, and with China's WTO membership and the right to stage the 2008 Olympics spectacle, foreign capital now has a vested interest in the stability of the Chinese state and its effort to contain social threats from below. The political economic relationships between the Chinese state, transnational media capital, and the different social classes in China have been significantly reconfigured. Rather than providing a political voice to voiceless social groups in China, the dual compulsion of political control by the Chinese state and market imperative ensure that transnational media capital will concentrate on delivering entertainment and consumer information to China's affluent consumers.

Thus far the cumulative effects of political control and the inherent bias of the market, as well as the relentless use of a repressive state apparatus, have contained domestic dissent even as the Chinese state continues to deepen market reforms and accelerate China's integration with global capitalism (Zhao and Schiller, 2001: 151). This, of course, does not mean that the current integration between the Party state and market forces in the Chinese media is total and stable. The ruling elite is divided and prone to self-paralysing power struggles. Meanwhile, it collectively faces many challenges in media control. To remain in power, the Party must constantly update its strategies and renegotiate the parameters of control. These challenges are multi-faceted and of a different political order: some must be brutally suppressed, while others can be contained and neutralized with less repressive measures. They range from the unfiltered dissenting voice waiting to exploit a technical loophole in a live phone-in programme to the angry laid-off state enterprise workers attempting to seize a local television station to broadcast a call for a general strike, from *Falun Gong* believers demanding favourable coverage in the state media to radical intellectuals of liberal, nationalist, and leftist persuasions, an enterprising journalist aiming to uncover a good investigative story, and domestic and foreign capitalists wanting their share of the lucrative Chinese media market. The WTO membership, which inevitably leads to further layoffs of state enterprise workers and accelerated displacement of farmers from China's agricultural heartlands, will further intensify these tensions. As the Party is consolidating its own media capital and negotiating within its own ranks over political openness, and with private and foreign capital over market shares, the majority of the Chinese population remains largely voiceless in a commercialized, conglomerated, and increasingly globalized media system.

References

Ang, Peng Hwa (2003) 'Critical Looks: How and Why China is Regulating the Internet'. Paper presented at the China and the Internet: Technology, Economy, and Society in Transition Conference, Los Angeles, 30–31 May 2003.

Associate Press (2003) 'Beijing Paper Critical of Gov't shut down'. Internet accessed on 20 June.

Baokan guangli (Press Management) (2000) '*Muqian woguo baokanshe zichang junshu guoyouzichang* (All Capital in Our Country's Press Organizations Is State Capital)'. 1 January 1. p. 8.

Barmé, Geremie (1998) 'Spring Clamor and Autumnal Silence: Cultural Control in China'. *Current History*, September. pp. 257-262.

Barmé, Geremie (1999) *In the Red: On Contemporary Chinese Culture*. New York: Columbia University Press.

Bobin, Frederic (2002) 'China's Anti-Globalisation Voices Struggle to be Heard'. *The Guardian*, 3 January. p. 9.

Chan, Vivien Pik-Kwan (2001) 'Provincial Media "Allowed to Grow After Policy Shift"'. *South China Morning Post*, Internet edition accessed on 6 November.

Chang, Leslie (1999) 'A Phoenix Rises in China: Rupert Murdoch's Satellite TV Thrives, Legalities Notwithstanding'. *The Wall Street Journal*, 26 May. p. B4.

Chen, Huailin and Lee, Chin-Chuan (1997) 'Press Finance and Economic Reform in China', in Joseph Y.S. Cheng ed., *China Review 1997*. Hong Kong: Chinese University Press. pp. 557-609.

Cheng, Anne S.Y. (2003) 'The Business of Governance – China's Legislation on Content Regulation in Cyberspace'. Paper presented at the China and the Internet: Technology, Economy, and Society in Transition Conference, Los Angeles, 30-31 May 2003.

China Mainland Marketing Research Co. (1998) *Fenghua Weishi Zhongwentai dalu shoushi qingkua diaochanggaisu* (An Overview of Phoenix TV's Audience Rating in Mainland China.) March.

Chu, Henry (2001) 'Middle Kingdom's Middle Class'. *The Los Angeles Times*, 18 June. http://www.latimes.com/new/nation/20010618/t000050617.html.

Curran, James (1981) 'The Impact of Advertising on the British Mass Media'. *Media, Culture, and Society* 3:1. pp. 43-69.

Duan, Shiwen, and Kuan, Yanpeng (2000) '*Minjian dianshi zhizhou jiguo fengchi yuanyong* (A Surge of Private Television Production Companies)'. Xinhuanet accessed on 12 July 2000. http://www.bj.xinhua.org.

Gilley, Bruce (2001) 'Jiang's Turn Tempts Fate'. *Far Eastern Economic Review*, 3 August. pp. 18-20.

Guo, Zhenzhi (1991) *Zhangguo dianshi shi* (A History of Chinese Television). Beijing: Zhongguo renmin daxue chubanshe.

Hachigian, Nina (2001) 'China's Cyber-Strategy'. *Foreign Affairs* 80:2, March/April. pp. 118-133.

Hallin, Daniel C., and Papathanassopoulos, Stylianos (2000) 'Political Clientalism and the Media: Southern Europe and Latin America in Comparative Perspective', Occasional Paper, Center for German and European Studies, University of California, Berkeley, CA.

He, Zhou (2000a) 'Chinese Communist Press in a Tug of War: A Political Economy Analysis of the Shenzhen Special Zone Daily', in Chin-Chuan Lee ed., *Power, Money and Media: Communication Patterns and Bureaucratic Control in Cultural China*. Evanston, IL: Northwestern University Press. pp. 112-151.

He, Zhou (2000b) 'Working with a Dying Ideology: Dissonance and its Reduction in Chinese Journalism'. *Journalism Studies* 1:4, pp. 599-616.

Herman, Edward, and McChesney, Robert (1997) *The Global Media: The New Missionaries of Global Capitalism*. London and Washington: Cassell.

Hu, Zhengrong (2003) 'The Post-WTO Restructuring of the Chinese Media Industries and the Consequences of Capitalization'. *Javnost/Public*. 10:4. pp. 19-36.

Huang, Chenju (2000) 'The Development of a Semi-Independent Press in Post-Mao China: An Overview and a Case Study of Chengdu Business News'. *Journalism Studies* 1:4, pp. 649-664.

Kalathil, Shanthi (2000) 'Cyber Censors: A Thousand Web Sites Almost Bloom'. *The Asian Wall Street Journal*, 29 August. p. 10.

Kemenade, Willem Van (1998) *China, Hong Kong, Taiwan, Inc*. New York: Vintage Books.

Lee, Chin-Chuan (2000) 'China's Journalism: The Emancipatory Potential of Social Theory'. *Journalism Studies* 1(4), pp. 559-575.

Li, Clara (2002) 'Shenzhen Firms to Merge in Newspaper Shake-up'. *South China Morning Post*. Internet edition accessed on 15 February 2002.

Liu, Yong (2000) *Meiti Zhongguo* (Media China). Changduo: Sichuan Renmin chubanshe.

Lynch, Daniel (1999) *After the Propaganda State: Media, Politics, and Thought Work in Reformed China*. Stanford, CA: Stanford University Press.

Manthorpe, Jonathan (2002) 'Liberals Take a Cue from Beijing with Their Internal Bloodletting'. *The Vancouver Sun*, 13 February. p. A15.

McChensey, Robert (1999) *Rich Media, Poor Democracy: Communication Politics in Dubious Times*. Urbana and Chicago: University of Illinois Press.

Meisner, Maurice (1996) *The Deng Xiaoping Era: An Inquiry into the Fate of Chinese Socialism, 1978-1994*. New York: Hill and Wang.

Meng, Yan (2001) 'Bertelsmann plans China foray with magazines'. *The China Daily*. http://www.chinadaily.com accessed on 28 November.

Mitchell, Tom (2000) 'Mainland Ties Bind Pioneer Publisher'. *South China Morning Post*. Internet Edition, accessed 12 July.

Nain, Zaharom (1996) 'Rhetoric and Realities: Malaysian Television Policy in an Era of Globalization'. *Asian Journal of Communication* 6:1. pp. 43-63.

Policy and Regulation Research Office, Central Party Propaganda Department (1998) *Xuanchuan wenhua zhengce fagui xuanbian*. (A Selection of Rules and Regulations in the News Media and Culture Fields). Beijing: Xuexi chubanshe.

Qiu, Jack Linchuan (1999) 'Virtual Censorship in China: Keeping the Gate Between the Cyberspaces'. *International Journal of Communication Law and Policy* 4. pp. 1-25.

Robison, Richard, and Goodman, David S.G. (1996) 'The New Rich in Asia: Economic Development, Social status and Political Consciousness', in Richard Robison and David Goodman eds., *The New Rich in Asia: Mobile phones, McDonald's and Middle-Class Revolution*. London and New York: Routledge. pp. 1-16.

Rosenthal, Elisabeth (2002) 'China Changes Approach in Espionage Incident'. *The New York Times*. Accessed on the web on 27 January 2002.

Shi, Wenhuan (2002) 'Li Penghuanqian, weizi huanzhai (Li Peng Pays Back, Pays Back Your Son's Debts!)'. *Kaifang* (Open), February. pp. 12–14.

State Press and Publications Administration, PRC (2000) '*Xinwen chuban ye 2000 nian ji 2010 nian fangzhang guihuo.* (Plans for the Development of the Press and Publication Industries in Year 2000 and Year 2010)'. *Zhongguo xinwen nianjian 1999.* (China Journalism Yearbook 1999). Beijing: China Journalism Yearbook Press. p. 57.

Tan, Ziyi (1997) '*Baoye jituan yantao hui zhongshu* (A Summary of the Seminar on Press Groups)', in *Zhongguo xinwen nianjian 1997* (China Journalism Yearbook 1997). Beijing: Zhongguo xinwen nianjian chubanshe. p. 254.

The Straits Times (2002) 'Chinese Media to Remain under State Ownership'. Internet Edition accessed on 18 January 2002.

Tian, Chongming (2000) '*Qianshi jiaqiang xunchuan guangli quebao diaoxiang zhengque he bochu anquan* (Resolutely Strengthening Propaganda Management, Ensuring Correct Guidance to Public Opinion and the Security of Broadcast Transmission)'. *Reference to Broadcasting Decision-Making,* January. p. 3.

Wang, Jifang (2000) '*Dazhao yulejie de "xinwen lianbo"* (Forging A "Joint News Broadcast" for the Entertainment World)'. *Nanfang Weekend,* 9 November. p. 21.

Wang, Xi'ai and Zhang, Ximing (2000) '*Wangluo xinwen chuanbo: Xinshiqi yulun diaoxiang de yige zhongyao zhigoadian.* (Internet News Transmission: An Important New Command Height in Directing Public Opinion in the New Era)'. *Geige* (Reform) 4. pp. 27–30.

Wu, Guoguang (2000) 'One Head, Many Mouths: Diversifying Press Structures in Reformed China', in Chin-Chuan Lee ed., *Power, Money, and Media: Communication Patterns and Bureaucratic Control in Cultural China.* Evanston, IL: Northwestern University Press. pp. 45–67.

Xu, Guangchun (2000) 'Speech at the National Broadcasting Bureau Chiefs Conference, 11 August 2000'. *Reference for Broadcasting Decision Making,* September. p. 11.

Xu, Guangchun (2000) '*Yi "shange daibiao" wei zhizheng, yi "shange chuangxin" wei dongli, jiakuai guangbo yingshi shiye de gaige he fazhan.* (With "Three Representatives" as Guiding Principle and "Three Innovations" as Motor, Accelerate Reform and Development in Broadcasting)'. *Reference for Broadcasting Decision-Making,* October. p. 10.

Ya, Ge (2000) '*Kankan Hunan weishi de ren he shi.* (A Look at the People at the Hunan Satellite Television and Their Stories)'. *Weishi zhoukan* (Satellite TV Weekly), 19 December. pp. 6–9.

Zhang, Le (2000) '*Zhejiang youxian wuxian jiaoyu shantiai hebing.* (Zhejiang Merged over the Air, Cable, and Educational Television Stations.)' *The People's Daily,* 16 December. p. 5.

Zhang, Weiguo (1999) '10 Years in Jail for Providing Information to Radio Free Asia on Labor Protests inside China'. *The Christian Science Monitor,* 24 February. p. 6.

Zhang, Yong (2000) 'From Masses to Audience: Changing Media Ideologies and Practices in Reformed China'. *Journalism Studies* 1:4, November. pp. 617–635.

Zhao, Yuezhi, and Schiller, Dan (2001) 'Dances with Wolves? China's Integration with Digital Capitalism'. *Info* 3:2. pp. 137–51.

Zhao, Yuezhi (1998) *Media, Market, and Democracy in China: Between the Party Line and the Bottom Line*. Urbana and Chicago: University of Illinois Press.

Zhao, Yuezhi (2000a) 'Watchdogs on Party Leashes? Contexts and Limitations of Investigative Journalism'. *Journalism Studies* 1:4. pp. 577–97.

Zhao, Yuezhi (2000b) 'From Commercialization to Conglomeration: The Transformation of the Chinese Press within the Orbit of the Party State'. *Journal of Communication* 50:2. pp. 3–26.

Zhao, Yuezhi (2001) 'Media and Elusive Democracy'. *Javnost* 8:2. pp. 21–44.

Zhao, Yuezhi (2002) 'The Rich, the Laid-off, and the Criminal in Tabloid Tales: Read All about It!' In Perry Link, Richard Madsen, and Pual Pickowicz, eds., *Popular China: Unofficial Culture in a Globalizing Society*. Lanham, MD: Rowman and Littlefield. pp. 111–35.

Zhao, Yuezhi (2003) 'Enter the World: Neo-liberal Globalization, the Dream for a Strong Nation, and Chinese Press Discourses on the WTO'. In Chin-Chuan Lee ed., *Chinese Media, Global Context*. London and New York: RoutledgeCurzon. pp. 32–56.

Zhao, Yuezhi (2003a) 'Falun Gong, Identity, and the Struggle for Meaning Inside and Outside China'. In Nick Couldry and James Curran eds., *Contesting Media Power: Alternative Media in a Networked World*. Lanham, MD, Rowman and Littlefield.

Zhao, Yuezhi (2003b) 'Transnational Capital, the Chinese State, and China's Communication Industries in a Fractured Society'. *Javnost/Public* 10: 4. pp. 53–74.

Zhongguo gongshang shibao (2001) 'Guangdian jituan huanxi ziben tuidong (Broadcasting Conglomerates Need Further Push by Capital)'. 26 December. Accessed at http://www.sarft.gov.cn on 8 January 2002.

Zhongguo xinwen geige, zhongyang zhibaoliu sijiabaozhi (Press Reform in China, Central Party Authorities Keep only Four Press Outlets), http://www. creeder.net/headline/newsPool/25A172861.html. Accessed 26 June 2003.

Zhongguo Jizhe (The Chinese Journalist) (1996) '*Tansuo yitiao Zhongguo xinwen gaige yu fazhan de xinlu* (Exploring a New Road for Reform and Development of the Chinese Press)'. April. pp. 16–17.

Zhou, Wei (2002) '*Meiti Qianyan Baogao* (Front Reports on the Media)'. *Beijing, Guangming ribao chuanbanshe*.

Media Ownership and Communication Rights in India

Pradip N. Thomas

As one of the key generators of profit in the current economy, the media in India today is an extension of big business and consequently, of class/caste interests. These interests are maintained, extended and reinforced by a dominant politics that has periodically embarked on a witting dispossession of minorities, supported the reinvention of the Indian intellect in line with the requirements of a majoritarian (Hindu) Indian identity and aggressively courted accommodation with global capital. The media are clearly implicated in this project.

The emergence of the media as a business in its own right has led to the establishment of a variety of 'media interpretation' enterprises. Today, journalists and academics, activists and business writers contest and interpret the media in India in publications, through on-line discussions and web sites, videos, workshops and seminars. The publishing house Sage India currently publishes a variety of books on communication in India of varying quality – from the empirical investigation *Satellites Over South Asia* to the anthology *Critical Issues in Communication* to the many celebratory readings of information technology (IT) including *India's Communication Revolution* and others of that ilk. Media news and stories are carried in a variety of business and trade magazines inclusive of *BusinessWorld* and *Business India*, financial newspapers such the *Economic Times*, a range of glossy film magazines, the major newspapers in the vernacular and English languages, current affairs magazines such as *India Today*, *Outlook*, media-dedicated magazines such as *Satellite and Cable TV* and *Advertising and Marketing* (A&M), a slew of IT-related magazines, alternative media magazines such as *Voices* and *Madhyam*, scholarly journals such as the *Economic and Political Weekly*, activist publications such as the *Lokayan Bulletin*, in websites ranging from that of the mainstream software trade association NASSCOM (http://www.nasscom.org) and of the software company Tata Infosys, to numerous sites along the alternative media spectrum (http://www.thehoot.org, http://www.sarai.net, among others). This flurry of channels and space for media-related stories is a comparatively recent phenomenon coterminous with the Indian media industry's tryst with neoliberalism and privatization.

The media as a commodity in India is part of a multimillion dollar industry. There are, however, numerous contestations and a range of media interests. The government, business and to a lesser extent, civil society, are currently locked into many contestations over media futures in India.

Some features of the neoliberal economic landscape

The major beneficiaries of the current media environment in India – in terms of access, choice and employment opportunities – are the politically significant middle and upper middle classes who remain the political partners of the incumbent coalitional government headed by the BJP and the Congress Party that is currently in opposition. The ruling government and its allies have been vociferous proponents of economic liberalization. It enacted a series of legislations oriented towards the opening up of every productive sector of the Indian economy – insurance, finance, banking, agriculture, manufacturing, industry, services – to foreign capital. These measures have been complemented by the creation of a domestic legal framework supportive of the expansion of capital, the easing of restrictions on cross media ownership, the deregulation and privatization of public utilities and the harmonizing of legislative environments in India in line with World Trade Organization (WTO) stipulations including its provisions related to the Trade Related Intellectual Property Rights (TRIPS).

The extent of this capitulation to global economic agendas is reflected in the numerous TRIPS-related accommodations that include the following: India became a signatory to the Paris Convention and the Patent Cooperation Treaty on 7 December 1998. It was a signatory to the Berne Convention and the Universal Copyright Convention. Other legislative changes include the Patent (Amendments) Act, March 1999, the Copyright (Amendment) Act, December 1999, the Trademark Act, 1999, the Geographical Indications of Goods (Registration and Protection) Act, and the Designs Act, 2000. Legislations on the anvil include the Semiconductor Integrated Circuits Layout-Design Bill, the Protection of Plant Varieties and Farmer's Rights Bill and the Bill on Biodiversity.

This set of priorities was graphically reflected in the government's budget for the year 2002–2003. This budget reflects a commitment to the further opening up the agricultural sector, increased allocations for the telecommunication sector in the region of a massive Rs. 19,463 crores (US$43 billion), the slashing of taxes on IT related capital goods, cellphones, TV studio equipment and computers and increased military budget by 30% amounting to Rs. 65,000 (US$144 billion) crores. At the same time the budget has increased taxation on essentials for the poor such as kerosene (for cooking), fertilisers, pulses (dal) along with a withdrawal of the Minimum Price Support for wheat, rice and other essential crops (Slater, 2002). With interest payments (29.5%), defence (16.3%) and government salaries (18.7%) taking up nearly 70% of the annual budget, it is not surprising that very little is left over for development projects (Chatterjee, 2002). These changes in development policy are by no means of recent vintage. While enormous investments have been made in priority areas such as telecommunications, there has been a corresponding decline in the annual budget outlays in areas such as health, education, family planning and poverty alleviation during the last decade. By way of an illustration, while the budget for telecommunication in the Eight Five Year Plan (1990–95) was revised from Rs. 19,200 crores (US$40 billion) to Rs. 40,555 crores (US$84 billion), in the 1992 budget, there was a 40% decline in allocations for rural water supply programmes, 60% reduction in support for central hospitals and dispensaries, a 25% reduction of support for employment schemes as well as cutbacks in education, rural development, labour welfare and land reform (Chawla, 1992). These trends are in line with the proposed development budget freeze for the next five years, recommended by the Planning Commission at the current level of Rs. 35,000 crores ($8 billion) per year allocated to the Centrally Sponsored Schemes (CSS) in education, health, employment and income generation (http://www.geocities.com: 2001).

The reasons for and the consequences of poverty in India – landlessness, unemployment, a rapid increase in the price of grain and pulses leading to starvation-related deaths in some of the most prosperous states in India – rarely feature in mainstream media reports. Instead, media space has been taken over by business news, blow by blow accounts of corporate contestation by domestic and transnational firms for the Indian market and business advertorials. These stories are revealing, not least because they are a record of the gradual parcelling off of the Indian economy to a select group of players. The recent announcement of the takeover of then erstwhile state-owned long-distance carrier, Videsh Sanchar Nigam Limited (VSNL), by the Tata family-owned conglomerate, is a reflection of the government's policy on the privatization of public utilities. Heralding the eventual dis-investment, the VSNL, had to earlier relinquish its role as the sole Internet service provider (ISP) in India.

Creeping concentration

While competition remains a rallying call for the proponents of economic liberalization, this has not led to the establishment of a level playing field. All signs point to increased concentration. The Tatas by taking over VSNL reinforced their already established presence in the telecommunication sector. With the take-over of the VSNL, this firm now has substantive interests at every stage of the telecommunication value chain in cellular, basic, long-distance services, and is also poised to take over national long distance services in the country. This conglomerate's telecommunications interests are represented by six companies: Tata Teleservices, Birla-Tata-AT&T, Broadband Division of Tata Power, Tata Intranet Division of Nelco, Tata ISP and Tata Telecom (http://www.timesofindia.com, 2002). Furthermore, Tata Consultancy Services (TCS) is the leading software company in India and exporter of Indian software. In the 2001–2002 period, TCS closed with revenues of Rs. 4,800 crores (US$999 million) with a profit of Rs. 1250 crores (US$325 million). It had an annual revenue of Rs. 2033.01 crores ($484 million) and export revenues of Rs. 1820.35 crores ($440 million) in 1999–2000 (http://www.nasscom.org, 2000). Other Tata-owned IT companies include Tata Infotech, Tata Elxsi, Tata Interactive Systems, Tata Technologies, and Nelito Systems. They also own control systems – Tata Honeywell and Nelco and also have interests in publishing – Tata McGraw-Hill Publishing Company and Tata Infomedia. These companies are part of a stable of eighty companies involved in engineering, materials, energy, chemicals, consumer products, communications and IT and the services sector (http://www.tata.com).

Business families in the consolidation game

Deregulation, privatization and the easing of restrictions on monopolies and cross-sectoral media ownership have led to the emergence of a breed of local entrepreneurs but also to business convergences between old business families and new economic opportunities. The Tatas, the Ambanis, the Thapars, the Modis and the Birlas are among venerable business families in India that today have substantial interests in the telecommunication and media sectors. In fact, these groups have cornered large sectors of the media market. Consolidation is the name of the game today. After a brief flurry of players in the cellular phone market, there has been consolidation and/or planned mergers between the few remaining players. The biggest of the mergers between BPL, AT&T, Tata Cellular and Birla, has led to the formation of BPL-BATATA, the largest cellular service provider in the country with 24% of the country's cellular subscriber base. Most of the lucrative cellular phone markets have been bought out by either the BPL combine or by other players, notably Bharti Telecom and Hutchinson-Essar (Singh, 2001). The attempts to licence fixed line operators to operate wireless services using Wireless in Local Loop (WiLL) technologies will strengthen existing monopolies – Tata Teleservices, Reliance Telecom, Himachal Futuristic Communication and the public-sector Bharat Sanchar Nigam Limited – in key states such as Maharashtra and Gujarat.

This very same pattern of consolidation has affected the ISP market. Out of the 437 players who applied for an ISP licence in the late 1990s, only 75 were active in December 2000, only five remained at the end of 2002. The dominant five accrued from the ranks of the already advantaged, those already providing basic services, Hughes Telecom and Tata Telecom Consolidation also characterized the FM radio market in India. In August 2000, the government auctioned 108 frequencies for which there were originally 37 bidders. Today 10 players operate 71 stations with Music Broadcast Private Limited holding FM licences in six key cities in India including Delhi, Mumbai and Bangalore (Lobo, 2001). Vanita Kohli et al. (2001: 6) observed that the government received ". . . 360 applications, though the minimum cost of setting up infrastructure is Rs. 4 crore ($952,380) . . . almost all the publishing houses – Bennet, Coleman & Co., Living Media, Hindustan Times, Observer Network, Indian Express, Mid-Day – have applied for FM licenses. The *Times of India* which is the flagship of the media conglomerate Bennet, Coleman & Co. [*sic*] was the top newspaper in the year 2000 with 31.91% readership among urban net users in India. Among the electronic media players are the usual suspects – Zee TeleFilms, Udaya TV, Jain Studios, Asianet, Nimbus Communications and Modi Entertainment Network. Zee and the Times group have both applied for 40 licenses each, while Mid-Day has applied for six". The satellite and cable television market has also been affected by consolidation. The Zee TV empire, which is the largest of the homegrown media empires, became even larger following their acquisition of the South-India based Asianet channel. In the year 2000, Zee TV was ranked third in terms of viewership among urban net users (55.70%) and fifth in terms of urban non-net users (26.69%). A survey of the top 50 TV shows revealed that Zee TV owned 32 of these shows. Zee TV's stocks trade at a price to earnings ratio of 200 which is even higher than what some blue-chip software stock have been able to command (Kohli, 2000). The acquisition by Zee Telefilms of a significant stake in Padmalaya Film's, a leading entertainment house in India, is a significant move. It is an attempt to corner this market and add to Zee's ownership of ZICA, one of India's top animation production units. As reported in the *Hindu*

International Edition (23 March 2002), "This acquisition (will) help create India's number one animation software production house through the coming together of Padmalaya's Hyderabad-based studio and Zee's Mumbai based ZICA. Further, it gives Zee an important stepping-stone into the South Indian market. It also provides Zee with ready software of 300 movies in various languages and over 1,500 hours of television software . . . in several languages".

There is also an-on-going process of consolidation in the domestic cable market, through fair means and foul, by major players determined to wrest control of the "last mile". There are five major players in the cable industry: Siticable owned by the Zee TV empire, IndusInd Media owned by the Hindujas, Hathway Cables owned by the property tycoons the Rahejas, Sumangali Cable Vision owned by Kalanithi Maran of Sun TV and the network owned by Harsh Goenka of RPG.

Advertising, consumerism and the making of the global Indian

Front-runners in the Rs. 8,500 crores (US$1.7 billion) Indian advertising industry currently include Hindustan Thompson Associates, Mudra Communication Ltd., owned by the Ambanis, McCann-Erickson India Ltd., Ogilvy & Mather Ltd and Rediffusion – DY&R, a blend of local and multinational agencies. It is in the advertising industry that consolidation is at its peak. The world's largest agglomeration of advertising agencies, the US$40 billion Interpublic Group, plans to consolidate the buying power of all its Indian agencies with an integrated media services unit called Magna Global which "will represent the aggregate media negotiating interests of Interpublic's Indian entities with a total media spend of 1700 crores" (US$354 million). The world's second largest ad agency WPP formed Mindshare, which brings together four of India's top ad agencies that control a Rs. 3000 crores (US$624 million) billing (Ramalingam, 2001; Kohli, 2001). Given such developments, it would seem likely, that before too long, media buying power in India will be in the hands of two major players, each sharing a substantial transnational base, along with three smaller groups.

Advertising has become a primary means for expanding the consumer product market into rural and urban India. In the consumer product market the extent of corporatization is most visible. Today, in a little more than a decade, the average middle class Indian has turned into a consumer of branded, global goods symbolized by their choice of food products, clothes, cars, television sets and television channels, among other goods. From a middle class perspective, the availability of consumer choice has been welcome. Indian consumers, who had previously had no choice but to accept consumer products manufactured by the 75 local business families that dominated the private sector, now have other options. The business columnist and editor, TN Ninan (1999, 48) used findings from the magazine *Advertising and Marketing* (A&M) to illustrate the extent of corporate presence in India today. "Year after year, the magazine A&M does a survey of . . . the leading Indian brands; and year after year, the findings are the same. The foreign controlled companies that operate in India control the dominant brands. Of the top 30 brands listed by the magazine, 19 were foreign-owned/controlled, and only 11 were *desi* (locally-owned). Of the next 30, only 10 were *desi*, the rest were MNC-controlled. So two-thirds of the 60 leading brands are MNC controlled". Available reports also indicate that the rural consumer market too is being taken over by MNCs who have creatively adapted products to the sensibilities and purses of rural customers.

However, such trends are in themselves part of larger trends that have changed the texture of the Indian economy. Every sector of the Indian economy is now open to MNC led competition. Take for instance the leisure and entertainment industries. The big Indian marketing firms such as ORG-MARG and IRMB are, like the advertising industry, beholden to foreign shareholders. The leading Indian travel firms, Travel Corporation of India and Sita Travels, have been taken over by the UK based Thomas Cook and the Germany-based Kuoni. Franchising has become an established aspect of the leisure industry, as the fast food industry (McDonalds, SubWay, Starbucks), the entertainment industry (multiplex cinemas, game parlours, bowling alleys), and the health industry (hospitals, laboratories and fitness centres), function as extensions of the global market (Rao, 2000).

The digital economy in India

The services sector has begun to dominate earnings in the Indian economy and contributed to more than half of the national income, 52.4% in the 1999–2000 period. It earned US$6 billion in revenue in 2000, is projected to grow to a US$87 billion industry in 2008 and to employ 7 million people (Saran, 2001). The key sectors that contribute to the digital economy in India today are (1) IT and in particular software and allied services and (2) the entertainment industry. Much has been written about the software industry in India. The value of the sector to the Indian economy is illustrated by the following observation. The software exports during March–September 2000 alone earned £1.9 billion (US$3 billion). This represented 12.5% of India's total export earnings over the same period (Merchant, 2000a). A decade ago, this industry was worth US$150 million. Today it is worth US$5.7 billion and it is projected that in the year 2008 software export earnings alone will be in the region of US$8 billion. A total 184 of the Fortune 500 companies outsourced their software development to India in the year 2000. Today there are nearly a thousand companies involved in software exports alone. All the major software companies from the US are established actors in India, either on their own or in partnership with an Indian company. The IT industry employs nearly 430,114 people, second in number to the US (*Hindustan Times Online*, 2002).

India has become the global manager of the round the clock office that is based on the exploitation of numerous opportunities related to tele-work. (Taylor, 2000, Merchant, 2000b). Today there are more than 14,000 employees working in the remote-processing business. US-based hospital chains, insurance companies, credit card companies and law firms are outsourcing low value processing work to countries like India. For example, the multinational medical transcription firm Healthscribe, headquartered in Virginia, provides services to 18 US-based hospitals. It organizes all its transcription services from its set-up in Bangalore at costs that are roughly 20 times cheaper than if they were done in the US (Mukerjea and Dhawan, 1999). Such opportunities for local employment and export earnings must however be seen in the light of the fact that this fast growing sector of the Indian economy is tied to and nurtured by a particular market, that of the US, which accounted for 60% of software exports from India in the year 2000. This over-reliance on the US market does have its limitations – the recent example of the contraction of the dotcom market in India is a direct reflection of dotcom fortunes in the USA that have taken a battering since 2000.

A potentially powerful, emerging industry is the entertainments sector, in particular animation. The March 2000 Ficci-Arthur Anderson report on the Indian entertainment industry estimates revenue figures of Rs. 8,445 crores (US$18.8 billion) in the year 2000 and predicts that it will reach Rs. 33,984 crores (US$755.1 billion) in the year 2005, of which Rs. 14,692 crores (US$32.6 billion) will come from film exports alone (Dutta, 2001). With an average yearly production output of 800 films in regional languages, the Indian film industry produces more films than Hollywood each year. Film and film-based spin-offs such as film music have become the basis for a multi-million dollar, regional language centred satellite and cable television industry. There are three potential growth areas in the entertainments sector in India:

1. An overseas market for Indian film, music and entertainment software: There is a booming film export business to the Middle East, Europe, North America and South East Asia. In the year 2000, US$800 million was spent by overseas Indians on Indian movies, serials and music. India movies earned over Rs. 400 crores (US$88 million) in the international market and it is expected that that film exports will grow over 80% by the year 2003. In recent years, Indian films such as the Oscar nominated *Lagaan*, *Asoka* and *Kabhi Kushi Kabhie Gham* (*K3G*) have contributed to film export earnings that are projected to reach US$349 million in 2005. Film export earnings grew from "Rs 200 crores (US$41 million) in FY 1998 to Rs 450 crores (US$93 million) in FY 2000 with the UK, USA and Canada accounting for 55 per cent of export revenues. In the week December 14–21, 2001, K3G was the third highest gross earner among films in the UK" (Joshi, 2001). As Rao (2000: 3571) observed " . . . the entertainment industry . . . is expected to see in five years, film exports grow from Rs. 400 crores (US$88 million) to Rs. 1000 crores (US$2.2 billion), cable and satellite advertising from Rs. 1,366 (US$ 3.0 billion) to Rs. 2,050 crores (US$ 4.6 billion), music from Rs. 1,700 crores (US$3.8 billion) to Rs. 3,000 crores (US$6.7 billion) . . . Entertainment software is expected to export US$20 billion by the year 2008 and employ 15 million people".

2. Animation: Specifically the outsourcing of products for global studios. Leading companies include the Mumbai-based Unilazar Group and the Chennai-based Pentafour.

3. Investments in domestic broadbanding services by multi-channel companies who are poised to take advantage of the demands for entertainment in the domestic market. Today regional media moguls like Subhash Chandra of Zee TV, Kalanithi Maran of SunTV and Ramoji Rao of Eenadu are creating new regional entertainment pipelines via satellite television and cable television. Their ambitions are linked to providing a host of services including Internet, telephony, video-on-demand and other services. Others like the Modi group have invested in giant multiplex cinemas. There are 6,000 production houses in India involved in creating software for this thriving, growing market (Kohli, et al. 2000).

Poverty in the new economy

In spite of remarkable developments in the media industry in India, a significant proportion of Indians have not benefited from this growth, except as passive consumers of the media. Take for instance the IT scenario in India that is inextricably linked to key cities, notably Bangalore that has been referred to as the Silicon Valley of India. Bangalore is the capital city of the state of Karnataka, the eighth largest state in India with a population of 45 million. It has become a success story, the home of software exports and the generator of export earnings for the country. The city employs 65,000 IT professionals. From being a relatively unknown player in the global information economy, this city has contributed substantively to the US$3.9 billion earned through software exports by IT firms in India in the year 2000. All the information on Bangalore's IT success – the statistics, the stories, the downturns and upturns – are easily available in the media. What is relatively inaccessible is information on the other side of the IT revolution in Bangalore, its marginal impact on communities existing within a city that is considered to be one of the hubs of the IT revolution in the South.

A majority (70%) of the population of Karnataka is involved in agricultural or allied activities. The incidence of urban poverty in Bangalore is not worse than any of the big cities in India although it is on the increase and in all probability reflects the poverty index of India that is in the region of 35%. There are more than 750 small or large urban shantytowns in the city and an estimated 65,000 street children. While the city corporation breezes through infrastructure development projects on behalf of the IT sector, some of these developments takes place at the expense of massive displacements of the already poor. A recent example of this is the making of the Bangalore-Mysore Infrastructure Corridor, a development project intended to benefit the IT industry and its employees. Plans include the making of a six-lane express highway linking Mysore and Bangalore, and a real estate venture related to the building of five townships with an 18 hole golf course and other luxury facilities for Bangalore's nouveau rich. The corporation has acquired 20,000 acres of land, of which 13,000 acres are currently being used for agricultural purposes. It is estimated that 168 villages will be depopulated by this development. Job opportunities in the IT sector have scarcely benefited the urban poor except in a very marginal sort of way. As one observer (Rao, 1998) pointed out "Bangalore provides a good example of the wide range of opportunities arising in the wake of the setting up of numerous hi-tech industries, precisely the scenario visualised by the proponents of economic reform ... And yet, a study done in 1996 indicates that the poor households living in villages in the close vicinity of the city could hardly benefit ... from the rising temperature of its economic activities excepting access to low-paid informal sector employment". The poor who have benefited from this economy are more usually than not in low-paid, assembly-line employment, characterized by job insecurity because their employers have been guaranteed non-unionized labour. Women workers in particular are victims of poor working conditions, are often exploited and suffer from health problems as a result of contact with hazardous material. In a real sense, this example is a metaphor for development, of the exercise of power in India and of the selective, sector-specific development priorities of both the central and state governments. Arundhati Roy (1999: 61), in one of the best written accounts of development in contemporary India, observed, "Power is fortified not just by what it destroys, but also by what it creates. Not just by what it takes, but also by what it gives. And Powerlessness is reaffirmed not just by the helplessness of those who have lost, but also by the gratitude of those who have (or think they have) gained".

Such downbeat stories rarely hit the headlines in the South and the North. It is one example of the turn away from serious reporting of concerns that ought to be in the public eye. The reporting of poverty in general has become a low priority throughout the world. As news media have transformed into commercial entities, rural reporting and rural reporters are fast becoming a thing of the past. It is interesting to note that while in the 1990s, newspapers in South and South East Asia assigned reporters by the dozen to cover fashion, design, entertainment, eating out and financial and business news, not a single reporter was intentionally assigned to cover poverty related issues. This trend is in all probability global rather than merely regional. There are occasions when features of the Old Economy such as starvation, famine, and destitution get out of hand and reporters are forced to deal with the real world. Such realities affected at least three of the "richest", IT-savvy states of Andhra Pradesh, Gujarat, and Maharashtra in the year 2000.

The control state

The Indian government's support for the media industry stands in marked contrast to its stance on the right to communicate. Every single attempt to reform broadcasting, to democratize access to information, to create an autonomous, independent broadcasting agency and to create regulatory bodies has been scuttled, shelved, or seriously diluted to maintain government control. Take for instance the creation of an autonomous broadcasting corporation – the Prashar Bharati – that has been on the cards since 1979. The process of creating this institution was stalled by the present government and placed on track only after its board was staffed by acolytes sympathetic to the "saffron" agenda of the BJP. Government dithering over the Freedom of Information Bill is another example of the exercise of state control over its citizens. The Freedom of Information Bill, if passed by parliament, will make it mandatory for all rungs of the government to be open to public scrutiny of their accounts, to be accountable to their electorate. This is a brave piece of legislation, although at this moment in time no one is sure if it will become a Bill given the stakes involved, and the many potential embarrassments to the government bureaucracy and the political system if government complicity and corruption become targets for contestations. The government has tried to dilute this piece of legislation through the creation of a variety of caveats citing "national security" and secrecy, thus exonerating certain departments from its purview. Article 19, the Global Campaign for Free Expression, in a Memorandum on the Indian Freedom of Information Bill, 2000 (2000: 1–10) pointed out some of its major flaws – including its failure "... to provide for independent review of refusals to disclose information", the "blanket exclusion of key intelligence and security organisations" and "an excessively broad range of exemptions". The March 2002 Prevention of Terrorism Ordinance (POTO), hastily passed in the light of the 11 September incident, has been rightly criticized for the power that it gives the government to rein in dissenters, including journalists. Such attempts to further government control needs to be seen against recent exposes of the deep correspondences between politics, money and power through a 'sting' operation that was carried out by an investigative journalism website 'Tehelka' (http://www.tehelka.com). Posing as representatives of a fictitious arms company, Tehelka's journalists struck an arms deal by bribing among others, the ex-President of the BJP, the defence minister, other government functionaries, including defence personnel. It was recorded and the entire transcript and videoed excerpts are available on the Tehelka website. Instead of taking decisive action against the bribe takers, the journalists involved including Tarun Tejpal have been targeted for severe repression.

Redeeming alternatives

While the government has, in the recent past, hinted at "freeing the airwaves" and creating space for community broadcasting, this is not a cause for optimism given the government's past record. There are, however, signs that technological convergence has granted civil society opportunities to creatively bypass government restrictions. The US-based digital radio consortium World Space, has been in negotiations with NGOs to provide development programmes, and local government too has been negotiating with this company for a satellite-based digital radio service. There are possibilities for Internet-based community radio although to date they remain experimental broadcasts and in very localized regions.

The single most challenging obstacle to media reform is large-scale public apathy over information/communication rights. While there are numerous media-based NGOs that have organized around a variety of enthusiasms, their activities have not reached critical mass. Ordinary Indian citizens continue to remain unsympathetic to communication rights related issues and concerns. This apathy is illustrated by the fact that not a single consortium of NGOs in India had contributed to national, regional or global efforts linked to ensuring maximum civil society participation at the first phase of the UN-sponsored World Summit on the Information Society (WSIS) held in Geneva in 2003 and the second phase scheduled to be held in Tunis in 2005. When contrasted with other mobilizations on human rights-related issues, this lack of interest is striking. It will take a nation-wide media reform movement to stem media concentration and consolidation. For the moment, however, the status quo remains intact.

References

Article 19 (2000) Memorandum on the Indian Freedom of Information Bill, 2000. http://www.article19.org

Chatterjee, A. (2002) 'Common man will be hit'. *Hindu Online* 1 March. http://www.hinduonnet.com.

Chawla, V. et. al. (1992) 'The great switching saga'. *Computers and Communication*, December. pp. 53–81.

Deccan Herald Online (2002) 'Sinha flatters only to deceive'. 1 March. http://www.deccanherald.com.

Dutta, S. (2001) 'Real life, reel woes'. *BusinessWorld* 15 January. pp.1-3. http://www.businessworldindia.com/archive.

Hindustan Times Online/Press Trust of India (2002) 'Software export to grow by 30% to Rs 37,000 cr in 2001–02'. 14 March.

Hindu, International Edition (2002) 'Zee to buy stake in Padmalaya'. 23 March. p. 11.

Joshi, N. (2001) 'Exporting dreams: Frontier mail'. http://www.outlook.com, 14 January.

Kohli, V. (2000) 'India media patterns – 2000'. *Satellite and Cable TV* January. pp. 1–2.

Kohli, V. (2001) 'Collective muscle'. *Business World* 6 August. p. 19.

Kohli, V. et al.(2001) 'It's showtime folks'. *BusinessWorld* 10 January.

Lobo, A.(2001) 'In tune with the times'. *Business India* 23 July–5 August. p. 94.

Merchant, K. (2000a) 'India's software exports surge'. *Financial Times* 2 November. p. 21.

Merchant, K. (2000b) 'Hard sell for software'. *Financial Times Survey: Indian Information Technology* 4 January. pp. i–iv.

Mukerjea, D.N. and Dhawan, R. (1999) 'Teleworking: The hottest business opportunity for India'. *BusinessWorld* 7 January. pp. 1–6. http://www. businessworldindia.com/archive.

NASSCOM (2003) 'Software exports'. http://www.nasscom.org.

Ninan, T.N. (1999) 'Chequered past, uncertain future'. *Seminar*, 482, October pp. 46–51.

Ninan, T.N. (1992) 'Manmohanics; Whats in store'. *Voices*, Vol. 1. pp. 3–6.

Ramalingam, A. (2001) 'Consolidation is the name of the game'. *Business Today*, 19 August. p. 52.

Rao, S.L. (2000) 'India's rapidly changing consumer markets'. *Economic and Political Weekly* 30 September. pp. 3570–3572.

Rao, V.M. (1998) 'Economic reforms and the poor: Emerging scenario'. *Economic and Political Weekly* 1 July. pp. 1949–1954.

Roy, A. (1999) *The Greater Common Good*. Bombay: India Book Distributors Limited.

Saran, R. (2001) 'The new economy: Services sector, growth engine'. *India Today* 19 February. http://www.india-today.com. pp. 1–3.

Singh, S. (2001) 'The shakeout begins now'. *Business World* 23 July. pp. 24–27.

Slater, J. (2002) 'Ever so slowly'. *Far Eastern Economic Review* 14 March. pp. 48–49.

Tarraqqi, M. (2001) 'Second generation economic reforms: Proposal to freeze social spending budget allocations'. http://www.geocities.com. April–June.

Taylor, P. (2000) 'New pioneers at the helm'. *Financial Times Survey* 2 November. p. iii.

The Times of India Online (2002) 'Tatas to invest over Rs.10,000 cr in telecom'. 14 February. http://www.timesofindia.com.

Times of India Online (2002) 'It hits who it hurts the most'. 2 March. http://www. timesofindia.com.

The Political Economy of Media Ownership in Nigeria

Mohammed Musa and Jubril Mohammed

Introduction

This chapter examines the two broad, but interconnected, issues of ownership and control in the mass media sector in Nigeria. In doing this, we highlight the character of the economy and attendant social structure of the country as a necessary framework for examining the condition for the foundation of the mass media in Nigeria. Subsequently, we focus specifically on the character of ownership and control dominant in the mass media sector. The implication of the latter to democracy and freedom for the majority, who are labouring, poor and disadvantaged in the extant distribution of power, is extrapolated.

Economy and society in Nigeria

When the British formally colonized the country, the main thrust of their economic policy was essentially the successive transformation of the colony into an exporter of primary goods and consumer of manufactured imports. It was also to create a vast reserve for cheap labour to facilitate huge returns on British colonial investments.

For instance, in the agricultural sector, British policy emphasized the cultivation of cash crops mainly for exports, notably palm oil and kernel, cocoa, groundnuts, rubber, citrus fruits, kola nuts, cotton, beneseeds, shea butter, and hides and skins. Added to this was the ruthless exploitation of cheap labour for tin and coal mining and the introduction of a common currency as legal tender by the British.

The construction of the colonial economy also witnessed the ruthless liquidation of indigenous middlemen. In the coastal flanks of the oil rivers, indigenous middlemen such as King Jaja of Opobo, Nan Olomu of Ebrohimi in Itsekiriland, and the Brassmen of Nembe for instance, sometimes called "oil princes" emerged by 1860 to mediate in the palm oil and palm kernel trade between producers in the hinterland and

European traders along the coast. These oil princes, nay heads of trading houses, resisted the British incursion in the second half of the 19th century, a posture the colonialists refused to countenance. Through a combination of dubious treaties and physical might, these middlemen were totally subdued and their roles taken over by foreign trading companies. Notable among these were United African Company (UAC), John Holt, Lever Brothers, Company of African Merchants, Anglo African Company, African Merchants of Bristol, Royal Niger Navigation and Trading Company and Merchants of London-Liverpool Trading to West Coast of Africa were all British (see Dike 1960 for more on this).

The trading companies relied on the various commodity marketing boards established by the colonial administration to control the sources of production, rule out any competition and manipulate the pricing mechanism in their favour. Among them include Cocoa Marketing Board, Groundnut Marketing Board and Palm Produce Marketing Boards, all established in 1949 (Onimode, 1985: 50). These Boards were later regionalized depending on the commodities and their respective areas of production.

Under the marketing board system, a new form of middlemanship emerged. The producers were expected first of all to sell their produce to individuals who, very often pay prices lower than official rates. These individuals, who operated as agents, turned over what they purchased to the trading companies who were the official and accredited agents of the marketing boards. These trading companies would feed the marketing boards that were all organized under the central marketing board in Lagos. At the international level was the London based Nigerian produce marketing company which arranged shipment for onward sale at the so-called world market (Onimode, 1983: 50). African middlemen were at best incorporated into the colonial commercial network as junior agents supervised by the trading companies.

To accelerate the transportation of bulk produce to the coastal areas, the colonial administration embarked on the construction of roads and rail lines across the country. These projects were executed through a combination of forced labour and high taxation. By 1992, a total of 1,265 miles of rails had been laid (Ekundare 1973) in addition to over 6,000 miles of road network already in place by 1926 (Onimode; 1983: 45).

In the mining and mineral sector, foreign multinational companies were involved as early as 1900. Tin and columbite were mined in the Bauchi-Jos Plateau, coal in Enugu, salt in Muri and on a smaller scale silver, lead, petroleum and diamond (Onimode, 1983: 53–54).

Thus, on the whole, contrary to what was evident in the pre-colonial economy which was predominantly based on internal dynamics of operation, the new colonial economy, based on capitalist production relations, was now essentially responsive to external dynamics, i.e., the moods of the British economy. This situation marked the effective incorporation of the Nigerian economy, as a producer of primary goods, cheap labour source and consumer of western manufactured products cheap labour and consumer of western manufactured products, into a global capitalist economy.

On the basis of this colonial political economy, it may be argued that Britain controlled the economic, political and cultural life of Nigeria. It had absolute jurisdiction by virtue of conquest, over the material wealth, real and political, of the country. It supplanted, through forceful means, the assortment of slave and feudal modes of production dominant in the kingdoms and city-states out of whose demise the colony and protectorate of Nigeria was forged.

Consequently, the British imperialist state deployed its agents such as the Governor-General, Regional Governors, Lt. Governors, Residents and Divisional Officers in addition to several directors and heads of administrative departments, to exercise formal political authority in the country. These were joined by agents of leading imperialist commercial/ industrial firms operating as produce buyers and sellers of manufactured goods, banking representatives, representatives of private capitalist mining companies and hordes of missionaries. These came together to constitute the colonial state in Nigeria.

The British imperial bourgeoisie, aided though to a lesser extent by those of France, Germany, Portugal along with Lebanese, Syrians, Yamanis, constituted the dominant class in the Nigerian colonial political economy. This class owned, in various ways, the means of production. It had absolute authority over land and mineral resources and technology (though this was largely left undeveloped) and using state policy, controlled the deployment of labour. In addition, by virtue of this control, it exercised the capacity to appropriate the surplus labour of the working classes.

Beneath this class there was the class of those people who were created by and or co-opted to serve the needs of the imperialist state. This class included the educated Nigerians who met the requirements for middle level bureaucrats to man the expanding administrative structures of the state, their counterparts at the middle levels of the colonial commercial concerns as well as the traditional rulers, the Emirs, Obas, Warrant Chiefs, who now collected taxes for the colonial administration and conscripted forced labour for the mines, construction projects and the colonial army. All these which formed the colonial petite bourgeoisie were bound together as a class by their role as employed servants of the imperial state, a means through which they all derived their income.

The third social class within the colonial political economy was the working class. Central here were the peasant farmers who were the subsistence cultivators and producers of cash crops such as palm oil and kernel, cocoa, rubber, cotton, groundnuts, etc. that formed the bases of the colonial economy and the key items of the legitimate trade. This stratum of the working class was the most ruthlessly appropriated more so, as subsistence agriculture took a back seat to cash crop production. The imperial state made insignificant efforts to tranform the productivity of the subsistence farmers.

Workers of the rich mineral mines and infrastructure construction projects formed the second stratum of the working class in the colonial political economy. Like their counterparts in agriculture, they were ruthlessly exploited. As conscripts they were forced to live in camps and to work long hours on barely subsistence wages. Until the dawn of the Second World War these workers were not unionized and unable to fight for improved working conditions, better wages, a pension scheme and humane working hours among others.

These were the three major social classes borne of the colonial political economy. Given the process of its construction, and the subsequent consolidation and development of new capitalist production relations there were bound to be numerous intra and inter class disagreements, conflicts, frictions, in other words, contradictions. These contradictions, which sometimes broke into open confrontations, existed at various levels. For instance, the violent confrontations and wars spanning several decades across the country between the new dominant capitalist class and the erstwhile feudal lords and slave masters of the obsolescent feudal and slave modes prevalent in the erstwhile pre-colonial Kingdoms and city states that resulted in the defeat of the latter. Similarly, the contradiction between the colonial capitalist class and the indigenous petite bourgeoisie nurtured the seeds of the nationalist struggles from the 1920s.

However, the principal contradiction of the colonial political economy was between the colonial state and the working classes over the effective attainment of the goal of imperialist colonial acquisition to exploit the material and human resources of the colony to serve the needs of British imperialism.

The foundation of the press

Although students of media studies in Nigeria have written copiously on the origin of the mass media in the country there are, unarguably, areas of agreement as well as disagreement in their respective accounts.

For instance, there is marked agreement on the chronology of events from 1846 when the first printing press in Nigeria was established in

Calabar in the South East by the Reverend Hope Wadell of the Church of Scotland Mission to the foundation of the *Iwe Irohin fun awon ara Egba ati Yoruba* (the newspaper for the Egba people and Yoruba) in Abeoukuta, South Western Nigeria by the Reverend Henry Townsend of the English Church Missionary Society in 1859, and to the contemporary proliferation of newspapers in the country. Again, there is high concurrence on the identity of personages associated with the foundation of various newspapers within the same period.

However, there appears to be room for divergence of opinion on the interpretation of the historical significance of the founding of the newspaper in the country was and its significance to the future of both the country and the West African coast.

For example, writing about the Reverend Townsend and the process leading to the foundation of the newspaper, Duyile said

> On 17th December 1842 he arrived at Badagry and worked with many Sierra Leonian freed slaves and natives of Badagry . . . Rev. Townsend left for Abeokuta where he lived the rest of his missionary life, and there in 1854 he established a small printing press. Five years after he set up an African Christian newspaper the 'Iwe Irohin ...' His motive among others was to excite the intelligence of the people in his area of operation and to get them read. (Duyile 1987: 6)

Similarly, Omu has also written about the missionary linkage in the genesis of the newspaper press in Nigeria. He stated that the missionaries

> Embarked upon programmes of western education and general enlightenment in Sierra Leone and subsequent in what became the colonies of Nigeria, Gold Coast, Gambia. Their most enduring weapon was the school but journalism played important role. The newspaper had been established as an essential instrument of mission work outside Britain as a result of the effective use, which the British humanitarian movement made of it in mobilizing support for their programmes. (Omu, 1978: 6)

Both scholars appear to conceive of the newspaper merely as an instrument for the attainment of the goal of missionary activity, specifically evangelism and humanitarianism. Even on the few instances when allusion is made to the political role of the *Iwe Irohin*, it is done, more often than not, in the narrow context of Egba politics (for instance, see Duyile, 1987: 16)

Again, it seems both scholars do not recognize the extraordinary connection between the activities of the Christian missions and the goals of colonialism. In other words, they conceive of Christian missionary work as purely for the mind and soul while colonialism was for the politics and economy as a result of which their relationship is depicted in a superficial, and at best, administrative manner.

As both scholars have hardly gone beyond the Christian Missionary activity in explaining the origin of the newspaper press, they interpret the historic foundation of the newspaper and its significance to the future course of events in that limited context too. Consequently, their account, which we term as the ecumenical theory of origin of the press, tends to miss the essence of the development and thus, stopped short of being properly historical.

To understand the foundation of the newspaper press, indeed the entire mass media, it must be situated in a proper historical context, specifically in the context of the class struggle that engendered colonialism and the establishment of the capitalist mode of production in Nigeria. Accordingly, we shall attempt to show that the foundation of the *Iwe Irohin* just like the deployment of Sierra-Leonian ex-slaves to Badagry and subsequently, Lagos and Abeokuta was part of the process of establishing the structures of colonialism. Thus, notwithstanding the missionary background of its founders, the *Iwe Irohin* was primarily, though not exclusively, a political instrument for the articulation, propagation, coordination and defence of imperialist ideology in Egbaland. *Iwe Irohin* was, in essence, established "to mobilize the minds and ideas of people, over time to accept and adopt capitalist values and practices" (Ibrahim, 1981).

Elsewhere, Mohammed has suggested that if the goal of colonialism was the rabid appropriation of the human and material resources of the colony, then British incursion and intervention into local African affairs in the 19th century, which was widely hinged on humanitarianism and evangelism, in effect merely found ideological legitimation in them (Mohammed, 2000: 72).

Thus, the second half of that century witnessed intensive imperialist bickering with coastal middlemen. Through tricky treaties combined with gunboat diplomacy various European powers were able to extend their spheres of influence into the hinterland. The 1884/85 Berlin conference for the partition of Africa among the leading imperialist powers was conceived primarily to regulate intra-imperialist rivalries in the process of African colonization.

For Britain, therefore, with an established role as anti-slavery crusader and, with traditional commitment to the settler colony of Sierra Leone which it founded in 1787, it evolved a policy of utilizing these ex-slaves who had widely attained literacy and proficiency in various trades and, along with these, attained exposure to imperialist ideology and values to promote British imperial interest along the coast and in the hinterland. It was therefore not surprising that barely 14 years after the foundation of

Sierra Leone company, the officers of the Sierra Leone company (who were administering the territory before it was redesignated a colony in 1808) established *The Royal Gazette* in 1801 (Omu 1978: 5). This newspaper, which was the first along the West African coast, existed up till 1827 (Omu, 1978: 5).

Fyfe reported that at its best, *The Royal Gazette*, which was later renamed *The Royal Gazette* and *Sierra Leone Advertiser* in the 1920s, carried local news, advertisements, poems, letters and accounts of fashionable life in Freetown (Fyfe, 1957). These undoubtedly capitalistic reports related the activities of the Europeans and the settlers rather than those of the local inhabitants.

It was probably the successful experience of Sierra Leone that encouraged General (Sir) Charles Macarthy, Governor of the Gold Coast settlements to establish *The Royal Gold Coast Gazette* in 1822.

Thus, both in Sierra Leone and Gold Coast (now Ghana) the administration effectively pioneered the foundation of the newspaper. It was probably due to the successes of these government initiatives in both Sierra Leone and Gold Coast, that the British imperialist state devised a new strategy (probably to conceal its direct involvement at this early attempt) at penetrating the hinterland, by relying on Christian missions assisted by Sierra Leonian emigrants in Badagry, Lagos and Abeokuta in Yorubaland to prosecute the twin ideological function of education and evangelism, indeed journalism, for future colonial penetration. For as Onimode noted,

> . . . the impact of Christian ideology imposed on West Africa after the 15th century which facilitated the penetration of imperial values also effected cultural alienation to the extent that it still persists today, Christian missionaries were cultural agents of mercantilist imperialism. (Onimode; 1983: 25)

In 1842, both Rev. Hope Wadell and Rev. Henry Townsend, who had both been in Sierra Leone, left for Badagry to continue to work among Sierra Leonian emigrants. From Badagry, Rev. Wadell moved to Calabar in the south-east where he established the first printing press in Nigeria in 1846. Townsend moved to Abeokuta in the south-west, and in 1854, like Wadell, he established a printing press. Five years later he began publishing the *Iwe Irohin* as a vernacular newspaper for the Egbas and the Yorubas. The initiative was so successful that a year later an English supplement was added (Omu, 1978: 7).

Allusions have also been made about the quality of the content of *Iwe Irohin*, which was said to favour the Egba point of view. In an account in which Ade Ajayi lamented the destruction of the *Iwe Irohin* in the anti-European Ifole riots of 1867 in Egbaland, he said;

> It was a spontaneous uprising . . . libraries were destroyed, harmonium broken down, and the printing works where the "Iwe Irohin" had so often proclaimed the Egba point of view was destroyed. (Ajayi, cited in Duyile, 1987: 21)

Similarly, Suburi Biobaku has commented on Townsend's activities in Egbaland in the following words:

> Townsend's prestige reached its zenith. He was not only the amanuensis of the Egba 'nation' but he was regarded as the author of their deliverance from the Dahomi. Henceforth, he must be acknowledged as the real architect of Egba policy toward the British. His objective was peace in which missionary and other civilizing influences might flourish and the great obstacle which must be overcome was the foreign slave trade. (Biobaku cited in Duyile 1987: 25)

But if as it has been claimed that *Iwe Irohin* was even the amanuensis of the Egba nation, then why was it victimized in the Ifole anti-European riots of 1867? If it had so much as defended Egba against Dahomi as Biobaku claimed, why was *Iwe Irohin*, indeed Townsend, reluctant to support the same Egba in their claim to areas near Lagos as part of their frontier against the British, by now firmly entrenched in Lagos?

A statement by George Townsend's brother to Henry Townsend and one of his biographers, is revealing at least in establishing the initial motive behind the establishment of *Iwe Irohin*.

> The publication of Iwe Irohin shows what was attempted among the secondary means of introducing new life and thought in Africa, Thus **leading up to the grand idea of substituting lawful tariff for that of the trade in human creatures**, with all its horrible commitments, a consummation devoutly to be wished. (Our emphasis) (Townsend, cited in Duyile, 1978: 23)

Thus, from George it is clear that *Iwe Irohin* was in fact, primarily a means of introducing new life and thought, i.e., those acquiescent of the goal of British imperial presence in the west coast and in Nigeria, and "leading up to the development of British economic activities" substituting lawful tariff for that of the trade in human creatures. Thus the promotion of the ideology and economic prosperity of (British) imperialism were the twin factors underlying the foundation of the *Iwe Irohin* as the first newspaper in Nigeria.

The development of the mass media, 1850–1937

Duyile reported that after *Iwe Irohin* the birth of Robert Campbell's *The Anglo-African* on 6 June 1863 introduced slightly a critical element in newspaper content. He stated that *The Anglo-African* devoted its front pages to publish advertisements, notices and announcements. It carried local news, and a lot of editorials dealing with issues of those years. It was ahead of Townsend's *Iwe Irohin* "in news coverage and editorial issues" (Duyile, 1987: 29). It must be pointed out that Campbell's slightly critical posture may have been informed by the frustrating ordeals of the educated African intelligentsia, the colonial petite bourgeoisie, in the face of discrimination – an experience which, for instance explains why Campbell was highly critical of Townsend in the latter's conflict with Bishop Samuel Ajayi Crowther (Omu, 1978: 21). Omu observed that:

> In the 1860s the African intellectuals who had hitherto cooperated with the missionaries as the only means by which they could pave way for the creation of a modern African nation were becoming disillusioned and frustrated. They were finding it increasingly difficult to reconcile missionary proclamations of Christian ethics with evidences of glaring hypocrisy . . . (Omu, 1978: 21)

Following the demise of the *Anglo-African* on 30 December 1865 no publication was issued until the 1880s (Duyile 1987: 31). It must be pointed out that during this period the internal politics of Yorubaland, Benin, the Aro country, the oil rivers and Old Calabar display evidence of massive internal decay while the British colonial state was not prepared to brook any African leader impeding their advancement into the hinterland.

Thus from the annexation of Lagos in 1862 the struggle between these two social classes within the colonial political economy was eventually to be resolved in favour of the imperialist colonial bourgeoisie. Formal colonial authority was proclaimed throughout the colony and protectorate of Nigeria was formed by the first decade of the 20th century.

During this process, the African intelligentsia was predominantly acquiescent of the calculations of the imperialist colonial state. For, having been socialized into western capitalist values through education, the African intelligentsia initially took up jobs within the colonial bureaucracy, at the ports and commercial establishments, schools and Christian missions. Others opted to be self-employed either as technicians, legal and medical practitioners and journalists among others.

The intelligentsia was led, through their process of immersion into aspiring in the future, to enjoy the rights and privileges of their contemporaries in Europe such as equality of opportunities, freedom against discrimination, freedom of speech and assorted liberal democratic values. Their experience of discrimination in the colonial service, commerce and even in the missions was to push them into radical reappraisal.

> ... the frustrations of educated Africans which had been gathering momentum from the 1860s, and the keen competition which became a feature of commerce from the 1870s was added the growing circulation of learning and the eruption of nationalist and intellectual fervour in the 1880s and after ... (Omu, 1978: 21)

Thus, the 1880s through to the 1920s and 1930s saw the beginning of sporadic agitation by the colonial petite bourgeoisie especially the intelligentsia. Excluded from the colonial executive council, repressed in the legislature, frustrated in the bureaucracy, commerce, and the missions and schools, these educated Africans turned to journalism to challenge their oppressors. In the first phase which lasted up to the Second World War, they were agitating for fairness, justice and equity within the colonial order, but in the second phase which proceeded from the post war years they demanded for national independence, to be free and sovereign within the comity of nations. It is against this background that the establishment of a plethora of newspapers in the country from the 1880s should be perceived and appreciated.

In this period a total of 58 publications with varying frequencies were issued. This figure did not include Christian missionary publications. In Lagos 42 newspapers were published while 16 were based in the hinterland. Of these newspapers, only seven were vernacular papers. The vast majority were in English language. Thus, most of the country's newspapers were concentrated in Lagos, a situation which has continued till today. Again, with English as the dominant language of communication in Nigerian newspapers, it means that during the period under review, readership was limited to those literate in the English language, a proportion undoubtedly insignificant in relation to the overall population of the territories these newspapers were meant to serve.

Furthermore, all the 58 newspapers issued in the period under review were owned by members of the petite bourgeoisie, specifically the African intelligentsia. In very many cases, they served as owners and editors of their respective newspapers. Being educated and skilled in various occupations, the views of various African intelligentsia were considered weighty in shaping public opinion. This is primarily because of their knowledge of the colonial system having been employees at various times in its service. Some of them had crowned their educational attainments with degrees from England. These and many more were to broaden their focus relative to their under-privileged compatriots, thereby ascribing to them the duties of opinion leadership.

Thus, from the advent of the 20th century into the fist two decades, the dominant themes in newspaper activity were cultural nationalism and anti-racism. Cultural nationalism found expression in the popularization of traditional African names, symbols, attire, vernacular press and literature and the eventual Africanization of the church.

As for anti-racism, scores of skilled Africans resigned their appointments in the colonial service in favour of journalism, now seen as a thriving alternative occupation. But more importantly, journalism became the latest avenue, after the schools and churches, for decisive "counter-hegemonic" campaigns within the colonial order. Such campaigns were eventually significant in adding pressure on the colonial authorities to make some constitutional concessions.

In addition to bowing to pressure through constitutional reform the colonial state sought other ways of staving off the vociferous press. Three methods may be discerned.

First, inducements to win the friendliness of newspaper owners. This was manifest in granting advertisements to augment the journal's financial base. For example, *The Eagle* and *Lagos Critic*, a monthly publication founded by Owen Emerick Macaulay, a grandson of Bishop Samuel Ajayi Crowther and brother of Herbert Macaulay, on 31 March 1883 was partially sustained by the advertisements inserted by the administration of Lt.-Governor W.B. Griffith, Moloney's predecessor (Omu, 1978). Similarly, Governor G.T. Carter was said to have arranged to place government notices worth 150 pounds sterling per year in the *Lagos Weekly Records*, a foremost example of bellicose public opinion in the last decade of the 19th century. The arrangement survived Carter's departure from Lagos in 1896 and was not terminated till 1900 (Omu, 1978: 31–34).

The second method was for the colonial authorities to encourage friendly educated Nigerians to establish newspapers, understandably with an editorial policy that would not be caustic. Examples here include *The Nigeria Pioneer* and *Daily Times*. The *Pioneer* was established by a successful Lagos lawyer Sir Kitoyi Ajasa. Omu reports that he was the most celebrated "Black Englishman" of his time having had his post primary through university education in England. He was cricket captain in his grammar school days where he won the respect of his peers. In Lagos, he endeared himself to the European population, who reposed so much confidence in him that most of the merchants among them employed him as their counsel. For Ajasa, peaceful persuasion was a better way of getting government to redress grievances than violence and vituperations which displeased those in authority and destroyed all chances of success (Omu

1978: 44–45). According to Allister Macmillan, *The Pioneer* was founded following persuasion from Governor Egerton to get Ajasa to start a newspaper that would voice the opinions of both whites and blacks (Allister Macmillan cited in Omu 1978: 48). *The Daily Times* was founded in 1926 by Adeyemo Aladja, a successful Lagos lawyer who was foundation chairman of the Board, Richard Burrow, Chairman of the Lagos Chamber of Commerce and Ernest Ikoli who was founding editor. Ikoli once said that their aim was to found a daily in the tradition of *The Times of London*: "our policy is to support government as much as possible" (Ikoli cited in Omu, 1978: 62).

The third method of silencing the critical press was through the law. Notable here were the Newspaper Ordinance, 1903 and the Seditious Offenses Ordinance, 1909. The former imposed stiff financial requirements before establishing a newspaper while the latter made an editor liable for reports that cause or were likely to cause disaffection in the minds of readers against the colonial administration (Elias, 1964).

On the whole, however, the struggle of the African intelligentsia in this period was not geared at a fundamental restructuring of the colonial status of Nigeria nor was it aimed at a radical transformation of the colonial system. They essentially needed equity, justice and fair play within the colonial order.

Development of the mass media, 1937–1960

During the phase 1937–1960, the Second World War was perhaps the most critical event of the period with far-reaching impact on the country. In 1937, Nnamdi Azikiwe, then 33 years old, returned to Nigeria having successfully trained as a political scientist at Lincoln University in the US and distinguished himself as a university professor, publicist and journalist. He founded the *West African Pilot* in November as a newspaper chain that was to play a very active role in the future political process in the post-war years. His paper became very successful and was a strong moulder of public opinion against Nigeria's commitment to the war.

The colonial administration in 1932 established a BBC relay station in Lagos and upgraded the facility into a Rediffusion station in 1936. Similarly facilities were commissioned in Ibadan, Enugu, Kaduna and Kano all in a bid to strengthen official propaganda media. In 1951 these stations were reorganized into stations of the newly formed Nigeria Broadcasting Service (NBS). By an Act of Parliament in 1956, the NBS was further reorganized into the Nigeria Broadcasting Corporation (NBC) allegedly to give it a semblance of independence from direct government control (Nigeria Broadcasting Corporation Ordinance, 1956).

In Northern Nigeria where the effect of the press was still not felt, the colonial administration took giant preemptive strides with the establishment in 1939 of the *Gaskiya Tafi Kwabo*, a vernacular mouth piece of the then Lt.-Governor of the region (Ibrahim 1981). It was issued under the aegis of the Northern Literature Agency in Zaria. In 1944, Dr Rupert M. East was commissioned by the colonial administration in the region to set up the Gaskiya Corporation to promote the printing and publication of vernacular reading matter on a large scale.

In 1948, *The Citizen* was established as an English version of the *Gaskiya Tafi Kwabo*. In 1966 *The Citizen* was renamed *New Nigeria Newspaper*. Both *Gaskiya Tafi Kwabo* and *New Nigeria Newspaper* were being issued at the instance of the colonial government and, have to this day retained their pro-government posture.

When Second World War ended in 1945, the USA and USSR emerged as global superpowers. Both powers supported the struggle for self-determination of the colonial people of Africa and Asia, a development which instantly went against the grain of British colonial policy. This posture of the superpowers, more especially the US, was a manifestation of the post-war contradiction within the international capitalist system. Britain, now a relatively weaker power, was anxiously looking forward to increased American aid for her post-war reconstruction. It therefore, set in motion series of constitutional reforms that were meant to lead to the independence of its overseas domains.

In 1948 both India and Pakistan attained independence. In 1954 Morocco, a French colony followed suit. Three years later Ghana and a year later Guinea all became independent. These international developments were to serve as tonic for the nationalist struggles in Nigeria in which the press were to serve as veritable instruments of political struggle.

Constitutional reforms such as Richard's constitution of 1946, McPherson's constitution on 1951 and Lyttleton constitution of 1954 opened greater vistas for electoral politics. The colonial petite bourgeoisie, especially the intelligenstia, who were the main beneficiaries of these constitutional developments, formed political parties and, along with those newspapers, to compete for political power. However, notable members of this class, who had earlier distinguished themselves as journalists and astute anti-colonial agitators, now each assumed power in their regions from 1951. In the 1959 Federal elections the NPC narrowly emerged with more seats in the legislature than the AG and NCNC. NPC's Abubakar Tafawa Balewa became Prime Minister. AG's Awolowo became leader of Opposition and NCNC's Nnamdi Azikiwe, the Governor-General. Nigeria thus attained (political) independence on 1 October 1960.

In all these processes the colonial petite bourgeoisie, now close to power, turned rather hostile to radical ideas associated with the politics of the working class. They unanimously, regardless of party differences, preferred to close ranks with the colonial administration than countenance the radical politics of the Zikist movement rooted in the working class and in the trade union movement. They would rather concentrate on how to win political power from the British, as a means to deploy national resources towards their transformation into a post-colonial bourgeois class.

In summary, what we have attempted to do in the preceding discourse was to establish the historical framework to appreciate the subsequent development of the Nigerian press. We have extensively dwelt on what is essentially a reinterpretation of crucial historical landmarks in the emergence, growth and activities of the mass media in the period under review. These reinterpretations derive more from our reliance on the theory of class and class struggle which lent more insight into the essence of such developments.

Central to the endeavour has been the desire to resolve three crucial issues. First, what form and manner of relationship did the mass media maintain with the dominant class? Here, we have been able to establish that both the imperialist colonial state and the colonial petite bourgeoisie effectively founded, owned, and operated the mass media to articulate, propagate and defend their respective class interest in the context of the colonial political economy. From the 1930s through till independence, the mass media had virtually become, perhaps, the hottest theatre of hegemonic contestations between the two classes.

Second, what form and manner of relationship did the mass media maintain with the dominated classes? Here, to the extent that we are referring to the working classes – workers and peasants – they were at best treated as subjects rather than objects of history. Their class interests, aspirations and opinions were not the primary contents of the dominant press as their support in the struggle of each of the two classes.

Third, what was the pattern of property relationship in the media sub-sector? Here we have shown that the media were owned by the two classes, i.e., the dominant imperialist colonial bourgeoisie as well as the colonial petite bourgeoisie. Reflective of the activities of capitalist property relations, their newspapers tended to be concentrated in the areas of high economic activity, particularly Lagos and subsequently Ibadan, Enugu, Kaduna and Kano, which all became industrial centres.

Ownership and control of the mass media

It was noted in the preceding discussion that the mass media in colonial Nigeria were established, owned and maintained on the one hand by the state and on the other by the colonial petite bourgeoisie. The former needed the institution primarily to articulate, promote and defend bourgeois imperialist values, ideas and world outlook, and to counteract nationalist agitation. The colonial petite bourgeoisie viewed the institution of the press as an instrument to agitate for accommodation within the bourgeois state by championing the cause of national independence. Thus, these two social classes, engaged in fierce political struggle, mobilized their respective media of mass communication, which now became instruments and theatres in their struggle.

But contradictorily enough, the fear of "politicizing" the mass media in terms of reducing the institution into the megaphones of powerful political and other partisan interests in the country had been expressed many years before independence. This fear was, for instance, inherently articulated in the justification for the establishment of the Nigerian Broadcasting Corporation via an Act of Parliament in 1956 and the desire to insulate broadcasting from politicization and/or ethnicization.

> . . . The Corporation should be modeled on the British Broadcasting with a national and regional orgnanization and that so far as the regional organization is concerned there should, within the lines of the Corporation policy, be a large share of regional autonomy, in deciding the content of programmes. The detailed arrangements, when they have been formulated will be subject to the approval of House of representatives. Among other provisions there would be laid upon the Corporation the obligation of impartiality. Controversial broadcast could be given by the Corporation provided that all reasonable points of view are represented. It should be the particular care of the Corporation to ensure that reasonable expression shall not be denied to minority groups, whether cultural, religious or political. (Mackay 1964: 2)

In contrast to the NBC, both newspaper organizations and broadcast stations had been the convenient targets of anti-colonial mass media activity. Concomitantly in place of the quest for independence which organically unified the pre-independence political groupings, there was now, in the post-colony, a veritable struggle between these different regional power groupings and centres for involvement, equity, fairness and justice in access to the spoils of office in the regions and at the centre. Accordingly, several organizations were mobilized to articulate the views of the Action Group (AG) controlled Western regional government. These were the government owned Western Nigeria Television Service (WNTV) founded in 1959, and the government owned *Daily Sketch* and *Sunday Sketch, Daily Tribune* and *Sunday Tribune* newspapers established privately in 1960 by Chief Obafemi Awolowo founder of the Action Group now in government in the region and himself as leader of Opposition at the Federal Parliament.

The NCNC, now in government in the Eastern Region, founded the Eastern Nigeria Television Service in 1960 and some newspapers all in addition to the West African Pilot group of newspapers which were privately owned by NCNC leader Dr Nnamdi Azikiwe himself then Governor-General.

Not to be left behind, the Northern People's Congress (NPC), then in government at both the regional and federal levels, founded the Radio television Kaduna (RTK) based in Kaduna, the regional capital, as well as the *New Nigerian* newspaper equally based there.

The 1967 Nigerian civil war resulted in the restructuring of the country into 12 states in 1969 in place of the three regions (later four with the creation of the Mid-West out of the Western region). Many of these states later established their own television and radio stations in addition to newspapers, particularly in the aftermath of the civil war through to the period of oil boom throughout the 1970s. In this period, all the regional government owned television stations, notably WNTV in Ibadan, ENTV in Enugu and RTK in Kaduna in addition to a few others owned by states were all taken over by the Federal Military Government (FMG) and reconstituted into a single Nigerian Television Authority (NTA) in 1977. The creation of seven more states that year, bringing the figure to 19, also saw the establishment of more television stations within the NTA framework.

Similarly, the FMG also took over all radio stations hitherto established and operated by the regional governments of old and now inherited and managed by the group of states curved out of the defunct regions, and reconstituted them into the Federal Radio Corporation of Nigeria (FRCN) in 1976.

In addition, the FMG founded the nation's only wire service, the News Agency of Nigeria (NAN), in 1978 with responsibility of procuring news from major international agencies for dissemination free of charge to local mass media organizations. It also had the duty of projecting Nigeria to the rest of the world by supplying news and features about the country to external users. Local news media were, in this period, banned by the FMG from subscribing to major international news agencies. Furthermore, the NTA, FRCN and NAN became agencies with a Board of Governors for each but answerable to the Minister of Information.

As for the printed news media, there is also a strong correlation between the oil boom and the creation of additional states on the one hand and the proliferation of newspapers and magazines in 1970s. For instance, increased oil rvenue meant more resources to support federal and state administrations. Accordinly, ten of the 19 states of the Federation came to have their own daily and weekly newspapers. However, *New Nigerian Newspapers* in Kaduna and the *Daily Times* group of newspapers and magazines were taken over by the FMG in 1975. A few private individuals such as Chris Okoli, a businessman, founded *Newsbreed*, a weekly news magazine that became very critical of the military government and was subsequently banned in 1978.

Nevertheless, the period of the 1980s though critical and tough in the country's political economy was however, a period of massive growth in the mass media, particularly, the news magazines. This period witnessed the overthrow of the civilian administration of Alhaji Shehu Shagari on 31 December 1983 and a counter-coup against the military government of Major-General Muhammadu Buhari on 27 August 1985 after barely 20 months in office. The new military government with the populist Major-General Ibrahim Babangida as President and Commander-In-Chief was to rule the country till 1993.

Still in this period, the Babangida administration embarked on the implementation of a World Bank inspired programme of Structural Adjustment in the economy. One of the critical aspects of this was the commercialization and privatization of public enterprises including, of course, the mass media. Commercialization and privatization have been defined respectively as "the re-organization of enterprises wholly or partly owned by ... government in which such ... enterprises shall operate as profit making commercial ventures without subvention from ... government ..." and "the relinguishment of part or all of the equity or other interests held by ... government or its agency in enterprises whether wholly or partly owned by government" (Privatization and Commercialization Decree, 1988).

Furthermore, by early 1992, General Babangida had dropped hints of his personal commitment "to go down in history as the first Nigerian President to make private broadcasting possible" and assured that his administration would do everything to fulfill this pledge by the end of the year (NTA Network News, 1992). Shortly afterwards, the administration established the Nigerian Broadcasting Commission to oversee the deregulation of broadcasting in the country. Part of the Commission's duties include receiving, processing and considering applications for the private ownership of radio and television stations including cable television services, direct satellite broadcast and other medium of broadcasting; recommending applications through the Minister to the President for the grant of radio and television licences and, establishing and disseminating a national broadcasting code and setting standards with regards to the content and quality of materials for broadcast (NBC Decree, 1992). Since the promulgation of this decree and the foundation of the NBC, several *private individuals* have been licensed to establish private radio and television, including cable, stations nationwide.

With regards to the print media, the resistance to hardship occasioned by liberalization of imports and corresponding collapse of local industries and eventual unemployment coupled with the massive devaluation of the national currency, were favourable conditions to found a number of private news magazines. Notable examples are *Tell*, *The News*, *The Week Source*, *Hotline* and *The Sunday Magazine* (TSM) as well as critical weekly newspapers such as *Tempo* and *Razor*. Other than these critical magazines, the sector witnessed the proliferation of soft sale publications.

Thus, by 1996, Nigeria had 60 daily and weekly newspapers and 25 news magazines, both privately and publicly owned. In addition, there were 14 radio and 15 television (including cable) stations, all privately owned and 36 radio and 40 television stations all government owned.

The return to party politics preparatory to the fourth republic which took off with the 29 May 1999 triangulation of Chief Olusegun Obasanjo, a former general and head of state between 1976–1979, also created some positive conditions for the expansion of the mass media sector. As usual of Nigerian politicians, some of them found media organizations to boost their standing in the polity preparatory to their active participation in partisan politics. At least two instances may be recalled here. Chief Mike Ajaegbo, who founded the Minaj cable television in 1995, later became a stalwart of the People's Democratic Party (PDP) and successfully contested election as a senator of the Federal Republic. The other is Mr James Ibori, who established the *Diet* daily and Sunday newspapers, joined the PDP and successfully contested election to become the Governor of Delta Sate. Until they founded their respective media, both Ajaegbo and Ibori were hardly reckoned with as politicians either at national, state or local levels.

Arising from the situation above the following points may be made about the character of media ownership and control in contemporary Nigeria. First, government at federal and state levels remain the major owner of radio and television stations in the country. This is notwithstanding the foundation of the NBC to regulate the establishment of private broadcast stations in the country. Government also wholly owns the country's only wire service to the total exclusion of private interests. The ratio of government to private broadcast media ownership at current reckoning stands at about three to one.

Second, in relation to the printed press, notably newspapers, private individuals constitute major owners. In fact, of the 36 states and Federal Capital Territory, only 14 own newspapers in addition to the *New Nigeria*, *Daily Times* and *Sunday Times* owned by the Federal government. In the case of both *Daily Times* and *Sunday Times*, government maintains a 60% share holding. The rest of over 42 titles are all owned by private individuals. Thus, while public ownership is dominant in the broadcast/ wire services, private owners predominate in respect of newspapers.

Third, in respect of news magazines, which have proliferated since the mid 1980s, there is not a single issue owned by government either at state or federal levels. All 25 of them, as at 1996, are owned privately.

Fourth, in terms of control, which is a philosophical and class issue, the bourgeois post-colonial state as well as the bourgeois class whose dictatorship the former represents, exercise firm control of the mass media, both broadcast and print. This is notwithstanding the instances of malevolent confrontations between the private press on the one hand and the government, particularly during the military regimes, on the other. The subjects of these confrontations have always been reformist such as human rights, constitutional governance, corruption and economic crises. In fact, Mohammed (2000) has argued rightly that given the origin and development of the mass media in the country since 1859 to date, the institution has become so steeped in the bourgeois notion of the press that it lacks the capacity, as presently constituted, to serve as veritable vehicles of revolutionary social transformations in favour of the working and oppressed citizens.

Fifth, that throughout the nearly one and a half century of media history in Nigeria there has not been much showing by the revolutionary press. Almost without exception, the virulent anti-colonial press succumbed to the successful incorporation of their hitherto militant and anti-colonial owners into the post-colonial state and soon after became pro-establishment media rooted either as arms of regional power centres or as mouthpieces of reformist fractions of the "national" bourgeoisie. The few attempts by progressive individuals and groups did not result in much of a success story. The most resilient here was perhaps the *New Horizon* news magazine founded in 1978 and operated by some pro-Soviet socialists with USSR funding. Soon after the dissolution of the Soviet union and the deaths in 1989 and 1990 respectively of the two founding members Comrades Wahab Goodluck, a trade unionist, and Ibidapo Fatogun, a veteran professional journalist, the *New Horizon* ceased to exist by 1991.

Conclusion

These five points, taken collectively, have serious implications for diversity of interests and opinions, so much proclaimed in liberal democracy. Given the character of ownership and control in the Nigerian mass media sector little is heard of the opinions and interests of the working classes in relation to the existing social order and those issues that are daily making the news. As institutions, government and its leading officials, notably the president and governors, constitute most news sources in both the public and private presses, these are the sources of political news in most Nigerian media. Added to this are sports and to some extent, economy and business reports. This narrow sourcing of media content is further confounded by the equally narrow dimension of reports that are most often the news of one party in the story.

Many journalists in Nigeria do not possess degree level journalism training, yet even those that have are products of a heavy dose of western classical notions of the place and role of the press in a democracy. Often these professionals are unable to adjust to glaring discrepancies between their training and their actual experience in the industry. The result is the continuing culture of one-sided-information supply type journalism, and at best a potential for damning criticism, almost bordering on anarchism, in the name of reform. Both, however, have little value either for the consolidation of liberal democracy or the radical reconstitution of society with attendant redistribution of power in favour of the majority working citizens.

Furthermore, a truly diversified media system must go beyond ownership as currently constituted or conceptualized, i.e., between government and private individuals. After all, fundamentally speaking, the bourgeois government is but the representative of the bourgeois class which is dominant in the country. So the kind of diversity of opinion and/ or interest engendered by the extant character of ownership is, at best one between factions of the same dominant bourgeois class, and therefore not threatening to the present social order and the accompanying distribution of power. Therefore, for diversity to be truly visible in both ownership and control, the former must be extremely liberalized to include organizations of the poor and under privilegdged such as the Nigeria Labour Congress, women groups, peasant cooperatives and allied non-governmental groups. This way, ownership and control would assume true diversification in the mass media sector, thereby creating the necessary condition for true expression of fundamentally diverse social (therefore class) interests.

These developments will combine to give a perfect blend necessary for the development of a sound democratic tradition and provide a true meaning for ownership and control of the mass media in Nigeria.

References

Dike, K.O. (1960) *Trade and Politics in the Niger Delta, 1830–1885*. Lagos: Federal Ministry of Information.

Duyile, D. (1987) *Makers of Nigerian Press*. Lagos: Gong Communications Ltd.

Ekundare, O. (1973) *The Economic History of Nigeria, 1860–1960*. London: Macmillan.

Elias, T. (1954) *Nigeria: The Development of its Laws and Constitution*. London: Stevens and Sons.

Elias, T.O. (1964) *Nigerian Press Law*. Lagos: University of Lagos Press.

Federal Republic of Nigeria Official Gazette (1992) *National Broadcasting Commission Decree 1992: No 33*. 4 September 1992. Lagos.

Fyle, C. (1957) *A History of Sierra Leone*. Oxford: Oxford University Press

Ibrahim, J. (1981) 'The structure of dependence and media production in Nigeria'. Paper presented at the Nigerian Political Science Association Conference Kano 13 April.

Mackay, I. (1964) *Broadcasting in Nigeria*. Ibadan: Ibadan University Press.

Mohammed, J.B. (2000) 'The Crisis of Hegemony in Nigeria: State-Press Relations in the Babangida Years'. Unpublished PhD thesis.

Omu, F. (1978) *Press and Politics in Nigeria. 1880–1937*. London: Longman.

Onimode, B. (1983) 'Nigeria: The dynamics of the challenge of underdevelopment'. In Kayode, M.O. and Usman, Y.B. eds., *The Social and Economic Development in Nigeria*. Proceedings of the National Conference on Nigeria since Independence, March 1983. Vol. 11. Zaria: Gaskiya Corporation.

Onimode, B. (1985) *Imperialism and Underdevelopment: The Dialectics of Mass Poverty*. London: ZED Press.

Ownership, Control and the Malaysian Media

Zaharom Nain and Wang Lay Kim

Introduction

For virtually a decade prior to the East Asian financial crisis of 1997–98, the Malaysian economy had been experiencing annual growth rates of almost 9% – impressive by any standard. Together with other Southeast Asian countries like Thailand and Singapore, Malaysia was seen as a "Tiger" economy, fast catching up with the Asian "Dragon" economies of Japan, Taiwan and South Korea. However, despite being hailed by local and international magazines, journals, politicians and even academics as a major economic success story, Malaysia's political system and, certainly, its media were not looked upon as being exemplary. If anything, Malaysia's political and media systems were seen as being heavily controlled, with little room for dissenting opinions. Our aim in this chapter is to locate the development of the Malaysian media within numerous interlinking contexts of political expediency, strategy and control and, equally important, economic motivations. By so doing, we argue and illustrate how both the actions of the state and the motives of the market continue to limit the representativeness of the Malaysian media.

The contemporary structure of the Malaysian media, especially the press and broadcasting, is very much a product of two major developments in the country's history. The first is the May 1969 riots which rocked the country and the second is the 22-year premiership of Dr Mahathir Mohamad, which began in 1981 and ended on 31 October 2003.

The May 1969 riots

In the 1969 general election, the ruling Alliance coalition almost failed for the first time to gain a two-thirds majority in the *Dewan Rakyat* (House of Representatives). The opposition parties, on the other hand, managed to encroach into many Alliance strongholds (Lee, 1995: 13). The ruling party's popularity suffered a setback, particularly that of its Chinese component party, the Malaysian Chinese Association (MCA). This caused severe strains within the ruling Alliance coalition (Means, 1991: 6–7), more so when Chinese-based Democratic Action Party (DAP) as well as the multi-ethnic Gerakan party were able to gain more votes from the non-Malays.

What caused the ethnic riots, according to government, were "the inflammatory speeches made by political candidates from various parties during the election campaigns, and the victory processions staged by some opposition parties" (Lee, 1995: 13). These events alarmed the government. To contain the situation, the King, on the advice of the government, declared a state of emergency for the whole of Malaysia. At the same time, the government made a decision to suspend the publication of all newspapers for two days starting from 16 May 1969 (Mohd Safar, 1996: 272) supposedly in an attempt to curb further spread of ethnic violence. Subsequently, all the major papers were permitted to publish but with the provision that the government had the right to censor items that were deemed "dangerous to national security".

The imposition of a state of emergency meant that the Federal Constitution and Parliament were suspended, while elections in Sabah and Sarawak were postponed for a period of time. While a new government was eventually formed, the real powers to administer the country lay in a newly established body, the National Operations Council (NOC), which was headed by the Deputy Prime Minister, Tun Abdul Razak Hussein. In a sense, this was how the Prime Minister Tunku Abdul Rahman was eventually marginalized.

The NOC was entrusted to find ways and means to revive parliamentary democracy, restore public confidence and cultivate ethnic harmony. To purportedly contribute towards political stability and harmonious relations between the ethnic groups in the country, the NOC issued an emergency decree to amend the Sedition Ordinance (1948). This 1971 amendment curbs freedom of speech and of the press, particularly on the (sensitive) issues of rights of citizenship, Malay special rights, the status and powers of the Malay Rulers, the status of Islam, and the status of Malay as the sole national language. It also prohibits any act, speech, or publication that has a tendency to bring about feelings of ill-will and enmity between the various ethnic groups. The Act was further amended when Parliament reconvened.

The emergency period provided the opportunity for the ruling party, whose political support was eroded in the 1969 general election, to strengthen its position and, more importantly, enhance the powers of the executive (Means, 1991: 16). The ruling Alliance, in the professed pursuit of national harmony and socio-economic development, managed to attract a number of Opposition political parties into its fold, thereby enabling it to form a larger political coalition called the Barisan Nasional (BN) or National Front.

In the aftermath of the 1969 riots the government amended the Control of Imported Publications Act (1958) in 1972. This amendment enables the Minister of Home Affairs "to ban or censor any imported publication deemed prejudicial to public order, national interest, morality, or security" (Means, 1991: 138). It empowers the state to impose stringent controls over imported material, supplementing existing legislation which allow for similar control over local material. Suffice it to say that even before the 1972 amendment, the Act was already draconian in nature.

The period of uncertainty and instability arising from the ethnic riots in 1969 also provided justification for the government to introduce the Official Secrets Act (OSA) in 1972. This law prohibits a person from getting information that is deemed "official secret" by the government which, so goes the official argument, can be used by enemies of the country. In effect, the law continues to discourage citizens from demanding their right to information, and casts doubts about the transparency of the government of the day. (It is perhaps more than fortuitous that this Act was further amended and strengthened in 1987, at a time when the government of the day was facing a crisis of confidence, particularly just before and after the big political clampdown of October 1987 called *Operasi Lalang* [see, for example, Singh K.S., 1987; CARPA, 1988].) Equally serious and ominous is the legal control that the OSA imposes on investigative journalism in particular, and press freedom in general.

These Acts a notwithstanding, since 1969 both the electronic media of radio and television in Malaysia are expected to transmit programmes that reflect the aspirations of the government, to promote national harmony and integration, and also to encourage the people to appreciate the government's policies. In short, these programmes are to assume that the government can do no wrong.

The New Economic Policy

The New Economic Policy (NEP), introduced in 1971, was yet another outcome of the events of May 1969. It came about because the NOC felt that one of the main reasons for ethnic suspicion and enmity in 1969 was the socio-economic imbalances between ethnic groups, in particular the gap between Malays and non-Malays. The NEP was to address the socio-economic problems faced by the ethnic groups in the country so that national development, harmony and unity eventually could be achieved.

Under the NEP (1971–90), the government designed a series of five-year plans that merged economic growth with the redistribution of economic opportunities to the Malays. It had a two-pronged strategy: (1) to reduce and eventually eradicate poverty; and (2) to restructure society so that the identification of economic functions with ethnicity could be reduced and eliminated.

Through the NEP and the related desire to increase Malaysian participation in the national economy, the dominant political partners in the ruling coalition started to invest in the country's major newspapers and began to control and influence the newspapers (Loh and Mustafa, 1996: 101–104). The government-owned trading company, Pernas, for example, acquired 80% control of the *Straits Times* (Means, 1991: 136), which was originally held by Singaporean investors. Later a majority of the shares were transferred to Fleet Holdings, an investment arm of the dominant partner in the BN coalition, United Malays National Organisation (UMNO). The transfer of ownership was then followed by a change of name to the New Straits Times Press (NSTP). Fleet Holdings subsequently set up an investment company called Fleet Group that oversaw its subsidiaries such as the NSTP. This corporate move was of great political significance because the take-over involved major mainstream newspapers under the NSTP stable.

This, of course, was a strategy that followed in the wake of UMNO's earlier success in gaining control of *Utusan Melayu* in 1961. *Utusan Melayu*, which began publication in 1939, had been advocating Malay rights, articulating issues pertaining to Malay interest and development and had given much support to UMNO's efforts in opposing the Malayan Union.

However, when an UMNO man, Ibrahim Fikri, was appointed director of operations, the newspaper workers staged a strike to protest the appointment. *Utusan Melayu* stopped publishing for one day on 20 July 1961, because the new appointee was given specific instructions to make *Utusan Melayu* support the ruling coalition. Journalists protested the appointment on the principle of press freedom. The strike lasted for 93 days. After the strike, a substantial amount of the company's shares were bought over by UMNO, enabling the party to have full allocative control over the newspaper (Mohd Safar, 1996: 247). Sadly, this large-scale protest was the only instance in Malaysia where newspaper workers resisted a political party take-over in order to protect the independence of the press.

Following in the footsteps of UMNO, the other component parties in the coalition also began acquiring media organizations. These acquisitions have been both business ventures as well as attempts at controlling the content of the media. The Malaysian Chinese Association (MCA), through its official holding company, Huaren Holdings, currently has a 58% stake in Star Publications, which publishes Malaysia's top selling English daily *The Star*. Star Publications, in turn, in 2002, acquired the Chinese daily *Nanyang Siang Pau* amidst much protests from a split Chinese community supporting two opposing factions within the MCA.

The Malaysian Indian Congress (MIC) owns a substantial portion of the Tamil press, often used to publicize its President Samy Vellu's campaigns, thoughts and projects. Through its investment arm, Maika Holdings Bhd., it has had investments in other media such as television.

The introduction of the NEP certainly influenced the ownership and control structure of the media in Malaysia. Gomez (1994) pointed out that while it is not unusual for political parties to own business concerns and be actively involved in corporate business, in the case of Malaysia, what is unusual is the extent of such political involvement in business in general and in the media in particular.

Through a complex web of nominee companies, investment arms and individuals aligned to it, UMNO currently holds controlling shares in two of the largest media conglomerates in Malaysia, New Straits Times Press (NSTP) and Utusan Melayu (Malaysia) Berhad (UM). NSTP publishes the Malay dailies such as *Berita Harian* and *Harian Metro*, and the English dailies, *New Straits Times Press*, *Malay Mail* and *Business Times*, and the Chinese daily, *Shin Min Daily News*. UM, on the other hand, publishes Malaysia's top selling Malay daily, *Utusan Malaysia* and Malaysia's only Jawi newspaper, *Utusan Melayu Mingguan*. It also publishes a popular women's magazine, *Wanita* and the equally popular entertainment magazine, *URTV*, both of which are in the Malay language.

Hence, what is clear is that the 1969 riots and the subsequent NEP, which was introduced to address the problems, have had a great impact on the structure of Malaysian media. On the pretext of restructuring and increasing *Bumiputera* (indigenous) participation in the economy, much of the Malaysian media continue to be transferred to the hands of political elites and their business allies.

Mahathir and the need to privatize

When Mahathir Mohamad became Prime Minister in 1981, he chose to achieve economic development through a more consolidated centralized executive power and liberalization policies. During his tenure, privatization and liberalization plans were at the top of his agenda and the privatization of key industries was carried out with the intention of integrating Malaysia into the global economy and to fully realize the NEP objectives by promoting *Bumiputera* capitalism. His liberalization plan gained him electoral support from the non-*Bumiputeras* because the Chinese capitalists saw minimal state intervention as a boon to business and opportunities for inter-ethnic business cooperation were further enhanced (Gomez 1999: 135). Mahathir's privatization process not only encouraged *Bumiputera* domination in particular industries, but it also created a new network of patronage. For example, Daim Zainuddin, the UMNO Treasurer at that time, handed out benefits to Ting Pek Khing to administer the largest Bakun dam project in Sarawak in return for support during election. Daim also handed out benefits to his close business associate, Halim Saad, head of Renong, to administer the second Malaysia-Singapore causeway (Hilley 2001: 96). Strategically, these alliances and consociational politics allowed the powers that be to control or regulate other potential agencies for political representation and for UMNO to strengthen its hegemony in the ruling coalition (Verma, 2000).

By 1983, Mahathir had his long-term policies in place, as outlined in the *Mid-Term Review of The Fourth Malaysia Plan 1981–85*, namely "Privatization" and the notion of "Malaysia Inc." The ultimate objective was to reduce the size and presence of government and to expand the role of private enterprise. This, it was felt, could be achieved through cooperation between the government and the private sector, with the government providing the policy framework and the private sector forming the "commercial arm of the national enterprise" (Government of Malaysia, 1984: 22–25).

For the media, what this supposedly meant was that there would be less state involvement and control economically over media organizations, encouraging private media organizations to emerge and develop. In reality, however, control and influence over media organizations increasingly shifted to political parties. Where UMNO moved into the newspaper industry in an earlier era, in the 1980s, there was greater movement of this nature by similar political parties in the ruling coalition into the electronic media. As we have indicated more comprehensively elsewhere (Zaharom, 2002; Wang, 1998) this is precisely what happened with TV3, Malaysia's first commercial television station, and, as we illustrate at the end of this chapter, such consolidation of control continues virtually unabated.

Operation *lalang*

The year 1987 is widely regarded as a watershed year in Malaysian politics, a crucial juncture for Mahathir as the head of UMNO. The first six years of Mahathir's premiership had witnessed a spate of financial scandals which forced the administration on to its back foot. To make matters worse for the administration, the vicious UMNO in-fighting between what has been called "Team A" (headed by Mahathir) and "Team B" (headed by former Finance Minister and now bitter rival, Razaleigh Hamzah) culminated in UMNO being declared illegal by a Kuala Lumpur High Court in early 1987. In the same year, questions raised in public regarding Chinese education in Malaysia and the financial problems faced by Chinese depositors led to inter-ethnic tensions between UMNO and Chinese-based parties, particularly coalition member MCA and opposition party, DAP. Added to this, the opposition parties at this point had been pressuring the government to investigate numerous financial scandals. All these developments culminated in a major crackdown called *Operasi Lalang* (Operation *Lalang*).

In this major political crackdown on 27 October 1987, more than 100 individuals, including opposition politicians, social activists, academics, religious and human rights activists and social workers were detained under the Internal Security Act (ISA). Three mainstream national newspapers, *The Star, Watan,* and *Sin Chew Jit Poh,* had their publishing permits or licences suspended (CARPA, 1988). The suspension of *The Star* came as a shock to many, as it was widely acknowledged that this immensely popular English tabloid was – still is – owned by the MCA, a BN coalition member and, hence, was believed to be free from any threat of having its permit suspended. For others, its suspension was merely illustrative of the fact that UMNO, under Mahathir, was indicating to its coalition partner, MCA, that in this tense period, it was the dominant party and could, indeed would, dictate terms. The suspension of *The Star* was lifted some months later, but what returned was a pale copy of the original newspaper. It was clearly much less critical, and popular columnists who had been critical of the government, such as Malaysia's first prime minister, Tunku Abdul Rahman, and former Opposition leader, Dr Tan Chee Koon, had become more subdued and, soon after, stopped writing their columns.

The events surrounding *Operasi Lalang* and the operation itself marked a purging by Mahathir and his faction, a successful and concerted attempt at overcoming a crisis of leadership, a hegemonic crisis that required coercive measures. As far as the media were concerned, in 1988, the Printing Presses and Publications Act (PPPA) (1984) was amended. These amendments clearly illustrate the tightening stranglehold the government has on the media. Under the amended Act, all mass circulation newspapers in Malaysia need to have a printing permit, granted by the Ministry of Home Affairs, before they can be published. A new permit needs to be applied for every year. Section 13A of the amended Act totally empowers the Home Minister to reject applications for a printing licence (popularly known as the "KDN") and to revoke or suspend a permit. The Minister's decision is final and cannot be challenged in a court of law. As stated under Section 13, Subsection (1) of the Act (emphasis added):

Without prejudice to the powers of the Minister to revoke or suspend a licence or permit under any other provisions of this Act, **if the Minister is satisfied that any printing press in respect of which the licence has been issued is used for printing of any publication which is prejudicial to public order or national security or that any newspaper in respect of which a permit has been issued contains anything which is prejudicial to public order or national security, he may revoke such licence or permit.**

On top of this, Section 7 of the amended Act empowers the Minister to prohibit the printing, sale, import, distribution or possession of a publication. The Minister may do this if he believes that the contents of a publication threatens morality, public order, security, public or national interests, conflicts with the law or contains provocative matters. Thus, one has this situation where the decisions of one Minister are binding and, strictly speaking, the Minister is under no obligation to explain these decisions.

In the same year, The Broadcasting Act (1988) was introduced clearly in anticipation of the further commercialization of broadcasting, especially television. The Act as it stood was both stringent and inflexible, and bestowed enormous powers on the government to determine the type of television made available to the Malaysian public. Indeed, in the midst of the supposed "deregulation" of broadcasting, the Broadcasting Act gave the Minister of Information virtually total powers to determine who will and who will not broadcast and the nature of the broadcast material. Under the Act, any potential broadcaster would need to apply for a licence from the minister beforehand. On paper, this meant that one individual had the power to decide. Further, Part III, Section 10, Subsection (1) of the Act (emphasis added), stated that "It shall be the duty of the licensee to ensure that the broadcasting matter by him complies with the direction given, from time to time, by the Minister."

In October 1996, amendments were made to this already-stringent piece of legislation aimed at taking into account the introduction of new services, such as cable and satellite television, satellite radio, pay TV and video on demand. In 1998, the Act was repealed with the proclamation of the Communications and Multimedia Act.

Consolidation and control

After the period of purging in the late 1980s, the water seemed to become less choppy for the administration under Mahathir. In 1988, after UMNO had been deregistered as a political party, it was reformed as UMNO Baru or New UMNO and the dissidents of Team B were excluded. Despite losing some seats and states to the opposition in the 1990 general election, the outcome was not as painful for the ruling coalition as many had anticipated (see Mustafa, 1990). In 1991, Mahathir unveiled his Vision 2020,[1] indicating a new agenda. At the same time, the National

---

1. The Vision is based on nine challenges facing the nation in its attempt to attain fully developed status by the year 2020. These challenges (Mahathir, 1991: 2–4) may be summarized as follows:

Development Policy (NDP) was introduced to replace the oft-criticized New Economic Policy (NEP).

Subsequently, the privatisation policy started gaining momentum and became standard practice. What is evident is that the privatization exercise thus far had been a selective one. In broadcasting, following the introduction of the first commercial television station, TV3, in 1984, the 1990s saw the numbers quadruple, with the introduction of free-to-air stations Metrovision (1995), ntv7 (1998), cable television, Mega TV (1995), and a satellite TV service, Astro (1996). Mega TV and Metrovision have since folded, but a new free-to-air station, Channel 9 (2003) has since joined the fray, albeit on a test basis, and in early 2004, 8TV is scheduled to start operations. Meanwhile, Astro has been growing rapidly and is now listed on the Kuala Lumpur Stock Exchange (KLSE). But, it is also clear that these companies were each approved licenses more on the basis of who owned them.

In early 1994, the local media giant closely aligned to UMNO, the Utusan Melayu Group (UM), became part of a consortium of four companies that was awarded a tender by the government to operate Malaysia's second (and now defunct) commercial television station, *MetroVision* (Zaharom, 1994). Yet another company in the consortium was Melewar Corporation, controlled by Tunku Abdullah of the Negeri Sembilan royal house and a longtime close associate of Prime Minister Mahathir.

i.   Establishing a united Malaysian nation with a sense of common and shared destiny ... at peace with itself ... (and) ... made up of one *Bangsa Malaysia*.

ii. Creating a psychologically liberated, secure and developed Malaysian society with faith and confidence in itself ... psychologically subservient to none and respected by the peoples of other nations.

iii. Fostering and developing a mature democratic society, practising a form of mature, consensual, community-oriented Malaysian democracy that can be a model for many developing countries.

iv. Establishing a fully moral and ethical society ... strong in religious and spiritual values and imbued with the highest of ethical standards.

v.   Establishing a mature, liberal and tolerant Malaysian society.

vi. Establishing a scientific and progressive society ... innovative and forward-looking.

vii. Establishing a fully caring society and a caring culture, a social system in which society will come before self.

viii. Ensuring an economically just society ... in which there is fair and equitable distribution of the wealth of the nation.

ix. Establishing a prosperous society, with an economy that is fully competitive, dynamic, robust and resilient.

The third commercial television company, ntv7, launched in April 1998, also has strong links with the state. Its original chairman, Mohd Effendi Nawawi, served as managing director in the Sarawak State Economic Development Corporation (SSEDC) (Cheong: 1993: 57) and is a member of the BN coalition. After the 1999 General Election, he was appointed the Malaysian Minister of Agriculture. However, his links to ntv7 are still clear, based on the latest company profile for Encorp Berhad, ntv7's holding company which indicates that his children, Efeida and Mohd Ezra Effendi are directors of the company and hold majority shares in the company (http://www.klse-ris.com.my/CDB/owa/lcd.genchq).

Before it folded, Malaysia's first cable television service, *Mega TV*, which began operating in the third quarter of 1995, was run by a consortium using the company name Cableview Services Sdn. Bhd. The largest shareholder in the consortium, with a 40% stake, was Sistem Television Malaysia Berhad or TV3. The Malaysian Ministry of Finance had a 30% stake, while Sri Utara Sdn. Bhd., a wholly-owned subsidiary of Maika Holdings Bhd. (the investment arm of the MIC, another component of the BN coalition) had a 5% stake (Zaharom and Mustafa, 1998).

Malaysian satellite television effectively began on 13 January 1996, when the Malaysia East Asia satellite, Measat-1, was launched from Kourou, French Guiana. Described by one newspaper as "marking the country's historic entry into space technology", (*New Straits Times*, 14 January 1996), Measat-1 is owned by Binariang Sdn. Bhd. which, in turn, is owned by trusts associated with three Malaysians, most prominent of whom is manufacturing and horse racing tycoon, T. Ananda Krishnan. Ananda has been politely referred to by one Malaysian daily as "a businessman who enjoys the confidence of Prime Minister Datuk Seri Dr Mahathir Mohamad". (*The Star*, 9 January 1996) And the chairman of Binariang's board of directors is the former Inspector-General of the Malaysian police force, Hanif Mohamad Omar. Binariang, in turn, owns and controls the Astro All Asia Networks PLC (effectively Astro) (http://www.klse-ris.com.my/CBD/owa/compchq).

Hence, as far as television – including satellite television – is concerned, the situation in Malaysia for the past decade has been one where the selective privatization exercise by the state has continued to extend the control of the ruling coalition and its allies even wider across the Malaysian economy, adding economic and cultural control to what is already virtual political domination.

Similar growth has been experienced in the radio industry. Apart from those stations owned and run by the government, new ones emerged in the mid-1990s, including the hugely popular Hitz FM (1997), Mix FM (1997), Time Highway Radio (1994), and Light and Easy FM (1997), all of which concentrate on airing popular music and disc jockeys engaging in light banter. In terms of ownership, concentration is quite evident, with Hitz, Mix FM and Light and Easy all being owned by Astro (*Media Guide Malaysia 2003*: 284). Leaving aside concentration of ownership, it is evident that Malaysian commercial radio was – and remains – a means of channelling music, advertising and other forms of entertainment and has never been seen as being anything more than that. The strict licensing laws and other acts, such as the Sedition Act, continue to make sure that the situation remains that way.

By the mid-1990s, just prior to the 1997 East Asian financial, crisis, the Mahathir administration seemed unshakeable. Apart from the increase in media organizations and products, the administration itself had been spending greatly, more so during the first five years of the 1990s, on mega projects, such as the Kuala Lumpur International Airport (KLIA), the Petronas Twin Towers, the new administrative capital of the country, Putrajaya, and the proposed information technology (IT) hub of Malaysia, Cyberjaya. In 1996, Mahathir unveiled the Multimedia Super Corridor (MSC), which he proclaimed "Malaysia's gift to the world" (Mahathir, 1998: 7).

The MSC is located in an area of 750 sq. km, which is larger than insular Singapore. It spreads from the Kuala Lumpur City Centre in the north to Sepang in the south where the newest and largest international airport in the region, the RM9 billion Kuala Lumpur International Airport (KLIA), is situated. Two "Smart Cities" are still being developed in the MSC: Putrajaya, the new RM20.1 billion administrative capital of Malaysia where the concept of electronic government is being introduced; and Cyberjaya, a place that accommodates multimedia industries, research and development centres, the Multimedia University, and operational headquarters for transnational corporations which are expected to direct their worldwide manufacturing and trading activities using multimedia technology. These are indeed some of the key incentives and attractions that the MSC has provided for interested corporations.

The ambitious RM5-billion project was spurred primarily by the administration's desire to propel Malaysia to the status of a developed country, as envisaged in Mahathir's celebrated Vision 2020. The MSC is viewed as helping Malaysia enter into an "Information Age" where, so goes the assertion, "information, ideas, people, goods and services move across borders in the most cost-effective and liberal ways" (Multimedia Development Corporation [MDC], 1998). It is a project, in other words, to help Malaysia transform itself from being an industrial-based economy to one that lays emphasis on information, which in turn facilitates greater industrialization, and trade and commerce.

By the mid-1990s, Vision 2020 and state spending on mega projects appeared to have been accepted by the people, given the fact that in the

1995 general election, the administration was given a fresh mandate, sweeping back into office with an increased majority – the biggest majority since Mahathir first became premier in 1981. In this election, the Opposition, especially the DAP, was badly defeated, compared to previous elections when it managed to garner more parliamentary and state seats. The 1997 Asian financial crisis and the ouster of Mahathir's deputy somehow changed things, albeit momentarily.

Crises, *Reformasi* and the media

In the heady days of late 1998, the streets of Malaysia's capital, Kuala Lumpur, reverberated with chants of R-E-F-O-R-M-A-S-I. Thousands of demonstrators took to the streets almost weekly, demanding changes, including justice (especially for Anwar Ibrahim, the sacked former Malaysian deputy prime minister, who was later detained, beaten up by Malaysia's top policeman, charged in court, convicted and sentenced to 15 years incarceration), greater transparency, and accountability on the part of the Mahathir administration.

It was, to borrow from Charles Dickens, the best of times and the worst of times. The 1997 Asian financial crisis had started biting the Malaysian economy. Many businesses were facing bankruptcy while other, more privileged ones, were being bailed-out by the administration. Words like "transparency" and "accountability" were being being bandied about by the likes of the IMF and the World Bank and becoming popular in Malaysia. Awkward questions (awkward for the administration) about why the bubble had burst, why the miracle had become a debacle, were being asked. Suddenly, it seemed as though social and political consciousness had replaced decades of political apathy and civil society was finally starting to assert itself. But of course it was not as simple as that.

On 2 September 1998, barely a week after they shared the same platform in the state of Penang, celebrating Independence Day on 31 August, Mahathir sacked his deputy and also finance minister, Anwar Ibrahim, amidst sleazy allegations of sodomy, adultery, and abuse of power. Cornered and badly battered, Anwar, a former Islamic student leader and a fiery orator, decided to go on the offensive. He initially held daily gatherings at his residence, reportedly attended by hundreds, explaining why he was sacked from office, detailing corrupt practices within the administration of which he was once a member, and alleging that he was the victim of a top-level conspiracy, headed by Mahathir who, Anwar asserted, had been locked in a power struggle with him. This power struggle was later confirmed on frequent occasions by Mahathir himself.

As if aware that he needed to get across to a wider audience, more so because the mainstream Malaysian media had blocked out reports of the gatherings at his residence, and also because, prior to his dismissal, newspaper and television editors closely aligned to him had been ousted,[2] Anwar's next move was to go on a nationwide campaign to explain his side of the story. His aim was to reveal to the people at the grassroots level the continuous abuse of power by powerful ministers in the administration. Taking his cue from the Indonesian experience, Anwar and his supporters began to popularize the terms, *Korupsi, Nepotisme, Kronisme* (KNK).[3] Through his campaign, Anwar detailed cases of nepotism (especially those involving Mahathir's family) and cronyism, involving business friends of the prime minister and the previous finance minister, Daim Zainuddin.[4]

Anwar's arrest under the ISA on 20 September, his subsequent "black eye" and his anticipated conviction created splits, especially within the Malay community, the likes of which Malaysia had not seen since the 1987 *Operasi Lalang* crackdown. Opposition political parties, NGOs and religious groups began forming a loose coalition, *Gerak*, demanding wide-scale reforms in the system of governance. With Anwar especially as its symbol, and his arrest, charge, court cases and convictions as illustrations of everything that had gone wrong with the Mahathir administration, the *reformasi* movement thus gained momentum.

There appeared "to be an overwhelming feeling that something had gone wrong with our country – and determination for change in the future". (Sabri, 2000: 191). If nothing else, the decimation of Malaysia's number two political leader and the blatant manner with which he was virtually destroyed laid bare to most Malaysians the fact that "rights and freedoms which they once took for granted can be so easily taken away,

---

2. Just weeks before his dismissal, two top editors in the *Utusan Malaysia* and *Berita Harian*, Malaysia's main Malay language newspapers, aligned to Anwar resigned and so did a top executive from TV3, also aligned to Anwar. This signalled the beginning of the end for Anwar.

3. The terms had been uttered earlier, when Anwar was still in office, at the 1998 UMNO General Assembly in an attempt to embarrass Mahathir. Unfortunately for Anwar, Mahathir had anticipated this move and at the Assembly had revealed a list of the names of Anwar cronies and family members who were alleged to have received financial and business kickbacks. Equally damaging for Anwar then, copies of a book, *50 Dalil Mengapa Anwar Tidak Boleh Menjadi Perdana Menteri* (50 Reasons Why Anwar Cannot Be The Prime Minister), were distributed to all delegates at the Assembly in the official bag which they received.

4. As in the best soap operas, Daim was later reappointed finance minister and, after a reported falling out with Mahathir, relinquished his position and has since found himself in the political wilderness.

ignored or abused. They have seen how easy it is to misuse the institutions that are supposed to protect our freedom and turn them into tools to repress, silence and curtail that freedom". (Sabri, 2000: 192). More specifically for the Malay community, the community Mahathir's party, UMNO, depends totally on for support, "they have witnessed every shred of dignity stripped away from a well-respected leader and his family. This is cultural outrage for a race whose ancient *Annals*, the *Sejarah Melayu*, have decreed that 'if subjects of the ruler offend, they shall not, however grave the offence, be disgraced or reviled with evil words'" (Sabri, 2000: 192).

It was during this period that the mainstream media began to lose its credibility. Throughout the economic crisis and, certainly, throughout the political crisis which followed, official denial and media censorship seemed the order of the day. The degree to which the economic crisis affected Malaysia and different segments of the Malaysian public was never deemed an important question for the media to ask. Policy decisions by the administration to "address" the crisis – such as pegging the value of the Malaysian ringgit to the American dollar, the imposition of capital controls and, equally controversially, the government bail-out of selected companies, particularly those belonging to Mahathir's children and friends – were never discussed, let alone criticized by the print or broadcast media. It was as if both mass media were sticking jealously to one of the infamous directives which had been handed down by the political masters to broadcasting organizations after 1969, namely that television (and now radio and newspapers as well) needs to provide extensive coverage of government policies and programmes to stimulate public interest and opinion in line with the requirements of the government.

During this period also, whatever little space there was in the media for alternative viewpoints was further curtailed. The *New Straits Times*, for example, axed the popular literary column, *Perforated Sheets*, written by a young writer, Amir Muhammad, for being too critical of the administration and, at the same time, made life quite uncomfortable for its literary editor, who later left the organization.

Politically, if general election results are anything to go by, the financial and economic crises left a terrible toll on the administration. In the 1999 general election, the Opposition, especially the Islamic party, PAS, made considerable inroads, winning more seats than previously, some in what were previously safe UMNO constituencies. It became the biggest opposition party in the Malaysian parliament and its twice-weekly party newspaper, *Harakah*, then boasted a circulation of more than 350,000, easily making it the best-selling Malay or English language newspaper in Malaysia.

Not surprisingly, virtually immediately after the November 1999 general elections, the crackdown on dissent began. First, there was a clampdown on the alternative media, with the arrest of the editor and printer of *Harakah*. Both were arrested under the Sedition Act, purportedly for publishing seditious material. Then, two prominent opposition politicians were also arrested under the same Act, one, Anwar's lawyer, Karpal Singh, for allegedly uttering seditious words in court in the course of his duty as Anwar's counsel.

A variety of other pro-*reformasi* and pro-Opposition publications (*Detik, Al-Wasilah,Eksklusif*) also had their printing permits revoked. On 1 March 2000, *Harakah* was also punished, when its frequency of publication was slashed from twice a week to twice a month.

With all these restrictions, attention shifted to the Internet. Indeed, despite the fact that computer penetration is still low among the Malaysian public, and despite the fact that access to and usage of the Internet were even lower, *reformasi* groups nonetheless opted to utilize it, possibly aware of its potential. Initially, it was also because the administration had promised to keep the Net relatively "free" and unregulated in an attempt to attract foreign investors to the MSC, and make it a success.

Into this scene came Malaysia's first web-based daily newspaper, *Malaysiakini*. Launched just prior to the 1999 general elections, on 20 November, *Malaysiakini* was initially funded largely from a grant that it received from the Southeast Asian Press Alliance (SEAPA). It (http://www.malaysiakini.com/aboutmalaysiakini/About%20Us.htm) describes itself as "an Internet media project featuring independent news coverage, investigative journalism and in-depth news analysis ... conceived by journalists unhappy with the sorry state of our mass media." Within a year of its launch, *Malaysiakini* received rave write-ups in international newspapers and magazines such as the *Far Eastern Economic Review, The Wall Street Journal* and *The Australian* and won numerous international awards, including the International Press Freedom Award, which was awarded to its editor, Steven Gan.

The way the Anwar saga was conducted by the administration offended many. The way it was so uncritically reported by the mainstream media insulted the intelligence of many more. These factors, coupled with the fact that UMNO's hegemony over the Malay community was broken during this period, help to explain the temporary shift towards alternative forms of explanation, alternative media such as *Malaysiakini*.

Post-crisis media-restructuring and realignment

The unpopularity of the mainstream media during the 1997–98 crisis contributed to the *New Straits Times, Berita Harian* and TV3 incurring heavy financial loses and having to downsize their activities. 'The financial figures tell the story: two companies (TV3 & NSTP) struggling through the storm, buffeted on all sides – poor management and corporate decisions, (perceived) biased content, political interference, the currency and financial crises ... and the list goes on' (http://theedgedaily.com.my, 22 September 2003). In October 2001, two top executives were appointed to the board of Malaysian Resources Corporation Berhad (MRCB), the majority stakeholder in the NSTP Group, one as the CEO and the other as the executive director. Their task was to restructure MRCB, "shedding 350 jobs and trimming overhead costs by almost half, selling major assets while bolstering its next to nil future order book to RM800 million" (*Star Bizweek*, 11 January 2003: 14). MRCB at the point had debts totalling RM4 billion (RM1=US$0.263).

The restructuring scheme was completed in August 2003, with a new company, Media Prima Berhad (MPB), replacing TV3. On 22 October 2003, MPB was listed on the Kuala Lumpur Stock Exchange (KLSE) and TV3 was delisted on the same day. Under the restructuring scheme, MPB acquired 100% equity interest in TV3 and 43.5% stake in New Straits Times Press (Malaysia) Berhad (NSTP). The restructuring made MPB Malaysia's largest listed media company, combining the TV3 television network with NSTP, Malaysia's largest newspaper publishing company.

The restructuring of MPB also involved the appointment of Kamarulzaman Haji Zainal, the former press secretary to the new prime minister of Malaysia, Abdullah Ahmad Badawi as the Executive Director. Kamarulzaman also sits on the board of directors of Malaysia's other media conglomerate, UM.

It appears that during this period of transition of power from Mahathir to Abdullah Ahmad Badawi, key decisions regarding the media were also being affected. Prior to the MRCB restructuring exercise, rumour was rife that prominent businessman – and a purported Mahathir ally – Syed Mokhtar Al-Bukhary, was attempting to gain control of and merge the two media conglomerates, NSTP and UM. When this did not happen, there was speculation that Abdullah Ahmad Badawi's people in UM had prevented the merger, mainly to block off any consolidation of power by any particular political group within UMNO, just prior to Abdullah becoming prime minister on 1 November 2003.

UM, by the same token, remains very much in the hands of UMNO. This is very much evident with its board of directors comprising an Executive Chairman who was a Senator, a member who is an UMNO member of Parliament, another who is a former Deputy Chief Minister of the state of Kelantan and an UMNO member, and Mahathir's and Abdullah Ahmad Badawi's former political secretaries (http://www.utusangroup.com.my/bods.html).

The tragic event of 11 September 2001 somehow was a godsend for Mahathir and his administration both internationally and, more so, locally. PAS's ambivalent stand on issues of terrorism and its insistence on the setting up of an Islamic state governed by Islamic laws, especially Hudud laws, seems to have worked against it. This has not been helped by the arrest, under the ISA, of alleged Malaysian Islamic terrorists linked to PAS. Mahathir's nurturing of an image of UMNO being the face of a 'tolerant Islam', on the other hand, appears to have placated the non-Malay, non-Muslim population of Malaysia.

For the alternative media, especially *Malaysiakini*, the initial heady days were somehow not translated to hard cash to keep them providing a free Internet newspaper. In 2001, it had to start a subscription service to increase its revenue. Despite the fact that it is still operating, it is suffering financially and politically. Its journalists have been refused press accreditation by the administration, disqualifying them from covering official government meetings. In 2002, after having earlier been heavily criticized by the government television station, TV1, the offices of *Malaysiakini* were raided by the police and its computer equipment detained by the police. This happened because of a police report lodged by UMNO Youth about a letter published on *Malaysiakini*'s website which was purportedly seditious in nature. Following this, their landlord threatened to evict the journalists from their rented premises. In the end, most of the equipment were returned, no one at *Malaysiakini* was charged, and their landlord backed down. But threats of further harassment continue.

Conclusion

As a new prime minister assumes power in Malaysia, there is much talk about a new era, one that is more compassionate and open-minded about the development of democracy in the country. Abdullah Ahmad Badawi himself, in one of his first speeches as prime minister, urged Malaysians "not to work for him but to work alongside him for the country" (*The Star*, 2 November 2003). However, it is difficult to see how one individual, no matter how sincere and honest, can do much to dismantle structures which have come about due to the logic and the demands of a wider capitalist system and a development policy that embraces such a system.

Nonetheless, there needs to be less concentration of media ownership, and greater encouragement for new actors to enter the industry, leading to wider – and more varied – participation and competition in the production of information and meanings. In a sense, if, indeed, there is a call by the administration to work with it rather than for it, there would certainly need to be a movement towards a more balanced and equal flow of information and opinions between the administration and Malaysia's citizens.

Of course there is a need to remind ourselves that present hierarchies, present structures, did not emerge out of nothing, but were deliberately created by groups in power to enable them to maintain their power. And history has shown that human beings in power do not enjoy losing that power and will resist challenges, even if these challenges were accepted as changes that would democratize society further.

Attempts to reform media ownership would also most certainly not go down too well with the current circle of media owners in Malaysia who, in many cases, are closely linked to politicians and political parties in the ruling coalition. Concentration of media ownership – and concentration in the hands of politically affiliated companies and individuals at that – has been the norm in Malaysia for a long time. Media reform places much importance on the need to disperse ownership, the need to break down monopolies and oligopolies. Going by the experience of more established capitalist economies, there will be much resistance to such reforms. Our contention, however, is that despite the resistance, reforms are necessary. The process of democratization, contrary to the myths propagated in Malaysia, does no simply entail looking at party politics and political practices in a narrow sense. It entails democratizing every major sphere of activity, including the economy and the media.

References

Broadcasting Act 1988. Kuala Lumpur: International Law Book Services.

CARPA (1988) *Tangled web: Dissent, deterrence and the 27 October 1987 crackdown in Malaysia,* Sydney: Committee against repression in the Pacific and Asia.

Cheong, S. (1993) *Bumiputera companies in the KLSE* (2nd Edition). Petaling Jaya: Corporate Research Services.

Faruqui, S. and Ramanathan, S. (1998) *Mass media laws and regulations in Malaysia,* Singapore: AMIC.

Gomez, E.T. and Jomo, K.S. (1997) *Malaysia's political economy: Politics, patronage and profits,* Cambridge: Cambridge University Press.

Gomez, E.T. (1999) *Chinese business in Malaysia: Accumulation, accommodation and ascendance,* London: Curzon Press.

Gomez, E.T. (1994) *Political business: Corporate involvement of Malaysian political parties,* North Queensland: James Cook University of North Queensland.

Government of Malaysia (1984) *Mid-Term Review of The Fourth Malaysia Plan 1981–85,* Kuala Lumpur: Economic Planning Unit.

Hilley, J. (2001) *Malaysia: Mahathirism, hegemony and the new opposition,* London: Zed Books.

Khoo, Kay Kim (1988) 'English newspapers in Malaya 1900–1941: History and historiography', in Mohd Sarim Hj. Mustajab et al., eds. *Akhbar dan majalah di Malaysia: Sejarah dan perkembangan*, Bangi: Jabatan Sejarah UKM, 69–89.

Lee, H.P. (1995) *Constitutional conflicts in contemporary Malaysia*, Kuala Lumpur: Oxford University Press.

Loh, K.W. and Mustafa, K. A. (1996) 'The press in Malaysia in the early 1990s: Corporatisation, technological innovation and the middle class', in Muhammad Ikmal Said and Zahid Emby, eds., *Critical perspectives: Essays in honour of Syed Husin Ali*, Petaling Jaya: Malaysian Social Science Association, 96–131.

Mahathir Mohamad (1991) *Malaysia: The way forward*, Kuala Lumpur: Malaysian Business Council.

Mahathir Mohamad (1998) *Mahathir Mohamad on the Multimedia Super Corridor*, Subang Jaya: Pelanduk Publications.

Means, G.P. (1991) *Malaysian politics: The second generation*, Singapore: Oxford University Press.

Media Guide Malaysia 2003, Kuala Lumpur: WhiteKnight Communications.

Mohd Safar, Hasim (1996) *Akhbar dan kuasa* (The press and power), Kuala Lumpur: Universiti Malaya Press.

Multimedia Development Corporation (MDC) (1998) Extracted from http://www.mdc.com.my

Mustafa K. A. (1990) 'The Malaysian 1990 general election: The role of the BN mass media', *Kajian Malaysia* 8, 2, 82–102.

Printing Presses and Publications Act 1984. Kuala Lumpur: International Law Book Services.

Sabri Zain (2000) *Face off: A Malaysian reformasi diary (1998–1999)*, Singapore: BigO Books.

Singh K.S., Gurmit (1987) *No to secrecy: The campaign against 1986's amendments to the OSA*, Petaling Jaya: Aliran, SGS, EPSM, DAP, MAE & CRC.

Verma, V. (2000) 'Malaysian elections 1999: Unfinished journey', *Economic and Political Weekly*, 29 July 2717–2724.

Wang Lay Kim (1998) 'Malaysia: Ownership as control', *Development Dialogue*, 2, 61–83.

Zaharom Nain (1994) 'Commercialization and control in a "Caring Society": Malaysian Media "Towards 2020".' *SOJOURN*, 9, 2, 178–199.

Zaharom Nain and Mustafa K.A. (1998) 'Ownership and control of the Malaysian media'. *Media Development*, 14, 4, 9–17.

Zaharom Nain (2002) 'The structure of the media industry: Implications for democracy', in Loh, K.W. and Khoo, B.T. eds., *Democracy in Malaysia: Discourses and practices*, London: Curzon, 111–137.

Democratic Communication Futures

The Whole World is Watching: Online Surveillance of Social Movement Organizations*

Sasha Costanza-Chock

Introduction

Heightened cooperation between law enforcement and military intelligence is currently advancing at both the domestic and international levels under the rhetoric of the "war against terror". While information sharing between police, military, and intelligence agencies, as well as between state, corporate, and other bodies is not new, such practices have recently been amplified and extended. For example, sweeping legislation passed in the wake of 11 September as the "USA Patriot Act" expands the information-gathering powers of various government agencies, broadens authority to conduct wiretaps and electronic surveillance, and erodes judicial oversight that previously served to check state surveillance powers (ACLU 2001).

In this chapter, I pose the question: what are the implications of heightened state surveillance of electronic communications for Social Movement Organizations (SMOs), especially those participating in the global justice movement (also known as the movement for "another" globalization), in terms of their use of the Internet and other new communications technologies?[1]

I will proceed from a review of the ways in which activists have employed new communications technologies as aids to diffusion, mesomobilization, and other social movement interaction processes, to a short historical overview of state surveillance of social movements within the USA. I will then discuss the dangers activists are exposed to when

---

* Special thanks to Dr Oscar H. Gandy, Jr. and to all the students of his seminar on Privacy in the Information Age, who helped me develop these ideas.

1. SMOs communicating online risk surveillance by corporate and countermovement actors as well as by the state. I will return to this later.

they use new communications technologies in the heightened surveillance context of the Bush administration's Infinite War. Finally, I will consider possible responses to online surveillance and virtual infiltration.

SMO use of new communications technologies

Literature on the use of new communications technologies by social movements is already significant and is rapidly expanding. SMOs and other movement actors from all across the spectrum – left to right, large to small, highly bureaucratized to radically decentralized, from the One-Third World ("global North" plus Southern elites) and from the Two-Thirds World ("global South" plus Fourth World and internally colonized peoples) – have embraced, to varying degrees, communications technologies including the Internet (especially the world wide web (www), email, bulletin board services (BBS), and chat), cell phones and pagers, and digital photo and video cameras.[2] Early SMO use of the Internet (pre-www) included information-sharing between activists worldwide via usenet groups like PeaceNet, EcoNet, and GreenNet (see www.igc.org). There is extensive scholarship on the use made of the Internet by the EZLN, or Zapatistas, to capture the attention of global civil society and create international pressure that raised the stakes too high for the Mexican government to continue their initial plan of all-out counterinsurgency warfare (for example see Schulz, 1998; Keck and Sikkink, 1998; Kumar, 2000). Many authors have also described the use of the Internet and cell phones as mobilization tools by the broad labour/environmental/anarchist coalition at the 1999 Seattle protests against the World Trade Organization (WTO) (Smith, 2001; Eagleton-Pierce, 2001), as well as the rise of the Independent Media Center that was first deployed to provide alternative coverage of Seattle and since has spread into a global network of over 80 open-source newswires (http://www.indymedia.org). There is work on the uses of the Internet and digital video by environmental movements (Pickerill, 2001); the free Burma movement (Troester, 2001); and online feminisms (Vogt and Chen, 2001; Tamina, 2001). Movement actors have used the Internet to organize nomadic protests against EU immigration policies (http://www.noborder.org) and to maintain communication between poor people's movements within the broader global justice movement (KWRU, 2002), and there is emerging legal scholarship on labour organizing rights in the virtual workplace (Spognardi and Hill, 1998; Malin and Perritt, 2001).

---

2. It is not my intention to downplay the vast imbalances in access to communications technology between global "North" and "South," and within each along lines of class, gender, ethnicity. However, I am focusing here on the potential dangers of using such technology, assuming SMO access.

Not all SMO use of new communications technologies is limited to the various kinds of information-sharing. A few authors describe disruptive electronic tactics such as electronic civil disobedience, hacktivism, or infowar (for example see Denning, 2001; Critical Art Ensemble, 1996; Dominguez, in press). I have attempted elsewhere to develop a typology of what I call the *repertoire of electronic contention* that divides SMO use of new technologies into three (overlapping) categories: conventional electronic contention, disruptive electronic contention, and violent electronic contention (Costanza-Chock, in press).[3]

While much of the work mentioned above focuses on case studies of individual SMOs, some of it is analysis of the importance of Internet technology (IT) to broader movement coalition building, especially across national boundaries. Most authors mentioned here would agree with Keck and Sikkink, who argue that IT has been used to help accelerate and strengthen transnational social movements but caution against the idea that communication technologies "drive" transnational movement activity. They emphasize instead the long history of transnational advocacy networks, detailing how the abolitionist and the feminist movements, for example, were always transnational (Keck and Sikkink, 1998). Other scholars developed terms to specify different kinds of interaction within and between individual activists, SMOs, coalitions, and movements. I will draw here on Silke Roth's concept of *social movement interaction* processes in order to lay the ground for a better understanding of the mechanisms by which electronic surveillance might affect movement activity.

Social movement interaction

Roth uses this term to describe the ways in which movement personnel, tactics, organizations, campaigns, ideologies, discourse, mobilizations, and histories may overlap, influence, constrain or otherwise affect one another (Roth, in press). Social movement interaction includes subprocesses elaborated by other social movement scholars: for example, *mesomobilization* (Gerhards and Rucht, 1992), meaning the process by which certain kinds of SMOs (umbrella organizations, for example) do "bridging work" to mobilize broad coalitions of organizations to act collectively; or *spillover* (Meyer and Whittier, 1994), meaning ways in which one movement may influence another through overlapping SMOs, strategies, and membership or by altering political opportunity structures and influencing cycles of

---

3. I also question how changing political opportunity structures and differing levels of repression affect the diffusion of contentious electronic tactics between SMOs. I will return later in this chapter to the idea that diffusion of tactics may be constrained by the kind and degree of surveillance.

protest. In the context of this chapter I prefer Roth's term, since it emphasizes multidimensional flow rather than a one-way diffusion process, and also because Roth nicely articulates the intersection between individual activist life-paths and broader movement processes.[4] This emphasis is important since it reminds us that the potential "chilling effects" of surveillance may operate at the level of the individual, but that such effects then impact SMOs and movement networks by altering a variety of processes including mesomobilization, spillover, bridging, diffusion, and other types of movement interaction.

Surveillance of SMOs in the USA

What exactly are we talking about when we discuss surveillance of SMOs in the US context? In a 1998 article, Diffie and Landau provide insight into the "national security" climate where SMOs continue to be considered important targets of surveillance.[5] They provide a useful overview of "intelligence" technologies employed by the state, and they also show how "national security" in the USA has come to mean not only the maintenance of military forces and intelligence on foreign military powers, but also "provision of intelligence on the capabilities and intentions of all powers, both friendly and hostile, sufficient to inform foreign policy and military action. Such powers ... include organizations representing landless peoples, revolutionary movements, terrorist groups, organized crime, trans-national political movements, and multi-national corporations" (Diffie and Landau, 1998: 78). To discern the path that has led law enforcement and intelligence agencies towards this formulation of "national security", with ever-increasing information gathering capabilities and aims of "predictive policing" (Marx, 1998) based on "total information awareness" (http://www.darpa.mil/IAO/ 2002), it is important to locate electronic surveillance of SMOs in historical perspective.

---

4. Roth pays attention to the fact that individual activists are often engaged not only in one SMO or even in just "one" movement; rather, individual activist life-paths often trace looping and intersecting lines through multiple organizations, coalitions, and movements.
5. Their perspective is useful, although in statements such as "on balance, the impact of technology is so weighted on the side of law enforcement as to make it remarkable that crime has survived at all," (Diffie and Landau, 1998: 121) they appear to buy into a modernist discourse of techno-optimism that bears a straight line to futurist or fascist dream of perfect control, linked to the imagined possibility of a "sanitized" world.

COINTELPRO

Past US government surveillance and repression of domestic social movements have been well documented, most famously through the release of internal intelligence agency documents via Freedom Of Information Act (FOIA) requests. Ward Churchill and Jim Vander Wall's (1990) "The COINTELPRO Papers" gathers internal memos obtained via FOIA that document the breadth and scope of the FBI Counter Intelligence Program (COINTELPRO) extensive campaign of surveillance, disinformation, infiltration, and other activity against the Communist Party USA, the New Left, the Black Liberation Movement, the American Indian Movement, the Socialist Workers Party, the Puerto Rican Independence Movement, and others. They document systematic illegal operations by the FBI against domestic SMOs, including literally thousands of taps, bugs, mail openings, and other COINTELPRO actions between 1957 and 1974 (Churchill and Vander Wall, 1990).[6]

Church Committee

During the 1970s, COINTELPRO and other programmes aimed at domestic surveillance and repression of SMOs came under scrutiny in the Senate investigation known as the Church Committee, which uncovered details of "domestic intelligence activities [that] threaten to undermine our democratic society" (Church Committee, 1976: 1) and concluded with a recommendation that the "CIA, NSA, the Defense Intelligence Agency, and the armed services be precluded, with narrow and specific exceptions, from conducting intelligence activities within the United States, and that their activities abroad be controlled so as to minimize impact on the rights of Americans" (Diffie and Landau, 1998: 121). However, the limits on internal surveillance and on information sharing between agencies that were put in place at the time have by now been greatly eroded. This erosion began well before the events of 11 September 2001. For example, a 1994 Memorandum of Understanding between the Department of Defense and the Department of Justice notes "a growing convergence between the technology required for military operations and the technology required for law enforcement" and calls for the "sharing and joint development ... of technology and systems applicable to both" (DOD and DOJ, 1994).

---

6. Lest we mistake the current use of "war against terror" rhetoric for an innovation, Churchill and Vander Wall also document that as early as 1972, the FBI began using the term "terrorist" in place of "activist", "radical", "agitator", and "political extremist".

2001 FBI statement before Senate

More recently, it is clear that groups that have played large roles in organizing street protests at the meetings of multilateral organizations like the WTO, Internationl Monetary Fund (IMF), World Bank and World Economic Forum (WEF) have come under close scrutiny by various arms of US and foreign law enforcement and intelligence agencies. In a statement on "the domestic terrorism threat" to the 2001 US Senate Committees on Appropriations, Armed Services, and Select Committee on Intelligence, Director of the FBI Louis J. Freeh remarked: "Anarchist and extremist socialist groups – many of which, such as the Workers' World Party, Reclaim the Streets, and Carnival Against Capitalism – have an international presence and, at times, also represent a potential threat in the United States ..." (Freeh, 2001). In accordance with Freeh's view, many have noted that the actions of police around recent large protests recall COINTELPRO and earlier government crackdowns on domestic dissent (see Scher, 2001).[7]

The 2001 USA Patriot Act

In the wake of 11 September, the 2001 USA Patriot Act was pushed through Congress with almost no opposition. The bill allows greatly expanded wiretaps and secret searches, and further enables information sharing between agencies. In relation to "computer crime", the act allows voice taps of suspected hackers/"cyberterrorists", access to voicemail, and interception of electronic communication (email); it also broadens the scope of allowable subpoenas to service providers to include information such as "records of session times and durations", IP addresses, and credit card numbers, in addition to already existing provisions for telephone numbers. The Act also includes nationwide search warrants for email (2001 USA Patriot Act).[8]

I invite the reader to keep in mind the above-mentioned explicit admissions that social movements are still considered legitimate targets

7. "The collaboration of federal and local police harks back to the height of the municipal Red Squads, renamed 'intelligence units' in the postwar period ... Local citizen action won curbs on Red Squad activity in the 70s and 80s after scandals revealed political surveillance of the ACLU, antiwar and civil rights activists, among others." (Scher, 2001).

8. For a more comprehensive review of legislation regarding wiretap and electronic surveillance, see Young (2001).

of state information-gathering activity throughout the following discussion of surveillance actors, technologies, and modes. Such admissions can serve as a kind of base "motive" from which we assume that the state can and will gather any and all possible information about social movements, using any and all tactics and technologies at its disposal, in a legislative climate that has steadily removed checks and blocks on such activity.

The double-edged sword

Seth F. Kreimer points out that the new communication technologies are a mixed blessing for "insurgent social movements" (Kreimer, 2001). Although he does little to define or locate "insurgency" within the wide spectrum of varying social movement styles, tactics, goals and outcomes, his point is well taken: use of new communication technologies may make social movements vulnerable to heightened surveillance by a wide array of state and other actors. The whole world is watching, indeed: "[P]recisely the qualities of the Internet which enable insurgents to reach previously unaffiliated constituencies allow opponents to track and counter insurgent activities" (Kreimer, 2001).

"Opponents" of social movements may include government agencies, private agencies, corporations, and countermovements. Although I will focus here primarily on government agencies, it is useful to briefly touch on these others – not least because (as we will see) the Defense Advanced Research Projects Agency (DARPA) is actively developing technologies that would increase government access to information they gather.

Private agencies

Government agencies have a long history of working with private agencies that don't face the same legal restrictions on information gathering and that don't face the threat of FOIA requests. For example, "The tax-exempt ADL has 30 regional offices in the U.S. (and offices in Canada, Paris, Rome, and Jerusalem), a staff of 400, and an annual budget of $32 million. For many decades they have been gathering information on U.S. citizens, using public sources as well as paid infiltrators, informants, investigators, and liaison with local law enforcement and the FBI" (Brandt, 1993). Meredith Everson has also outlined this terrain (Everson, 2002). Although she speaks mostly about the online monitoring of individual anticorporate speech, it seems that coordinated anticorporate social movements would be subject to equal or greater levels of surveillance by target corporations or their specialized subcontractors.

Countermovements

SMOs should also expect at least their open online communications (websites, BBS, listservs) to be monitored by opposing groups, and probably (depending on the resources of the countermovement) to be subjects of dataveillance as countermovements conduct more sophisticated investigations or hire corporate infomonitors to do so.

Government agencies

The US Government agencies involved in surveillance of social movements are too numerous to list here, but include the FBI, CIA, and NSA as well as local, state, and federal police units. All are increasingly coordinated under the newly formed Office of Homeland Security (http://www.whitehouse.gov/homeland). In addition, after 11 September, the Defense Advanced Research Projects Agency announced the creation of a new office to aid dataveillance: convicted guns-for-hostages dealer John Poindexter was appointed director of the Information Awareness Office (http://www.darpa.mil/iao). Under Poindexter's control, the office will work to develop data-mining systems focused on identifying "potential terrorist organizations" (Markoff, 2002).

Methods of surveillance

To specify and differentiate between the various kinds of electronic surveillance carried out against SMOs by these multiple agencies, I will draw on Diffie and Landau's (1998) categorization of the spectrum of intelligence gathering activity. They describe open source intelligence (OPSINT), gathered from unconcealed sources; operations intelligence (OPERINT), gathered by observing the target's actions; human intelligence (HUMINT), gathered by interviewing, interrogating, or infiltrating with agents or informers; and signals intelligence (SIGINT), gathered by analyzing signals emitted by the target. While SIGINT may be "limited" to observation of information traffic nodes, rates, and flow patterns, this category also contains the subset communications intelligence (COMINT), gathered by analyzing the content of the target's communications (Diffie and Landau, 1998). All these forms of surveillance have potential implications for SMOs, but I will limit concern here mostly to OPSINT and COMINT, while touching on SIGINT and outlining a possible new category: virtual human intelligence, or VHUMINT.

Open source intelligence (OPSINT)

While I have spent some time above outlining various undercover, illegal, and invasive forms of intelligence gathering practised historically and currently by US law enforcement and intelligence agencies, the vast majority of intelligence activity falls under the category of Open Source Intelligence, or OPSINT. To put it simply, OPSINT is in some ways akin to what those of us in the academic community call "research": information gathered from publicly available sources is gathered and analyzed to make inferences about the subject, or in this case, "target". Obvious examples of online OPSINT facilitated by SMO use of the Internet include website, listserv, and BBS monitoring. Police monitoring of these sources of SMO communications might be contextualized as part of a learning process by law enforcement agencies in the wake of the 1999 Seattle protests. During that mobilization, over 50,000 people representing labour, environmentalists, anarchists and a wide range of other movement organizations took to the streets and were violently repressed by what one commentator called a "police riot" where city, state, and federal agents (and later the national guard) used rubber bullets, pepper spray, tear gas and CS gas on peaceful protestors.[9] The Internet had been used extensively by organizers during the pre-event mobilization as a way to distribute calls to action and information about the WTO, as a way to arrange rides and housing for protestors from around the country and around the world, and to develop and disseminate a schedule of protest actions, meetings, alternative conferences and teach-ins, and other events (Eagleton-Pierce, 2001). By all accounts, police had not followed the Internet traffic closely and were not expecting such a large mobilization. During the week of protests, the Internet was used to provide constant updates of eyewitness accounts, photos, video, and audio via the Independent Media Center. In addition, organizers in the streets used cell phones to coordinate direct action, civil disobedience, march logistics, and so on. It seems that police were unprepared for the high level of tactical communication between different affinity groups, blocs, and organizations in the street, and were left unable to deal with simultaneous actions in multiple locations (Eagleton-Pierce, 2001; Smith 2001).

---

9. The violent police response has been described as the result of Seattle police being unprepared for the scale and coordination of the protests, in part since it runs counter to a general trend in liberal democracies away from violent protest policing and toward deescalation, crowd control, prediction and management. For more on policing protest see della Porta (1998).

By the time of the 16 April 2000 IMF/World Bank protests in Washington, DC, however, police and intelligence agencies had gone through a learning process. DC police openly discussed how they monitored activist websites for updated information on protest plans, and activists described intimidating visits by intelligence agents who showed up on cue for planning meetings that had been announced online (Montgomery and Santana, 2000).

In an ominous parallel, Egyptian police began a crackdown on gay men in Cairo that was facilitated when police found a website used by the gay community to organize parties and social events. Police used information there to coordinate a raid on a boat party (Eslinger, 2001). While not SMO surveillance *per se*, this case illustrates the problem faced by marginalized or disempowered groups that use IT to coordinate group activity. In addition, it is telling that 52 men arrested in the raid are now being tried for "organizing to undermine the state", tantamount to terrorism (Krisberg 2001). In essence, Egyptian law enforcement is using the "war against terror" to justify a crackdown on the gay community, facilitated by OPSINT gathered from community websites.

While the state may have historically gathered a great deal of information about SMOs through OPSINT, and more recently through monitoring activity as described in these examples, the evolution of data mining technology is dramatically shifting just what kind of information can be characterized as "open source". Part of what I like to suggest here is that even SMOs that are aware that their websites and listservs are monitored, and even those that are wary of covert monitoring, infiltration, and other forms of state surveillance, may not understand the degree to which new (or projected) information gathering and analysis technologies, combined with permissive legislation and a paranoiac political will that flourishes in the climate of the "war against terror", make their use of IT risky inasmuch as such use feeds new OPSINT technologies.

Government databases and data mining

These new technologies are aimed at achieving what DARPA terms "total information awareness". The Information Awareness Office (IAO) call for proposals (BAA 02-08 Information Awareness Proposer Information Pamphlet, 2002) explicitly describes a goal of incorporating *all* existing state databases into one massive distributed database that will automatically update itself, gathering and analyzing information about any and all potential "threats to national security" (DARPA 2002).

I do not mean to suggest that database consolidation has not been taking place outside of the IAO. On the contrary, since 1967 the FBI

National Crime Info Center (NCIC) has combined juvenile offence, gang,[10] terrorist, and many other categories of membership in a centralized national database system.[11] However, the vision and call for proposals of the IAO is marked by language like "[I]n the context of this BAA, the term 'database' is intended to convey a new kind of extremely large, omnimedia, virtually-centralized, and semantically-rich information repository ... we use "database" for lack of a more descriptive term" (DARPA, 2002). Such an "omnimedia" database makes current fears about state monitoring of medical and employment records, book purchase records, and Internet search terms into the mere tip of the iceberg. It suggests, among other things, a vision of linkage to CCTV systems[12] as well as to information gathered in ways other than "open source".

Signals intelligence (SIGINT)

Movement actors should be aware of the new kinds of OPSINT described above, and also recognize the extent to which even information not publicly available is accessed by state agencies.

---

10. "In 1992, Denver's gang database listed eight of every ten young people of color in the entire city ... in some places, all you have to do to get in the database is be down with hip-hop style" (Chang, 2002). Such databases are justified post- 9.11 as essential to 'homeland security'. The racialized development of such databases, and application of gang laws to youth of color, is critical here. You can't talk about surveillance and policing of the movement for global social justice without talking about the criminalization of people of color, especially youth of color.

11. While such database linkage is taking place within the US between local, state, and federal law enforcement, military and other intelligence agencies, I invite further research into the factors that determine whether such links are made across national boundaries. There has been a broad push by the US for information sharing between national intelligence agencies under the rubric of "war against terror", but sustained analysis would be necessary to describe the complex ways in which information sharing between national agencies actually is implemented – or blocked.

12. More work is needed on the relationship between digital video technology and surveillance of social movements. There is much written on the spread of CCTV systems and image-recognition software; in addition, the "double edge" comes into play here as activist-produced videos might be used by police and intelligence agencies to feed image databases that later link to CCTV systems installed in areas at "high risk" for protest.

Server logs

Server log subpoenas are one method used by the state to gather SIGINT on SMO targets. In 2001, the FBI unsuccessfully tried to subpoena the server logs of IMC Seattle when anti-corporate-globalization activists in Quebec stole a memo on protest policing tactics from the back of a squad car and posted the contents to the Seattle Independent Media Center. Seattle IMC soon found itself with an FBI server log subpoena plus a gag order on the request (McCullagh, 2001). While IMC refused to turn over the logs and eventually overturned both the gag order and the subpoena in court, the danger represented by this case is clear: SMO exchange of tactical information, facilitated by IT, exposed Indymedia and all the activists who use it (and by extension, any SMOs they were affiliated with) to increased monitoring by law enforcement.

Cell phones

The use of cell phones by activists provides another example of communications technology that exposes movement actors to increased risk of SIGINT. I refer here not to the monitoring of phone conversations (I will touch on that below) but to the fact that an in-use cell phone provides law enforcement or intelligence agents with the ability to physically pinpoint the user. What's more (although this may be stretching the limits of Signals Intelligence), activists at the Philadelphia Republican National Convention were arrested for having cell phones on charges of "possession of an instrument of crime" (Wells, 2000). Although these cases were later thrown out of court, the police may continue to make such arrests as part of predictive protest policing strategies.

Large scale SIG/COMINT systems

Although OPSINT makes up the majority of intelligence gathering, COMINT is probably the most written about of all state surveillance activity against SMOs. For that reason I will refer the reader on to more in-depth discussions of the technologies and systems involved. Very briefly, then:

Carnivore

Carnivore is the FBI's system for monitoring electronic communications, technically a filtering software package installed on a PC that can be switched back and forth between SIGINT (pen trap) and COMINT (content capture) modes. Privacy advocates charge that Carnivore provides the capability for overbroad and invasive monitoring of communications. (For an excellent technical and legal discussion see Haas, 2001). More information about the system was requested under FOIA and is available from the Electronic Privacy Information Center (http://www.epic.org/privacy/carnivore/foia_ documents.html).

ECHELON

ECHELON is a computer system used to sift through all communications intercepted by the worldwide UKUSA SIGINT apparatus, possibly in conjunction with other surveillance networks. Currently, ECHELON is thought to monitor and sort cellular, satellite, microwave and fibre-optic traffic, potentially including all faxes, telexes, email, and computer traffic. Inadequate voice-to-text technology is apparently a current hurdle to automating the analysis of all phone traffic. Sorting is done using complex word-order algorithms (for more see Richelson 2001, or http://www.aclu.org/echelonwatch).

Monitor emissions and keystroke loggers

Other invasive COMINT tools that the state may deploy against SMOs are screen emissions detection, in which particles emanating from a computer screen can be captured at a distance and used to "view" the screen remotely (Goodman, 2001), and Trojan horse key logging software, designed to hide on the targeted PC and transmit every keystroke to a remote data collector (Krim, 2001).

Virtual human intelligence (VHUMINT)

State targeting of SMOs for message interception has been extensively discussed, online undercover operations less so. Police and intelligence agency practices of infiltration in meatspace have of course made their way online as well. In any unmediated forum, such as many BBS systems, open email lists, chat rooms, or hybrid news/discussion venues like Indymedia, the only cue to the identity of participants is often a short text "handle". Users of these fora sometimes create alternate identities, switching gender, race, and other categories. In this environment, it becomes very difficult for social movement actors to determine whether opposition – corporate, governmental, or countermovement – is monitoring their discussions. In fact, it would potentially be easy for opposition not only to monitor but also to attempt to influence movement activity by proposing events, tactics, strategies, and so on. There's no room here for a more extensive examination of the possibilities of virtual undercover operations, but Gary Marx provides a (dirty) laundry list of problems caused by meatspace undercover operations conducted in the name of crime control or intelligence gathering. These include damage to the public trust, to peripheral innocents, and to third parties, as well as potential difficulties and ethical dilemmas that arise when law enforcement attempts to "manage" informants (Marx, 1988). I suggest that these and other problems also apply to undercover operations in the virtual sphere.

Netwar

While not a category of surveillance, it is worth mentioning here that use of the Internet may also make SMOs vulnerable to various kinds of communication disruption, or netwar. For example, the fundamental strength of the Indymedia centers – their open publishing format – also seems to be a fundamental weakness, as hackers mounted attacks on Indymedia Palestine by placing destructive scripts in place of news stories as well as by simply clogging the newswires with hate-text posts (palestine.indymedia.org). In addition, SMO use of disruptive electronic tactics can make them vulnerable to retaliation, as in the case of a "hostile applet" developed by the Pentagon and deployed against participants in the "Netstrike for Acteal" (Ronfeldt, Arquilla et. al., 1998). More recently, when the Pentagon forced the entire Somalian Internet to shut down under the pretext that the providers were supporting terrorism, NGOs and human rights groups in Somalia that had been using the Internet to coordinate food and clothing distribution with international partners and to ferry documentation of human rights abuses were caught unawares and with no backup coordination system (Electronic Frontier Foundation, 2002).

Consequences

What consequences might all this online surveillance, infiltration and disruption have on individual activists, SMOs, and on social movement interaction processes?

Selective prosecution

Kreimer points out that activists who utilize the Internet may be vulnerable to selective prosecution. For example, "If members of insurgent political groups are less than scrupulous about complying with intellectual property laws, hostile authorities can invoke intellectual property prosecutions selectively against dissidents, in the same way that ubiquitously violated traffic regulations are invoked against suspected drug couriers" (Kreimer,

2001). In a related example, he notes that the Internal Revenue Service (IRS) has recently launched an initiative to revoke the non-profit status of some organizations that were engaged in web-based activism, arguing that they be considered "lobbyists" (Kreimer, 2001).

Persistence of data

Since digital information can be stored for indefinite periods of time, it is not hard to imagine a multitude of scenarios where information gathered at one point in an individual's life returns to haunt them in a new, damaging or incriminating context.[13] Persistence of data is relevant for all social movement participants (or even observers-at-a-distance), since all electronic communications are potentially permanent, monitored, and searchable. As agencies increasingly deploy artificial intelligence programs to sift through email, chat room, BBS and other online communications looking for statements supporting "terrorist" organizations, and as the pool of searchable material extends further back in time, we might expect algorithmic surveillance (Norris et. al 1998) and automated justice to implicate SMOs and individual activists in retroactive webs of "terrorist activity". In the extreme case, this might be analogized to "automated blacklists" that impact movement participant's life-chances. This might also occur if, say, prospective employers were able to check on an individual's history of political activism.

Chilling effects

Beyond the problems of selective prosecution, persistence of data, and the general effects of the violation of individual privacy rights and dignity, what might all of this add up to? Concerns arise about the deterrence of legitimate political expression and activism; the disruption of social movement networks; the delegitimation of social movement individuals, organizations, and movements; a general political climate of fear, lack of tolerance for dissent, the further entrenchment of unjust power; and the destruction of trust, both within and between movement organizations and between targeted individuals and the state. Here I would like to reiterate that online surveillance and virtual infiltration of SMOs and other movement actors may affect not only individuals but also bridging processes, mesomobilization, diffusion of tactics, social movement

---

13. For example, Dr Sami Al-Arian, a UF professor, was recently fired for comments made over 10 years ago in support of armed resistance movements in occupied Palestine – groups that later were labelled terrorist by the Department of Defense (Jacoby, 2002).

spillover, and other kinds of social movement interaction processes. While analysis of effects on all these processes is beyond the scope of this paper, I will illustrate with the example of diffusion.

Diffusion of the electronic repertoire of contention

One possible outcome of heightened online surveillance of SMOs is a decrease in the rate of diffusion of the electronic repertoire of contention. For example, conventional electronic contention may be affected as SMOs grow hesitant to adopt, say, chat room planning meetings from fear of government or countermovement monitoring (VHUMINT); or some SMOs may become less likely to set up open-membership listservs or online event calendars due to risk of exposure to OPSINT operations.

Most likely, disruptive tactics (for example netstrikes, virtual sit-ins, site defacement, email and form flooding) will be avoided by most SMOs in the current legislative and discursive climate: such tactics, especially if deployed against government sites, are actionable under "cyberterrorism" laws and are likely to be framed as "cyberterror" by the media even if not so prosecuted. Smaller SMOs are unlikely to adopt such tactics for lack of legal resources, while larger SMOs that might be able to afford extensive legal support against "cyberterror" charges are for the most part dependent on broad membership bases (for example Amnesty International, NOW, NAACP, or most trade unions) and are unlikely to employ disruptive electronic tactics for fear of alienating membership.[14]

I invite further discussion of the effects of online surveillance and virtual infiltration on other kinds of social movement interaction processes. For now, though, I will move on to the question of possible responses.

Responses

Given the current playing field, what can SMOs and other movement actors do?

Jump ship

SMOs might abandon certain uses of communication technologies, or choose not to adopt them if not already in play. While it seems unlikely

---

14. On the other hand, there exist legal organizations like the Electronic Frontier Foundation that would likely take on any case of "cyberterrorism" charges brought against an SMO. This creates an opportunity for small SMOs or other actors to employ disruptive electronic tactics in a bid to gain large amounts of media attention, if they are willing to risk incarceration under cyberterror law.

that many SMOs would abandon electronic communication (though there may be some who do so), there are examples of organizations choosing not to engage in certain uses of communication technologies based on fears of heightened surveillance. Many gay websites and listservs in Cairo were shut down by their owners in the wake of the Queen Boat raids (Eslinger, 2001). Some activists carefully avoid sending critical information via email, preferring to relay such information face-to-face or via snail mail. Also, consistent with my analysis of the rate of diffusion of disruptive electronic tactics, netstrikes and other forms of "electronic civil disobedience" were toyed with by some SMOs before 11 September but then abandoned, based on a (probably accurate) perception of heightened surveillance or repressive action that such tactics might expose them to. Communications Workers of America, who had been planning a netstrike against Verizon as a protest against Verizon's refusal to let Puerto Rican telecom workers form a bargaining unit, abandoned this plan after 11 September (Communications Workers of America, 2001).

Keep tabs

SMOs might work more closely with organizations that focus on monitoring state abuses of surveillance, and dispute such surveillance in court. Groups like the Electronic Frontier Foundation (http://www.eff.org), the Electronic Privacy Information Center (http://www.epic.org), chillingeffects.org, and others help to keep tabs on state surveillance technologies, legislation, and abuses.

School themselves

SMOs and other actors might inform themselves and their networks about the dangers of surveillance they become exposed to when they use electronic communications. Organizations like Privaterra (http://privaterra.cpsr.org) and Human Rights Tech (http://www.humanrightstech.org) exist in order to train human rights organizations how to transmit sensitive information without being observed. These groups primarily help to diffuse PGP or other Privacy Enhancing Technologies among small human rights SMOs, who then transfer the knowledge to human rights workers.

Mash it up

Certain SMOs or individual "hacktivists" may engage in direct disruption of surveillance systems. This is analogous to disruption of the surveillance apparatus in meatspace – for example, spraypainting the lenses of CCTV cameras. Disruption of online surveillance systems or of databases might be accomplished through the introduction of viruses, worms, or Trojan horses into state or corporate databases. These kinds of activities will generally be limited since they are actionable under a wide range of laws, from destruction of property to cyberterrorism statutes.

Disruption of databases or of automated online surveillance can also be accomplished through certain kinds of mass-participation coordinated online actions. For example, in June 2001 thousands of people flooded the US Navy recruitment database by filling online Navy enlistment form "name" and "address" fields with protest messages demanding a military withdrawal from the island of Vieques, Puerto Rico (see http://www.freespeech.org/provieques). However, it seems unlikely that databases used to monitor SMO activity online will be publicly accessible via forms. Using a related mass-participatory strategy, online activists called for a "Jam ECHELON Day", urging all opponents of the automated communications surveillance and sorting system to attach a file containing "suspect" keywords in an attempt to overwhelm the system's capabilities (see http://www.cipherwar.com/echelon). When pressed by critics who claimed that simply copying lists of keywords would be unlikely to have an effect on Echelon's sophisticated word-order algorithms, organizers granted that the purpose of the action was mostly to inform and educate, not to disrupt (McAuliffe, 2001).

One of the most daring database disruptions to date was performed during the summer of 2002 in Strasbourg, where activists from the No Borders network physically dug up the street and tapped into a cable to access the Schengen Information System (a pan-European immigration, deportation, crime, and terrorism database). They then hacked into the system and made all information in the database publicly available and open to modification (http://www.dsec.info).

Legislate

SMOs must be involved in pushing for legislation that limits and checks surveillance of social movements, as part of the broader attempt to enact legislation on privacy rights in the information age. Unfortunately, for a variety of reasons, omnibus privacy legislation of the kind developed in the EU has not been successful in the US. As we have seen, the trend is quite the opposite, with a series of acts broadening intelligence and law enforcement powers and eating away at protections against wiretaps, interagency infosharing, and so on, culminating in the USA Patriot Act and the funding of agencies such as the IAO. From here, the legislative road looks like a very long uphill path.

Conclusion

I have tried to show that, while SMO interaction processes of many kinds may be aided by the affordability and speed of new communication technologies, use of such technologies also exposes SMOs and other movement actors to the possibility of increased OPSINT, SIGINT, COMINT, and VHUMINT by a wide range of state intelligence agencies, including automated systems. New surveillance technologies and legislation enabling unprecedented levels of online surveillance and virtual infiltration, designed to allow preemptive arrest or other action against suspected terrorist groups, may be applied to social movement organizations with chilling effects on legal dissent and on social movements. SMOs that choose to use new communications technologies therefore need to consider how such use might frustrate, facilitate, or otherwise interact with the efforts of state or other actors to monitor and repress. In addition, it is in the interest of SMOs to join the push for comprehensive privacy legislation both at the national and transnational levels.

References

American Civil Liberties Union (ACLU). 'Echelonwatch'. http://www.aclu.org/echelonwatch.

American Civil Liberties Union (2001) 'USA Patriot Act boosts government powers while cutting back on traditional checks and balances'. 1 November, 2001. http://www. aclu.org/congress/l110101a.html.

Bellia, Patricia L. (2001) 'Chasing bits across borders'. In *The University of Chicago Legal Forum 35.*

Brandt, Daniel (1993) 'Cyberspace wars: Microprocessing vs. big brother'. In *NameBase NewsLine,* No. 2, July–August 1993.

Chang, Jeff (2002). 'Styling and profiling: Privacy and the hip-hop generation after 9/11'. Presentation at Media Bistro Salon, 19 March.

Church Committee (1976) Final report of the senate select committee to study governmental operations with respect to intelligence activities, Book II, Intelligence Activities and the Rights of Americans. USS 94d.

Churchill, Ward and Vander Wall, Jim (1990) 'The Cointelpro papers: Documents from the FBI's secret wars against domestic dissent'. Boston, MA: South End Press.

Communications Workers of America (2001). Personal correspondence, 12 November.

Costanza-Chock, Sasha (2003) 'Mapping the repertoire of electronic contention', in Andrew Opel and Donnalyn Pompper, eds. *Representing resistance: Media, civil disobedience and the global justice movement,* Westport: Praeger Greenwood, in press.

Critical Art Ensemble (1996) *Electronic civil disobedience*. New York: Autonomedia/ SemioText(e).

DARPA. 'BAA 02-08 information awareness proposer information pamphlet'. Defense advanced research projects agency 2002, http://www.eps.gov/ EPSData/ODA/Synopses/4965/BAA02-08/IAPIP.doc.

della Porta, Donatella and Reiter, Herbert eds. (1998) *Policing protest: The control of mass demonstrations in Western democracies*. Minneapolis: University of Minnesota Press.

Denning, Dorothy (2001) 'Activism, hacktivism, and cyberterrorism: The Internet as a tool for influencing foreign policy'. Presentation at the Terrorism Research Center, February, http://www.terrorism.com/documents/ denning-infoterrorism.html.

Department of Defense (DOD) and Department of Justice (DOJ) (1994) 'Memo of understanding between DOD and DOJ on operations other than war and law enforcement'. 1994.

Diffie, Whitfield and Landau, Susan (1998) *Privacy on the line: The politics of wiretapping and encryption*. Cambridge: MIT Press.

Dominguez, R. (2004) *Hacktivism: Network art activism*. New York: Autonomedia.

Eagleton-Pierce, Matthew (2001) 'The Internet and the Seattle WTO protests.' In *Peace Review*, 13, 3, September.

Electronic Frontier Foundation (2002) 'Chilling effects of anti-terrorism'. http:// www.eff.org/Privacy/Surveillance/Terrorism_militias/antiterrorism/chill.html.

Electronic Privacy Information Center (2002) 'The carnivore FOIA litigation.' http://www.epic.org/privacy/carnivore.

Eslinger, Bonnie (2001) 'Uncertain future: The ongoing prosecution of the "Queen Boat" defendants has Cairo's gay community laying low'. *Cairo Times*, 5, 19, July.

Everson, Meredith (2002) 'Monitoring the electronic water cooler: Internet discussion mining and its social consequences'. Unpublished.

Freeh, Louis J. (2001) 'Statement for the record, Louis J. Freeh, Director, FBI, on the threat of terrorism to the United States'. United States Senate Committees on appropriations, armed services, and select committee on intelligence, 10 May.

Gerhards, Jurgen and Rucht, Dieter (1992) 'Mesomobilization: Organizing and framing in two protest campaigns in West Germany'. *American Journal of Sociology* 98, 3, 555–595.

Goodman, Cassi (2001) 'An introduction to TEMPEST'. SANS Institute, 18 April. http://rr.sans.org/encryption/TEMPEST.php.

Haas, Trenton C. (2001) 'Carnivore and the fourth amendment'. In *Connecticut Law Review* 34, Fall, 261.

H.R. 3162, 2001 USA Patriot Act.

Human Rights Tech. http://www.humanrightstech.org.

Independent Media Center. http://www.indymedia.org.

Information Awareness Office. http://www.darpa.mil/IAO.

Institute for Global Communication. http://www.igc.org.

Jacoby, Mary (2002) 'Fighting terror: Muslims hit raids linked to Al-Arian'. In
St. Petersburg Times, 22 March, 1A.

Jam Echelon Day. http://www.cipherwar.com/echelon.

Keck, Margaret E. and Sikkink, Kathryn (1998) Activists beyond borders: Advocacy
networks in international politics'. Ithaca, NY: Cornell University Press.

Kensington Welfare Rights Union (KWRU) (2002) Presentation at the University of
Pennsylvania, 17 February.

Koopmanns, Ruud (1997) 'Dynamics of repression and mobilization: The German
extreme right in the 1990s'. In Mobilization, 2, 2, 1997, 149–165.

Kreimer, Seth F. (2001) 'Technologies of protest: Insurgent social movements and
the first amendment in the era of the Internet'. In University of Pennsylvania Law
Review, 150, 1, 2001, 119–171.

Krim, Jonathan (2001). 'Privacy advocates question FBI's keystroke logging'. In
Washington Post, 14 August.

Krisberg, Kim (2001) 'Egyptian defendant accused of terrorist link'. In Washington
Blade, 19 October. http://www.washblade.com/national/011019b.htm.

Kumar, Chetan (2000) 'Transnational networks and campaigns for democracy.' In
Ann M. Florini, ed. The third force: The rise of transnational civil society, Tokyo/
Washington: Japan Center for International Exchange/Carnegie Endowment
for International Peace.

Markoff, John (2002) 'Chief takes over new agency to thwart attacks on US'. In
New York Times, 13 February.

Martin, H. Malin and Perrit, Henry H. (2001). 'The national labor relations act in
cyberspace: Union organizing in electronic workplaces'. In University of Kansas
Law Review, 49, 2000. http://www.bnabooks.com/ababna/nlra/2001/perritt.doc.

Marx, Gary T. (1998) Undercover: Police surveillance in America. Berkeley and Los
Angeles, CA: University of California Press.

McAuliffe, Wendy (2001) 'Activists target US surveillance system'. ZDnet, 27 July.
http://www.zdnet.com.au/printfriendly?AT=2000020814-20250982-1.

McCullagh, Declan (2001) 'Journalists protest gag order'. In Wired News, 25 April.
http://www.wired.com/news/politics/0,1283,43339,00.html.

Meyer, D. and Whittier, N. (1994) 'Social movement spillover'. In Social Problems
41, 2, 1994, 277–298.

Montgomery, David and Santana, Arthur (2000) 'Rally web site also interests the
uninvited: DC police are monitoring information posted online'. Washington Post
2 April, A14.

Netstrike for Vieques. http://www.freespeech.org/provieques.

No Border Network. http://www.noborder.org.

Norris, C. and Moran, J. et. al. (1998) 'Algorithmic surveillance: The future of automated visual surveillance'. In C. Norris, J. Moran and G. Armstrong, eds. *Surveillance, Closed Circuit Television and Social Control.* Aldershot, England/ Brookfield, VT: Ashgate.

Office of Homeland Security. http://www.whitehouse.gov/homeland.

Palestine Independent Media Center. http://palestine.indymedia.org.

Pickerill, Jenny (2001) 'Environmental Internet activism in Britain'. *Peace Review* 13, 3, 2001, 365–370.

Privaterra. http://privaterra.cpsr.org.

Ronfeldt, David F. and Arquilla, John et. al. (1998) 'The Zapatista social netwar', in Mexico. Santa Monica, CA: Rand http://www.rand.org/publications/MR/ MR994.

Roth, Silke 'Social movement interaction, bridging organizations, processes of political socialization: A case-study of the coalition of labor union women ', in press.

Richelson, Jeffrey (2001) 'Desperately seeking signals'. In *Peace Research Abstracts,* 38 3, 2001.

Scher, Abby 2001) 'The crackdown on dissent'. In *The Nation* 19 January 2001.

Schulz, Markus S. (1998) 'Collective action across borders: Opportunity structures, network capacities, and communicative praxis in the age of advanced globalization'. In *Sociological Perspectives* 41, 3, 1998, 587–616.

Smith, Jackie (2001) 'Globalizing resistance: The battle of Seattle and the future of social movements'. In *Mobilization* 6, 1, 2001, 1–19.

Spognardi, Mark A. and Hill, Ruth Bro (1998) 'Organizing through cyberspace: Electronic communications and the national labor relations act'. In *Employee Relations Law Journal* 23, 4, Spring. http://www.mbc.com/db30/cgi-bin/pubs/ MAS-Organizing_Through_Cyberspace.pdf.

Tamina (2001) 'RAWA: Empowering Afghan women'. Lecture/Presentation at University of Pennsylvania, 28 November 2001.

Troester, Rod (2001) 'Using the Internet for peace in isolated Burma'. In *Peace Review* 13,3, 2001, 389–394.

Vogt, Christina and Chen, Peiying (2001) 'Feminisms and the Internet'. In *Peace Review,* 13, 3, 2001, 371–374.

Wells, Janet (2000) '$1 Million bail ordered for protesters: Berkeley-based activist allegedly led mayhem'. In *San Francisco Chronicle,* 5 August 2000, A3.

Young, Mark G. (2001) 'What big eyes and ears you have!: A new regime for covert governmental surveillance'. In *Fordham Law Review* 70, December, 1017.

Agendas for Research
and Strategies for Intervention

Pradip N. Thomas

The background to many of the articles included in this volume is the looming presence and impact of the neoliberal economy on media structures and media processes throughout the world. In a post-Cold War era, characterized by the global dominance of US power, the decline of countervailing power, and the advancement of a global market economy, it would seem that there is very little left of civil society and/or the space for initiatives linked to the popular reclamation of cultural and media space, in spite of the many expressions of the anti-globalization movement and initiatives such as the Global Social Forum. One can concur with the view that the relentless pace of media privatization and the steady retreat of the state from its public media commitments have contributed in no small measure to this state of affairs.

If one were to take stock of global media and democracy, there will be little to celebrate. While there are, at any given time, a "million mutinies" at local levels aimed at reclaiming cultural space, these are, for the most part, specific, small-scale initiatives that have typically not led to any sustainable enlargement of democratic media or cultural space at national levels. Organizing around enthusiasms does not, in other words, necessarily lead to or result in a social movement, although most actors related to civil society media initiatives think otherwise and assume that their actions automatically contribute to what is almost always a rather glibly referred to as a "social movement".

Local expressions of community media, linked to the empowerment of local communities – through the setting up of media watch groups, media education foras, and community media initiatives – have advanced the cause of media democracy. However, while "small may be beautiful" and there are many lessons to be learned from these expressions, it is clear that this accent on the local has been made at the expense of the global, that for all practical purposes has been hijacked by a corporate-government-multilateral combine. In other words, the policies and frameworks related to the planning, development, and implementation of global media and information futures – the larger picture, for the most part – remains conspicuously bereft of inputs from civil society.

To mention just a few of these universal trends: social clauses that once limited media monopolies have now been revoked at national levels, intellectual property rights especially copyright and patents have been used by industry to reinforce property rights in the media, new media such as the Internet, that in its inception promised to be a people's communication tool, is now firmly advancing down the commercial track, the audio-visual spectrum is in danger of migrating from the hands of government to that of a handful of media combines and people's right to information is being compromised by post-11 September policies that have enhanced public and private surveillance, resulted in restrictions to the public scrutiny of certain government institutions, ostensibly for reasons of national security, the manufacture of wall to wall, 24 hours media propaganda and to palpable efforts aimed at curbing the media's right to independently report in the context of war situations such as in Afghanistan and Iraq.

It is clear that in a post-NWICO world, the relative absence of civil society as a global player in media policy making has made it very much easier for corporate media institutions to cut a swathe through the world's media while aided by mergers and alliances, the weakening of pro-social media laws and the steady commercialization of public sector media.

CRIS and the politics of civil society

There have been the occasional civil society related attempts linked to global media advocacy. Take for example the Communication Rights in the Information Society (CRIS) campaign. Borne out of a coalition of international media organizations – the Platform for Communication Rights (PCR) – that were formed in London in 1996, the CRIS campaign was launched to ensure maximum civil society participation and input into the UN-sponsored World Summit on the Information Society (WSIS) organized by the International Telecommunication Union (ITU) on behalf of the UN. This summit is scheduled to be held in two phases: Geneva 2003 and Tunis 2005. The PCR had, prior to the launching of the CRIS initiative, campaigned for non-governmental organization (NGO) participation at the ITU, one of the last of the UN organizations to recognize the involvement of NGOs. This effort, along with the pre-existing work of the UN Gender IT Task Force and the growing importance of the global NGO movement, arguably led the ITU to include civil society along with governments and the private sector in the organizing of the WSIS.

The objectives of the CRIS campaign are to ensure maximum participation of civil society at the WSIS, to broaden the agenda of the WSIS from its present emphasis on connectivity, technology and the globalization of IT products, to critical issues in communication rights related to content, process, audiences and structures, from within a critical political economy perspective. Towards this end, CRIS is presently involved in mobilizing regional, national and local networks on the WSIS and creating awareness on key issues related to communication as a human right. There are no guarantees that this effort will be taken seriously. The ITU, while on the one hand has granted civil society a role in organizing the WSIS, it is, on the other hand, under intense internal and external pressure to maintain the status quo and keep the deliberations firmly in the hands of governments.

While CRIS is a laudable initiative, its success will depend on the energies it expends on this initiative over the long term, the synergies that it creates at various levels, advocacy efforts at local and international levels and support it attracts over the long term. Key to the success of this project is advocacy at a local level where issues such as communication as a human right and the right to communicate are yet to become issues worthy of local concern. It would be off target to generalize this reality. While there are numerous initiatives around the world specifically linked to communication rights issues at any given moment, this issue has not reached "critical mass" in any country. For most people communication means televised infotainment. The term communication lends itself to multi-accentual meanings and that remains an obstacle to conveying the meaning of communication as a human right. While the global media education movement has, to some extent, succeeded in including communication and media issues in school curricula and helped raise media awareness among local communities, this movement has a long way to go before it becomes an accepted and legitimate aspect of education both in formal and non-formal settings.

The term civil society is often used in a loose way to refer to organizations and people working to ensure the sustainability of non-state and non-private environments. As such, the civil society umbrella is home to a variety of organizations and people motivated by diverse political persuasions and expectations. Internet-focused NGOs are a good example of this diversity. They range from the conservative, well endowed US based Markle Foundation to the Bill Gates Foundation to NGOs involved in wiring the nation in their capacity as foot soldiers for private industry, to those involved in the sometimes well-intentioned but politically inept attempt at tackling the "digital divide" to those involved in supporting the information rights of marginal communities to libertarians like the

Electronic Frontier Foundation and their brand of Net-freedom. In the context of organizing a campaign such as the CRIS, this diversity raises questions related to the nature of partners and alliances. Unlike the environmental movement which is concerned with diverse issues and yet manages to communicate a core set of universally recognized concerns, the multi-accentuality of terms such as communication and for that matter human rights along with the existence of a variety of perceptions, interests and investments in communication hinder the recognition, at global and local levels, of a set of identifiable, common, universal concerns in communication. While those of us involved in a day-to-day basis on such issues blithely refer to the right to communicate, there is to date, not a single resource that clearly explains to ordinary people what the right to communicate is all about. Charters and statements have their own validity but these have to be complemented with easily accessible material. It would seem that a global educational strategy is absolutely central to universalizing issues such as the right to communicate.

While efforts at global advocacy may be few and far between, there exist a number of efforts at a local level to claim media rights and media space. There are efforts in Latin America to legitimize the community radio movement, the media education movement in South Korea, the many efforts throughout the world to initiate the right to information bills, to recognize the validity of gender and communication issues on local agendas, to make governments accountable for their policies. All these are critical initiatives that have connected local with global issues. These strategic initiatives have contributed to democratizing communication environments throughout the world. Many of these initiatives are nurtured through global, regional and local networks as is the case with the work of the Association for Progressive Communications (APC), World Association of Community Radio Braodcasters (AMARC), World Association for Christian Communication (WACC), Latin American Information Agency (ALAI), Latin American Association of Educational Radio (ALER), ISIS International Manila (ISIS) and other organizations. However, these initiatives, individually and collectively, have typically been unable to contribute to changes that make a difference at the level of media policy. Given other pressing immediate needs, advocacy is often a luxury that most networks can ill afford. And yet, advocacy is critical to social change.

The Niue affair

One of the objectives of the series of workshops on media ownership that was supported by the WACC was to map the different permutations and patterns of media ownership in order to create resources to be used in media advocacy efforts. One of the case studies that was highlighted at the workshop that was held in Nadi, Fiji, concerned the small Pacific island of Niue. Niue had been assigned the top-level Internet domain name '.nu' in the late 1990s. A government minister was approached by an American media entrepreneur, Bill Symitch, who offered to buy this domain name in return for US$10,000. After the sale, .nu was managed by the Internet Users Society of Niue (IUSN), which then redelegated the management and marketing responsibilities to a US-company NU Domain Ltd. There have, since this sale, been more than 200,000 .nu registrations and substantive sales related income, none of which was shared with the government of Niue. Niue, a former protectorate of New Zealand, with a population of less than 2,000 people, is a relatively poor nation, dependent on tourism and fishing. They could have used .nu to earn valuable foreign exchange. The government of Niue, who were duped into parting with their assigned domain name, have, as a result of advocacy by the Pacific Region-WACC, taken up the issue and have approached the Internet Corporation for Assigned Names and Numbers (ICAAN) to settle this dispute and to take back control over .nu. The Government Advisory Committee (GAC) of the ICAAN has recommended that the domain name be handed back to the government of Niue. This has been contested by NU Domain Ltd. who, along with other players in the private sector, placed pressure to hand control of ICAAN to the private sector. This dispute has dragged on for a few years and has been complicated by the on-going politics at the ICAAN, including attempts to divest its board of representatives from the global Internet community.

This dispute reflects a global reality. Prospecting for the world's information resources and its privatization is an unchecked, global trend. It is ironic that while the piracy of cultural products is condemned, and WIPO, the WTO and national and regional IPR regimes have invested in a raft of anti-piracy measures, there are no comparable initiatives linked to curbing the global prospecting for information resources.

IPR

One of the areas that is in need of critical political economy-based explorations are IPR and communication-related issues at local and national levels. There is very little research work on issues related to IPR and communications in the South. In an era characterized by the increased concentration of media ownership by a handful of transnational, regional, domestic firms and in some instances the state, and the pressure to harmonize IPR laws under the TRIPS agreement, governments in the South have had no option but to frame a raft of IPR-related legislations in compliance with TRIPS. It will be interesting to watch the response from China to IPR issues after its accession to the WTO. So far, the WTO's support for the audio-visual trade has been restricted to the opening up of quotas for Hollywood film. In the areas of telecommunications, the Internet, software and hardware, it has, along with other international agencies such as WIPO and supported by the updated Copyright Treaty (1996) that came into effect in May 2002, the ITU and governments, expanded a proprietorial approach to IP and encouraged enclosures via patents and copyright. In the US, as it has been pointed out, Congress had extended the term of copyrights eleven times during the last forty years "The 1998 (digital copyright) law alone extended copyright by 20 years: works copyrighted by individuals since 1978 were granted a term of 70 years beyond the life of the author; works made by or for corporations were protected for 95 years. The extension applied to existing works even if the author was dead or the work long out of print" (Waldmier, 2002: 15). WIPO received a record 104,000 international patent applications from the information industries in 2001 with the US heading the list with 38.5% of all applications while developing countries as a whole barely managed 5% (Williams, 2002). This is a fraction of the total 7.1 million patent applications filed in 1999. In Europe, Philips filed 2,010 patents in the year 2000 while British Telecommunications had amassed 13,000 patents protecting 1,700 inventions by that same year. In the US, companies make major profits from licensing IP. IBM, the top filer of patents at the US Patent and Trademark Office over the last eight years (2,886 patents in the year 2000) made profits of $1.7 billion from licensing intellectual property (IP) the same year (Kenward, 2001). The US earned $38 billion in royalties from outside of the country in 2000. Since the emerging knowledge economy is extensively based on a specific model of growth that is advantageous to the Global North rather than to the Global South – there is bound to be an increase in the import bills of countries in the South – as IP legislations are used to earn incomes from the sale of formats, screenings, software licensing. At the same time, this is bound to result in barriers to the democratization of knowledge as already cash strapped libraries are denied free use of digitized knowledge, the space for cultural appropriation is restricted and knowledge that was once freely available becomes available for a fee.

As a result of multilateral pressures, many countries in the South have invested a lot more in combating piracy than creating socially friendly IP laws. The clarifications regarding "compulsory licensing" that were issued at the Doha WTO meetings in 2003 set an important precedent for developing countries in their struggle to gain access to and/or manufacture cheaper drugs against AIDS. The same type of exceptions were not granted for "culture" and "cultural products" in spite of the attempts made by the Canadian and French governments to advocate for a cultural exception clause related to trade in cultural products.

Canada, in the aftermath of loosing a trade dispute with the USA over a magazine split-run, adopted an interesting strategy related to culture as trade. In 1999 the Canadian Minister for International Trade convened a Cultural Industries Sectoral Advisory Group on International trade (SAGIT) towards developing a New International Instrument on Cultural Diversity as a means to achieve global consensus and leverage in the matter of culture as trade. The five objectives of the report are as follows:

- Recognize the importance of cultural diversity.
- Acknowledge that cultural products and services are significantly different from other products.
- Acknowledge that domestic measures and policies intended to ensure access to a variety of indigenous cultural products are significantly different from other policies.
- Set out rules on the kind of domestic regulatory and other measures that countries can and cannot use to enhance cultural and linguistic diversity.
- Establish how trade disciplines would apply or not apply to cultural measures that meet the agreed upon rules. (Goldsmith, 2002).

The Canadian government used the International Network on Cultural Policy (INCP) forum to pursue these goals. This network met in Switzerland in 2001. There is a need for research to explore and further such initiatives and that can be used for advocacy in the South.

There are other global initiatives linked to imbuing culture as trade with local meanings. The Chinese government's post-WTO moves to consolidate its existing seven domestic telecommunication players into four monolithic full service providers is arguably a ploy to keep control of a changing, competitive telecommunication environment and to restrict possibilities for foreign players to find suitable local partners – a requirement for licensing (Leahy, 2002). While countries with robust cultural industries such as the film industry in India may be able to creatively extend protection of its domestic industry while simultaneously accommodating the surge in Hollywood exports, it is doubtful whether nascent domestic cultural industries in the smaller nations will be able to withstand the swamping that is inevitable. Hopeton Dunn pointed out in his chapter on the media in the Caribbean that despite a small local film industry, Hollywood films remain dominant.

IPR's impact on traditional culture/heritage, mass communication, digital media and local cultural environments have the potential to affect a country's sovereignty and its ability to maintain its cultural diversity and creativity and adapt specific technologies and technological systems to its own social, demographic and economic requirements. Lawrence Lessing (2001: 21) in his book *The Future of Ideas* refers to the Internet forming an *innovation commons*. This commons is being depleted by new norms and architecture that are proprietorial in nature. "What has determined the commons is the *character of the resource* and how it *relates to a community*. In theory, any resource might be held in common ... But in practice, the question a society must ask is which resources *should be*, and for those resources, *how*". Most countries in the South are no longer in a position to even ask that question, let alone answer it. This is one aspect of a larger tragedy related to IPR.

The political economy of cross-sectoral convergences

The potentially larger issue for research is the need for an in-depth, wide ranging analysis of convergence, in particular the political economy of inter-sectoral applications of information technology. This is an area that has not received enough critical scrutiny. And yet, the marriage between IT and other technologies and multifarious IT applications across sectors remains a key feature of the contemporary technological and economic landscape. It is not merely a source for substantive profits for a select group of companies. Its products have begun to impact life itself and the products and processes that are essential to the quality of life – food, health, security. There is a need for more focused research on information as a constitutive element related to all life processes, the role of information in contemporary modes of production, not simply because there is a need to explore the cross-sectoral consequences of IT applications, but because there is a need to understand the commodification of knowledge in our brave new world. Dan Schiller's (1994: 102) remarks on the correspondences, convergences and centrality of IT in the life sciences, points to a research agenda that is yet to be explored in earnest:

> Agribusinesses, pharmaceutical giants, energy and chemical firms, and medical complexes – all essentially concerned with diverse biological information streams – are in the midst of a continuing technological transformation of the means of information production that is every bit as relevant to our understanding as the parallel trend toward digitization in telecommunications. The convergence and overlaps between genres traditionally of interest to communication research – television shows, newspaper reports, computerised data streams – and genes now subject to unprecedented manipulation and control via bio-engineering, compel consideration as parts of a single conceptual and historical process.

It is not at all surprising that bioinformatics – "the making sense of all the information about the sequence, structure and function of genes and proteins" is at the heart of a projected $6.7 billion market in the USA in 2007. All the leading global IT firms are now involved in the life sciences industry. This includes Compaq, Hewlett Packard, Motorola, Sun, Fujitsu and IBM (Cookson, 2001). The biotech industry is already in the throes of a series of mergers and consolidations with the world's largest biotechnology company Amgen acquiring Immunex for a record US$16 billion in late 2001 (Dyer and Griffith, 2001).

Communications and debt

The relationship between communication and debt is a significantly under-theorized area, and yet debt-related borrowings and debt-servicing affect the nature of information/communication environments in the South. If one were to look at the nature of borrowings today, a significant component of it is related to investments in IT, the development of telecommunication infrastructure and towards making environments suitable for commercial and business activities linked to the New Economy. As high-return investments, such borrowings have attracted a range of financial investors from multilateral organizations such as the World Bank and the IMF, to private investment banks, venture capitalists and government lending institutions such as import-export (EXIM) banks. These borrowings, in turn, are accompanied by loan conditionalities and high interest rates that often result in the siphoning of sizeable export earnings to service the national debt. UNDP's *Human Development Report 2000* indicates that Brazil has increased its percentage of debt servicing from its exports of goods and services from 39.1% in 1985 to a massive 74.1% in 1998 (UNDP, 2000) While it is true that in Latin America and the Caribbean as a whole, total debt service as a percentage of exports of goods and services had dropped from 36.8% in 1985 to 33.7% in 1998, it still indicates a large-scale siphoning of earnings from the South.

Altruism does not figure in bank-lending philosophies. Take for instance the case of telecommunication financing by the Export-Import Bank of Japan which made credit commitments totalling US$1,649 million in the 1986–1991 period. These loans were "provided to the countries which Japan deem[ed] politically and economically essential" and were linked "to such purposes" as the promotion of "direct investment from Japan"(Agata, 1991: 141–145). Perhaps the most under-theorized area is the role played by private venture capitalists in the financing of IT projects in the South. The downside of private financing of telecommunication ventures are high interest rates and stringent penalties for defaulters. Many of these firms, including VenGlobal Capital, RFC Capital Corp., DynaFund Ventures and Zacson Corp., to name a few, are also specialists in market-based, debt conversion schemes. In other words, if you were to default on payments they would help you get into a hole larger than the one you were previously in. They specialize in an array of debt-reduction schemes such as debt-equity swaps, debt paybacks, debt securitization, debt for exports, debt for nature, debt for development, debt for arms, etc. Debt-equity swaps have led to the disappearance of local assets, often at fire-sale prices. Susan George (1992: 75), the celebrated critic of global debt, cites the example of the Argentinian telephone company ENTEL. In her words, "In late 1990, Citicorp made the biggest single debt-equity deal in history, buying 60 per cent of ENTEL's southern division in partnership with Telefonica de Espana for $114 million in cash and $2.7 billion in debt. Manufacturer Hanover got the northern half of the same phone company in partnership with Atlantic Bell and on roughly the same terms: 4100 million in cash and $2.7 billion in debt". As another critic observed (Petrazzini, 1995), on the ENTEL deal, Argentina received "the lowest price per main line of companies privatised in developing countries" at the moment of sale.

Structural Adjustment Programmes, a direct result of debt-related borrowings, has in turn affected the quality, prioritization and extent of national development. Take for instance the scenario in India. Up until the mid-1980's, the country followed a policy of import substitution. But a weakening fiscal and balance of payments crisis in the late 1980's, led to renewed borrowings from the IMF and the World Bank, to the liberalization of the economy and to India's tryst with economic globalization. That led to the easing of a variety of controls in import-export restrictions, currency regulations, foreign equity caps, restrictions on monopolies, and foreign investments, along with a move away from public sector investments and support for the welfare economy. The government's commitment to new priorities such as wiring the nation, export-led growth and the privatization of essential services has been made at the expense of welfare measures and investments in the public sector. While enormous investments have been made in priority areas such as telecommunications, there has been a corresponding decline in the annual budget outlays in areas such as health, education, family planning and poverty alleviation. To belabour the point, while the budget for telecommunications in the Eighth Five Year Plan (1990–95) was revised from Rs. 19,200 crores (US$40 billion) to Rs. 40,555 crores (US$84 billion), in the 1992 budget, there was a 40% decline in allocations for rural water supply programmes, 60% reduction in support for central hospitals and dispensaries, a 25% reduction of support for employment schemes as well as cutbacks in education, rural development, labour welfare and land reform (Chawla, et al., 1992; Ninan, 1992). Simultaneously, there was a decline in public investments in research and development (R&D). As Lakhwinder Singh (2001: 2922–2924) observed, "... in the post-reform period, public sector industrial R&D expenditure recorded a negative growth rate of 7.08 per cent per annum". Singh links this trend to India's adoption of a liberalised economic and technology policy, World Bank (WB) and IMF loan conditionalities, and the government's engagement with the neoliberal economy.

To belabour the point, there is a need for research to map relationships between debt and communication including, for instance, a global mapping of the scale of IT-related borrowings, the political-economy of IT financing, the extent of media take-overs in the South by these venture capitalists, and the impact of IT borrowings on the nature of emerging media environments in the South, especially in relation to issues such as access, participation and affordable use.

Labour in the IT and media industries

A critical area of concern and one that is not getting the attention that it deserves is the changing role of labour in the IT and media industries in the context of globalization, outsourcing of products, the establishment of IT hubs in different parts of the world, the restructuring of telecommunications, and the privatization of media. These trends have affected large numbers of people previously employed in the public-sector along with those employed as non-unionized labour in hundreds of small, medium and large IT manufacturing and assembling firms. More often than not, employment statistics related to the IT industries fail to account for the men and women who work on assembly line jobs in a variety of IT-based industries. There may be 350,000 software engineers in India but there are as many or more mainly non-unionized unskilled employees toiling in poor working environments and prone to a variety of health hazards. The downturn in the telecommunication industry has led to decreases in employment in the state telecommunication sector. International Labour Organization statistics reveal a fall in employment in France Telecom from 157,000 in 1994 to 143,000 in January 1999, in Deutsche Telekom from 233,000 in 1993 to 172,000 in 1999 and British Telecom from 250,000 in 1991 to 130,000 in 1996. Unionized employees have been hardest hit and companies like AT&T lost more than half of its unionized employees between 1984–1992. With rapidly changing technologies, reskilling is a must although in a context characterized by a contracting market, employment in this industry is at a real premium.

This has effected employees in the South harder in the contexts of SAPs and the accelerated pressures resulting from economic liberalization. Reskilling is a luxury in most contexts in the South and often times such opportunities are just not available. The downturn in the telecommunications market, in particular the bursting of the dotcom bubble, also affected employment: low level employment predominantly occupied by women contracted as a result of the need for IT skilled employees (Murray, 2001). There is a need for research to explore the many ramifications for international labour, both skilled and unskilled, in the context of economic liberalization and the new global IT economy.

Conclusion

The foci for research that have been highlighted – namely IPR, the political economy of cross sectoral IT applications, communications and debt and the labour in the IT economy – can of course remain as stand alone research concerns. There is a continuing need for both theory and empirical knowledge in these areas. However, what is perhaps most necessary is the need to forge enduring links between theory and advocacy. I would like to think of critical political economy as an active collaboration between theory and practice, and conclude with a statement by Graham Murdock (1980: 151–152) on the objectives of radical theatre. While the context may have been different, critical scholars in communication will have a lot in common with the principles outlined:

> It aims to lay bare the structures of power and privilege and to show how they permeate everyday life, limiting and curtailing opportunities for self realisation and social change ... (it) probes the idealisations and rationalisations that justify the present order. It challenges taken for granted assumptions and prises open the gaps between ideological promise and institutional performance, and ... it investigates the dynamics of social change and transformation and explores the politics of possibility.

References

Agata, M. (1991) 'Financing Telecommunications Investment, Perspective of a Bilateral Official Financer'. In *Economic Symposium: Telecommunications as a Catalyst for Development and Growth*, Part 4. Proceedings of the 6th World Telecommunication Forum, 13–15 October. Geneva: ITU. pp. 141–145.

Chawla, V. et al. (1992) 'The Great Switching Saga'. *Computers and Communication* December. pp. 53–81.

Ninan, T.N. (1992) 'Manmohanomics: Whats in Store'. *Voices*, Vol. 1. pp. 3–6.

Cookson, C. (2001) 'Scientific buzz surrounds test bed of ideas in supercomputing'. *Financial Times Survey: Biotechnology*, 27 November. Part II. pp. 3–6.

Dyer, G. and Griffith, V. (2001) 'Growing Together'. *Financial Times*. 19 December. p. 20.

George, S. (1992) *The Debt Boomerang: How Third World Debt Harms Us All*. London/Amsterdam: Pluto Press/Transnational Institute.

Goldsmith, B. (2002) 'Cultural Diversity, Cultural Networks and Trade: International Cultural Policy Debate'. *Media International Australia Incorporating Culture and Policy* No. 102, February. pp. 35–53.

Kenward, M. (2001) 'When the finest minds are up for sale'. *Financial Times* 4 July. p. 12.

Leahy, J. (2002) 'Telecoms – A lucrative new market is calling'. *Financial Times Survey: China and the WTO*. Part IV. 15 March.

Lessing, L. (2001) *The Future of Ideas: The Fate of the Commons in a Connected World*. New York: Random House.

Murdock, G. (1980) 'Radical Drama, Radical Theatre'. *Media, Culture and Society* 2.2. pp. 151–168.

Murray, S. (2001) 'More jobs are on the line as sector restructures'. *Financial Times* 19 September. Part IX.

Petrazzini, B.A. (1995) *The Political Economy of Telecommunications Reform in Developing Countries: Privatisation and Liberalisation*. London: Praeger.

Schiller, S. (1994) 'From Culture to Information and back Again: Commodification as a Route to Knowledge'. *Critical Studies in Mass Communication*. March. pp. 93–115.

Singh, L. (2001) 'Public Policy and Expenditure on R&D in Industry'. *Economic and Political Weekly* 4 August. pp. 2920–2924.

UNDP (2000) 'Aid and Debt by recipient Country'. *Human Development Report, 2000*. New York/London: Oxford University Press. pp. 219–222.

WACC Communication Resource (2000) 'Key Issues in Global Communication: Communication and Debt'.

Waldmier, P. (2002) 'If technology switches to the side of copyright'. *Financial Times* 10 January. p. 15.

Williams, F. (2002) 'Copyright Protection Enforced'. *Financial Times*, 6 March. p. 12.

Contributors

Sasha **Costanza-Chock** is a graduate student at the Annenberg School for Communication, University of Pennsylvania. He was the recipient of the first Herb Schiller Award at the International Association for Media and Communication Research (IAMCR) 2002.

Hopeton S. **Dunn** is Senior Lecturer at the Caribbean Institute of Media and Communication (CARIMAC), University of West Indies, Jamaica. He has written widely in the area of communication policy and co-authored with Keyan Tomaselli (2001), *Media Democracy and Renewal in Southern Africa.*

Ana **Fiol** is Librarian and Assistant to the Global Studies Programme, WACC. She is a journalist by profession with an interest in the political economy of communication. She has written articles on the media in Latin America most recently on "ALCA and the Media" in the journal *Chasqui.*

Peter **Golding** is Professor of Sociology and Head of the Department of Social Sciences at Loughborough University, UK. He is co-chair of the European Science Foundation programme, Changing Media – Changing Europe, editor of the *European Journal of Communication*, and chairs the media research network of the European Sociological Association. He has published widely on communication and media policy issues.

Cees J. **Hamelink** is Professor of International Communication at the Universiteit van Amsterdam and also Professor of Media, Religion and Culture at the Vrije Universitiet in Amsterdam. He is an internationally renowned scholar and activist and author of numerous books and articles on communication including *The Ethics of Cyberspace*. He is the chief editor of the media journal *Gazette.*

William **Heuva** is a PhD candidate in Culture, Communication and Media Studies, University of Natal, Durban. He was previously head of the Department of Communication, Windhoek Polytechnic, Namibia, and is author of *Media and Resistance Politics: The Alternative Press in Namibia, 1960–1990.*

Robert W. **McChesney** is Professor of Communication at the University of Illinois at Urbana-Champaign. He is a leading scholar in the political economy of communication, is a co-editor of the *Monthly Review* and has written numerous books and articles on the media including *Rich Media, Poor Democracy*.

Jubril **Mohammed** obtained his Masters degree from University of Lagos, Nigeria and his PhD from ABU Zaria, Nigeria. He lectured Mass Communication at the University of Maiduguri where he was Head of Department until his untimely death in a car crash in Nigeria in June 2001. Dr Mohammed had published in areas such as Journalism and Society, Press and Politics, Communication and Development and Media and Social Change.

Mohammed **Musa** lectures in the Department of Mass Communication and Journalism, University of Canterbury, New Zealand. Dr Musa has published on news agencies, media and globalization, news flow, media and national identity as well as media and health issues. His current research interests are on media and the construction of terror, corporatization of the Internet and media and globalization.

Francis B. **Nyamnjoh** is Associate Professor at the Department of Sociology at the University of Botswana. He has written widely on media issues in Cameroon and Africa including *Media, Belonging and Democratisation in Africa*.

Seán **Ó Siochrú** is a researcher, writer and activist in media and communication. He is director of the Nexus Research Cooperative in Dublin. His most recent publication, co-authored with Bruce Girard, is *Global Media Governance: A Beginner's Guide*. He is a founder member of the Platform for Communication Rights.

Dan **Schiller** is Research Professor of Communications at the Graduate School of Library and Information Science, University of Illinois at Urbana-Champaign. A renowned media scholar, he has written extensively on the history and the political economy of communication, including *Digital Capitalism: Networking the Global Market System*.

Slavko **Splichal** is Professor of Communication at the Faculty of Social Sciences, University of Ljubljana, Slovenia. Founder of the European Institute for Communication and Culture and editor of the media journal *Javnost*, he has also written widely on numerous media issues from public broadcasting to public opinion.

Ruth **Teer-Tomaselli** is Associate Professor in the Media and Cultural Studies Program at the University of Durban, Natal. She has written extensively on broadcasting history and policy formation and is a Board member of the South African Broadcasting Corporation.

Pradip N. **Thomas** is Director of the Global Studies Programme, WACC. He has written extensively on the political economy of communications in India and is the joint-editor of the WACC journal *Media Development*.

Keyan **Tomaselli** is Professor and Director of the Graduate Program in Cultural and Media Studies, University of Natal, Durban. Editor of the journal *Critical Arts*, and author of numerous books and articles, he is one of the leading media academics in Africa.

Wang Lay Kim is Senior Lecturer in Communications at the School of Communication, Science University of Malaysia, Penang. She is a Board member of the Asian Network for Women in Communications (ANWIC) and is author of numerous book chapters and articles, particularly on women and the media.

Zaharom Nain is Associate Professor at the School of Communication, Science University of Malaysia, Penang. His interests lie principally in the political economy of communications, especially in Malaysia, having published extensively in this area. He is co-editor of *Communication and Development: The Freirean Connection*.

Yuezhi **Zhao** is Assistant Professor at the School of Communication, Simon Fraser University, Vancouver. She is an authority on the media in China and is the author of *Media, Market and Democracy in China: Between the Party Line and the Bottom Line*.

Index

Abdul Razak Hussein, 250
Abdullah Ahmad Badawi, 264–5
Abdullah, Tunku, 257
Abubakar Tafawa Balewa, 239
accountability, 18; ECE lack, 61
adaptation, social, 54
ADL, surveillance sub-
contractors, 277
Advance Publications, 13
advertising, 25, 30, 37–8, 53, 159,
187, 189–90; China TV, 200;
competition for, 191; consumer
tracking, 164; corporate
concentration, 12; few
regulations, 151; India
industry, 218–19; intensified,
138; media financing, 201–2;
new platforms, 161; 19th
century, 237; political, 147;
public service broadcasting,
114; subsidies, 185
Afghanistan, war on, 173
Africa: aid reduction, 99; Berlin
Conference partition, 232;
cultural nationalism, 237;
foreign journalists privileged,
126; government press control,
125; Independence
Declarations, 239; Information
Society Initiative (AISI), 102;
intelligensia, 235–6; journalism
repression, 123–4; media
ownership, 122, 128;
victimhood resistance, 129,
132

AIDS, drugs against, 298
Air Jamaica, 75
Ajaegbo, Chief Mike, 244
Ajasa, Kitoyi, 237–8
Aladja, Adeyemo, 238
Alfonsín, Raúl, 147
Algeria, revolution, 129
All China Federation of Workers,
189
Allende, Salvador, 142;
overthrow, 143, 149
Alliance for Progress 1961, 140
Alvarado, Velazco, Peruvian
government of, 142
Ambani family, India, 216
American Broadcasting
Company, 163
Amgen, Immunex takeover, 301
Amnesty International, 286
Anderson, Benedict, 141
Angola, 8
animation, outsourced to India,
221
anti-defamation laws, 53
Anwar Ibrahim, 260–1, 263
AOL–Time Warner, 9–10, 15, 18,
72, 163, 198, 203–4;
advertising revenue, 164
Arbenz, Jacobo, 142
Argentina: cinema boom, 140;
ENTEL privatization scandal,
148, 302; film production, 151;
inequality, 145; media
oligopoly, 153; populist
governments, 142; pro-
dictatorship media, 146;

publishing industry, 141; the
"disappeared", 138
Asia: censorship, 15; East Asia
1997 financial crisis, 160, 167,
170, 249, 259–60
Association for Progressive
Communications (APC), 32,
296
Astro, Malaysian media company,
257, 259
AT&T corporation, 18, 88, 93,
152–3, 167, 171; debt spiral,
169; /Liberty Media, 9
Atlantic Bell, 302
Australia, 19
Austria, 56
Awolowo, Obafemi, 239, 242
Azcarraga, Emilio, 17
Azikiwe, Nnamdi, 238–9, 242
Aznar, Jose Maria, 149

Bangalore: IT industry, 221;
Mysore Infrastructure
Corridor, 222; poverty, 222
Bank of China, 202
banks, EXIM, 301
Banyan Productions, Trinidad and
Tobago, 85
Barakat organization, 171
Barbados, 71; C&W assets 86;
Caribbean Media Corporation,
92; CBU, 81; Digital
Information Systems Limited,
87; Rediffusion, 76; Reuters,
82; video rental, 84
Barber, Benjamin, 56
Barco, Virgilio, 147
Barisan Nasional (BN), Malaysian
coalition, 250, 252
Barmé, Geremeie, 182, 186
Bart, Peter, 16
BBC (see British Broadcasting
Corporation)

Beckford, G., 74
Beijing: International Television
Week 2000, 199; Light
Television, 198
BellSouth, 153
Beltrán, Luis Ramiro, 142
Bennet, Coleman & Co, 217
Bennet, Louise, 81
Berlusconi, Silvio, 13, 63
Berne Convention and the
Universal Copyright
Convention, 214
Berne Convention for the
Protection of Literary and
Artistic Works, 43, 47
Bertelsmann, media company,
9–10, 13, 45, 72; China
operations, 203
Bill Gates Foundation, 295
Biobaku, Suburi, 234
Biondi, Frank, 9, 15
bioinformatics, 301
biotech industry, mergers, 301
Birla family, India, 216
BJP party, India, 214; "saffron"
agenda, 223
Blackburn, Robin, 66
Bolivia: coca growers movement,
147; Miners' Radio Movement,
142; popular movement, 139
Bonnier, Sweden, 13
Bosnia and Herzegovina,
parliament, 61
Botswana, 105; Bosnet, 110;
national television station, 127;
Telecommunications
Authority, 107; television, 116
brands, 219
Brassmen, of Nembe, 227
Brazil, 11; "cable TV war", 157;
"cordel literature", 140; debt
servicing, 301; Globo (see
Globo); inequality, 145; media

oligopoly, 34, 152; media weight, 151; MST, 139; music, 17, 141; satellites, 146; Vargas government, 142
Bretton Woods meeting, 1944, 99
bribes, to journalists, 187
British Broadcasting Corporation (BBC), 72, 76, 80, 83, 93, 127; Lagos Relay station, 238; World, 77; World Service radio, 203
British Rediffusion Group, 76–7
British Telecommunications plc (BT), 171, 298
Broadcast Relay Services (overseas) Ltd, 76
broadcasting: ownership rules, 105; regulation process, 5
Brutus, Dennis, 131
Bucaram, Abdala, 139
Bulgaria, 53, 56
"bureaucratic capitalism", Chinese newspapers, 190
Burrow, Richard, 238
Bush Radio Cape Town, 127
Bush, George W., administration, 155, 163, 172–3, 272
business news, media space occupation, 215

Cable & Wireless (C&W): Caribbean media ownership, 85–8; VSAT litigation, 90–1
Cable News Network (CNN), 72, 78, 83, 93
cable technology, 191
cable television: 16, 137, 150, 243, 256–7; Brazil, 154; Caribbean, 79; India consolidation, 218; monopoly rights, 4
Cameroon, 120, 130; media repression, 123; Union des Populations du Cameroun, 129

Campbell, Robert, 235
Canada, 13, 19, 154–5; Cultural Diversity initiative, 299
Canal Horizon, France, 127
Cancun, WTO meeting, 28
Canelini, N.G., 141
CanWest Global Communications, Canada, 13
Capital Radio Malawi, 106
Capital Research & Management, 10
Cárdenas, Cuaehtémoc, 148
Cardozo, Fernando Henrique, 156
Caribbean, the: Broadcasting Union (CBU), 81–2, 92; Communication Network (CCN) Trinidad, 75; Caribbean Community and Common Market (CARICOM), 71, 81, 83; cooperative media ventures, 81; C&W ownership levels, 87; decolonisation, 77; diversity, 70; electronic media nationalization, 76; English-speaking, 69, 71; film industry, 84–5, 91, 299; imported TV content, 79–80; internet uptake, 89; ISPs, 89; Media Corporation collapse, 82, 92; News Agency (CANA), 82–3, 92; online newspaper editions, 75; TV ownership, 78; USA TNCs, 72
Carmona, Alberto, 149
Carter, G.T., 237
cartoons, 131
Castro, Fidel, 156
CCTV, 199; systems linkage proposal, 281
cellular phones, 86; African industry, 110; Indian mergers, 216–17; location pinpointing,

282; operators, 106–7; political
mobilization use, 272
censorship: China, 182, 184,
205–6; Malaysia, 250–1;
"passive", 181; self-, 215, 262
Centennial, US telecoms
company, 87
Chandra, Subhash, 221
Chase Manhattan, 9
Chavez, Hugo, 156; attempted
coup against, 149
Chernin, Peter, 10
Chile, 150, 154; indigenous
organization, 139; inequality,
145; pro-Pinochet media, 146;
TV station ownership, 153
China, 16; backdoor media
financing, 200; Bank of, 202;
broadcasting sector, 194;
Central Party Propaganda
Department, 179, 196; Central
Television (CCTV), 183, 191;
elite business magazines, 188;
foreign media investment, 202;
IPR issues, 298; leftist criticism
marginalized, 184; market
embrace, 159, 165, 185; mass
appeal papers, 190; media
advertising revenue, 186;
media consolidation, 201, 299;
media piracy, 45; Mexican
soaps, 153; municipal
broadcasters, 195; Newspaper
Association, 193; newspaper
licensing system, 189; party
media dominance, 197–8,
204–5; party political
struggles, 206; party–state
relationship, 179, 196; Phoenix
TV, 10; protest reporting
repression, 185; public opinion
polls, 181; Radio, Film and TV

Group, 195, 197; recent
newspaper shutdowns, 183;
State Press and Publications
Administration, 180;
Taiwanese entertainment
shows, 191; television product
studios, 199; underground
media production, 182; WTO
membership, 203, 207–8
China Computerworld, 202
Chinese Academy of Social
Sciences, Industrial Economy
Research Institute, 199
Chomsky, N., 138
Church Committee, USA, 275
Church of Scotland Mission, 231
Church, the, media ownership, 65
Churchill, Ward, 275
Ciespal's Media Inventory, 151
cinemas, Caribbean, 84;
multiplexes, 12, 221
Cisneros Group, Venezuela,
14–15, 150–1; size of, 153
Citicorp, 302; Equity Investments
(CEI), 153
Civil Society Summit, Montreal
1999, 32
Clarín (Grupo Clarín), Argentina,
14, 148, 150–3
Clarke/Ashenhein families,
Jamaica, 75
class struggle, 240–1
CNN (see Cable News Network)
Collor de Mello, Fernando, 147
coca growers movement, Bolivia,
147
COINTELPRO, USA, 275–6
Colgate-Palmolive, 151
collective work, cultural products,
46
Colombia: literacy, 140; 1994
election, 149

colonialism, residual effects, 70
Columbia Pictures, 44
Commonwealth Caribbean Heads of Government Conference, 82
Communication Rights in the Information Society (CRIS), 294–6
Communication Workers of America, 286
community radio, 128; internet-based, 224; Latin American movement, 296
Compaq, 301
CONAIE movement, Ecuador, 139, 147
conglomerates, China media, 192–7; regional, 13
Congo, telecoms company, ONPT, 111
Congress Party, India, 214
copyright, 4, 28, 154; 'fair use' doctrine, 47; web, 34
Copyright Treaty 1996, 298
corporate media (see also media ownership), 3, 7–8; equity joint ventures, 15; legitimacy deficit, 6, 37; lobbying, 5, 40; multinational, 29
corruption, 224; China reporting, 184; privatization process, 137; US lobbies, 5
Crawford, Gordon, 10
Creative Televison, Jamaica, 78
cricket, Test, 81
'cross-fertilization', 62
cross-media ownership, restrictions removal, 163
cross-subsidization, 28
Crowther, Bishop Samuel Ajayi, 235, 237
Cuba, 155; revolution, 142

Cui, Z., 58
cultural dependency theory, 55, 143
Cultural Revolution, China, 205; commercial recuperation, 186
"cyberterrorism" laws, 286–7
Czech Republic, 51, 56; newspaper foreign ownership, 64; regulation, 60
Czechoslovakia, journalism, 58

Dahl, Robert, 56
Daim Zainuddin, 253, 261
data, persistence of, 285
database disruptions, 287
debt: –equity swaps, 302; servicing, 301; US telecoms boom, 168–9
DeCSS case, 48
Defense Advanced Research Projects Agency (DARPA), 277–8
Delo, Slovenian newspaper, 57
democracy, 3, 18, 52, 246; imitation, 56; media, 293; political culture of, 4; quality of, 128; weak, 6–7
Democratic Republic of Congo, telecoms infrastructure, 106
denationalization, 53, 62
Deng Xiaoping, 184–5; "no debate" decree, 181
Denmark, 11, 13
depoliticisation, 17
deregulation, 19, 72, 103, 159, 214, 216; Latin America, 148
Deutsche Telecom, 106
developmental strategy, dissociation phase, 100
Dicey, Albert Venn, 55
Diffie, Whitfield, 274, 278
diffusionist theories, 55

Digital audio broadcasting (DAB),
    77
"digital capitalism", 159; outlay
    scale, 166
digital communications, 11;
    technology, 44
"digital divide", 31, 295
Digital Eastern Caribbean Fibre
    Systems (DEFCS), 88
Digital Millenium Copyright Act,
    USA (DMCA), 47
digitization, 161; knowledge
    commercialized, 298
Direct TV, 84
Disney Group, 9, 72, 203, 207;
    Disneyfilms Pay-TV rights, 44
disruptive electronic tactics, 273
Dixon, Christopher, 8
Doha, WTO round, 28
Domain Name System (DNS), 27
domestic media protection, 11
Dominica: Broadcasting
    Corporation, 78; C&W
    ownership, 86; telecoms, 88;
dotcom bubble burst, 304
Dow Jones, 13
Duncan, H., 58
Dunn, H., 127
Dunn, Hopeton, 299
Duyile, D., 231

Earth Summit 1991, 32
East, Rupert M., 239
East-Central European countries
    (ECE), 51, 54;
    commercialization, 63; dual
    broadcasting system, 53;
    imitative nature, 58, 65; media
    ownership, 52, 54–7; Mexican
    soaps, 153; public service
    media, 59; state media
    involvement, 60–5

Eastern Nigeria Television
    Service, 242
ECE (see East-Central European
    Countries)
ECHELON, surveillance system,
    283
Econet, Zimbabwe, 106, 110, 272;
    fast growth, 111
economies of scale, 196
Ecuador, 150; CONAIE
    movement, 139, 147
educational publishing, 9
Eenadu, Indian media company,
    221
Egmont, Denmark, 13
Egypt: gay men website
    crackdown, 280; Orascom
    Telecom, 110
Electronic Frontier Foundation,
    286, 296
Electronic Privacy Information
    Center, 283, 286
elite(s): Chinese Communist
    Party, 182, 205–8; Chinese
    media, 187, 189; ECE political,
    61–2, 65; global
    communication policy, 7;
    landowning settler, 75;
    Malaysia, 253; new power,
    137; opinion, 6; policy making
    forums, 11; regional power,
    136;state broadcasting need,
    114; unelected, 30
email, search warrants, 276
EMI, 44
English Church Missionary
    Society, 231
English, language, 16, 236
Enron, 19
Eurnekian, Eduardo: Media
    Group Argentina 148
European Community, 149

European Union: Commission,
12; Global Information Society
concept, 31; privacy
legislation, 287
Everson, Meredith, 277
Export–Import Bank of Japan,
301

Fabris, H.H., 64
Falun Gong, 182, 200, 203, 206,
208
Fanon, Frantz, 129
Fatima Meer, 131
Fatogun, Ibidapo, 245
Federal Bureau of Investigations
(FBI); Carnivore system, 282;
National Crime Information
Center, 281
Federal Communications
Commission (FCC), 164–5, 170
Federal Radio Corporation of
Nigeria (FRCN), 242
fibre optics, 111; USA circuitry,
167
Ficci–Arthur Andersen report,
India entertainment, 220
film industry: Argentina, 151;
Caribbean, 84–5, 91, 299;
domestic, 11; India, 17, 220–1,
299
film libraries, 44
financial scandals, Malaysia, 254
FM radio: India oligopoly, 217;
Jamaica, 77; Malaysia, 258–9
"forced privatization",
Mozambique, 106
foreign affairs reporting, US
decline, 163
foreign direct satellite
broadcasting, 31
Fortune Forum, Shanghai 1999,
203

Fourth Estate, publishing imprint,
13
Fox TV network, 10
Fox, Vincente, 139
France, 16, 19
franchising, India, 219
"free press", 3–4
Free Trade Area of the Americas
(FTAA–Alca), 69, 140, 155–6
Freedom of Information Acts:
India, 224; USA, 275
Freeh, Louis J., 276
FreeSpeech TV, 33
Frondizi, Arturo, 142
Fuentes, Carlos, 135
Fujimori, Alberto, 147, 149
Fujitsu, 301
Fyfe, C., 233

G7, Information society summit
1996, 34
G8, 30–1, 39; Information Society
and Development Conference,
102
Galperin, Hernán, 154
Gan, Steven, 263
Gannett, media company, 13
García, Alan, 147
Gaskiya Corporation, Nigeria,
239
Gates, Bill, 119
General Agreement on trade and
Tariffs (GATT), 99; Uruguay
Round, see Uruguay Round
General Dynamics, 172
General Electric, 9
Gentino, Octavio, 151
George, Susan, 302
geo-stationary orbit, 26
Germany: News Agency (DPA),
83; TV ownership, 13
Gide, Andre, 48

Gilder, George, 167
Gilley, Bruce, 184
Girvan, N., 69, 74
Gleaner, 75, 83; Jamaican
   newspaper, 75
Global Business Dialogue on
   Electronic Commerce, 32
Global Campaign for Free
   Expression, 224
global governance, institutions, 25
Global Information Infrastructure
   Commission/ concept, 31–2
global justice movement, 271
global media education
   movement, 295
Global Social Forum, 293
globalization, uneven impact, 98
Globo group, Brazil (Rede
   Globo), 14, 141, 150, 153;
   dicatorship support, 146; Brazil
   TV dominance, 151–2
Goenka, Harsh, 218
Golding, P., 74
Goldman Sachs, 15
Gomez, E.T., 253
Goodluck, Wahab, 245
Goodman, Davis S.G., 205
Gordon, Ken, 74–5
Gramsci, Antonio, 157
Great Leap forward 1958, 188
GreenNet, 272
Grenada, 78; C&W media
   ownership, 86
Griffith, W.B., 237
Guangzhou Daily Group, 192–4
Guatemala: CIA coup, 142;
   Mayan genocide, 138
Guyana, 71, 75; Broadcasting
   Corporation, 76; cinemas, 84

Habermas, J., 52
Halim Saad, 253

HarperCollins, 10, 13
Hathaway Cables, 218
Healthscribe, USA, 220
Hearst, media company, 13, 153
Herman, E., 138
Hewlett Packard, 301
Hicks, Muse, Tate and Furst,
   USA, 13
Hinduja family, India, 218
Holmes, L., 51
horizontal integration, 111
Hoyte, Harold, 75
Hughes Telecom, India, 217
Hu Jintao, 182–3
Human Rights Tech, 286
human rights, activists, 42
Hunan Broadcasting Bureau, 200–
   1
Hundt, Reed, 170
Hungary, 8, 56; government
   media interventions, 60;
   newspaper foreign ownership,
   64

IBM corporation, 301; patents,
   298
Ibori, James, 244
Ibrahim Babangida, 243
Ibrahim Fikri, 252
Ikoli, Ernest, 238
IMF (see International Monetary
   Fund)
import substitution
   industrialisation policies, 140
imported content, 91; geopolitics,
   79–80
Independent Media Centers
   (Indymedia), 33, 272, 279, 283;
   Palestine, 284; Seattle, 282
India, 16, 19, 303; Bollywood, 17;
   budget composition, 215;
   Independence, 239; film

exports, 220–1, 299; media buying power oligopoly, 218; media interpretation business, 213–14; media sector, 34; Mexican soaps, 153; poverty non-reporting, 223; Prevention of Terrorism Ordinance, 224; privatization, 302; public sector R&D, 303; software industry exports, 219–20; Tata family cross sector media conglomerate, 216

IndusInd Media, 218

Infochannel Limited, 91

Infochan, 90

information and communication technologies (ICTs), 30; Information Awareness Office, USA, 278, 280, 287

information, right to compromised, 294

"information subsidies", 64

"innovation", Tarde's notion of, 59, 62

intellectual property rights (IPRS), 18, 25, 30, 38, 43, 45, 72, 154, 161, 294, 299, 304; laws, 284; monopolistic, 44; protection, 46–7; regional regimes, 297

Inter-American Development Bank, 148

International Data Group (IDG), 202, 204; China investment, 201

International Federation of Phonograph Industries, 45

International Monetary Fund (IMF), 73, 99, 101, 123, 136–8, 146, 148–9, 165, 260, 276; 301–3; April 2000 protests, 280; loan conditionalities, 303

International Network on Cultural Policy (INCP), 299

International Press Freedom Award, 263

International Telecommunication Union (ITU), 12, 25–6, 29, 165–6, 298, 294; accounting rate system, 28; diminished power, 30

Internet, 17–18, 27, 31, 59, 79, 93, 110, 131–2, 167, 182–3, 195, 204, 224, 271, 294; access points US control, 171; African private ISPs, 109–10; Caribbean uptake, 89–90; China, 181, 203; copyright issue, 29; democratic potential, 161; Indian ISP oligopoly, 217; ISP subpoena risk, 276; Jamaican ISPs, 90; SMO use, 272; surveillance, 277, 279

Internet Corporation for Assigned Names and Number (ICANN), 25, 27–8, 31, 297

Internet Information Management Bureau, China, 180

Interpublic Group, India, 218

inter-sectoral applications, 300, 304

investment banks, 15

Irie FM Jamaica, 77

ISIS International Manila, 296

Italy, 11, 13; media model, 62–3

Ivory Coast, 11

Iwe Irohin, newspaper, 231–5

Jakubowicz, K., 58–9

Jamaica, 71; Broadcasting Commission, 77; Broadcasting Corporation, 76, 78, 92; C&W, media ownership, 86; cinemas, 84; Creative Production and Training Centre, 78, 85;

public radio, 76; first
newspapers, 74; ISPs, 90;
satellite dish statistics, 79;
Scientific Research Council,
90; telecoms business, 73, 88–
9;Telecommunications
Advisory Council, 87
James, C.L.R., 81
Jamil Mahuad, 139
JAMINTEL, 90
Japan, 58; deflation, 170
Jefferson, O., 74
Jefferson, Thomas, 4
Jiang Zemin, 182–4
Johansen, Jon, 48
journalism: Africa, 236; African
repression, 124–6; Czech, 58;
investigative repression, 224;
Nigeria, 237; political
influence, 64;
professionalisation, 7, 53;
schools of, 6; training, 246
journalists, Malaysia strike 1961,
252
just-in-time inventory systems,
168

Kalathil, Shanthi, 204
Kamarulzaman Haji Zainal, 264
Keck, Margaret E., 273
King Jaja, 227
Kirch, Leo, 44
Kitch Group, 13
Knight-Ridder, 13
knowledge, commodification, 300
Konaré, Alpha Omar, 34
Kreimer, Seth F., 277, 284
Krishnan, T. Ananda, 258
Kundun, 203

labour, IT industries, 303; US job
losses, 169

Landau, Susan, 274, 278
Latin America: Association of
Educational Radio, 296;
censorship, 15; cinema
production, 151; debt crisis,
146; Information Agency
(ALAI), 32, 296; land-owning
oligarchs, 142; military
dictatorships, 143; piracy, 154;
political advertising, 147;
politics "disappearance", 137;
state terror, 139; wage levels,
145
Latin American Association of
Educational Radio (AWER),
296
Lee, P., 119
Lent, J., 72, 74
Les Penelopes, 32
Lesotho, 108; Siemens contract,
107; television, 127; Vodacom,
106
Lessig, Larry, 47
Lessing, Lawrence, 300
Levin, Gerald, 9
liberalization "demobilized", 186
Liberation Daily Group,
Shanghai, 193
libraries, 4
life science industries, IT firms,
301
Lincoln University, USA, 238
Linux, operating system, 48
Li Peng, nepotism exposure
Li Yuanjiang, 193, 194
Liu, Changle, 202
lobbying, corporate media, 5, 40
Lockheed Martin, 172
Love FM, 77
Lui Yong, 187
Lush, D., 124
lustration, 56–7

M-Cell, Mozambique, 106
M-Net: Namibia, 105; South
    Africa, 127
Macarthy, General Charles, 233
Macaulay, Herbert, 237
Macaulay, Owen Emerick, 237
Macmillan, Allister, 238
Mahathir Mohamad, 249, 253–6,
    258–60, 262, 264–5; nepotism
    accusation, 261
Malawi: brodcasting ownership,
    106; Malawinet, 110; national
    TV station, 127; partial
    privatization, 108
Malaysia, 104; government/party-
    owned newspapers, 252–4;
    media credibility loss, 262;
    media licence control, 257,
    259; media ownership, 258,
    264; Official Secrets Act, 251;
    repression, 255, 263; state
    media control, 256;
    transnational media
    corporations, 204
Malaysiakini, web-based daily
    newspaper, Malaysia, 263, 265
Malaysian Chinese Association
    (MCA), 249; Hauren
    Holdings, 252
Malaysian Indian Congress,
    Maika Holdings, 252
Mali, 34
Malthus, Thomas, 74
Mandela, Nelson, 34
Manley, Michael, 76
Manley, Norman, 76
Manufacturer Hanover, 302
Maoist era, China, 186, 188
Maran, Kalanthi, 218, 221
Marinho family, Brazil, 152
Markle Foundation, 295
Marley, Bob, 81

Marpin TV station, Dominica, 78,
    90
Marshall Plan, 99
Martín-Barbero, J., 141, 146
Marx, Gary, 284
Marx, Karl, 74, 156, 184
Mattelart, Armand, 141, 143
Mbembe, A., 130
McChesney, Robert, 119, 203
McIntyre, Arnold, 73
Measat-1, satellite, 258
Media Institute of Southern Africa
    (MISA), 107, 112
media ownership (see also
    corporate media): Africa, 128;
    China concentration, 196;
    concentration, 9–11, 14, 72,
    137, 161, 265–6; global
    oligopolies, 119; Indian
    concentration, 216;
    monopolies, 294; tax cuts, 215
Media Prima Berhad company,
    Malaysia, 264
media products, special nature of,
    24
media technology, US innovation,
    160
MediaChannel, 33
MediaMix, Jamaica, 85
Mediaset, 13
Mega TV, Malaysia, 257–8
Melody, W.H., 69, 88–9
Mencinger, J., 58
Menem, Carlos, 148
Mercosur, 156
mergers and acquisitions, 9, 72
mesomobilization, 273, 285
"Metro papers", China, 190
Mexico, 11, 16, 139, 154; *barrios*,
    145; Cardenas governments,
    142; cinema boom, 140; film
    production, 155; media

oligopoly, 152; media weight,
151; 1988 election, 148;
Partido Revolucionario
Institucional, 141; satellites,
146; Televisa, 14, 17
Miami, Latin American media
capital, 138, 151
Microsoft, 18, 153; antitrust case,
164
Middlehoff, Thomas, 9
Mill, J.S., 74
Minaj cable TV, Nigeria, 244
missionaries, West Africa, 231–5
modernization "reactionary", 165
Modi family, India, 216
Mohammed Buhari, 243
Mohammed, J.B., 232, 245
Mona Information Systems Unit
(MISU), 90
monopolies: broadcasting rights,
4; copyright, 19; licenses, 5
Montesinos, Vladimiro, 149
moral rights, copyright, 43
MoRE group, 48
Morgan Stanley, 15
Morishima, M., 58
Mosco, V., 74
Mossel, Irish phone company, 86
Motion Picture Association of
America, 48
Motorola, 153, 301
Movement of Landless Peasants,
Brazil (MST), 139, 147
Mozambique, cellular phone
operators, 106
MTN, South Africa, 106
Mueller, M., 73–4
Muhammad, Amir, 262
multi-Choice, 127
Multilateral Agreement on
Investments (MAI), proposed,
32, 154

multilateral governance structures,
39
Multimedia Super Corridor,
Malaysia, 259
multiplex cinemas, 16; India, 221
Murdoch, James, 203
Murdoch, Rupert, 10, 13, 15, 119,
202
Murdock, G., 74, 120, 304
music industry, 17, 33; Brazil, 17,
41; Caribbean, 80

NAFTA (see North American
Free Trade Agreement)
Namibia: Broadcasting
Corporation, 114;
Communications Commission,
107; electricity utility, 111–12;
Internet Development
Foundation, 109; Mobile
Telephone Company, 110;
public payphone operator,
105; Tele2. 105; Telecom
Namibia, 106, 108, 110, 112
Napster, 45
NASSCOM, India, 213
Nation Group, Barbados, 75
nation state, 29; censorship, 15;
media governance, 41; press
suppression, 4, 8; sovereignty,
100
National Association of
Broadcasters, USA, 45
National Security Doctrine, Latin
America, 143
National Union of Mineworkers,
South Africa, 106
NATO, see North Atlantic Treaty
Organization
Nawawi, Mohd Effendi, 258
neoliberalism/ 'Washington
Consensus', 10, 17, 19, 73;

economic imperatives, 98;
Latin America, 135–6
netwar, 284
Neves, Tancredo, 147
New World Information and
Communication Order
(NWIC), 7, 26, 76, 143, 294
New Zealand, 19; newspaper
ownership, 13
News Agency of Nigeria (NAN),
242
News Corporation, 9–10, 14–15,
72, 203–4
newspapers: China ownership,
200; early West African, 231–
3; government owned, 75;
Malaysian licensing system,
263; Nigeria, 238–9, 243–5;
party–state ownership/control,
253–5; web-based, 263
NGOs/civil society, 29, 32
Ngwane, Trevor, 131
Nicaragua, Sandinista revolution,
142
niche markets, 12, 194
Nigeria, 130; Broadcasting
Commission, 243;
Broadcasting Corporation,
238, 241; cellular phone
market, 106; colonial
economy, 227–30; first
printing press, 233; Labour
Congress, 246; missionaries,
231–2; newspaper cartoons,
131; newspapers, 236, 238–9,
243–5; press, 125; satellite
communications, 111; state
media control, 242; Television
Authority (NTA), 242
Ninan T.N., 219
Niue, Internet domain name
dispute, 297

Njeuma, Dorothy L., 121
Non-Aligned Movement, 33
North American Free Trade
Agreement (NAFTA), 11, 18,
140, 154
North Atlantic Treaty
Organization (NATO),
Chinese Embassy bombing,
184
Norway, 11

O'Reilly, Tony, 13
Obasanjo, Chief Olusegun, 244
OECD (see Organization of
Economic Cooperation and
Development)
Office of Homeland Security,
USA, 278
"official nationalism", 141
Okoli, Chris, 243
Olomu, Nan, 227
Omu, F., 231, 235, 237
Operasi Lalang, 254–5, 261
Oracle, 172
Organization of American States
(OAS), 89
Organisation of Economic
Cooperation and Development
(OECD), 30–1, 39
Orwell, George, 17

PaineWebber, investment firm, 8
Palace Amusement Company,
Jamaica, 84
PANOS Institute, 32
Paraguay, 150; indigenous
organizations, 139
Paramount, 44
Paris Convention and the Patent
Cooperation Treaty, 214
Paris Convention for the
Protection of Industrial
Property, 43

partisanship, 62; journalism, 6
PAS, Malaysian Islamic party, 262
Pasquali, A., 141
patent applications, 298
paternal–commercial media system, 63
"paternalist commercialism", 66
Patten, Chris, 203
Pay TV, 152, 256; Latin America, 150
PeaceNet, 272
Pearson, media company, 13
peasant farmers, Nigeria exploitation, 230
Pentafour animation studio, 221
People Communication Charter, 32
People's Daily, for-profit accounting system, 185
Pernas, Malaysian government company, 252
Peron, Juan, 142
Peru, General Bermudez government, 142
Pew Center for People and the Press, 160
Philadelphia Republican National Convention, arrests, 282
Philips company, 298
Phoenix TV, 202
phone-in talk shows, China, 183, 191
Pinochet Augusto, 143, 145; 1988 plebiscite, 147
piracy, 45, 298; Latin America, 154; China, 45
Platform for Communication Rights (PCR), 32, 294
Poindexter, John, 278
Poland, 56; newspaper foreign ownership, 64; Solidarity revolution, 58

'political capitalism', 66
postal systems, 53
poverty: Bangalore, 222; globalization of, 131; India, 215; Mexico, 155; non-reporting, 223
Prashar Bharati, stalled, 223
print media, distribution, 53
Prisa, media company, 13
Privacy Enhancing Technologies, 286
Privaterra, 286
privatization, 19, 53, 57, 59, 63–4, 66, 99, 103, 104, 214–16, 243, 253–4, 297; Colombia, 149; corruption, 137; global scale, 166; Latin America, 146, 148; partial, 108, 110; selective, 257–8
profits, 3–4, 38
Progressive Era, USA, 5
propaganda, commercial, 186–7
protective technologies, 47
public domain information, 25, 36
public service media, 11–12, 35–8; broadcast, 7, 113; advertising, 114; Caribbean demise, 92; retreat from commitments to, 239
Puerto Rico, 72

quasi-governmental organizations, 31

Rádio Boca, 130
Radio Demerara, Guyana, 76
Radio Distribution, Barbados, 76
Radio France International, 127
Radio Jamaica, 78
Radio Jamaica and Rediffusion Ltd (RJR), 76
Radio Mille Collines, Rwanda, 128

Radio Mona, 77
radio spectrum, allocation, 25–6, 35, 38; ownership, 164
Radio Television Kaduna (RTK), 242
Radio Trottoir, 130–1
Radio Wave, Namibia, 105
Raheja family, India, 218
Rao, Ramoji, 221
Rastafari, 80
Rather, Dan, 207
Raytheon, 172
Razaleigh Hamzah, 254
Reagan, Ronald, 7
Recording Association of America, lobbying, 45
Rede STB, Brazil, 152
Rediffusion Group, 76
Redstone, Sumner, 9
Reed Elsevier, 13
reggae music, 80
regionalisation, 104
regulation/regulators, 24, 38, 66, 180, 244; ECE countries, 60–1, 65; failures, 31; forms of, 25; global, 42; "independent", 103, 107, 113, 115; US elimination, 162
remote processing business, India, 220
Reuters News Agency, 13, 83, 92; Barbados, 82
Ricardo, David, 74
Richardson, W., 103
ridicule, power of, 130
right to information bills, 296
RJR group, 92
Robinson, Mansfield, 76
Robison, Richard, 205
Rodney, Walter, 74
"role model" reporting, 187
Romania, 51, 53

Rosenbaum, J., 58
Roth, Silke, 273–4
Roy, Arundhati, 223
royalties, 46
rumour, 130
Russia, 8, 51; media, 60

Sage India publishing house, 213
Salinas de Gortari, Carlos 148
Samper, Ernesto, 149
San José meeting, Costa Rica, 143
Sandals hotels, chain, 75
Sao Tomé and Príncipe, 130
SARFT, China, 197, 201
SARS (see Severe Acute Respiratory Syndrome)
satellite: Africa TV, 127; direct broadcast TV, 79, 243; dishes, 202; orbital slots, 26; technology, 72; television, 146, 256, 258; transmission facilities, 81
Saudi Ogre company, 106
SCADA system, 111
"Scar literature", China, 188
Schengen Information System, 287
Schiller, Dan, 300
screen emissions detection, 283
Seattle: WTO protests, 272, 279; Independent Media Center, 282
second-tier media firms, 12, 150; Asian market, 14; globalization, 13
selective prosecution, 284–5
self-censorship: India, 215; Malaysian media, 262
self-government, informed, 8
September 11th 2001, consequences, 265
Service de Presse du Front de Liberation Nationale, 129

service economy, integrated, 70
Severe Acute Respiratory
    Syndrome (SARS), reporting
    of, 182–4
Shagari, Alhaji Shehu, 243
Shanghai Culture and
    Broadcasting Group, 195
Shenzhen Stock Market, 200
Siemens, 106; African
    subsidiaries, 107
Sikkink, Kathryn, 273
Silicon Valley, Defence
    Department contracts, 172
Singh, Lakhwinder, 303
Sky Latin America, 152
SkyGlobal Networks, 10
Slovenia, 51, 56; Ministry of
    Information, 57; self-
    management, 61
Smith, Adam, 74
social democracy, 12
Social Movement Organizations
    (SMOs), 271; Internet use, 272;
    surveillance, 274
software, Trojan horse, 283
Sony corporation, 9–10, 13, 45,
    72; global film production, 16;
    local subsidiaries, 17
South Africa, 11, 34; AIDS drugs
    victory, 131; broadcasting
    ownership, 105; Independent
    Communication Authority,
    107; M-Net, 127; Mineworkers
    Investment Company, 106;
    partial privatization, 108–9;
    press, 125; transport and
    electricity companies, 111;
    television, 116
South East Asian Press Alliance
    (SEAPA), 263
South Korea, 11; media education
    movement, 296

South–South trade, 104
Southern African Broadcasting
    Association, 116
Southern African Development
    Community (SADC), 101–2,
    108; media market, 104; mixed
    broadcasting system, 97, 113;
    Protocol on Transport,
    Communication and
    Meteorology, 103; regulatory
    bodies, 107; state in
    involvement in print media,
    114; strategic partnerships,
    110; television newness, 116
Soviet socialism, collapse, 159,
    165
Spain, 11; Sogecable, 15
Sparks, Colin, 54, 64
Spilchal, Slavko, 136
sports coverage, 81
St Vincent, 78
Stabroek News, Guyana, 75
Star Publications, Malaysia, 252
Star TV, Asia, 10, 202–3
state broadcasting sector, Latin
    America, 150
State Council Administrative
    Affairs Bureau, China, 200
State Council Information Office,
    China, 180
State Press and Publications
    Administration, China, 186,
    189, 193, 196, 200
Stewart, Gordon "Butch", 75
Stone, C., 74
structural adjustment programmes
    (SAPs), 99, 101, 122–3, 138,
    302; Nigeria, 243
submarine cable systems, 167
subsidies, 12; China severance,
    185; film industry, 11; postal,
    4; state, 186

Sumangali Cable Vision, 218
Sun, IT company, 301
Sun TV, 218, 221
surveillance: algorithmic, 285;
    electronic, 273; online, 272,
    286; online disruption, 287;
    SMOs, 274; state, 271;
    technologies, 288; types, 278
Swapo, Namibia, Kalahri
    Holdings, 105
Swaziland, television, 127
Sweden, 11, 13, 19
Syed Mokhtar Al Bukhary, 264
Symitch, Bill, 297

Tan Chee Koon, 255
Tanzania: Broadcasting
    Commission (TBC), 107;
    partial privatization, 109;
    television, 116
Tarde, Gabriel, 54–9
Tata family: conglomerates, 215;
    Indian media dominance, 21;
    Tata Infosys, 213; Tata Telecom
    Consolidation, 217
technical transfers, 100
'Tehelka', persecution of, 224
Tejpal, Tarun, persecution of, 224
telecommunications sector: Basic
    Service Agreement 1997, 101;
    Caribbean, 73; colonial
    control, 85; less developed
    countries, 31; private capital,
    301; regulatory structure, 88;
    surplus capacity, 99; world
    stock market value, 170; WTO
    agreements, 102
Telefé, Argentina, 148
Telefonica de Espana, 302
Telekom Malaysia Berhad, 109
Telemundo TV network, 150
"telenovelas", 140, 150; exports,
    141, 153

Televisa, Mexico, 139, 141, 150–3
television, 13; cable, 4, 16, 79, 137,
    150, 154, 84, 218, 243, 256–7;
    Caribbean production, 85; cost
    of, 147; digital, 150; pay-TV,
    150, 152, 256; sponsorship,
    151; subscriber, 78
Telkom Kenya, 111
Thapar family, India, 216
Thatcher, Margaret, 7
Third Caribbean Media
    Conference, Guyana 2000, 73
Third Summit of the Americas,
    Quebec 2001, 155
Thomas, P.N., 119
Tiananmen Square, PR debacle,
    181
time-delay equipment, 183, 192
Ting Pek Khing, 253
Togo, 130
Tomaselli, K., 127
"total information awareness",
    280
Townsend, George, 234
Townsend, Rev Henry, 231, 233–5
trade in services (TIS), 101
Trade Related Aspects of
    Intellectual Property Rights
    (TRIPS), 28, 100, 214, 297
trade-related investment measures
    (TRIMS), 100
Trans-Caribbean System,
    telecoms, 88
Trinidad and Tobago, 71;
    Broadcasting System, 76;
    cinemas, 84; telecoms
    divestment, 73;
    Telecommunications Services
    of, 86; Television (TTT), 78;
    television station ownership,
    153
Truman, Harry, Point Four
    Program, 99

TRW corporation, 172
Tunku Abdul Rahman, 250, 255
Turkey, Mexican soaps, 153
Turner, Ted, 15
Twentieth Century Fox films, 10

Uganda, cellular phone market, 106
Undercurrents, 33
UNESCO, 11, 25, 26, 81, 82; USA withdrawal, 7, 27, 33; weakness, 31; Windhoek Declaration 1991, 112
uneven liberalisation, China, 188
Unilazar Group, animation studio
Union Alliance Media (UAM), 106
Union of Soviet Socialist Republics (USSR), 53
United Artists/Warner Brothers, 44
United Fruit, 142
United Kingdom/Britain, 11; Caribbean diaspora, 85; Caribbean media presence, 77; colonialism, 74; Nigeria colonialism, 228–32; UNESCO withdrawal, 7, 33
United Malays National Organisation (UMNO), 253, 255, 257, 262, 264–5; newspapers control, 254; re-formation, 256
United Nations system, 29, 37; agencies weakness, 30, 109; Economic and Social Council (ECOSOC), 32; Gender IT Task Force, 294; transparency need, 39; World Intellectual Property Organization (WIPO), 28, 30, 47, 297–8; WSIS conference, 225

United States of America (USA), 11, 17, 37, 39, 45, 59, 154–5, 274; Afghanistan war, 162; Caribbean diaspora, 85; Caribbean media presence, 72, 79; changed China reporting, 207; Constitution, 4, 43; copyright 18–19, 47, 298; corporate system, 8; cultural imperialism, 16; educational publishing, 9; emergency legislation, 171; Federal Communications Commission (FCC), 89; global power, 293; hegemony, 138; Hispanic market, 150; India software companies, 220; Latin America relationship, 136; military spending, 160; network-related investment, 167; Office of Homeland Security, 172; overseas royalty earnings, 298; Patriot Act, 271, 276, 287; State Department, 149; surveillance agencies, 275, 278; Telecommunications Act 1996, 163; telecoms de-unionization, 168; telecoms overcapacity, 169; UNESCO withdrawal, 7, 27, 33; USAID, 103
universal access, rhetoric, 116
universal service, 103; affordable access, 100; instruments, 35; obligations, 31; policies, 28
University of Buea, Cameroon, 120–1
University of Puerto Rico, 90
University of Technology, Caribbean
University of West Indies (UWI), 77; website, 90

Univision, 150
Uruguay Round, GATT, 28, 88;
    Annex X, 101, 109
utility companies, telecoms
    ventures, 111

Vargas, Getulio, Brazilian
    government of, 142
Variety, 15–16
Vartanova, E., 60
Vellu, Samy, 252
Venezuela: Bolivarian Revolution
    Centres, 139; Cisneros Group,
    see Cisneros; literacy, 140; oil
    industry, 149
venture capitalists, telecoms, 302
Verizon, 286
Viacom, 9, 72, 207; advertising
    revenue, 164
victimhood, African resistance to,
    120, 129, 132
video: digital, 272; outlets, 84–5
Videsh Sanchar Nigam Limited
    (VSNL), 215–16
virtual undercover operations,
    272, 284
Vivendi, 45, 72; advertising
    revenue, 164; Universal
    Studios, 9, 15, 44
Vodacom Tanzania, 106–7
Vodacom, South Africa, 110
Voice of America, Middle East,
    171
VSAT, 90–1

Waddel, Rev Hope, 231, 233
Waisbord, Silvio, 149
Wall, Jim Vander, 275
Wang, Changtian, 198–9
Wang, Guoqing, 200
Warner Brothers International
    Television, 106

Warner Music, 45
West Africa, first newspapers, 233
Western Nigeria Television Service
    (WNTV), 242
Wilson, Mark, 84
Windhoek Declaration 1991, 112;
    Charter, 113, 116
Windward Islands Broadcasting
    Service (WIBS), 77
Wireless in Local Loop (WiLL)
    technologies, 217
Witter, M., 74
World Association for Christian
    Communication (WACC), 32,
    120–2, 296; Pacific Region,
    297
World Association of Community
    Radio Broadcasters, 32–3, 296
World Bank, 73, 99, 101, 122–3,
    129, 136–8, 148, 165, 243, 260,
    276, 301–2; loan
    conditionalities, 303
World Commission on Culture, 27
World Economic Forum, 19, 31,
    276
World Social Forum: Porto Alegre
    2001, 32; Porto Alegre 2002,
    19
World Space, 224
World Summit on the Information
    Society (WSIS), 225, 294–5
World Trade Center, New York,
    167
World Trade Organization
    (WTO), 11–12, 18, 25, 27–8,
    31, 35, 39–40, 73, 88, 100, 108,
    119, 129, 131, 162, 195, 214,
    276, 279, 297–8; arbitration
    boards, 29; augmented power,
    30; Basic Telecommunications
    Agreement, 166; Cancun
    meeting, 28; China entry, 184;

commitments to, 101, 109;
Doha meetings, 28, 298;Seattle
protests, 272; telecoms
agreements, 102 trade-offs, 34
Worrell, D. 70–1
WPP advertising agency, 218
Wu, Guoguang, 189
Wuxi Broadcasting Bureau,
programme production, 195

Xinhua News Agency, 193
Xu, Guangchun, 197
Xu, Lei, 205

Yugoslavia, ex: former republics,
61; 'right to publish opinions',
57

Zaharom Nain, 204
Zaire, 130
Zambia: central bank private
network, 111; Independent
Media Association (ZIMA),
112
Zane Ibrahim, 127
Zapatistas, Mexico, 139, 147;
internet use, 162, 272
Zee TV, 221; PE ratio, 217;
takeovers, 218
Zhejiang Province, TV mergers,
195
Zikist movement, Nigeria, 240
Zimbabawe, 100; Broadcasting
Authority (BAZ), 107;
BroadcastingCorporation,
114–15; broadcasting sector,
104–5, 116; Econet,
110;satellite communications,
111; Siemens contract, 107

Printed in the United States
40987LVS00003B/88-306